Ecotherapy

Ecotherapy

Theory, Research, Practice and Education

Second edition

Edited by

Joe Hinds, Hayley Marshall and Martin Jordan

BLOOMSBURY ACADEMIC
LONDON • NEW YORK • OXFORD • NEW DELHI • SYDNEY

BLOOMSBURY ACADEMIC
Bloomsbury Publishing Plc, 50 Bedford Square, London, WC1B 3DP, UK
Bloomsbury Publishing Inc, 1359 Broadway, New York, NY 10018, USA
Bloomsbury Publishing Ireland, 29 Earlsfort Terrace, Dublin 2, D02 AY28, Ireland

First published in Great Britain 2016

This edition published 2026

Cover design: Terry Woodley
Cover image © Vicente Méndez/Getty Images

A catalogue record for this book is available from the British Library.

A catalog record for this book is available from the Library of Congress.

ISBN: HB: 978-1-3504-5984-7
PB: 978-1-3504-5985-4
ePDF: 978-1-3504-5987-8
eBook: 978-1-3504-5986-1

Typeset by Newgen KnowledgeWorks Pvt. Ltd., Chennai, India

For product safety related questions contact productsafety@bloomsbury.com.

To find out more about our authors and books visit www.bloomsbury.com
and sign up for our newsletters.

Joe Hinds

To Erin and Freya for memorable outdoor times together and for making me proud and to those clients and students who have taught me

Hayley Marshall

To Marnie, life made perfect; and to my guides and teachers from all realms, in deep gratitude

Martin Jordan

To Cara, Mary and Gemma, for all the happy times spent in nature, and to all the participants in my ecotherapy workshops, who taught me so much

Contents

Part IV Education

Figures

Ecotherapy: A preface to the second edition

Hayley Marshall, Joe Hinds and Martin Jordan

Since the first volume of *Ecotherapy* was published in 2016, we, in the West, are living through times of escalating trouble, through times of ecological and socio-political turmoil. While our kin in Indigenous nation cultures have already been suffering the long-lived impacts of colonialization (Ghosh 2021) and climate change, it is clear that these issues are now landing more distinctly on the doorsteps of Western societies. Therefore, the plurality of practice that forms the discipline of ecotherapy (applied ecopsychology) – ontologically rooted in ancient healing traditions with attention centred on the human–nature relationship – now seems even more essential and vital. The underlying aim being to heal the nested fractals of personal-social-ecological distress, thus aiding a broader planetary project of how to help humans find their 'proper' ecosystemic place.

It is in this spirit that the second edition of *Ecotherapy* is offered, updated and revised according to important personal, subject and global developments.

Beginning from the personal, we want to acknowledge the death of our beloved co-editor. Martin Jordan tragically lost his life in January 2017 – our time with Martin was unfortunately brief but greatly inspirational – we miss him. Without his drive, vision and insight there would have been no first edition let alone a second. We find ourselves tasked with continuing his legacy by developing this text through the introduction of important new chapters, the revision of existing ones and a brand-new section on ecotherapy and education. The latter reflects a rapidly growing interest in and importance of the kind of training and ongoing support twenty-first-century ecotherapists need. There is some suggestion here that the traditional ways of training psychological practitioners in particular may no longer be fit for purpose.

For a variety of reasons (including political events happening in the regions authors are based in), a few original chapters could not be included in the current edition, and some of the ones retained are re-presented in their original form. We also miss the inclusion of some proposed chapters – the 'ecotherapeutic' practice of working within indigenous human–nature relationships for instance. We look forward to future publications that can address this and other issues to add to an even broader and more critical cultural understanding of ecopsychotherapy.

Alongside this we note that the current edition is once again a finite text; we could not include all topics that are pertinent to such a wide-ranging field. So, like the original, this new volume is not a complete 'how to' text. While issues concerning ethics and moral obligations towards the client are similar in any psychotherapeutic work, the consideration of the therapeutic frame outdoors is always going to need some additional attention (Jordan and Marshall 2010) – there are important considerations that arise concerning human relationship with place and ecological intersectional practice, for example. While some of these matters are alluded to in the writings here, they are not followed fully but *are* dealt with in significant depth elsewhere (Jordan 2015; Brazier 2018). Rather, the emphasis in this edition is to offer a range of chapters that are a series of portals, providing deep pools of 'outsight' into many of the substantive possibilities in this work. The aim being to entice and support an impulse to explore, to discover what healing practices might, and indeed need to become in the times we are living through.

Much of the pioneering work done by Martin and others in the original volume still stands strong, forming the ground for our newer chapters. So, to honour these 'ancestors', and particularly the voice of Martin, we continue our preface with updated text from the original volume.

The use of nature to affect positive change in the well-being of people has been around in many forms for many years (e.g. Metzner 2009). An emphasis on the healing of the split between nature and human nature has long formed part of some psychological traditions (Jung 1989; Sabini 2008; Searles 1960). In the past forty years, however, there has been a growing interest in, and development of, ecopsychology as an explicit field (Roszak, Gomes and Kanner 1995). This has largely been orientated towards the 'greening of psychology' such as developing a human identity with, and compassion for, the natural world (Roszak 1995: 16), alongside the recognition that human psychological distress is bound with the ecological destruction inflicted by humankind upon the natural world. A strongly related concept that has adopted some key features from ecopsychology is ecotherapy (Buzzell and Chalquist 2009). Although both approaches have drawn on a number of different disciplines and perspectives in their development, particularly psychology, a central aspect to both is developing a reciprocal relationship with nature to ensure both psychological and environmental well-being. Whereas ecopsychology is about the psyche and the greening of psychology, ecotherapy focuses on the total mind–body–spirit relationship (e.g. Clinebell 1996).

Clinebell (1996) first coined the term ecotherapy, positing a form of 'ecological spirituality' whereby a holistic relationship with nature encompasses both nature's ability to nurture us, through our contact with natural places and spaces, and our ability to reciprocate this healing connection through our ability to nurture nature. Developments, particularly in North America, tend to describe ecotherapy as 'applied' or clinical ecopsychology, just as psychotherapy can be described as applied or clinical psychology (Jordan 2009). Ecotherapy is positioned as healing the human–nature relationship and includes a range of therapeutic and reconnective practices such as horticultural therapy, 'green' exercise, animal-assisted therapy, wilderness therapy, natural lifestyle therapy, eco-dreamwork, community ecotherapy and dealing with eco-anxiety and eco-grief with others (Buzzell and Chalquist 2009).

Ecotherapy may be seen as an umbrella term for nature-based methods of physical and psychological healing representing a new form, or a new modality, of psychotherapy that enlarges the traditional scope of treatment to include the human–nature relationship (Chalquist 2013; Hasbach 2012; Rust 2020). Traditional therapy approaches have not tended to explicitly recognize these relationships with the more-than-human world (Abram 1996; i.e. such as plants, animals, rocks) as an important part of how the client's story and healing intertwine (Hegarty 2010).

However, amid this variety, there remains a question concerning what 'nature' is. For this collection of essays on therapeutic and psychological effects of nature, we take the position that nature is both material in its form and a historical construct. Moreover, given that we as a species are part of nature, 'mind', in the form of interiors, and 'nature', in the form of an exterior, are not so easily separated. Nature can be understood through its processes and forms as a biotic and ecological system of interaction and also as a historically contingent understanding.

Furthermore, nature and people (although fully acknowledging that this is a false dichotomy) may be viewed as spiritual entities that are undeniably connected (e.g. Macy 2009; Wall-Kimmerer 2025). Nature has emerged historically through its articulation in the natural sciences (Latour 1993) and through the practices and economic developments of modernity (Bluhdorn 2001) as well as through ancient indigenous practices, beliefs and rituals (e.g. Abrams 1996), and therefore it is impossible to situate nature as a singular entity (Macnaghten and Urry 1998).

In these merging and emerging movements, we do not find a distinct 'mind' coming into contact with a distinct 'nature'; both are in a relational process. And undoubtedly these perceptions, and indeed changes in perceptions, of both nature and self are part of the therapeutic journey. The following collection of essays seeks to explore the relationship between humans and nature and the effect both have upon one another as an emerging and relational process.

Moreover, we are not advocating an anthropocentrism here in that nature is perceived as merely a 'resource' to be exploited for therapeutic ends. We take the position that the large majority of ecotherapy practices, including those in this book, fundamentally represent and practise a reciprocal relationship with nature, one that promotes and enhances sustainable practices (psychological and ecological). For some chapters this is in the foreground, and for others it is less so; nonetheless, it is the relational and reciprocal aspect of ecotherapy that we wish to acknowledge here that is genuinely healing for both people and the planet.

Our goal in this volume is to establish a grounding of ecotherapy in a theory-based understanding in order that this multifaceted discipline might grow further. We attempt to do so by developing epistemologies of a broad ecotherapy based on sound practice and coherent research. We are particularly interested here in how ideas from contemporary psychotherapy theory and practice interweave with ideas from the emerging fields of ecopsychology and ecotherapy, for instance, how conventional ideas regarding the therapeutic frame (e.g. the therapeutic hour) are challenged and managed by the practicalities of taking people into natural environments. Overall, we are keen to present and articulate the therapeutic effects of the natural world and our relationships to it from an ecotherapy standpoint while also acknowledging that this broad approach does not constitute a panacea: undoubtedly there are situations when ecotherapy will not be appropriate.

Nevertheless, the following chapters, we feel, are further step towards building a robust theoretical, experiential, practice-driven and educational understanding of ecotherapy by bringing together a diverse and international array of researchers and practitioners and thus drawing on a broad range of philosophies and positions. We recognize, however, that among the approaches presented some material will be at odds with certain readers' ideas of what constitutes evidence; on one hand, the richness of the more personal chapters may not be perceived as being part of an empirical evidence base; on the other hand, the phenomenological nature of these accounts may be seen as central to a depth understanding. Undoubtedly, this book is an endeavour that attempts to bring together both.

They of course interact and are part of the holistic process of understanding: both the positivist and inductivist positions of this growing discipline are important, and we cannot be without either. Moreover, although we recognize that the preceding chapters cover and contain aspects of one or more of the book's key areas of theory, research, practice and education, we have made a judgement regarding the main components or aspects of each chapter and allocated them to the most appropriate section: some chapters are stronger in one or more of these aspects than others. Again, this volume attempts to both unify the field under the umbrella term ecotherapy while also recognizing the idiosyncratic nature of each contribution.

Therefore, as with other aspects of human inquiry, how these various chapters both converge and diverge will be interpreted differently, and our aim is not to provide prescriptive direction here about these patterns of interrelation, but to provide, as far as possible, what we feel is an informed and deliberate attempt at buttressing the practice of ecotherapy. We now offer a brief synopsis of each chapter within its given section.

Theory

An important epistemological basis for the practice and theory of ecotherapy is ecopsychology, and Thomas Doherty's original chapter introduces some of the fundamental tenets to the growing practice and theoretical understanding of how and why ecotherapy works. Starting with a definition of ecotherapy as intrinsically linked to psychotherapy, he describes the fundamental ecological focus of ecotherapy at the planetary, societal, group and individual levels. Outlining some of the fundamental dichotomies in ecotherapeutic practice, his chapter gives an in-depth exploration of the history of the field, the practice and the underpinning epistemologies that inform ecotherapy, and it sets the scene for what is to follow.

In her updated chapter, Caroline Brazier explores nature-based therapeutic practice from a Buddhist perspective, placing particular emphasis on the role of mindfulness in the therapeutic relationship outdoors. She discusses the therapist's own quality of mindful attention and capacity for role modelling this quality for the client. Caroline draws from her own unique model, which she calls an other-centred approach, that sees the troubled person existing in an isolated and alienated condition which is then explored through embodied awareness, addressing the conditioned mind and how this drives perceptions, thoughts and relationships. She presents a thoughtful and well-researched chapter which will be of use to those seeking to understand ecotherapy from a Buddhist perspective.

Joe Hinds describes in his chapter an underpinning theoretical position which can account for the therapeutic power of human–nature connection. Drawing on the concept of eudemonia, in other words, attaining a good life and living well in accordance with one's own truth, he locates himself within humanistic and existential frameworks in order to explore how nature is central to promoting eudemonic well-being. However, within this philosophy, there is the recognition that experience of nature can promote fear, arduousness and suffering which may contribute to a more insightful shift in people's perceptions and understandings. This sense of 'terrible joy' captures something of the complexity of our relationship to nature in terms of holistic well-being and the challenges required to reconfigure world-views to elicit psychological and therapeutic benefits.

Martin Jordan explores ecotherapy as a psychotherapy in his original writing from 2016. He critiques the notion of what ecotherapy is, particularly within the UK, where it is still seen as more of an occupational therapy than a psychotherapy. He proposes that by understanding the place and process of early developmental experience in the aetiology of distress and trauma, and drawing in particular from the work of Donald Winnicott, we are better able to understand how space is felt emotionally in therapy. Martin concludes by locating nature as a 'third space' within which psychotherapy is conducted, and which can be a holding and containing space for both therapist and client alike.

Linda Buzzell offers a critical exploration of the role and position of ecotherapy, with particular reference to ecopsychology and makes a distinction between Level 1 and Level 2 ecotherapies.

Level 1 ecotherapies are located within traditional scientific world-views of human–nature relationships, where nature is viewed as a utility to be used by humans, thereby arguably continuing the psychic, social and emotional problems which underpin our current environmental crisis. Level 2 ecotherapies, in contrast, promote a reciprocal healing relationship between humans and nature. Drawing upon the work of several writers in the field of ecopsychology and deep ecology, she presents a multilevel version of ecotherapy in the service of healing both human and planetary distress as reciprocal circles of healing

Research

With the research section we wish to acknowledge the difference in the nature of research within therapy in comparison to more mainstream approaches. While more generic research is often concerned with the numerical, we would suggest that in the art of psychotherapy we do not follow the same research format of such disciplines as psychology – significantly because we are interested in the in-depth nature of human experience, our 'research' will often resemble singular case study material. Much ecotherapy research also follows this trend. Therefore, the research chapters here read like individual research papers, not necessarily synthesizing the broader research field.

The healing essence of human–nature connection and interaction has remained unchanged for millennia and while there are some updates to the research literature within this volume, we think that the older material continues to offer significant relevant support for the practice of ecotherapy. This is research carried out in order to understand further the depth of healing and psychological effects of contact with nature.

Deborah Kelly presents research which focuses on the area of palliative care and how nature can be used in working with this particular client group. Drawing upon Michael Kearney's work and the concept of Asklepian healing, the importance of symbolism and the idea that illness is a quest for healing, she articulates how nature represents a powerful space within which to explore the central issue of life and death in palliative care. Her research findings show that nature plays a central role in the healing and supportive work of palliative care and how it acts as a container for the work, in particular the rhythm of the seasons and the mirror of life and death reflected within these. Of special importance for ecotherapy practice and research is how nature can represent a sacred space through which rituals can be performed in order to make sense of life, death and illness.

Anna Maria Pálsdóttir also discusses research from Sweden's Alnarp Rehabilitation Garden project. Her focus is on how particular design aspects of the garden facilitate recovery in those experiencing mental health problems such as burnout and depression. Her chapter draws upon and further develops the significant body of research carried out in Sweden and Scandinavia into the healing effects of particular garden designs and spaces. She outlines how stages of recovery develop through a relationship to nature within the garden and describes a new and important concept of 'social quietness' which details a strong need to be alone in nature. This includes a profound non-verbal communication with nature which is not only a source of restoration but also seems to positively affect complex mental processes experienced by participants throughout the rehabilitation process.

Matt Adams and Martin Jordan discuss their research carried out with an organization called Grow, located in Brighton in the UK. Grow works with people experiencing mental distress and provides mental health support within a natural space. The project is unique in that it does not utilize horticultural therapy, but provides a safe, supportive group space in nature to aid recovery. An eight-week programme was evaluated in order to understand participants' experience of Grow. Although nature is articulated as an important context for recovery from mental health problems, this is contrasted with indoor mental health environments which are felt by some to be set up in ways that reinforce their symptoms and identity. Other important factors are the level of peer support found on the programme. The report highlights how a natural environment, in a socially supportive context, offers an alternative to the familiar routines and hierarchies of client's experiences of mental health services. In the right conditions, a natural environment supports the development of different and healthier identities, with the potential to aid recovery from psychological distress. Nature seems to play a role in this process, and this is explored in a discussion of the research.

Claire Lamont presents a heuristic study of the awareness of unconscious childhood experiences that are activated via the experience of gardens as an 'evocative object'. Of great interest to psychological practitioners, she focusses on an exploration of how being out in nature supports our 'knowing' of unconscious and tacit aspects of self.

Practice

Hayley Marshall's chapter outlines the roots of her understanding of nature-based psychotherapy from her own experience as a participant in therapy outdoors and from the perspective of transactional analysis and body psychotherapy. Drawing from both theory and case study examples, she positions the importance of the 'body' and embodied processes in nature-based therapy. Employing a range of contemporary psychotherapy theory, her chapter – only slightly amended from the original – stands the test of time in attempting to articulate how therapeutic processes can be understood in a natural environment.

We then re-present Ronen Berger's original chapter outlining his form of ecotherapy called 'Nature Therapy', an approach that is firmly embedded within arts therapies and in particular drama therapy. Berger sees Nature Therapy as a unique approach both related to ecotherapy and ecopsychology, but a further development of these. He outlines the theoretical underpinnings of Nature Therapy as an approach that draws upon creative processes as a therapeutic method with nature positioned as a central partner in the process and presents ideas and practices from shamanism and dramatherapy. Using case examples firmly embedded in practice, he illustrates the praxes and processes in relation to a hexagonal six-point model which incorporates the therapist–client–nature relationship with the group, art and the spiritual dimension on the six points of the star. Seeing Nature Therapy as a development of dramatherapy and other creative expressive therapies, his contribution firmly establishes the centrality of the link between ecotherapy and creative arts therapies.

Ecotherapy is not just about our relationship with the natural environment but also concerns our relationship with animals and their positive effect on our mental health. Joe Hinds and Louise Ranger discuss equine-assisted therapy (EAT). Positioning EAT as a unique form of animal-assisted therapy, they outline some of the important epistemological issues that underpin their understanding of this approach. Turning to the work of Prouty (2001), they show how his idea of pre-therapy may be seen as an important dimension to better understand how animals such as horses act as a therapeutic 'bridge' in determining psychological health. Human–animal relationships can provide a non-linguistic, cooperative connection that helps to define 'self' in reference to 'other'. These unique therapeutic associations also utilize transpersonal ideas to show how the relationship with a horse can provoke a sense of awe, enabling the horse to act as a transitional object to facilitate movement from one pattern of human relating and behaviour to another. The chapter represents an important step forward in developing knowledge about the therapeutic processes that come into play in this form of ecotherapy.

Elaine Thélier introduces the idea that working therapeutically outdoors can be an opportunity to explore a 'spirituality of the earth' and thus discover our own spirituality. She discusses how ecotherapy, an immersion in nature and a deep listening to the more-than-human world can develop the knowing and expression of a less explored part of ourselves.

Chiara Fortina Santin describes her own journey towards rewilding therapy and via a case study, utilizes ecosystemic ideas about working therapeutically in nature. She concludes with some reflections on the all-important subject of therapeutic activism and the urgency to harness imagination to promote new landscapes for mental health services that promote the benefits of spending time in nature for ecological well-being.

Education

The inclusion of education as a new section signals a step change since the first volume. As the number of ecotherapy practitioners has grown especially in Europe but also other parts of the world, a corresponding interest has developed in how ecotherapists find adequate, congruent training and supervision to support the kind of work they offer. Practitioners are often seeking 'something different' in terms of an educative process and in more-than-human places that could guide and support this. The chapters here are a foray into this cross disciplinary terrain – between them they offer a micro version of 'theory, research and practice' in the development of ecotherapists.

Alan Bainbridge draws on a range of theoretical disciplines to make useful and insightful connections between education and ecopsychotherapy. It will be argued the theory and practice of ecotherapy and education are founded on and supported by similar principles. He also suggests the need to rekindle an awareness of the wilder, less defended, aspects of the human condition and that both are motivated by anxiety.

Giles Barrow and Hayley Marshall present an extended education case study focused on developing ecological approaches for human relations practitioners. The programme they present combines embodied experiential encounters and direct application of theory for an educative ecological practice.

Natasha Sephton brings an evocative autobiographical account of nature experience and describes how these have been harnessed for therapeutic supervision. Natasha describes how the vibrancy and aliveness of an embodied supervision immersed in the more-than-human world elicits important relational awareness and the development of an ecological mind.

To bring our volume to a close, Mary Dees brings a powerful personal narrative of her journey of becoming an ecological psychotherapist. The chapter presents a route map, albeit a personal one, made up of many threads, including trainers, supervisors, teachers, peers, clients and the land itself, for aspiring practitioners to consider.

The growth of ecotherapy, and its allied variants – including new forms of psychotherapy (e.g. Buzzell and Chalquist 2009; Rust 2020), continues to grow and flourish globally. Consequently, alongside a proliferation of journals, journal articles, and reports (e.g. see Chapter 8: Matthew Adams and Martin Jordan) there have been several recent texts that have an ecopsychology or ecotherapy or ecopsychotherapy focus (e.g. Duncan 2018; Fortina Santin 2024; Key and Tudor 2023; Rust 2020).

Our aim in compiling and editing this book is to bring some of these emerging strands together to provide an overview of ecotherapy at this time. In outlining the theoretical, practice, research and educative strands of ecotherapy, we wish to show the important aspects of this fast developing and vibrant field of practice that, given the current state of mental health and the unfolding environmental crisis, is urgently required. We hope you enjoy the book and that new possibilities emerge as a result.

References

Abram, D. (1996), *The Spell of the Sensuous*, New York: Random House.

Bluhdorn, I. (2001), 'Reflexivity and Self-Referentiality: On the Normative Foundations of Ecological Communication', in C. B. Grant and D. McLaughlin (eds), *Language-Meaning-Social Construction Interdisciplinary Studies*, 181–201, New York: Rodopi.

Buzzell, L., and C. Chalquist (2009), *Ecotherapy: Healing with Nature in Mind*, San Francisco: Sierra Club Books.

Chalquist, C. (2013), 'Review of Ecopsychology: Science, Totems, and the Technological Species,' *Ecopsychology* 5 (1): 60–4.

Clinebell, H. (1996), *Ecotherapy: Healing Ourselves, Healing the Earth*, Minneapolis, MN: Fortress Press.

Duncan, R. (2018), *Nature in Mind: Systemic Thinking and Imagination in Ecopsychology and Mental Health*, Oxford: Routledge.

Fortina Santin, C. (2024), *Rewilding Therapy. Ecosystemic Theory and Practice*, Farnhill: Everything is Connected Press.

Ghosh, A. (2021), *The Nutmeg's Curse – Parables for a Planet in Crisis*, UK: John Murray.

Hasbach, P. H. (2012), 'Ecotherapy', in P. H. Kahn Jr. and P. H. Hasbach (eds), *Ecopsychology: Science, Totems, and the Technological Species*, 115–39, Cambridge, MA: MIT Press.

Hegarty, J. (2010), 'Out of the Consulting Room and into the Woods? Experiences of Nature-Connectedness and Self-Healing', *European Journal of Ecopsychology* 1: 64–84.

Jordan, M. (2009), 'Back to Nature', *Therapy Today* 20 (3): 26–8.

Jordan, M. (2015), *Nature and Therapy: Understanding Counselling and Psychotherapy in Outdoor Spaces*, Hove: Routledge.

Jordan, M., and H. Marshall (2010), 'Taking Counselling and Psychotherapy Outside: Destruction or Enrichment of the Therapeutic Frame?', *European Journal of Psychotherapy & Counselling* 12 (4): 345–59. https://doi.org/10.1080/13642537.2010.530105.

Jung, C. G. (1989), *Memories, Dreams, Reflections*, Knopf: Double Day.

Key, D., and K. Tudor (2023), *Ecotherapy: A Field Guide*, Bicester, Oxfordshire, UK: Karnac Books.

Latour, R. (1993), *We Have Never Been Modern*, Hemel Hempstead: Harvester Wheatsheaf.

Macnaghten, P., and J. Urry (1998), *Contested Natures*, London: Sage.

Macy, J. (2009), 'The Greening of the Self', in L. Buzzell and C. Chalquist (eds), *Ecotherapy: Healing with Nature in Mind*, 238–45, San Francisco: Sierra Club Books.

Metzner, R. (2009), 'Green Psychology, Shamanism, and Therapeutic Rituals', in L. Buzzell and C. Chalquist (eds), *Ecotherapy: Healing with Nature in Mind*, 256–61, San Francisco: Sierra Club Books.

Prouty, G. F. (2001), 'The Practice of Pre-Therapy', *Journal of Contemporary Psychotherapy* 31: 31–40.

Roszak, T. (1995), 'When Psyche Meets Gaia', in T. Roszak, M. E. Gomes and A. D. Kanner (eds), *Ecopsychology: Restoring the Earth, Healing the Mind*, 1–17, San Francisco: Sierra Club Books.

Roszak, T., M. E. Gomes and A. D. Kanner (eds) (1995), *Ecopsychology: Restoring the Earth, Healing the Mind*, San Francisco: Sierra Club Books.

Rust, M. -J. (2020), *Towards an Ecopsychotherapy*, Woodbridge, UK: Confer.

Sabini, M. (2008), *C. G. Jung on Nature, Technology, and Modern Life*, Berkeley, CA: North Atlantic Books.

Searles, H. (1960), *The Non-Human Environment in Normal Development and in Schizophrenia*, Madison, CT: International Universities Press.

Wall-Kimmerer, R. (2025), 'Becoming Earth – Experimental Theology', *Emergence Magazine*, https://emergencemagazine.org/essay/becoming-earth/, accessed 10 July 2025.

Contributors

Matthew Adams is Chartered Psychologist and Principal Lecturer in Psychology in the School of Humanities and Social Science at the University of Brighton, specializing in critical environmental and social psychology – particularly the psychological and relational dimensions of ecological crisis, human–animal relationships and the Anthropocene. He is an interdisciplinary researcher whose books include *Ecological Crisis, Sustainability & the Psychosocial Subject* (2016), and *Anthropocene Psychology: Being Human in a More-Than-Human World* (2020). Matthew's recent work, funded by an Arts and Humanities Research Council (AHRC) fellowship, explores arts-based and multispecies methods to challenge dominant narratives in psychology and amplify more-than-human perspectives.

Alan Bainbridge is Professor in Education at Queen Margaret University, Edinburgh and Visiting Reader in Education and Sustainability at Canterbury Christ Church University. He has an expansive view of education that ranges across ecology, psychology, politics and sustainability. He uses broadly narrative-based research methods to work qualitatively, exploring the development of education professional practice, and the transformative nature of human or more-than-human relationships. ORCID: 0000-0001-7783-7747

Giles Barrow has a background in education having worked in mainstream and special provision in south London as well as adult and community education. He has trained in transactional analysis in the educational field. He has also been a qualified mountain leader which is where he first started his professional career in outdoor practice. Giles has written widely on the themes of education, school culture, relational aspects of teaching and learning and ecological pedagogy. In 2023 he completed his doctoral study, 'Soil, Soul and Society in the Educational Encounter'.

Ronen Berger, PhD, is the founder of the Nature Therapy Center and the Nature Therapy Training Program at Tel Aviv University and is head of the Drama Therapy master's programme at the College of Arts and Social Work, Israel. He teaches nature therapy, art therapy and creative group work in Israel and around the world while researching, organizing and attending conferences and publishing on these topics. He lives on Kibbutz Snir in the north of Israel, where he tries to combine life as an academic and therapist with a close connection to nature, creativity and community. www.naturetherapy.org and ronenbw@gmail.com

Caroline Brazier is a psychotherapist and ecotherapy practitioner and trainer. She is the author of seven books on Psychotherapy, Ecotherapy and Buddhism. Her most recent book was *Ecotherapy in Practice: A Buddhist Model* (2017). She was course leader of Tariki Trust's therapeutic training programmes including the Ten Directions Training with its Certificate in Ecotherapy until 2021, and she now continues to teach on the programme, co-ordinating the Diploma in Ecotherapy.

Linda Buzzell has been a psychotherapist for fifty years. Since 2000 she has specialized in pioneering the fields of ecopsychology and ecotherapy. In 2009 she and Craig Chalquist edited a anthology, *Ecotherapy: Healing with Nature in Mind*. She is on the Editorial Board of *Ecopsychology*, a peer-reviewed journal in the field, and is adjunct faculty at Pacifica Graduate Institute. In 2023, she and Craig authored an influential article, 'From Eco-Anxiety to Eco-Resilience: Toward a Psychology of Care', in *Eco-Anxiety and Pandemic Distress: Psychological Perspectives on Resilience and Interconnectedness*. She and her husband Larry Saltzman has created a backyard food forest around her home that serves as her ecotherapy office.

Mary Dees, MSc PTSTA (UKCP Registered), is an ecological psychotherapist, supervisor and trainer working on the border of Greater Manchester/Peak District. She runs outdoor psychotherapy and supervision groups in the Peak District. She works systemically, including deep adaptation to the climate emergency and biodiversity crisis. Mary is also a master's degree Environmental Scientist and runs learning programmes, including Climate Change Programmes for NHS leaders. She is part of the Transition movement and runs Climate Cafes and Grief rituals.

Thomas Doherty is a clinical and environmental psychologist based in Portland, Oregon. His paper 'The Psychological Impacts of Global Climate Change', co-authored by Susan Clayton, has been cited over 1,300 times. He is a fellow of the American Psychological Association; past president of the Society for Environmental, Population and Conservation Psychology; and was founding editor of the journal *Ecopsychology* and founding director of the Ecopsychology program at Lewis and Clark Graduate School. Thomas Doherty co-hosts the Climate Change and Happiness podcast and is the author of *Surviving Climate Anxiety: A Guide to Coping, Healing, and Thriving* (2025). thomasdoherty.com.

Chiara Fortina Santin is an Italian woman in her fifties. Born in a middle-class family in a small village near the Swiss Alps and lakes, in 1998 she landed in Sussex (UK) with her partner as economic migrants. Chiara is a systemic family psychotherapist, supervisor and trainer, and director of Family Therapy Services and Rainbow CommUnity Projects CIC. She has been working as an independent psychotherapist with adoptive families since 2012 after ten years in social care. She has been teaching on systemic courses for twelve years. In the last ten years she has developed her ecosystemic practice in nature and is now focussed on community building and depathologizing mental health support. She also offers ecosystemic training, supervision and online groups for professionals. She loves nature, colours, creativity, dancing, doing and making. She is committed to social justice, self-reflexivity, multiple languages and diversity in dialogue. Chiara has written many academic articles, and she has published a book *Rewilding Therapy. Ecosystemic Theory and Practice*. www.rainbowcommunityprojects.co.uk

Joe Hinds is an integrative psychotherapist and group supervisor and a member of the BACP and UPCA (UKCP). He maintains a small therapeutic practice in East Sussex and is a Senior Lecturer in psychotherapy at the University of Greenwich in the UK. He has combined interests in environmental psychology and psychotherapy to extend and deepen his understanding of human–nature relationships and has published a number of papers relating to these. He has a passion for the outdoors and spends time in nature as a therapist, and for relaxation and inspiration as often as he can. JoehCP@yahoo.co.uk

Martin Jordan, PhD, was a HCPC-registered counselling psychologist, UKCP-registered psychotherapist and counsellor. Prior to his death in 2017, he was a key pioneer in the development of ecopsychotherapeutic practices, taking his therapeutic work outdoors into natural spaces. He also trained and worked with a range of mental health professionals who wanted to explore the healing potential of nature in their therapeutic practice. Dr Jordan's research and practice interests in this area culminated in the publication of *Nature and Therapy: Understanding Counselling and Psychotherapy in Outdoor Spaces* in 2014, the first book of its kind to explore the theory and practice of outdoor counselling and psychotherapy.

Deborah Kelly is an integrative arts psychotherapist, group facilitator and teacher. She has worked in end-of-life care for over twenty-five years, with individuals and groups. Her interests lie in working with nature and embodied imagination in her practice and academic research. She initiated two projects for palliative care groups, in and with nature and drawing on principles of Asclepian healing, which were the subject of her doctoral research. She has published works on ecotherapy, palliative care, environmental arts and transpersonal research. She also participates in groups in nature exploring belonging, aspects of deep listening as activism, and elderhood.

Claire Lamont is a psychotherapist and ecotherapist with a private practice in Edinburgh. After completing her MSc at the University of Greenwich in 2020, she started outdoor work with clients in London parks during the pandemic, before moving to Scotland and setting up an ecotherapy practice working in different green spaces across Edinburgh. She practises with gratitude for the rugged and often awe-inspiring landscapes of Scotland, alongside respect for clients' openness to outdoor therapy there through winter. Claire.lamont@gmail.com

Hayley Marshall, ESD, CTA, MSc, is one of the UK's leading clinical ecological specialists. Profoundly rooted in the broader network of the living world, her work is focused on awakening human relations practitioners' eco-spiritual development in alliance with the earth. In service of this she incorporates ecological movement and contemporary shamanic practices into all her trainings. She has written several book chapters, journal articles on clinical outdoor practice. She works exclusively outside in her private practice and also offers a variety of training courses and professional development groups for ecological practitioners at her own training centre. www.centrefornaturalreflection.co.uk

Anna María Pálsdóttir is an associate professor and senior lecturer at the Swedish University of Agricultural Sciences (SLU), specializing in environmental psychology and nature-based interventions. With a background in horticulture and landscape planning, her research focuses on sensory environments, stress recovery, and the design of health-promoting and sustainable landscapes, particularly through therapeutic gardens and nature-based rehabilitation. She has led several studies utilizing the Alnarp Rehabilitation Garden, as well as studies on vocational training, forest bathing and nature-based rehabilitation. As a co-founder of SLU's master's programme in Outdoor Environments for Health and Well-Being, she promotes interdisciplinary approaches to integrating nature into healthcare, urban planning and social services.

Louise Ranger (MSc, BA, PgDip) is a humanistic therapist and clinical supervisor with a specialist interest in animal-assisted therapy and pet bereavement. Her practice integrates equine-assisted therapy (EAT), exploring the transformative potential of therapeutic relationships with horses and the natural environment. Drawing on training in intergenerational mediation, Shiatsu (human and equine), and mindfulness-based approaches, Louise brings an embodied, relational awareness to her work. She also supports student well-being within higher education, fostering emotional resilience, and is passionate about the meeting point of nature, connection, and mental health. Louise continues to explore how ecotherapy can nurture healing and growth. Louise.ranger@outlook.com

Natasha Sephton has an established private practice spanning over twenty years, based among hills and woodlands on the edge of the Peak District, UK. Working outdoors and online she delivers drama therapy, lifespan integration and nature-based arts therapy. Trained in creative approaches to supervision and, as an approved Lifespan Integration consultant, she supervises a range of practitioners with their work in nature-based therapies, the arts therapies, lifespan integration, as well as clinical management roles and supervision. Previously, Natasha worked as a youth worker before qualifying as an outdoor development trainer delivering wilderness residentials for young people in South West England and Wales. On qualifying as a drama therapist in 2005, she worked in a CAMHS service in Yorkshire and as associate lecturer at the University of Derby before entering private practice. Natasha's trauma-informed practice follows a compassion-focussed, neuro-psychological and psychodynamic approach. Placing emphasis on embodiment and creative processes, engagement with ecological relatedness is central to her work. www.natasheseph ton.com

Elaine Thélier, originally from an educational background, has worked outdoors since 2006 as a horticultural therapist, counsellor, and now supervisor supporting other ecotherapists. Elaine managed allotment projects and community gardens and co-founded the Growing Works charity. Elaine's spiritual path has been long and varied, with an MA in Education and Religion in Contemporary Society. She is tutor and assessor on the Spiritual Coach and Caregiving Diploma delivered by the Spiritual Companions Trust. Elaine also works as an artist. www.elainethelier.co.uk

Part I

Theory

1

Theoretical and empirical foundations for ecotherapy

Thomas J. Doherty

Introduction

This chapter explores some of the theoretical and empirical foundations for ecotherapy. They are not meant to be definitive but rather to assist the reader in reflecting on their own practice and to better appreciate and critique the ecotherapy approaches detailed in this volume. The goal is to create a conceptual ground for ecotherapy and to identify some overarching theory, assumptions and findings that act as a shared commons.

There are hundreds of established psychotherapy and mental health counselling approaches (Prochaska and Norcross 2009). They promote differing visions of mental health and well-being. They use different tools to treat or prevent what, in their view, constitutes life problems or psychopathology. And, they intervene at levels of scale from individual neurophysiology, thoughts and emotions to the structure of daily life, to the level of intimate and family relationships, and on to group, community and population levels (Burns and Burns-Lundgren 2015; Roth and Fonagy 1996). So, once one becomes educated in this domain, it becomes clear that simply saying that one does 'counselling' or 'psychotherapy' is not enough to give an adequate description. This begs the questions: 'What kind of psychotherapy and for whom? How is human psyche and agency conceived? On what standard of health and well-being is it based? What are its methods? How are outcomes measured?'

So too with ecotherapy: The potential is great for approaches that apply existing therapeutic models in a natural ecological context and for the creation of others that constitute distinct innovations to therapy business-as-usual. In addition to the questions posed above, an ecotherapist might ask: 'How does the therapy involve the interplay of social systems *and* natural systems? What is the role of the physical context (the built space of the consulting room or the local natural environment) in the therapy? In what way does the therapy address the "client" or "patient" as a human animal, a social primate of the species Homo sapiens? How are other species recognized and involved in the therapy? How is relationship to community, bioregion or the planet recognized? What is the role of environmental ethics in the therapy and how are issues like global climate change or environment justice addressed? How do these factors figure into the conception of health outcomes and the methods of the therapy or not?'

These are profound questions that draw attention to basic assumptions people share about psychotherapy. There is a strong element of consciousness-raising inherent in surfacing them. To assert that nature or environmental issues *do not* figure into therapy can be perfectly reasonable and ethical given the issue addressed – and need not imply that these issues are not important to health. But, for our purposes, physical place, more-than-human nature, and global environmental issues *do* figure into therapy and counselling, and for good reason. And, while ecotherapy is still evolving in terms of variety and specialization, we can sketch out its theoretical and empirical underpinnings. This will allow for a more nuanced discussion of ecotherapy and set the stage for answering the question: 'What kind of ecotherapy do you do?'

The psychological territory of ecotherapy

To get a feel for the content of ecotherapy, consider the following questions, drawn from research questionnaires used in environmental psychology and sociology. Along with your intellectual responses, note the extent to which the questions elicit an emotional charge or a reaction. Also, notice how responding implicitly requires you to consider yourself in relation to others in your social group and to others in society:

- 'We are approaching the limit of the number of people the earth can support.' Agree or disagree?
- 'Like a tree can be part of a forest, I feel embedded within the broader natural world.' Strongly disagree, neutral or strongly agree?
- I have done this: 'Walk barefoot in a wild area; Hunt, fish, trap, raise and butcher my own meat; Navigate by the sun or the stars' Yes or no?
- Assuming global warming is happening, do you think it is
  (a) Caused mostly by human activities,
  (b) Caused mostly by natural changes in the environment,
  (c) Other,
  (d) None of the above because global warming isn't happening?

- 'I am worried about risks to human health from nearby environmental pollution.' Agree or disagree?
- Please indicate how often you have done each of the following in the last year (i.e. never, rarely, sometimes, often, very often, non-applicable):
  1. Composted food scraps
  2. Conserved gasoline by walking or bicycling
  3. Voted for a candidate who supported environmental issues, etc.

These survey items are meant to determine (1) whether respondents believe human activities are subject to or exempt from the natural order (NEP Scale, Dunlap 2008); (2) the extent to which someone perceives they are connected with nature (Connectedness to Nature Scale, Mayer and Franz 2004); (3) immersion and hands-on self-sufficiency in the outdoors, as in a hunter-gatherer context (Participation in Nature Scale, Scott, Amel and Manning 2014); (4) beliefs about human responsibility for global climate change (Global Warming's Six Americas Screening, Maibach et al. 2011); (5) emotions regarding felt impact of environmental changes (Environmental Distress Scale, Higginbotham et al. 2007) and (6) the frequency of various conservation behaviours (Proenvironmental Behaviour Scale, Schultz and Zelezny 1998). Your responding, both emotional and intellectual, gives a flavour of the mental activity associated with environmental perception, and how this is linked with identity, self-image, moral judgments about self and others, and expectations for responsible behaviour. It is in this realm of *ecological-self-in-relation* – to one's own ideals, to other humans as they utilize natural resources for survival, to other species and habitats, and to the planet Earth as a whole – that ecotherapy takes place.

Defining ecotherapy

For the sake of our work, *ecotherapy* will be defined as *psychotherapeutic activities (counselling, psychotherapy, social work, self-help, prevention, public health activities) undertaken with an ecological consciousness or intent.* These activities are considered *ecological* as they partake of natural ecology such as the local environment or the planetary biosphere, and not only the social ecology of human relationships and culture (Bronfenbrenner 2005; Cook 2012). Put in the language of conservation science, they concern coupled natural and human systems. While the human socio-cultural sphere, including the information technologies through which we can perceive global issues, is embedded in ecotherapy work, it is important to realize that the human need not be the basis or starting point of ecotherapeutic activities. In fact, a goal of many ecotherapies would be to bracket human culture and technologies, and look to the 'more-than-human' world (Abram 1996) for a holistic and fundamental experience of identity, mental health and well-being.

Put another way, ecotherapy, in terms of its orientation and moral compass, can be seen as 'ecocentric' (i.e. focused on systems, wholes and interdependence, with humans being one part of the natural order). This is in comparison to the more normative and unacknowledged 'anthropocentric' bias nature of psychotherapy and counselling (i.e. human-centred, and seeing all nature in terms of human ideas, uses and benefits). And as noted above, just as there is a great diversity in the form, content and scope of the anthropocentric psychotherapy approaches, there is a similar potential for diversity in the eco-psychotherapeutic enterprise, both in theory and based on a survey of extant approaches.

Defining ecotherapy

Psychotherapeutic activities (counselling, psychotherapy, social work, self-help, prevention, public health activities):

- Undertaken with an ecological consciousness or intent
- Often utilizing natural settings, activities or processes as an integral part of the therapeutic process
- Focusing on ecological aspects of self, identity and behaviour
- At various scales, from personal to planetary

Ecotherapy activities and scope

Ecotherapy often, but not necessarily, utilizes natural settings, activities, metaphors and processes as an ingredient of therapy. This can include conducting therapeutic conversations out-of-doors, or using walking, gardening or structured challenge and adventure. This may also involve bringing sense of place and other species into the therapeutic process (e.g. having a daily outdoor retreat space, engaging in animal-assisted therapy or simply considering the rights and well-being of other species and natural systems as a part of therapeutic goals). At its most basic, ecotherapy welcomes ecological aspects of self, identity and behaviour into the psychotherapeutic arena. Depending on the recipient(s) of the therapy, this ecological self may include direct or vicarious experience of natural or technological disasters, concerns about environmental toxins or degradation, or considerations of personal responsibility for larger global issues like climate change.

Most ecotherapy remains private and concerns the private sphere, just like traditional anthropocentric psychotherapies. However, like some anthropocentric therapies that are explicitly political in nature (e.g. feminist or liberation-based therapies), some ecotherapy approaches operate as a form of social and environmental activism – a sort of environmentalist therapy – and utilize individual therapeutic experiences to resolve a cultural-level split from wild nature in developed societies that is seen to impact health and identity, and to drive ecologically destructive behaviours.

Cultural competence and ecotherapy

Before moving forward, a caveat is important. Despite intuition and evidence that adding a natural ecological dimension to psychotherapy and counselling is a healthy progression, would-be ecotherapists need to be prepared for scepticism and resistance, both from other mental health providers and from the public. Some scepticism is to be expected of any new intervention and can be addressed by presenting clear rationale, evidence and outcomes for ecotherapy. However, the consciousness-raising aspect of ecotherapy can also activate cultural stereotypes about environmentalism and draw the discussion into often-polarized environmental debates. Whether someone may intellectually and functionally link the concepts of psychology, psychotherapy and nature has much to do with their environmental world-view, which in turn is informed by their cultural background, education and personal experience. So, in much the same way that cultural competency is essential to any psychotherapy (Sue et al. 2009), ecotherapists need to be culturally competent about the environmental world-views of those they serve, their colleagues and their communities. This is one rationale for including findings on environmental beliefs and attitudes drawn from environmental and conservation psychology as a theoretical and empirical touchstone for ecotherapy.

To give a personal example, writing as an able-bodied, heterosexual, white male, in the Pacific Northwest of the United States, my ecotherapeutic work more easily partakes of regional values and a commonly held, self-actualizing 'Go West' narrative in US culture (Nash 1992). Your region may be more or less receptive in terms or programmes, community uptake and institutional support, and have different cultural influences such as northern European countries versus Asian countries (Kellert 1993). Given your diverse personhood, and your social and cultural milieu, you may be able to be more or less 'out' with your ecotherapy philosophy. But, you can be confident there are resources available to ground your practice in a coherent theoretical and empirical structure.

The evolution of ecotherapy

Ecotherapy as a discrete endeavour, in the form of explicit environmental or ecological initiatives in counselling and psychotherapy, coalesced in the last decades of the twentieth century (Burns 1998; Clinebell 1996; Conn 1998; Howard 1993;

Macy and Young-Brown 1998; Roszak, Gomes and Kanner 1995; Swanson 1995). These advances, in turn, drew from many contemporary and historic sources, notably the nineteenth- and twentieth-century conservation and environmental movements (Adelson et al. 2008; Gottlieb 2005) and associated work in the peace, nuclear disarmament and environmental justice movements (Bullard et al. 2014; Macy 1983). Ecotherapy is also influenced by environmental spirituality of various kinds (Badiner 1990; Berry 1988), ecofeminism (Mies and Shiva 1993; Plumwood 1993), deep ecology (Drengson, Devall and Schroll 2011), early ecopsychology theorizing (Roszak 1978; Shepard 1982), and work on environmental literacy (Orr 1991; Thomashow 1995).

In recent years, there's been a flowering of ecotherapy initiatives of increasing sophistication and specialization. Theoretical innovations at the turn of the millennium (Fisher 2012; Kidner 2001; Weber-Nicholsen 2001) set the stage for broad-based surveys of ecotherapy practice and subculture (Buzzell and Chalquist 2009). More recently, unique integrations by scholars and practitioners (Hasbach 2012; Jordan 2015; Totton 2011) and development of targeted therapies have continued this trend, for example: coping with climate change (Randall 2009), addressing trauma in military veterans (Vella, Milligan and Bennett 2013), outdoor therapies for adolescents (Gass, Gillis and Russell 2012) and modern day rites-of-passage (Plotkin 2003). In the evolution of ecotherapy, one can discern a creative tension between grassroots innovations and institutional, research-based initiatives and integration of additional therapy perspectives (e.g. psychodynamic, cognitive-behavioural, mindfulness-based) into the gestalt, humanistic and transpersonal frameworks that were prominent in earlier waves of ecotherapy.

There are a number of parallel initiatives in mental and physical healthcare and social services that can be considered ecotherapeutic. These include environmental social work, horticultural therapy, animal-assisted therapies and disaster relief (Blazina, Boyraz and Shen-Miller 2011; Gray, Coates and Hetherington 2012; Haller and Kramer 2006; Jungerson et al. 2013). Differences between ecotherapy and these parallel initiatives are more often an artefact of the disciplinary silo in which they've developed than in the goals, practices or outcomes. Ecotherapists will find common ground in terms of actual practices by aligning with professionals in these areas.

As a counter to the apparent newness and novelty of ecotherapy, it's important to note that outdoor therapeutic activities, for example in the form of therapeutic camps, have been present in the United States and in other countries since the 1860s (White 2012) and therapeutic conversations while walking outdoors were a common practice in the early days of the psychoanalytic movement (Reik 1948). From the perspective of Western cultural history and environmental philosophies, the impulse towards holistic and therapeutic approaches to human's relationship with nature and wilderness are perennial (Oelschlaeger 1991). Most of today's modern ecotherapies can be meaningfully understood as responses to changes in Western Culture (e.g. a desacralized nature, urbanization, increased use of machines and technology) that date to the Enlightenment and the Industrial Revolution (Merchant 1980).

Empirical and theoretical basis in environmentally focused psychology

While ecotherapy as a field is rather new and relatively untested in many domains, there are a number of long-standing environmental initiatives in psychology that provide theoretical constructs and empirical findings useful to the practising ecotherapist. At times, locating these requires some effort and scholarly investigation. While original studies may not have been explicitly designed with psychotherapy in mind, findings on environmental topics that impact on human health and well-being, crowding, noise, the effects of information technology, impacts of natural disasters (Bechtel and Churchman 2002), will have obvious bearing on the creation of therapeutic contexts. Other studies, such as on the effective design of wildlife conservation programmes or ways to reduce barriers to pro-environment behaviour (Clayton and Myers 2009), provide guidance on how to support environmental engagement on the part of individuals and communities. On a deeper level, environmental psychology research provides insights on basic perceptions of nature and the natural environment and the development of environmental world-views.

There is great diversity among psychology-environment approaches in terms of epistemology, methodology and goals. The categories below (e.g. environmental psychology and ecopsychology) while useful in terms of conducting a literature review, are also somewhat arbitrary as these areas overlap and individual researchers and practitioners do not always hew to these labels. Various theoretical and practical debates among environmental psychology and ecotherapy scholars will broaden the personal and professional perspectives of would-be ecotherapists: certainly Thomas Doherty's interviews with Robert Greenway, Sherri Weber-Nicholsen, Joseph Reser (2009), Michael Cohen (2010), Andy Fisher, Riley Dunlap (2011) and Peter Kahn and Patricia Hasbach (2012) have aided this process.

There is a rich history of study of the dynamic interchange between humans and their environmental milieu, both built and natural, and how this relates to both basic psychological processes and the amelioration of social problems. This area coalesced into the subfield of 'environmental psychology' in the late 1960s and early 1970s (Ittelson et al. 1974). More recently, environmental psychology of the spatial and built environment has continued to grow and evolve in terms of focus and research methods (Gifford 2007) and interweave a more explicit conservation mission (Clayton 2012).

Some areas of environmental psychology that are of particular interest to ecotherapists are Stokols et al.'s (2009) theory and findings regarding contemporary polyfunctional environments (i.e. spaces that combine home, work and social settings and are linked through instantaneous global information technologies) and how these influence global environmental consciousness and mood and well-being. Also, research on links between clinical and environmental psychology, for example, in terms of aetiology and treatment of anxiety disorders (Anthony and Watkins 2002) and on the effective design of healthcare settings and psychotherapists' offices (Devlin 2014), have practical significance. Finally, environmental psychology has much to offer in terms of understanding the various aspects of global climate change as an existential reality, and in terms of disaster impacts and mitigation and adaptation responses (Doherty, 2015; Reser and Swim 2011).

Ecotherapy is probably most associated with taking therapy 'outdoors' (Jordan and Marshall 2010). Indeed, findings on the benefits of greenery and natural settings for psychological health and well-being through stress reduction, improved cognitive and emotional functioning, and the development of identity, efficacy and meaning, are some of the strongest in the social sciences (Kaplan and Kaplan 1989). This knowledge has been applied in the design of buildings and workspaces, healing gardens in hospitals, and in community-wide greening programmes (Frumkin 2012; Hartig and Marcus 2006; Ulrich at al. 2008). As I have argued, knowledge of the therapeutic effects of nearby and wild nature can be seen as a form of basic 'mental health literacy' in terms of self-help strategies and potential for psychological treatments (see Jorm 2012, cited in Doherty and Chen, 2016 .

Conservation psychology coalesced as an interdisciplinary, 'crisis discipline' modelled after conservation biology, in which social scientists partnered with natural resource and wildlife conservation colleagues (Saunders 2003). Conservation psychology theory and research is particularly useful to ecotherapy given its explicit focus and research findings on environmental identity (Clayton 2003) and the effects urban 'nearby' nature, human–wildlife interactions and the psychological basis for care of other species, for instance in terms of fostering the public education and conservation efforts of zoos and aquariums and in terms of managing wild lands (Clayton and Myers 2009).

Conservation psychology also provides examples of effective conservation behaviour change programmes and detailed studies of barriers and incentives to pro-environmental behaviours in complex, real-world contexts (McKenzie-Mohr et al. 2011). This includes the role of attention and mindfulness in making pro-environmental behavioural choices (Amel, Manning and Scott 2009). Given that the factors that promote successful conservation or sustainability programmes are often difficult to determine and counterintuitive (Nolan et al. 2008), the empirical studies of successful conservation programmes are very important for ecotherapists who seek to influence behaviour change or to promote programmes that have a higher likelihood of success.

In contrast to the more conventional disciplinary approaches associated with environmental and conservation psychology, ecopsychology can be seen as a transdisciplinary area that critiques normative, anthropocentric psychology in general where more-than-human nature remains effectively absent. This includes a critique of other environmental psychology approaches that operate on a reductive, experimental basis and downplay experiential and therapeutic aspects of nature-connectedness and lack a critical focus on systems of power and issues of social and environmental justice. In contrast, ecopsychology theorists seek to promote a more embodied, ethical interdependence with the natural world (Roszak 1992). While again quite diverse in terms of perspectives and approaches, most ecopsychology work can be characterized as holistic, departing from the basic Cartesian split associated with Western science and envisioning the human psyche and psychological processes as more fundamentally embedded in natural and wild systems (Kahn and Hasbach 2012; and Bragg's 1996 concept of 'ecological self'). Ecopsychology theorizing tends to be explicitly political, drawing from critical social theory and feminism to address issues of power, ideology and economic processes that drive humans' exploitation of other peoples, species and planetary resources (Fisher 2012). Ecopsychologists also tend to adopt a more explicit stance as therapeutic environmental activists, often working in grassroots settings (Macy and Young Brown 1998).

With its validation of the emotional impacts of environmental issues and normalization of environmental fears and anxieties, ecopsychology can be seen as helping to create ecotherapy as an endeavour. These areas are highly overlapped and for some practitioners, ecotherapy would be seen as an applied form of ecopsychology (Buzzell and Chalquist 2009). However, given the potential variety of ecotherapy settings and activities, philosophically diverse approaches to the theoretical and empirical basis of ecotherapy, and multi-culturally diverse practitioners, it's more useful to see ecopsychology as a key theoretical and practical contributor to ecotherapy but to keep some conceptual openness between these areas.

Theoretical synthesis: Identity, self, consciousness and setting

The environmentally focused schools of psychology described above provide measurable theoretical constructs that help us to understand the synergy of physical-environmental, social-behavioural and embodied-experiential phenomena that come into play in ecotherapy. From a non-reductive perspective, the cognitive and intellectual realm of beliefs, attitudes and attributions about the self and world (Clayton 2003) is continually influenced by actual experience of being in the world (Bragg 1996). Embodied experiences of ecological self are intimately influenced by the quality of one's moment-to-moment consciousness and focus of attention such as mindfulness, sense of flow, attention to patterns in nearby nature, or alternatively, immersion in communications technology or other human-centric stimuli (Amel, Manning and Scott 2009; Stokols et al. 2009). Identity, self and consciousness cannot be meaningfully separated from the design of the physical setting, whether built or natural, and whether restorative or stressful (Kaplan, Kaplan and Ryan 1998).

For example, a relaxing walk in a safe, forested park setting will provide opportunities to attend to natural views and stimuli (soft fascination) and facilitate an experience of ecologically embedded self that will influence one's cognitive appraisal of their identity and mood, and thoughts about the world at large. Conversely, a high intensity behavioural setting exhibiting hard fascination (e.g. driving in rush hour traffic), particularly a poly-functional setting with continuous access to global information technology, will provide a different set of stimuli to attend to and a different quality of consciousness and physiological arousal. This in turn is likely to be experienced as a different sense of self and to give rise to different thoughts

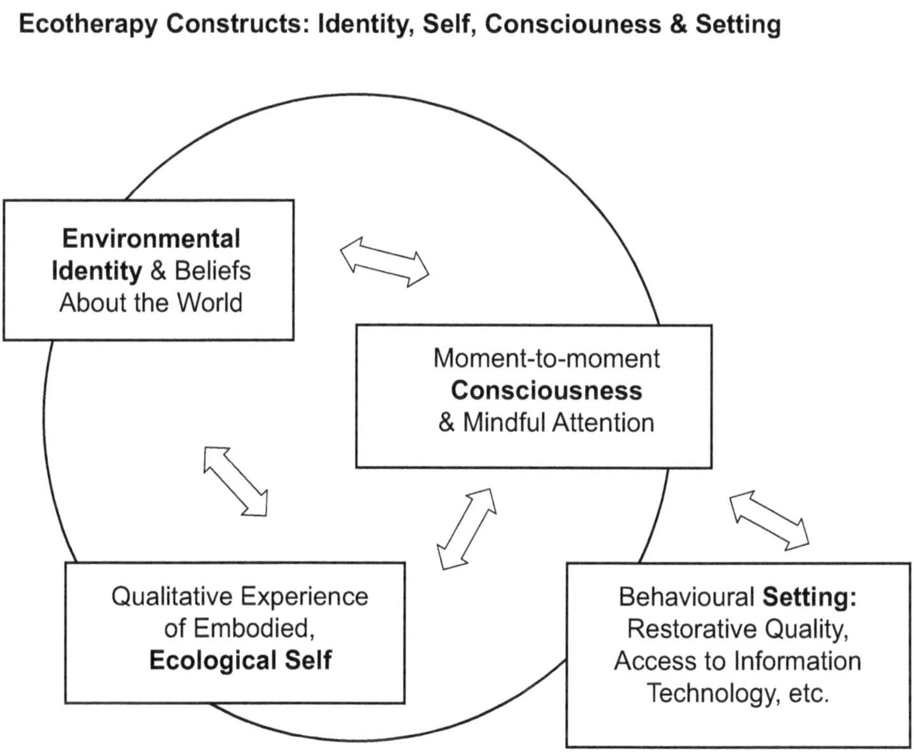

Figure 1.1 Key ecotherapy constructs.

about one's identity and one's sense of the world and their place in it. All of these factors – cognitive appraisals of identity, sense of embodied self, focused awareness and attention, and qualities of setting – can be utilized in the creation of ecotherapy interventions (see Figure 1.1).

Ecotherapy research

The study of ecotherapy can be approached in a number of ways, ranging from positivist or biomedical approaches that focus on symptom reduction, to more systems-focused biopsychosocial approaches; to humanistic, meaning-making approaches; to constructivist or critical approaches that recognize the role of cultural discourses and power in the social construction of eco-psychological problems (Marks and Yardley 2004). Ecotherapy programmes will have differing standards of evidence depending on their rationale and target goals. For example, expressive 'despair and empowerment' approaches (Macy and Young-Brown 1998) will have more qualitative and subjective outcomes than interventions designed to address symptoms (Faber-Taylor and Kuo 2009) that lend themselves to more quantitative methods.

Evidence-based ecotherapy programmes. As interest, funding and systematic study have increased, the evidence-base for ecotherapy has become more substantial. Practitioners are now fortunate to have some well-developed models to learn from (Doherty and Chen 2016). Academic research programmes that combine theory building, controlled study and intervention (see Landscape and Human Health Laboratory: http://lhhl.illinois.edu/) provide robust templates to build on, and have spurred their own interventions, such as outdoor-based treatment for children experiencing attention deficit disorder symptoms (Faber-Taylor and Kuo 2009). Private and public sector programmes have spawned ongoing research programmes as well. These include longitudinal outcome studies completed by the Outdoor Behavioral Healthcare Industry Research Cooperative http://obhic.com/research.html) sponsored by a consortium of residential wilderness therapy programmes in the United States and Canada. Forestry Scotland's 'Branching Out' programme, a community mental health programme that utilizes outdoor experiences, bushcraft and nature awareness, is also an exemplar (http://www.forestry.gov.uk/branchingout). On the individual level, the construct of eco-wellness – the subjective experience of wellness through one's perceived connection with nature – has found empirical support in counselling settings. A perception of eco-wellness is mediated by factors such as access to restorative settings, and sense of safety, efficacy, spirituality and community connectedness (Reese and Meyers 2012; Reese et al. 2015) (see Figure 1.2).

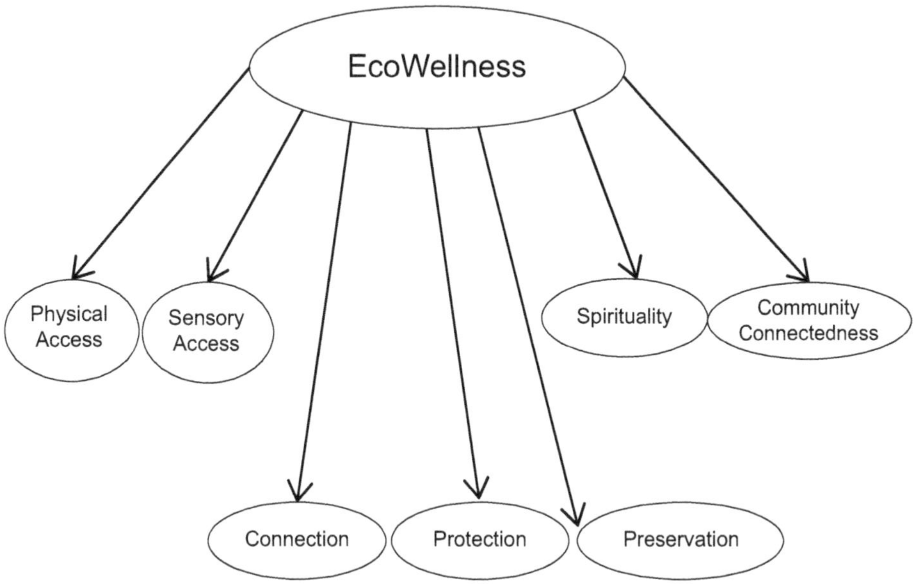

Figure 1.2 Ecowellness. Adapted from: Reese, R. F., J. E. Myers, T. F. Lewis and J. T. Willse (2015), 'Construction and Initial Validation of the Reese Ecowellness Inventory', *International Journal for the Advancement of Counselling* 27: 124–42.

Theoretical and empirical issues unique to ecotherapy

Competency in ecotherapy requires a nuanced understanding of commonly used terms such as 'nature' or 'natural'. While these terms can provide a useful shorthand for the out-of-doors or for objects or processes with minimal influence of humans (or explicitly valued for non-human attributes), this distinction can also present a false dualism that obscures the inherent naturalness of all human cultures and endeavours. From a perspective of environmental and conservation psychology (Clayton and Myers 2009), it is helpful to think of a spectrum from *domestic nature* such as plants in the home, to *nearby nature* such as parks and gardens, to *managed nature* such as tree farms and agricultural areas, to *wild nature* – native plants and animals, wilderness areas that are remote, challenging, or purposely left undeveloped, and 'wild' processes in the human body (Cryan and Dinan 2012). From the perspective of environmental philosophy and history, ideas of 'nature', 'wilderness' and 'the environment' are also social and cultural constructions whose meanings vary greatly based on the social context (Cronon 1995; Soule and Lease 1995). Conceptualizing nature has practical implications. When hypothesizing about ecotherapy outcomes, it is important to be clear about what aspects of 'nature' you intend to access and utilize, how these are to be operationalized, and in service of what therapeutic goal. Consider for example, doing so-called wilderness therapy. A place may be subjectively experienced as 'wild' given its remoteness, level of challenge or visible presence of other species. This can be assessed through a qualitative interview. A setting may also be considered wild based on its legal designation, or quantitative assessments of its size, number of visitors, or diversity of its ecosystem.

Working with systems and scale

An important ecological skill for ecotherapists is 'thinking at scale' the ability to track interdependent issues and phenomenon at different levels of local and global context, and to recognize the emotional and ethical ramifications. This can include understanding how 'distant suffering' (Boltanski 1999) associated with events at great physical remove can be personally experienced (Stokols et al. 2009). In the short term, this awareness can be disorienting and overwhelming. However, with patience and perseverance, simultaneously cultivating connections with local place and planetary awareness can also be comforting, a positive synergy of consciousness and dedication to daily efforts and local action.

Assessing psychopathology in an ecotherapy context

Expertise in assessment and diagnosis of psychopathology and psychiatric disorders and use of diagnostic criteria is beyond the scope of this chapter. But, this constitutes a necessary practical and ethical component of doing ecotherapy work. Some individuals seeking ecotherapy may be experiencing significant distress or impairment or suffering from psychiatric disorders. Others may be quite 'well' in terms of their general life functioning. Making a functional distinction between the concerns of someone who would be seen as normatively healthy by their cultural group but who is also suffering distress or concern regarding environmental issues, and another person who is impacted by a pre-existing interpersonal trauma, psychiatric disorder or psychosocial adjustment process that in turn makes them susceptible to environmental distress, requires some clinical sophistication. In practice, these situations are rarely clear-cut. Would-be ecotherapists are encouraged to make use of their existing training regarding psychopathology and psychodiagnosis. In fact, no special diagnostic criteria are needed to treat eco-therapeutic issues. For example, existing criteria for adjustment, anxiety and depression disorders can be applied to problems associated with the natural environment – both acute and secondary.

In terms of natural disasters or climate change, causal pathways for psychopathology or psychiatric impairment are relatively clear-cut. Geophysical effects such as flooding, heat waves, droughts and extreme weather events increase the likelihood of injury, trauma and anxiety-related responses in individuals and communities, and over time, the prevalence of chronic and severe psychological problems (see Doherty, in press). Indirect or vicarious mental health impacts of environmental issues are more difficult to assess and diagnose compared to acute disaster impacts. These tend to be gradual, diffuse and contingent on other aspects of a person's life functioning such as their exposure to media and information technology (see the discussion of the information-saturated polyfunctional environments in the environmental psychology section above) and their general level of environmental literacy.

In their treatment, ecotherapists are forced to make a difficult philosophical distinction between normal and expected worry about ecological threats and pathological worry that impacts their client's or patient's life functioning. Ecological worrying in and of itself does not correlate with pathology but rather with proenvironmental attitudes and positive personality traits such as altruism (Verplanken and Roy 2013). Anecdotes of 'eco-anxiety' symptoms in the popular press (Nobel 2007) including anxiety or panic, irritability, sleeplessness and malaise, signal the presence of diagnosable or subthreshold disorders of various kinds. Only a comprehensive diagnostic history and interview can sort these issues out with specific individuals.

Creative tensions in ecotherapy

The practice of ecotherapy becomes a radical endeavour when it calls into question assumptions of what philosophers might call the 'world in force', the normative anthropocentric-technological world of so-called developed human societies. In particular, ecotherapy questions seemingly obvious dichotomies in psychotherapy (and in general culture) between built and natural, inner and outer, global and local, wild and domesticated, backcountry and front country. Ecotherapy not only blurs distinctions between these concepts but also upends their assumed hierarchies and therapeutic values. This has philosophical and practical implications. For example:

A major insight of ecotherapy is that what are commonly seen as mental processes located 'in the head' (thoughts, emotions, behavioural impulses) are actually ecological products of environmental interactions. There is no psyche and no therapy without the physical setting. Ecological psychology in its physical-spatial framing (rather than its social and anthropocentric variations) has long conceived of human psychological processes as transactional, based on a systemic embeddedness in the physical environment, and taking form as patterns of action that continually attune people to that environment as an integrated behaviour-setting (Heft 2012). From the perspective of ecological psychology, certain settings provide affordances – physical properties of the environment that shape consciousness and behaviour. These spatial-systemic properties can also be understood from a phenomenological perspective and approached in the language of ecopsychology as 'turning the psyche inside out'

(Fisher 2012). This spatial-ecological thinking can also take on an evolutionary turn. When climbing a tree, finding a convenient branch that neatly fits one's hand is no accident. The human hand has been evolved to climb and has been shaped by such branches over millennia.

Ecotherapy involves practitioners who work in urban settings and those who act as guides or expedition leaders in more (un)managed or wild settings. Having done both types of work, I would encourage practitioners not draw too strict a line between the *backcountry* and the *front-country*. Approached from the perspective of physical challenge and risk management, a backcountry setting may be seen as more difficult than an urban setting. In some senses this is true. However, working out of doors and away from more mainstream settings offers greater space and freedom for doing ecologically focused and nature-based techniques without perceived stigma. Conversely, while front country activities may offer more infrastructure and convenience, they can also highlight the novel, political nature of ecotherapy with practices that question the therapeutic status quo. For example, trying to institute even the most benign ecotherapeutic initiative (e.g. a healthy plant or a window in every consulting office) in an urban, anthropocentric practice location can require laborious efforts to overcome scepticism; justify and seek support for the activity; and deal with the resources of the facility.

The development of the ecotherapist: Inside out and outside in

Rather than resolve these creative tensions in any essentialism about ecotherapy, I recommend that practitioners be mindful how their practice constitutes a synthesis of these dialectics and how this evolves during their career. I have observed in my own practice, and in the activities of others, a developmental trajectory in terms of ecotherapeutic practice that contains a tension between the indoors-and-outdoors and the level of risk-and-exposure in the activities (i.e. between sedentary, low risk activities in nearby nature such as doing walking sessions with clients vs. more physically active, challenging adventure activities requiring technical skills, specialized gear and explicit risk management thinking such as overnight outdoor retreats). Curiously, this trajectory can go in *either direction*, one can begin with office-style activities and then venture outward into more complex and challenging scenarios as they become empowered. Or, one can transition into an office-based practice from a career of doing high adventure activities (due to lifestyle changes). For a complementary perspective, see Kempton and Holland (2003) for an interesting study of the life development of environmental advocates.

Putting it all together

I have respect for inside and outside realms. My evolution as an ecotherapist, up until now, has gone more in an 'outside-in' direction. My conceptual baseline for ecotherapy was established during multi-week 'wilderness therapy' backcountry expeditioning in the western United States, in the late 1980s and early 1990s, and witnessing the standardization of grass roots backcountry outfitter and therapy programmes into the outdoor recreation and 'Outdoor Behaviour Healthcare' industries. The benefits of this shift included shared knowledge and resources, quality control and improved risk management. The losses included the passing of idiosyncratic regional programmes and homogenization of wildness therapy models. My growing edge has included the urban delivery of ecotherapy, teaching the science and craft of ecotherapy, and figuring out how to make a living doing this work in a personally and environmentally sustainable manner.

In my own work as an ecotherapist, I use a constructivist-developmental approach that fosters consciousness-raising and exploration of one's life history vis-à-vis nature (broadly, in the client's own cultural understanding), sense of physical and regional place, and how these influence environmental identity and diversity. I find that this tends to organically segue into a discovery of personal agency and curiosity about experimenting with new behaviours. This creates a need for a more precise assessment of readiness for change and deployment of conservation behaviour change strategies. Immersion in the world of action creates experience (i.e. new knowledge, setbacks and successes) that then can be reflected on, in an ongoing cycle of growth (Kempton and Holland 2003). I particularly enjoy doing this ecotherapy work in groups where the added complexity and synergy of different environmental identities and world-views comes into play (I imagine a similar enjoyment on the part of therapists who specialize in work with other species). Finally, I enjoy the challenge of risk management – risk in the sense of emotional risk as well as physical or practical risks. Rather than perceiving this as a burden, I see this as a signal that the therapeutic work I'm doing is truly real and adventurous and not simply abstract or removed from the joys and dangers of the physical and natural world. I wish you well on your own ecotherapy journey.

References

Abram, D. (1996), *The Spell of the Sensuous*, New York: Pantheon.

Adelson, G., J. Engell, B. Ranalli and K. P. Van Anglen (2008), *Environment*, New Haven, CT: Yale University Press.

Amel, E. L., C. M. Manning and B. A. Scott (2009), 'Mindfulness and Sustainable Behavior: Pondering Attention and Awareness as Means for Increasing Green Behavior', *Ecopsychology* 1: 14–25.
Anthony, K. H., and N. J. Watkins (2002), 'Exploring Pathology: Relationship between Clinical and Environmental Psychology', in R. B. Bechtel and A. Churchman (eds), *Handbook of Environmental Psychology*, 129–48, New York: John Wiley & Sons.
Badiner, A. H. (1990), *Dharma Gaia*, Berkeley, CA: Parallax Press.
Bechtel, R. B., and A. Churchman (2002), *Handbook of Environmental Psychology*, New York: John Wiley & Sons.
Berry, T. (1988), *The Dream of the Earth*, San Francisco, CA: Sierra Club Press.
Blazina, C., G. Boyraz and D. Shen-Miller (2011), *The Psychology of the Human-Animal Bond: A Resource for Clinicians and Researchers*, New York: Springer Science & Business Media.
Boltanski, L. (1999), *Distant Suffering*, Cambridge, UK: Cambridge University Press.
Bragg, E. A. (1996), 'Towards Ecological Self: Deep Ecology Meets Constructionist Self-Theory', *Journal of Environmental Psychology* 16: 93–108.
Bronfenbrenner, U. (2005), *Making Human Beings Human: Bioecological Perspectives on Human Development*, Thousand Oaks, CA: Sage Publications.
Bullard, R. D., G. S. Johnson, D. W. King and A. O. Torres (2014), Environmental Justice Milestones and Accomplishments: 1964–2014: A Report Prepared in Commemoration of the Twentieth Anniversary of the Environmental Justice Executive Order 12898. Barbara Jordan-Mickey Leland School of Public Affairs Texas Southern University. Retrieved from: https://orgs.law.harvard.edu/els/files/2014/02/Environmental-Justice-Milestones.pdf
Burns, G. W. (1998), *Nature Guided Therapy*, New York: Taylor & Francis.
Burns, T., and E. Burns-Lundgren (2015), *Psychotherapy: A Very Short Introduction*, Oxford, UK: Oxford University Press.
Buzzell, L., and C. Chalquist (2009), *Ecotherapy*, San Francisco: Sierra Club Press.
Clayton, S. (2003), 'Environmental Identity: A Conceptual and Operational Definition', in S. Clayton and S. Opotow (eds), *Identity and the Natural Environment: The Psychological Significance of Nature*, 45–65, Cambridge, MA: MIT Press.
Clayton, S., and G. Myers (2009), *Conservation Psychology: Understanding and Promoting Human Care for Nature*, Cambridge, MA: MIT Press.
Clayton, S. D. (2012), *The Oxford Handbook of Environmental and Conservation Psychology*, New York: Oxford University Press.
Clinebell, H. (1996), *Ecotherapy*, Minneapolis, MN: Fortress Press.
Conn, S. (1998), 'Living in the Earth: Ecopsychology, Health and Psychotherapy', *Humanistic Psychologist* 26: 179–98.
Cook, E. P. (2012), *Understanding People in Context: The Ecological Perspective in Counseling*, Alexandria, VA: American Counseling Association.
Cronon, W. (1995), 'The Trouble with Wilderness; Or, Getting Back to the Wrong Nature', in W. Cronon (ed.), *Uncommon Ground: Rethinking the Human Place in Nature*, 69–90, New York: W. W. Norton.

Cryan, J. F., and T. G. Dinan (2012), 'Mind-Altering Microorganisms: The Impact of The Gut Microbiota on Brain and Behaviour', *Nature Reviews Neuroscience* 13: 701–12.
Devlin, A. S. (2014), *Transforming the Doctor's Office: Principles from Evidence-Based Design*, New York: Routledge.
Doherty, T. J. (2009), 'Shierry Weber Nicholsen: The *Ecopsychology* Interview', *Ecopsychology* 1: 110–17.
Doherty, T. J. (2009), 'Joseph Reser: The Ecopsychology Interview', *Ecopsychology* 1: 57–63.
Doherty, T. J. (2009), 'Robert Greenway: The Ecopsychology Interview', *Ecopsychology* 1: 47–52.
Doherty, T. J. (2010), 'Michael Cohen: The Ecopsychology Interview', *Ecopsychology* 2: 53–7.
Doherty, T. J. (2011), 'Riley Dunlap: The Ecopsychology Interview', *Ecopsychology* 3: 219–26.
Doherty, T. J. (2011), 'Andy Fisher: The Ecopsychology Interview', *Ecopsychology* 3: 167–73.
Doherty, T. J. (2012), 'Ecopsychology Roundtable: Patricia Hasbach and Peter Kahn', *Ecopsychology* 4: 1–9.
Doherty, T. J. (2015), 'Mental Health Impacts', in J. Patz and B. S. Levy (eds), *Climate Change and Public Health*, Oxford, UK: Oxford University Press.
Doherty, T. J., and A. Chen (2016), 'Improving Human Functioning: Ecotherapy and Environmental Health Approaches', in R. Gifford (ed.), *Research Methods in Environmental Psychology*, Hoboken, NJ: John Wiley & Sons.
Drengson, A., B. Devall and M. A. Schroll (2011), 'The Deep Ecology Movement: Origins, Development, and Future Prospects (Towards a Transpersonal Ecosophy)', *International Journal of Transpersonal Studies* 30: 101–17.
Dunlap, R. E. (2008), 'The NEP Scale: From Marginality to Worldwide Use', *Journal of Environmental Education* 40: 3–18.
Faber Taylor, A., and F. E. Kuo (2009), 'Children with Attention Deficits Concentrate Better After Walk in the Park', *Journal of Attention Disorders* 12: 402–9.
Fisher, A. (2002), *Radical Ecopsychology*, 2nd Edition, Albany, NY: State University of New York Press.
Fisher, A. (2012), *Radical Ecopsychology*, 2nd Edition, Albany, NY: State University of New York Press.
Frumkin, H. (2012), 'Building the Science Base: Ecopsychology Meets Clinical Epidemiology', in P. H. Kahn and P. H. Hasbach (eds), *Ecopsychology: Science, Totems, and the Technological Species*, 141–72, Cambridge, MA: MIT Press.
Gass, M. A., H. L. Gillis and K. C. Russell (2012), *Adventure Therapy: Theory, Research and Practice*, New York: Routledge.
Gottlieb, R. (2005), *Forcing the Spring*, Washington, DC: Island Press.
Gifford, R. (2007), *Environmental Psychology*, Colville, WA: Optimal Books.
Gray, M., J. Coates and T. Hetherington (2012), *Environmental Social Work*, New York: Routledge.

Haller, R. L., and C. L. Kramer (2006), *Horticultural Therapy Methods: Making Connections in Health Care, Human Service, and Community Programs*, Philadelphia, PA: Haworth Press.

Hartig, T., and C. C. Marcus (2006), 'Healing Gardens: Places for Nature in Health Care', *Lancet* 368: S36–7.

Hasbach, P. (2012), 'Ecotherapy', in, P. H. Kahn and P. H. Hasbach (eds), *Ecopsychology: Science, Totems, and the Technological Species*, 115–40, Cambridge, MA: MIT Press.

Heft, H. (2012), 'Foundations of an Ecological Approach to Psychology', in S. D. Clayton (ed.), *The Oxford Handbook of Environmental and Conservation Psychology*, 11–40, New York: Oxford University Press.

Higginbotham, N., L. Connor, G. Albrecht, S. Freeman and K. Agho (2007), 'Validation of an Environmental Distress Scale', *Ecohealth* 3: 245–54.

Howard, G. (1993), 'Special Issue on Ecocounseling Psychology', *The Counseling Psychologist* 21: 4.

Ittelson, W. H., H. M. Proshansky, L. G. Rivlin and G. H. Winkel (1974), *An Introduction to Environmental Psychology*, New York: Holt, Rhinehart and Winston.

Jordan, M. (2015), *Therapy and Nature*, London: Routledge.

Jordan, M., and H. Marshall (2010), 'Taking Counselling and Psychotherapy Outside: Destruction or Enrichment of the Therapeutic Frame?', *European Journal of Psychotherapy and Counselling* 12: 345–59.

Jorm, A. F. (2012). Mental Health Literacy: Empowering the Community to Take Action for Better Mental Health. American Psychologist, 67, 231–43. https://doi.org/10.1037/a0025957

Jungerson, T. S., S. Daily, J. Uhernik and C. M. Smith (2013), 'All Trauma Is Not the Same', *Counseling Today*. http://ct.counseling.org/2013/03/all-trauma-is-not-the-same/.

Kahn, P. H., and P. H. Hasbach (2012), *Ecopsychology: Science, Totems, and the Technological Species*, Cambridge, MA: MIT Press.

Kaplan, R., and S. Kaplan (1989), *The Experience of Nature: A Psychological Perspective*, Cambridge, MA: Cambridge University Press.

Kaplan, R., S. Kaplan and R. L. Ryan (1998), *With People in Mind: Design and Management of Everyday Nature*, Washington, DC: Island Press.

Kellert, S. (1993), 'Attitudes, Knowledge, and Behavior Toward Wildlife Among the Industrial Superpowers: United States, Japan and Germany', *Journal of Social Issues* 49: 53–69.

Kempton, W., and D. C. Holland (2003), 'Identity and Sustained Environmental Practice', in S. Clayton and S. Opotow (eds), *Identity and the Natural Environment*, 317–41, Cambridge, MA: MIT Press.

Kidner, D. W. (2001), *Nature and Psyche*, Albany, NY: State University of New York Press.

Macy, J. R. (1983), *Despair and Personal Power in the Nuclear Age*, Philadelphia, PA: New Society Publishers.

Macy, J., and M. Young Brown (1998), *Coming Back to Life: Practices to Reconnect Our Lives, Our World*, Gabriola Island, BC: New Society Publishers.
Maibach, E. W., A. Leiserowitz, C. Roser-Renouf, C. K. Mertz and K. Akerlof (2011), 'Global Warming's Six Americas Screening Tools: Survey Instruments; Instructions for Coding and Data Treatment; And Statistical Program Scripts', New Haven, CT: Yale University and George Mason University. Yale Project on Climate Change Communication. Available at http://climatechangecommunication.org/SixAmericasManual.cfm.
Marks, D. F., and L. Yardley (2004), *Research Methods for Clinical and Health Psychology*, London: Sage Publications.
Mayer, F. S., and C. M. Frantz (2004), 'The Connectedness to Nature Scale: A Measure of Individuals' Feeling in Community with Nature', *Journal of Environmental Psychology* 24: 503–15.
Merchant, C. (1980), *The Death of Nature*, San Francisco, CA: Harper & Row.
McKenzie-Mohr, D. M, N. R. Lee, P. W. Schultz and P. A. Kottler (2011), *Social Marketing to Protect the Environment: What Works*, Thousand Oaks, CA: Sage.
Mies, M., and V. Shiva (1993), *Ecofeminism*, London: Zed Books.
Nash, R. (1992), *Wilderness and the American Mind*, New Haven, CT: Yale University Press.
Nobel, J. (2007, April 9). 'Eco-Anxiety: Something Else to Worry About' [Electronic version], *The Philadelphia Enquirer*.
Nolan, J. M., P. W. Schultz, R. B. Cialdini, N. J. Goldstein and V. Griskevicius (2008), 'Normative Social Influence Is Underdetected', *Personality and Social Psychology Bulletin* 34: 913–23.
Oelschlaeger, M. (1991), *The Idea of Wilderness*, New Haven, CT: Yale University Press.
Orr, D. (1991), *Ecological Literacy*, Albany, NY: State University of New York Press.
Plotkin, B. (2003), *Soulcraft*, Novato, CA: New World Library.
Plumwood, V. (1993), *Feminism and the Mastery over Nature*, New York: Routledge.
Prochaska, J. O., and J. C. Norcross (2009), *Systems of Psychotherapy*, Belmont, CA: Brooks / Cole.
Randall, R. (2009), 'Loss and Climate Change: The Cost of Parallel Narratives', *Ecopsychology* 3: 118–29.
Reese, R. F., and J. E. Myers (2012), 'EcoWellness: The Missing Factor in Holistic Wellness Models', *Journal of Counseling & Development* 90: 400–6.
Reese, R. F., J. E. Myers, T. F. Lewis and J. T. Willse (2015), 'Construction and Initial Validation of the Reese Ecowellness Inventory', *International Journal for the Advancement of Counselling* 36: 1–19.
Reik, T. (1948), *Listening with the Third Ear: The Inner Experience of a Psychoanalyst*, New York: Grove Press.
Reser, J. P., and J. K. Swim (2011), 'Adapting to and Coping with the Threat and Impacts of Climate Change', *American Psychologist* 66: 277–89.
Roszak, T. (1992/2001), *The Voice of the Earth*, Grand rapids, MI: Phanes.

Roszak, T., M. E. Gomes and A. D. Kanner (1995), *Ecopsychology: Restoring the Earth, Healing the Mind*, San Francisco: Sierra Club books.
Roszak, T. (1978), *Person/Planet*, Garden City, NY: Anchor Press.
Roth, A., and P. Fonagy (1996), *What Works for Whom? A Critical Review of Psychotherapy Research*, New York: Guilford Press.
Saunders, C. (2003), 'The Emerging Field of Conservation Psychology', *Human Ecology Review* 10: 137–49.
Schultz, P. W., and L. C. Zelezny (1998), 'Values and Proenvironmental Behaviors: A Five-Country Survey', *Journal of Cross-Cultural Psychology* 29: 540–58.
Scott, B. A., E. L. Amel and C. M. Manning (2014), 'In and of the Wilderness: Ecological Connection through Participation in Nature', *Ecopsychology* 6: 81–91.
Shepard, P. (1982), *Nature and Madness*, Athens, GA: University of Georgia Press.
Soule, M. E., and G. Lease (1995), *Reinventing Nature?: Responses to Postmodern Deconstruction*, Washington, DC: Island Press.
Stokols, D., S. Misra, M. G. Runnerstrom and J. A. Hipp (2009), 'Psychology in an Age of Ecological Crisis: From Personal Angst to Collective Action', *American Psychologist* 64: 181–93.
Sue, S., N. Zane, G. C. N. Hall and L. K. Berger (2009), 'The Case for Cultural Competency in Psychotherapeutic Interventions', *Annual Review of Psychology* 60: 525–48.
Swanson, J. (1995), 'The Call for Gestalt's Contribution to Ecopsychology: Figuring in the Environmental Field', *Gestalt Journal* 18: 47–85.
Thomashow, M (1995), *Ecological Identity*, Cambridge, MA: MIT Press.
Totton, N. (2011), *Wild Therapy*, Ross-on-Wye, UK: PCCS Books.
Ulrich, R. S., C. Zimring, X. Zhu, J. DuBose, H. Seo, Y. Choi, X. Quan, A. Joseph (2008), 'A Review of the Research Literature on Evidence-Based Healthcare Design'. http://edinnovation.com.au/documents/attachments/58-hcleader-5-litreviewwp.pdf.
Vella, E. J., B. Milligan and J. L. Bennett (2013), 'Participation in Outdoor Recreation Program Predicts Improved Psychosocial Well-Being among Veterans with Post-Traumatic Stress Disorder: A Pilot Study', *Military Medicine* 178: 254–60.
Verplanken, B., and D. Roy (2013), '"My Worries Are Rational, Climate Change Is Not": Habitual Ecological Worrying Is an Adaptive Response', *PLoS ONE* 8(9): e74708.
Weber-Nicholsen, S. (2001), *The Love of Nature at the End of the World*, Cambridge, MA: MIT Press.
White, W. (2012), 'A History of Adventure Therapy', in M. A. Gass, H. L. Gillis and K. C. Russell (eds), *Adventure Therapy: Theory, Research, and Practice*, 19–46, New York, NY: Routledge Press.

2

Nature-based practice: A Buddhist psychotherapy perspective

Caroline Brazier

Introduction

Ecotherapy is a broad-based field, as organic and diverse as the ecosystems it inhabits. Its practitioners are drawn from many backgrounds. Some are counsellors and psychotherapists, inspired to take their practice outdoors, while others come from a variety of other professions and interest groups. Some have worked previously in community mental health, others in a range of settings such as outdoor activities, education, the arts or earth-based spirituality.

Because ecotherapy is practised by people from different professional and other backgrounds, the challenges facing the aspiring practitioner will also vary. For practitioners coming from non-therapeutic fields, the challenges may be in coming to understand more of the psychological processes which may be unfolding beneath the surface of work that seems practical and familiar. Meanwhile, for those with a traditional psychotherapeutic background, the journey from the consulting room into natural surroundings can raise questions about boundaries and containment as working outdoors transgresses many of the norms of conventional therapeutic practice, inevitably inviting different approaches to time and space and to relating within them.

This chapter explores a particular model of outdoor working, namely other-centred approach. This is a Buddhist-based therapy (Brazier 2017) which is adaptable to this broad range of circumstances. The model provides the foundation for an ecotherapy training programme which has been run by Tariki Trust since 2011, where it has been developed over that time period through the work of staff and students who themselves reflect a broad spectrum of backgrounds.

We will start our exploration by reviewing the practice of mindfulness. Mindfulness offers a methodology that has been heavily drawn on in ecotherapy and therapeutic contexts, and which has its roots in the Buddhist teachings. We will then explore other aspects of the Buddhist thought and particularly the concept of conditionality. We will look at how these ideas underpin the other-centred model, which focuses particularly on ways in which conditioned view leads people to live in disconnected mind states, and at other-centred methods which address this disconnection. In particular we will explore the importance of the therapeutic alliance and the triangular relationship between therapist, client and the environment in which they are working. We will then look at some more general issues involved in adapting therapies to the outdoors, and, finally, at some other approaches based on Buddhist ideas which are currently informing ecotherapy practice.

Mindfulness and practice in nature

Buddhism offers a complex understanding of human psychology, developed across a number of Asian cultures over two and a half thousand years and now interfacing with Western ideas. In particular, in this chapter, I will be focusing on the approach which we have termed 'other-centred' which underpins our work at Tariki Trust. Before doing so, however, I will first explore the role of mindfulness in ecotherapy, since this Buddhist-inspired field has become widely known in therapeutic circles in the West and offers an important starting point for our exploration.

The mindfulness movement, spearheaded by Jon Kabat-Zinn (1990) and others (Segal, Williams and Teasdale 2002), has developed substantially over the past decades. Defined as 'paying attention in a particular way: on purpose, in the present moment, and non-judgmentally' (Kabat-Zinn 1994: 4), the practice of mindfulness is now applied in many therapeutic and related contexts. Mindfulness, according to this movement, is primarily concerned with developing awareness of immediate phenomena and changing people's experience through daily practice and through exercises that develop attention. Mindfulness practices of this kind are widely used in environmentally based therapies, and are particularly associated with developing calm, sharpening awareness and offering tools for grounding and embodied connection.

While such practices are important and valuable, this understanding of mindfulness does not reflect the full intent of the original teaching, and the practice of mindfulness, as commonly portrayed in secular settings, has come under scrutiny from the Buddhist community. A number of writers have questioned whether the models applied in most programmes of that name do justice to the roots of the teaching (Bazanno 2014), and whether understanding can be deepened by revisiting the original sources (Brazier 2013a).

The key Buddhist text on mindfulness is the Satipatthana Sutta, a text whose importance is perhaps reflected in the fact that it appears twice in the Buddhist canon (Majjhima Nikaya 10 and Digha Nikaya 22). The Satipatthana has four sections, each describing a layer of understanding which can be investigated through mindfulness practice. The four sections of the Satipatthana roughly translate as: body, reaction, mind and dhamma (basic elements). It outlines a progressive investigation which starts with body experience, then, as this stage is mastered, progresses to observing the body's tendency to reactivity, then to inquiring into mental structures and, finally, to the fundamental nature of things (Analayo 2003). The form of mindfulness commonly taught in Western secular settings mostly reflects the earliest stages in this process.

Mindfulness teaching, according to the Satipatthana, thus begins with a focus on the body. Attention is given to the body when sitting, walking, breathing and so on. These exercises teach embodied awareness in the present moment. As we will see, in our therapeutic model, we make considerable use of body scans and grounding exercises in working outdoors, often using them at the start of sessions to create a foundation for other work and, as sessions progress, to enable points of reflection and connection.

Western mindfulness exercises also focus on detailed observation of ordinary things which would otherwise be overlooked. By slowing the person down and concentrating attention, things are noticed which are normally missed. This too is foundational for therapeutic work and has obvious relevance to working in nature.

An aspect of mindfulness which is often missed in Western contexts, however, is the focus in the Satipatthana on the impermanence and conditionality of things. In each of the prescribed observations, the instruction in the text is to bring awareness to the dependently originated nature of the object of attention and to its provisionality and impermanence. These observations are fundamental to the Buddhist conception of experiencing. All things depend on certain conditions being in place. They are interdependent phenomena. All things are also transient. They are subject to change and ultimately to ending and decay. This aspect of the mindfulness teaching, less emphasized in secular contexts, supports awareness of existential aspects of human experience and the processes of change and impermanence in ourselves and others; themes which are also very relevant to working outdoors.

Engaging with the natural world, impermanence is everywhere. We see dead animals on the path or watch leaves fall in autumn, but we also watch the arrival of swallows in spring and young plants growing out of rotting logs. From the cycle of decay, new growth arises. Mindfulness is not just about finding calm; it is also concerned with gaining insight into this fundamental flow of things and their interdependence with one another. Working in nature, such observations can be particularly acute.

The first section of the Satipatthana Sutta involves mindfulness of the body. This is the longest section in the text. In addition to awareness of the body in motion and of the breath, it includes a number of other meditations, and particularly two which develop these themes of interdependence and impermanence.

The first of these two meditations involves contemplation of the elements. The elements in Buddhism are earth, air, fire and water. Practitioners reflect on each of the four elements in turn, recognizing how it manifests in the physicality of the body and also in things in the environment. Through these reflections, it becomes apparent that they and their surroundings are both composed of the same elements and depend on an interchange of material for their existence. The elements meditations are particularly suited to creating a framework for working outdoors (Brazier 2011). They invite a less personalized humancentric viewpoint and foster a more appreciative ecosystemic way of experiencing.

The other meditation found in this first section of the Satipatthana describes practices reflecting on the decomposition of a dead body. Commonly known as the charnel ground meditations, these meditations were originally practised by monks in ancient India, sitting in the charnel grounds where dead bodies were being burned. The somewhat gruesome reflections helped the meditators sharpen awareness of their own impermanence.

Although ecotherapy work does not usually involve reflecting on human corpses, examples of death and decay can be seen everywhere in the countryside and may be used as the focus for reflection on mortality and change. In this way, both the meditation on the elements and the charnel ground meditations can be directly adapted as group or individual exercises (Brazier 2017).

Mindfulness and grounded presence

Mindfulness practices are concerned with deepening insight, but they also involve improving the quality of attention by helping to develop groundedness and non-judgemental awareness. Mindfulness can be helpful to both therapist and client. It manifests in:

- the therapist's own level of mindfulness which allows deeper insight and empathy;
- mindfulness developed by the client as a result of indirect communication either through modelling or through activities which naturally invite more awareness; and
- direct teaching of mindfulness exercises.

In mindfulness meditations, the practitioner gives intense objective attention to subjective experience, observing thought patterns moment by moment with analytic rigour. Concepts such as internal and external become meaningless as all mental and physical processes are scrutinized with the same intensity. The mind, at least in theory, watches itself and everything else with equal attentiveness.

In the Ten Directions model which is used on the Tariki ecotherapy training programme (Brazier 2017), the first practice taught is embodied presence. Grounding and embodied awareness create a basis for developing empathic resonance with others as the student learns to hold psychological space in a calm and focused way. Broad, body-based attention is directed to clients, their perceptual worlds, and the physical space in which the work is taking place. This attention is concentrated, but non-directive. The therapist waits for participants to set the lead and follows attentively.

Embodied presence is particularly important in leading ecotherapy activities because working outdoors raises issues of psychological containment. Without the physical boundary of the therapy room, the work is in danger of becoming scattered and lacking depth or feeling unheld and uncontained for the client. Bringing this kind of presence to the work, the therapist themself becomes part of the therapeutic container.

By anchoring the therapeutic container in the therapist's presence rather than a physical space, the therapeutic work is not necessarily confined within one location. It can move as the therapist moves. Just as a baby monkey feels safe travelling with the troop so long as his mother is a constant presence for him, so too the client feels held while aware of the therapist's proximity.

The therapist's mindfulness underpins the attention given to the client's material. She provides a solid presence in which the work is held. As therapist and client attune to each other's processes, the client becomes less reactive to things and more interested in their felt quality. Therapy thus relies upon the therapist's way of being. As the client experiences the therapist's embodied presence, becoming more settled and mindful, a locus of trust and stability develops within them. Gradually the client finds their own containment and become less dependent on the therapist's presence – a process which has parallels in the work of Buddhist psychologist Gisho Saiko (Saiko 2018).

Buddhist psychology and conditioned mind states

Mindfulness is a practice taught in many Buddhist traditions. Buddhism sees ordinary mental process as a conditioned phenomenon, the product of past experience, current circumstances, culture and so on. The ordinary person's world-view is distorted by perceptual anomalies, brought about by personal biases and the mind's tendency to seek out things which are familiar or comforting, or to create illusions of familiarity where spontaneous connection is not to be found. Ordinary perception is thus described as *avidya*, literally meaning 'not seeing' or '*ignore-ance*'.

The reason for these distortions is primarily the creation and maintenance of psychological defences. At root, these are driven by a fundamental fear of change and impermanence and particularly of our mortality. The perceived threat, *dukkha*, is commonly translated as 'affliction' and consists of things like sickness, old age, death and disappointment, as well as the uncertain nature of the conditioned mentality itself. Processes of ordinary perception, commonly referred to as *clinging* or *attachment*, are thus driven by fear, which may be specific and immediate or more generalized existential anxieties. Conditioned perceptions create a kind of psychological bubble which supports the habitual mentality, rather as the algorithm feeds threads in social media to support and reinforce a person's preferences and interests.

So, the real world becomes a screen upon which personally meaningful stories are imposed. These stories, whose roots may be in the personal past or in collective mythology, give colouration to perception. They can enrich life, but mostly they distort perception, cutting the person off from raw reality and limiting their experiencing of their surroundings. Practices such as mindfulness therefore ideally aim to take the practitioner beyond *ignorance* toward a clearer relationship to the world.

The conditioned mind, embedded in memories and personalized perception, protects us from unsettling new experiences by creating an illusion of continuity, offering a semblance of control and solidity to the personal world. It also forms the basis for identity. But while the personal bubble may be protective, it is also isolating. It tends to prevent relationships from being real. Other people, creatures and objects are viewed through a veneer of projected self-material and not seen authentically. They are not fully experienced as having innate existence, but are viewed instead, at least to some extent, for their utility. At one level, then, ecotherapy can offer ways of challenging and expanding the world-view so that some of these habitual distortions come into question and a more direct encounter with others, human and non-human, becomes possible.

Greed, hate and delusion: Personal and global phenomena

The clinging which drives selective attention on an individual level, creating the self-bubble, is mostly based on positive attraction or negative aversion, commonly referred to as greed- and hate-type responses. These reactions feed tendencies towards consumption and accumulation on the one hand or alienation and hostility on the other. Such reactions are the foundation of self-building, as identity is formed through processes of identification with some things and differentiation from others. In this context, the self is seen as a delusory phenomenon, basically defensive in nature.

The theory of conditioned mentality which we have been describing does not, however, operate solely on the individual level. We can see all of these processes operating at the personal level, contributing to individual behavioural tendencies and character traits, but similar patterns of greed and hate responses also operate on a wider scale in groups and cultures. Indeed, they underlie many of the global problems which we currently face. Recognizing how these processes distort perception is not only beneficial in understanding individual psychology but also gives insight into the conditioned nature of the global trends in which we are all, at least to some extent, enmeshed, where consumption, hostility and identity building, often in the form of sectarianism and nationalism, are common responses to existential threat.

As ecotherapy practitioners, awareness and understanding of this collective level of process is important in helping ourselves and those with whom we work to make sense of, and perhaps challenge, the collective tendencies which contribute to the global environmental changes which we are now experiencing.

Other-centred approach as a model for nature-based therapy

Other-centred approach (Brazier 2009) is a model of psychotherapy, grounded in Buddhist psychology. Given the importance of conditioned view in shaping individual psychology, the distinctive tenor of other-centred therapy is that, rather than focusing introspectively, its primary exploration is of the client's relationship with the world. It explores ways in which the world-view is shaped and coloured by identifications and projections, and how experiencing can become more vivid, direct and authentic through exploration of the other-than-self viewpoint. While other-centred approach can be applied in the therapy room, the model lends itself in particular to exploring the relationship with the natural environment.

Other-centred methodology addresses the isolation and alienation of the conditioned mind through three fields of operation:

- Establishing the therapeutic container through embodied presence, involving grounded-ness, mindful accompaniment and authentic relationship
- Inquiring into the conditioned nature of mind and its manifestation in the world-view
- Inquiring into reality of 'others' and working to investigate other perspectives

Each of these areas is relevant to working outdoors (Brazier 2011, 2017).

Establishing the therapeutic container, as we have seen, requires relational skills, empathy and collaborative ways of working. This is described as embodied presence: a combination of grounded-ness and a particular quality of relationship. Working outdoors, however, the person of the therapist provides only a part of the therapeutic container. The environment itself is a significant other, also offering therapeutic containment for the process. Therapists learn to work in collaboration with this frame. The therapeutic relationship can thus be described as triangular, consisting of three elements: therapist, client and the environs. Within this triad, therapist and client adopt an outwardly orientated interest in both the client's process and the reality of surroundings.

In other-centred approach, the therapeutic relationship is founded on accompaniment and curiosity. It involves a shared exploration of a world of 'others'; a feature consolidated when therapy moves outdoors. Therapist and client walk together, relating to wild places, side-by-side, in a conscious and engaged way.

From this basis of containment, the two investigative fields of the model emerge. On the one hand, working together, therapist and client start to notice associations which the client makes with the things which they encounter and may observe how these colour perception through processes of projection and expectation. As therapist and client enter different spaces, the personal stories and mental frameworks that colour everyday experiencing become apparent and can be explored. On the other hand, it also becomes possible to explore, as far as is possible, the reality of the things which are encountered, seeking more objective perceptions of people, places and objects.

Outdoors, the attitude of inquiry becomes investigative and curious. Trees, walls and meadows are more evidently real than the stories and memories recounted in the therapy room. They do not have their own agendas in the way that other humans do, so are usually neutral subjects against which to explore projections. Even where natural features carry associations, these can be recognized and deconstructed or used as creative inspiration. Nature is capable of surprising us out of our assumptions.

In other-centred process, the concept of empathy can also be extended as it becomes a means of connection, not just for the therapist, but also for the client. Therapist and client work to develop a kind of empathy for 'others' in the client's perceptual field, often challenging simplistic initial assessments and embracing more complex perspectives which take into account the multiple conditions operating in any situation. This development of empathy for others can be expanded through creative work outdoors. Natural objects may be invited to 'find a voice' or materials used aesthetically as the client 'asks them what they would like to be'. Here imaginative and projective methods create new understandings of materials and objects, often leading to creative outcomes and fresh insights.

Triangularity in the therapeutic relationship

Other-centred approach views the therapeutic relationship as triangular (Brazier 2009). As we have seen, this relationship consists of three elements: therapist, client and the world. This conception of the therapeutic relationship as a triad rather than a dyad translates into ecotherapy in a number of ways. The other-centred model proposes that the dialogue between therapist and client is primarily a collaborative inquiry into a third element, and in ecotherapy, this third element is usually the natural environment in which therapist and client operate, the client's relationship to it, or objects within that environment. Also, however, the environment itself offers a therapeutic presence in which therapist and client operate together; a shift of focus which impacts on the nature of the therapeutic relationship itself.

In room-based other-centred therapy, the client's 'others' are largely present as objects of the mind-sense, that is the imagination. The therapist comes to know these 'others' by psychologically coming alongside the client and, through empathic resonance, developing a sense of the client's world-view. By exploring this world-view together, the client's perception of their others gradually comes into question and changes. Because the world-view and the identity are mutually conditioning, changes in the way things are viewed impact on the sense of self and affect behavioural patterns.

In nature-based therapy, the triangular quality of relationship is, in many ways, more obvious because the natural world is strongly present to both therapist and client. This renders the nature of the third element of the triangle complex. The environment is a real presence rather than a psychological phenomenon, but because both client and therapist's perceptions are coloured by their personal histories and biases, their experiencing of it will differ from each other's and from the actuality, if such a thing could be known. The presence of a real environment, however, allows for a much more explicit inquiry into the gap between both the therapist's and the client's conditioned views and reality.

Triangularity in the therapeutic relationship creates a dynamic between therapist and client which tends towards being collaborative and equalizing, a mode of discourse sometimes referred to as 'fellow feeling'. This change does not mean fudging boundaries or confusing projection with actuality. The distinction between empathy and identification is important in any therapeutic work, and this means recognizing when personal perspectives are contaminating one's ability to understand the client's world (Rogers 1980). At the same time, a sense of commonality provides an important condition for the work, as does the shared task of investigation. Face-to-face encounter is relatively uncommon outdoors while side-by-side working is common and naturally gives rise to a less formal style of relating in which open discussion flows more easily.

Differences of power and boundaries in working outdoors

Outdoor sessions differ from conventional therapy in many practical ways, which make the maintenance of traditional therapeutic boundaries challenging and often inappropriate. Sessions may be longer and interaction more fluid, with levels of intensity varying according to the activity. This inevitably affects the relationship style, whatever the therapeutic orientation of the therapist.

One factor which concerns many therapists moving outdoors is the maintenance of the therapeutic boundary. In an earlier article (Brazier 2013b), I discussed the therapeutic boundary in outdoor therapies. Working in the therapy room, it is usual practice to offer time-limited sessions in a contained, private space with standards governed by codes of practice and professional norms. Working in the natural environment, while these matters still have importance, time frames are generally less easily controlled; privacy may be intruded on by the unanticipated arrival of third parties or by unpredictable events, and the style of relationship may be affected by many uncontrollable factors. Maintenance of the therapeutic container can therefore seem to be a challenge.

Working outdoors does, however, offer compensating factors in this respect. As we have already seen, there are in fact two sources of therapeutic containment operating in nature-based therapies. Firstly, the therapist provides a source of containment. She is able to give a robust response if things become uncertain, and, by her quality of presence and personal boundaries, creates a solid reference point which holds the therapeutic process. Her presence also brings to focus the therapeutic agenda, reminding those with whom she works to remain reflective. With these qualities in place, a group or individual can respond fluidly to the environment. The therapist's personal boundaries and solidity anchor the work and those participating in it.

Secondly, however, the natural environment also offers containment. This happens at two levels. On the one hand, particular working spaces may be chosen because they are intimate and enclosed, providing a natural sense of holding. Reading the landscape in such a way as to select suitable working spaces is a skill that develops as we engage with the landscape more intensely. On the other hand, at a more profound level, a sense of containment arises from a deep engagement with the natural environment wherever this occurs. Through grounding exercises and encounter with nature in many places and ways, confidence develops. The earth is found to be trustworthy and solid, even when, at a more immediate level, things become uncomfortable or local environments are spoiled. Connecting with the wild, people discover intrinsic reliability of life and of the earth.

Changing conditions, changing mind states

Buddhism asserts that all things arise dependent upon causes and conditions (Jones 2011). Nothing exists independently and things only come into being, or continue to exist, as a result of the presence of numerous diverse conditions, some known and many unrecognized. The principle of conditioned arising is therefore central to any understanding of Buddhist psychology.

Changing conditions changes mind states and changing mind states change the way we experience the world. Some conditions are historic – the self-story, memories of past experiences and so on. Other conditions are immediate, circumstantial and environmental. While past conditions tend to persist, changing external conditions can also have immediate impact. On a sunny morning, for example, people often experience things more positively than on a wet one. On the other hand, some people may still not even notice the sunshine until it is pointed out because they are so caught up in old patterns of view. Such habitual reactions are often shaped by ways of thinking and feeling that have been carried for years, but they can be changed abruptly by unexpected experiences that shock us into new ways of seeing. We may suddenly feel joy – or rage – in spite of ourselves and so shift our habitual world-view.

Changing surroundings can therefore significantly influence mental states, refocusing attention and creating new patterns of perception which may then gradually become established as the norm over time. We take our old stories with us, but eventually new environments break through with new ones. If it remains sunny, a negative mood eventually starts to lift and perception of the things around changes. This is why being outdoors tends to improve people's mental health. Exposing people to fresh environmental conditions creates new mental and behavioural patterns which then tend to become self-replicating. We may learn to love the rain.

Reality is the teacher in other-centred method; the therapist the facilitator of the encounter. Thus, a fundamental question in the work is 'What is really true here?' Although rarely asked directly, collaborative inquiry implicitly questions habitual perceptions and interpretations, inviting the client to encounter the world with greater authenticity (Brazier 2009). As someone experiences the environment in all its rawness, physical experiences of weather and terrain impose themselves on the senses, and with this immediacy, the direct encounter with nature, though still mediated through reactions, tends to bring about healthier and less personally enmeshed experience.

Action as a condition

Working with conditions can enhance positive mental states by shifting predominant patterns and refocusing awareness. Taking people outdoors, in itself, creates new habit patterns, improving well-being. Creating wholesome living spaces and access to healthy environments provides important conditions for good mental health. For this reason, other-centred approaches sit well alongside practical interventions such as community work and mental health projects. Practical changes to people's circumstances constitute one important factor in facilitating change and, combined with more overtly psychological talking therapy, can be extremely powerful. Ecotherapy potentially combines such practical experience with psychologically orientated therapeutic interventions, working at a number of levels.

In the Buddhist understanding of mental conditioning, action plays a central role. This can be understood in terms of the workings of karma. Theory suggests that karma is created through intentional action. Each activity in which we intentionally engage creates action-traces, referred to as 'seeds' or *bija*, in the store mind. When similar conditions to those which surrounded the original action arise again, these seeds grow, leading to similar action responses to those which created the seeds in the first place. So, for example, if we respond to a stressful situation by withdrawing into silence, karmic traces of silent withdrawal will be created. The seeds of that response will then tend to be ignited by future similar experiences of stress, making it likely that we will withdraw again. This pattern tends to repeat over time as each stress event leads to further avoidant action, in turn creating more karmic seeds. Gradually we are likely to become increasingly withdrawn each time a stress arises, laying down more seeds each time which then condition future reactions.

At the same time, karma is not predestination. It involves tendencies. At each point where karmic seeds ripen, there is always a possibility that we may not act on them and a different seed may be sown which can condition different responses in the future. Some therapies which draw on Buddhist approaches focus particularly on changing action patterns in order to address mental distress. Morita therapy (Reynolds 1980) for example, places emphasis on the role of practical tasks in facilitating psychological change. It also offers methods for disrupting conditioned view through activities which reshape attention by deliberately avoiding habitual interests and seeking out different stimuli. For example, one commonly used exercise involves walking outdoors looking for all the things which are yellow, thus forcing the attention away from habitual biases towards a more direct encounter with real objects.

Experiencing awe

Fundamental to other-centred methodology is a valuing of connectedness. It is through our relationship with the world and our interdependence with others of every kind that we flourish. In particular, experiences of inspiration and wonder are powerful in evoking new reactions and in fostering a sense of connection, sometimes to particular people, places or living things, and sometimes to less tangible phenomena.

One therapeutic approach to working outdoors which has evoked interest in recent years is the deliberate cultivation of awe. Research into the psychological impact of awe is generally traced back to a paper written by Dacher Keltner and Jonathan Haidt (Keltner and Haidt 2003), who defined the experience of awe in terms of two factors: perceived vastness, and a need for accommodation, the latter representing a need for psychological adjustment. In this description we see that the experience of awe is one which both evokes wonder and challenges the current mental frame. By encountering something which is experienced as awesome, the person is changed in some way. This observation has obvious implications in terms of the Buddhist view that the rigidity of the world-view and the corresponding self-structures lie at the root of psychological problems as well as Buddhists theories about the way that mental states are conditioned by perception of the world.

From this appreciation of the beneficial impact of experiences of awe, a number of people have been developing the use of Awe Walks in which participants are invited to walk in nature with the deliberate intention of seeking out experiences of awe. One such researcher is Virginia Sturm (Sturm et al. 2022) who conducted a study of older adults taking weekly fifteen-minute walks outdoors over an eight-week period. Of the participant group, half were assigned as a control, receiving no specific instruction on how to behave on their walk, while the other half were asked to seek out experiences of awe. The latter group experienced measurable improvement on a number of factors relating to mental health.

An interesting feature of this research was that participants were asked to take selfies at intervals during each walk. When these were examined, it became clear that those who had participated in the awe walks portrayed themselves in increasingly small images against a larger backdrop of nature. The experience of awe seemed to reduce the separation between self and environment and contextualize them within the wider frame. As Sturm comments in an online article, 'One of the key features of awe is that it promotes what we call "small self," a healthy sense of proportion between your own self and the bigger picture of the world around you' (Sturm 2022).

Interdependence: An ecosystemic perspective

In emphasizing the conditioned nature of the self, Buddhism contextualizes the personal within a web of non-personal factors. Ideas of interdependence, oneness and inter-penetration of phenomena are variously proposed by different Buddhist traditions, particularly in Mahayana Buddhism. The theory of inter-penetration was probably most fully developed within the Huayan School in China through the mythic image of Indra's Net, which was described as a vast net which stretches to infinity in every direction through the universe and which has a jewel at each intersection. Each jewel reflects every other jewel so creating a world of infinitely interpenetrating mirrors.

The image of Indra's Net provides an illustration of the idea that everything in the universe contains elements of every other thing, expressing a fundamental understanding which is reflected in many teachings across all Buddhist traditions. For example, as we have already seen, it is traditional to meditate on the elements both inside and outside the body, revealing that the basic constituents, earth, air, fire and water, are present both within and without our physical form.

This way of thinking about the world and the place of humans within it has much in common with an ecosystemic view of humanity, seeing us as existing within a complex system of inter-dependent living and non-living things. Within the ecosystem, each creature holds a niche, placing it in a relationship of reciprocity with others within the system for as long as that system is in balance. Finding and honouring our niche as humans within the context of the whole is perhaps the greatest challenge which humanity currently faces (Maitney 2012).

The ecosystemic perspective in turn can inform our practice in ecotherapy. As we have already seen, the research on awe walks suggests that a move towards contextualizing the self in the greater picture is beneficial to mental health. Developing an appreciation for the complexity of life around us, the interconnections of which we are aware and those we are not aware of, is a challenge for all of us at many levels and is vital to addressing the larger issues associated with environmental crises, but it is also valuable in terms of our individual psychology.

Conclusion

The move from therapy room to the outdoors brings with it both challenges and opportunities. Exploring a Buddhist-based, other-centred methodology, in this chapter I have examined some different aspects of therapeutic work which are enabled in this context and have also noted some challenges.

Buddhist practice is primarily a phenomenological investigation of mental process. Some therapeutic applications of Buddhist thought have been popularized in mindfulness teaching, and others are being developed through a number of different psychotherapeutic models which are entering the field of ecopsychology and ecotherapy in various ways. In this chapter I have drawn on mindfulness teaching, Buddhist psychology, ecotherapy practice, group theory and other-centred therapy, both from my own experience and from theoretical sources.

What has emerged is a picture of the complexity which this work represents. The field of ecotherapy is broad, operating in different settings including counselling outdoors, mental health projects and other community-based initiatives. It incorporates therapies that are diverse in style and theoretical underpinnings. Buddhist psychology offers a unique integration and a depth understanding of human process and its moment-by-moment reinforcement, with models of therapy which combine environmental and behavioural approaches, an understanding of cognitive processing and theories of conditioned mind, which combine well with a psychodynamic perspective. With this diversity within the model, the approach can provide a useful vehicle for exploring the field of nature-based therapies and aiding in creating new integrations.

In addition to this, Buddhist psychology rests within a paradigm which is based on a view of the self as a constructed and often problematic phenomenon. In a world where ecological threat is perceived as a daily reality, it would seem that a model of therapy which brings into question assumptions of the importance of personal entitlement and autonomy is needed. As environmentally based therapists, we cannot ignore this moral challenge. It is only by seeing the small self in the bigger picture that we will address the urgent needs of our planet.

References

Analayo (2003), *Satipatthana*, Cambridge: Windhorse.

Bazzano, M. (2014), *After Mindfulness*, Basingstoke, UK: Palgrave Macmillan.

Brazier, C. (2009), *Other-Centred Therapy: Buddhist Psychology in Action*, Hampshire, UK: O-Books.

Brazier, C. (2011), *Acorns among the Grass*, Hampshire, UK: Earth Books.

Brazier, C. (2013a), 'Roots of Mindfulness', *European Journal of Psychotherapy & Counselling* 15: 127–38.

Brazier, C. (2013b), 'Sacred Space: Different Boundaries in Environmentally Based Therapies', *BACP Thresholds* Autumn.

Brazier, C. (2017), *Ecotherapy in Practice: A Buddhist Model*, Abingdon UK: Routledge.

Jones, D. (2011), *This Being, That Becomes: The Buddha's Teaching on Conditionality*, Cambridge: Windhorse.

Kabat-Zinn, J. (1990), *Full Catastrophe Living: Using the Wisdom of Your Body and Mind to Face Stress, Pain, and Illness*, Crystal Lake, IL: Delta.

Kabat-Zinn, J. (1994), *Wherever You Go, There You Are: Mindfulness Meditation in Everyday Life*, New York: Hyperion.

Keltner, D., and J. Haidt (2003), 'Approaching Awe, a Moral, Spiritual, and Aesthetic Emotion', *Cognition and Emotion* 17 (2): 297–314.

Maitney, P. (2012), 'Longing to Be Human: Evolving Ourselves in Healing the Earth', in M. Rust and N. Totton (eds), *Vital Signs: Psychological Responses to Ecological Crisis*, 47–60, London: Karnac.

Reynolds, D. (1980), *The Quiet Therapies*, Honolulu: University of Hawaii Press.

Rogers, C. (1980), *A Way of Being*, Boston: Houghton Mifflin.

Rust, M. J., and N. Totton (2011), *Vital Signs: Psychological Responses to Ecological Crisis*, London: Karnac.

Saiko, G. (2018), 'Dharma-Based Person-Centered Approach in Japan'. Available online: https://api.semanticscholar.org/CorpusID:198749238.

Segal, V., M. Williams and J. Teasdale (2002), *Mindfulness-Based Cognitive Therapy for Depression*, New York: Guilford Press.

Sturm, V. E. (2022), https://psychiatry.ucsf.edu/news/awe-walks-boost-emotional-well-being.

Sturm, V. E., S. Datta, A. R. K. Roy, I. J. Sible, E. L. Kosik, C. R. Veziris, T. E. Chow, N. A. Morris, J. Neuhaus, J. H. Kramer, B. L. Miller, S. R. Holley and D. Keltner (2022), 'Big Smile, Small Self: Awe Walks Promote Prosocial Positive Emotions in Older Adults', *Emotion* 22 (5): 1044–58. https://doi.org/10.1037/emo0000876.

3

Relational psychotherapy and eudemonic philosophy in nature experiences

Joe Hinds

Introduction

Orientated within a relational account of therapy, the present chapter focuses on how the natural environment is able to provide optimal conditions to elicit a eudemonic awakening; this is preceded by a summary explanation of eudemonia. Importantly, existential and transpersonal modes of understanding are examined to locate people's relational experiencing with nature. Of particular interest is the *quality* of reported emotional states as indicators of the transformative effect of nature on the human condition. Throughout, a simplistic interpretation of eudemonia is used, one that relates to a psychotherapeutic approach and that resonates strongly with nature-based experiences. Overall, the present chapter is intended to show that nature presents important opportunities that might contribute towards a eudemonic life developed through relational, reflexive and emotional mechanisms. Experiential accounts are presented to strengthen the argument for the inclusion of a eudemonic philosophy within nature-based therapies.

Eudemonia

The Greek philosopher Aristotle defined eudemonia (literally, 'good spirit') as well-being brought about by realizing and attaining what is worth having in one's life and 'living in truth to oneself' (Norton 1976: 216) in accordance with reason and contemplation (Huta 2013). It is further described as a moral or virtuous living (e.g.

exemplifying kindness, courage and honesty), one that stands in contrast to hedonic happiness, which is, essentially, the pursuit of pleasure and the avoidance of pain (Huta 2013). Moreover, eudemonia acknowledges effort and agency in value-based activities that are engaged in because they contribute to a purposeful existence and to a 'good life': a life that

> benefits (and, importantly, does not harm) others. Eudemonia is not achieved through momentary pleasure (hedonism) but is something that is developed over the life course – a good life *lived* well by developing, exercising and extending our human capacities. (e.g. Ryff 2013)

Although definitive 'lists' of various virtues thought to 'improve' individual well-being have been suggested (e.g. Seligman et al. 2005), these may be seen as rather prescriptive and, portrayed in terms of excellence, rather idealistic (Woolfolk and Wasserman 2005); moreover, there are 'manifold intangibles that make life worth living' (Haybron 2008: ix). The freedom to choose a path towards authenticity and responsibility is, within talking therapies, the individual's (e.g. Strasser and Clarke 2013), and indeed, this choice and subsequent behaviours are in themselves meaningful (Guignon 2002).

Importantly, the discovery of the 'true self' or *daimon*, that which is *intrinsically* worthy, cannot be entirely *extrinsically* driven (Vernon 2008). Drawing on Rollo May's (1969) interpretation, the daimon is a 'fundamental, archetypal function of human experience' (p. 123) that represents a 'unique pattern of sensibilities and powers which constitute the individual as a self in relation to [the] world' (p. 125). The daimon is usually experienced as a 'blind' urge to assert, affirm and perpetuate the 'self'. However, by being conscious of its presence and receptive to its totality, the daimon can be personally informative, directive and creative. Eudemonic 'well-being' is achieved by being in harmony with one's daimon (May 1969). Perhaps paradoxically, however, eudemonia develops from undertaking a pursuit that has some significance *outside* of the individual, one that is able to elicit an awareness and acceptance of a holistic understanding of one's self and one's place in the world (Vernon 2008). This way of being may not contribute to or involve 'happiness' per se, although undoubtedly there are prudential benefits; rather, it contributes to the development of values, worth and meaning in one's life (Vernon 2008).

Although some authors have made a distinction between eudemonic acting and feeling (Huta 2013), the present view posits that truly eudemonic states, despite Aristotle's emphasis on reasoning, are characterized by the convergence of contemplative, emotional and behavioural 'parts' of the self, prompting 'the fulfilment of human nature' and leading of a 'full life' (Haybron 2008: 35). This would be in alignment with Winnicott's (1965) concept of 'true self' which may be understood as a person's authentic, spontaneous, and alive sense of self derived from embodied experiences and sensations. The union of the physical, intellectual and emotional with an acceptance of finitude, to inform a value-based common good, has been expressed previously as *wisdom* (Kohut 1966; Sternberg 1998). Although beyond the scope of the present chapter, this convergence with eudemonia warrants elucidation.

Although there have been efforts to 'accurately' understand and apply eudemonic concepts in the modern world, for historical and cultural reasons this has led to differing interpretations (Vernon 2008). The contemporary psychological understanding of eudemonia, born from an individualistic, atomistic and capitalist culture (Midgely 2003), remains a less-than-holistic interpretation of what may be beneficial to human functioning and potential, with some indicating as problematic the absence of negative emotional states (Woolfolk 2002). Indeed, it is the integration of various aspects of the self (e.g. 'good' and 'bad') into our self-structure that allows for the possibility of living generatively and authentically in relation to the world (May 1969). A considered critique of a traditional eudemonia rejects some of its explicit and implicit tenets arguing, for instance, for a collectivist rather than an individualist perspective (e.g. Tantum 2014). Although Aristotle held contemplation of one's place in the world and the subsequent discovery of meaning in life to be essential (Vernon 2008), it is important to consider eudemonia as being 'less about navel gazing and more about understanding one's relation to the world' (Hamilton 2013: 486). Additionally, there is a need for recognition of the 'obliging social and physical context[s] to help shape the way we live' (Haybron 2008: 255). Exposure to the natural environment has been shown to be a valuable conduit for engendering at least some degree of human psychological benefit and potential (Annerstedt and Währborg 2011; Weinstein, Przybylski and Ryan 2009).

Existentialism

Aspects of eudemonia have been present in humanistic and existential accounts of the human condition in relatively recent history, including works by Nietzsche, Rogers and Maslow (Haybron 2008; Ryff 2013), together with more contemporary writings (e.g. Passmore and Howell 2014a; Schroll, Rowan and Robinson 2011). The idea that despair can be a catalyst for constructive action is embedded within existential philosophy (e.g. May 1981). Indeed, the natural world can evoke existential anxieties through the perception of it as threatening, disgusting and uncertain, and may make salient to people their mortality (Kellert 2002; Koole and van den Berg 2005). Certainly, embodied and challenging experiences in nature can contribute to a reconfiguration of people's world-view (Marshall, this volume; Skalski and Hardy 2013; Vernon 2008), mirroring the process of relationship with our environment (*Umwelt*) and the paradoxical acceptance of death in order to live (van Deurzen 2013; cf. Pienaar 2011). Moments of breakdown, replete with negative emotions, may be opportunities for therapeutic *breakthrough* that enable the self to develop through the integration of its various conscious and unconscious strands (Bollas 2013; Field 1996). A holistic and authentic notion of human functioning and eudemonia might therefore *include* those emotional states that are often portrayed as negative (Woolfolk 2002). Expressed differently, 'humanity's inherent negativity is the source for its development, where those contradictions which result in crisis and which are resolved lead to higher levels of Being' (Buss 1976: 9).

So although evidence suggests that nature affords people the opportunity to recover from depleted cognitive capacities (e.g. van den Berg, Hartig and Staats 2007) and for prevention against more affective conditions such as stress and anxiety (e.g. Maller et al. 2005), the degree to which these experiences lead to the development of a eudemonic awakening is debatable. Orr (1993), among many, has suggested that the reacquaintance of humans with nature is necessary to regain what it means to be *wholly* human. Although it is possible to develop a meaningful sense of self in relation to the world through emotional engagement with nature, without suffering (Milton 2002), finding harmony and meaning in and through nature has often been accompanied by fear and arduousness (Frankl 1959; Fredrickson and Anderson 1999; Hinds and Sparks 2011).

Eudemonia and nature

A growing body of evidence suggests that experiences associated with being in or engaged with nature induce a relatively unique group of emotional responses and states that may be aligned to the concept of eudemonia, particularly if a sense of connection (relatedness) to nature is considered (Davis and Gatersleben 2013; Passmore and Howell 2014a; Trigwell, Francis and Bagot 2014; see also Zelenski and Nisbet 2014). Research has indicated that activities motivated by eudemonic ideals tend to elicit feeling states of awe, inspiration and a sense of connection with a greater whole (Huta and Ryan 2010). For instance, developing a meaningful relationship with nature through gardening may be an important precursor to experiencing eudemonia (Webber, Hinds and Camic 2015).

Eigner (2001) suggests that the well-being associated with an embodied immersion in the natural environment may be a qualitatively different, 'higher quality' well-being compared to more hedonically construed well-being. Participants active in various voluntary environmental protective behaviours, such as the maintenance of local natural environments, have reported that the natural environment produced 'an amazing feeling of happiness', an 'inner sort of calm' and feelings of being 'really satisfied', more relaxed and more like themselves (Eigner 2001: 191–2). Participants exposed to natural environments in other studies have reported experiencing feelings of union with nature, joy, a sense of wonder and peace of mind (Jacob and Brinkerhoff 1999) and, after being introduced to a woodland environment, a sense of union with nature and tranquillity (Kjellgren and Buhrkall 2010). Indeed, Kaplan and Kaplan (1989) suggest that over time, contact with nature leads to 'deep reflection', or what might also be referred to as mindfulness; this has been found within a cohort of smallholders (Jacob and Brinkerhoff 1999), described here as a process whereby

> the anxieties of the future have space to recede to the background, and the past's residual fears can be replaced by peace of mind. The world for one moment appears whole and the mind moves towards a stillness. … One's being, then, is not seen as separate, apart from a world outside of consciousness; rather one, if only for an instant, appears to be drawn into the ongoing stream of a perceived universal reality, with the potential for finding tranquillity, union and wholeness. (Jacob 1997: 84)

There are also examples of mixed emotional responses reported by people in nature (Hinds and Sparks 2011). MacFarlane (2003) cites John Dennis's 1688 description of crossing the Italian Alps as 'a delightful horrour, a terrible joy' (p. 73), and empirical works have found that a large minority of respondents reported experiencing simultaneous states including, for example, elevated awareness and perception, and feelings of awe, respect, fear *and* happiness (van den Berg and ter Heijne 2005). Moreover, these emotional states resonate with notions that Maslow had regarding the actualized person for whom the appreciation for the 'basic goods of life', such as nature, are likely to be experienced with feelings of 'awe, pleasure, [and] wonder', (Maslow 1956: 177). Schneider (2003) proposes that experiencing awe equates to the human capacity 'for the thrill and anxiety of living … humility and boldness, reverence and wonder', (p. 135) which in turn allows for personal and interpersonal openness and dialogue.

Transpersonal relating and contemplation

As these deeply relational nature-based experiences seem to suggest, the natural environment is able to evoke relatively unique emotional and spiritual or self-transcendent experiences (Morrison 2009; Totton 2011; Williams and Harvey 2001) including eudemonic-like states such as contemplation and awe (Hinds and Sparks 2011). Akin to Maslow's later writings regarding the transpersonal (Koltko-Rivera 1998), self-transcendence may be characterized as a transpersonal identification with entities beyond the individual, such as a deep connection with nature (e.g. Kirk,

Eaves and Martin 1999). For instance, Fredrickson and Anderson (1999) discovered that direct and prolonged wilderness experiences elicited profound emotions such as awe, a deep sense of peace and an emotional connectedness to the natural environment that, at times, for some individuals, verged on the spiritual and therefore may be aligned with and indicative of a spiritual eudemonia (van Dierendonck and Mohan 2006).

Through the nurturance of a transpersonal relationship (Schroll, Rowan and Robinson 2011), one that demonstrates a deep sense of meaningful connection (Abram 1996; Ashley 2008), the natural environment can be a catalyst for a spiritual awakening. Indeed, the concept of eudemonia was conceived during a time when transcendent meaning was abundant (Haybron 2008); the Greeks of Aristotle's time revered the earth as a living goddess, expressing their awe, wonder and gratitude to her (Midgely 2003). Crucially, that which was taken for granted during Aristotle's time, namely a belief in a transcendent 'other', is largely missing in contemporary Western society (Vernon 2008) although the transpersonal has been acknowledged in psychotherapy and psychiatry (e.g. Jung 1995; Powell 2018).

Nature, in these circumstances, may be conceived as 'intimate other'; the third entity within an outdoor therapeutic encounter, one in which people can explore in an embodied, multisensory and sensuous way, a here-and-now experiencing (Adams 2010). Others have stressed the importance of exposure to the natural environment to build a sense of self that is orientated around a transpersonal relatedness (Jordan 2009). For instance, people's encounters with mountains have resulted in them experiencing their selves honestly, unguardedly and wholeheartedly by being aware of a transcendent 'higher reality' described variously as 'infinity, eternity, ecstasy, reverence, salvation, [and] humility' (Lester 2004: 96). Moreover, the mountains come to represent not just a good place but all that is 'noble, real, unselfish, and unselfconscious in life' (Lester 2004: 93). Climbers also talked of 'a mysterious harmony' and 'a purpose larger than myself' (Lester 2004: 96), complementing other research focused on white-water rafting (Arnould and Price 1993), extreme sports (Brymer and Gray 2009), forest encounters (Williams and Harvey 2001) and wilderness experiences (Hinds 2011).

Central to the ecotherapy understanding of healing trauma is the idea of developing a relationship with the natural world, a relationship which, in the modern Western and scientific world, has been seen in dualistic terms (Davis 2011; Macy 2009). Engagement with the transpersonal blurs the boundaries of self and other in a 'co-existence of opposites', permitting the simultaneous sense of 'self' and 'other' and (often held to be) opposite and intense emotions (Clarkson 2002: 148). Moreover, the ability to accept and synthesize these dichotomies is an important part of the process of personal growth and development (Weeks and L'Abate 1982). This degree of experiencing requires holistic and reciprocal patterns of connectivity (strong relationality) rather than individual or atomistic relationality (Wiggins,

Ostenson and Wendt 2013). Direct contact with nature may lead to a non-dualistic identification which is sometimes a confusing and paradoxical place where opposing emotions can co-occur and there is a blurring of 'self' and 'other' (Ashley 2008; see also Braud 2001).

Clear and unambiguous feedback from an embodied and multisensory experience where one may even feel discomfort, pain and tiredness (Reser and Scherl 1988) can be a powerful challenge to the status quo and has the potential to generate new insights about the self in relation to the world, effectively 'dislodging' or 'decentring' the self-concept (Clarkson 2002). The external environment impacts the internal (and vice versa), providing opportunities for different perspectives on the self, the immediate environment and the interaction between them (Reser and Scherl 1988). This person–environmental 'dialogue' seems to foster contemplative states (Davis 2011) via an emotional embodied experiencing (Abram 1996; see also Bohart 2011). These opinions seem to echo sentiments of philosophers such as Emerson: 'The lover of nature is he whose inward and outward senses are truly adjusted to each other' (1836/1982: 38); and Muir: 'I only went out for a walk, and finally concluded to stay out till sundown, for going out, I found, was really going in' (1966: 439).

Ethics

An important cornerstone of the eudemonic tradition is the idea of living a moral or ethical life. Modern life characterized by pervasive information technology tends to obscure a 'robust sense of reality' (Borgmann 1999: 15). Attempts to fill the modern crisis of meaning, the 'existential vacuum' (Frankl 1959), with modern consumer trappings and other inauthentic ways tend to have detrimental effects on well-being (Boyle 2003; Hamilton 2004). Recently, eudemonia has been wedded to proposed ethical guidelines reconceived to address current issues of environmental sustainability (Richards 2013). Others have found that living a simpler life in conjunction with the natural environment mitigates the negative effects of modern living and promotes an environmental consciousness (Brown and Kasser 2005; Kasser 2009). Additionally, immersion in natural environments seems to increase people's intrinsic value for community, intimacy and personal growth (Weinstein, Przybylski and Ryan 2009). Importantly, there is a corpus of research and informed opinion now to suggest that nature experiences, in many forms, may promote an environmental ethic (Collado, Staats and Corraliza 2013; Kellert 1993; Shapiro 1995). From a therapeutic position, healing individual trauma in the wild may liberate people's attention so that they can 'reconnect with their innate love and care for the other-than-human' (Totton 2011: 213; see also Greenway 2009).

Summary

It has been recognized that it requires 'direct encounters with nature ... for deeper emotional responses and spiritual understandings' (Koger and Winter 2010: 315). Moreover, the meanings we require to make sense of the world come not entirely from the words we use but rather meaning 'sprouts in the very depths of the sensory world, in the heat of meeting, encounter, [and] participation' (Abram 1996: 75). Thus, therapy outdoors may be considered a relatively unique therapeutic intervention with the potential to elicit profound insight and change and to awaken a gestalt of human functioning and being in order to live eudemonically (as a return to the original or true self; Winnicott 1965). It is therefore proposed that an embodied emotional immersion within a (sometimes physically as well as psychologically challenging) natural environment may elicit contemplative and transformative 'moments' that, although not resulting in the immediate uptake of a virtuous life (whatever that entails), do initiate a process of self-realization that fosters a better appreciation of one's place in the world.

With that in mind, I close with a poem presented to me voluntarily by a participant during a twelve-day wilderness experience in northern Scotland. Although this collective experience has been reported elsewhere (Hinds 2011), the following individual verbatim extract has not. It was an impromptu writing and is, I feel, an apt example of the eudemonic awakening which may be elicited from immersion in nature. Moreover, the poet had found the strength for the first time to confront and disclose personal trauma without an explicit therapeutic intervention, thus adding emphasis to the author's words and the transformative experience of the natural environment.

On the edge of the world, at the edge of the land, Standing facing
the sea, I look down to my hand It's brown with the wind, the sun
and the rain, It's wrinkled and lined with sand, ingrained

It's lined with a life that I thought I knew best, All my hopes and
my fears and a sum of the rest I look up to the sea and take a
sniff of air.

As the waves crash in, I'm remembering where I grew up and
who I've been,

Who I've touched and what I've seen. How I've cried
and laughed and joked, What I thought and what I
spoke.

A gull soars past, flying high,

Which takes my eyes towards the sky,

There clouds billow in, pushed along by the wind, a mix of whites,
greys and blues,

And when the sun sets, a hint of rouge.

I've been here before, on the edge of the world, Standing facing the sea, calling out without words, Looking towards a curved horizon,

Something for me to rest my eyes on. Somewhere for me to relax and remember, A place for then, for now, forever.

Now I know where my boundaries lie Where the waves touch the sky.

References

Abram, D. (1996), *The Spell of the Sensuous*, New York: Random House.

Adams, W. W. (2010), 'Basho's Therapy for Narcissus: Nature as Intimate Other and Transpersonal Self', *Journal of Humanistic Psychology* 50: 38–64.

Annerstedt, M., and P. Währborg (2011), 'Nature-Assisted Therapy: Systematic Review of Controlled and Observational Studies', *Scandinavian Journal of Public Health* 39: 371–88.

Arnould, E. J., and L. L. Price (1993), 'River Magic: Extraordinary Experience and the Extended Service Encounter', *Journal of Consumer Research* 20: 24–45.

Ashley, P. (2008), 'Toward an Understanding and Definition of Wilderness Spirituality', *Australian Geographer* 38: 53–69.

Bohart, A. C. (2011), 'A Meditation on the Nature of Self-Healing and Personality Change in Psychotherapy Based on Gendlin's Theory of Experiencing', *The Humanistic Psychologist* 29: 249–79.

Bollas, C. (2013), *Catch Them before They Fall*, London: Routledge.

Borgmann, A. (1999), *Holding on to Reality: The Nature of Information at the Turn of the Millennium*, Chicago: University of Chicago Press.

Boyle, D. (2003), *Authenticity: Brands, Fakes, Spin, and the Lust for Real Life*, London: Harper Perennial.

Braud, W. (2001), 'Experiencing Tears of Wonder-Joy: Seeing with the Heart's Eye', *The Journal of Transpersonal Psychology* 33: 99–111.

Brown, K. W., and T. Kasser (2005), 'Are Psychological and Ecological Well-Being Compatible? The Role of Values, Mindfulness, and Lifestyle', *Social Indicators Research* 74: 349–68.

Brymer, E., and T. Gray (2009), 'Dancing with Nature: Rhythm and Harmony in Extreme Sports Participation', *Journal of Adventure Education and Outdoor Learning* 9: 135–49.

Buss A. R. (1976), 'Development of Dialectics and Development of Humanistic Psychology', *Human Development* 19: 248–60.

Clarkson, P. (2002), *The Transpersonal Relationship in Psychotherapy*, London: Whurr.

Collado, S., H. Staats and J. A. Corraliza (2013), 'Experiencing Nature in Children's Summer Camps: Affective, Cognitive and Behavioural Consequences', *Journal of Environmental Psychology* 33: 37–44.

Davis, J. V. (2011), 'Ecopsychology, Transpersonal Psychology, and Nonduality', *International Journal of Transpersonal Studies* 30: 137–47.

Davis, N., and B. Gatersleben (2013), 'Transcendent Experiences in Wild and Manicured Settings: The Influence of the Trait "Connectedness to Nature" ', *Ecopsychology* 5: 92–102.

Eigner, S. (2001), 'The Relationship between "Protecting the Environment" as a Dominant Life Goal and Subjective Well-Being', in P. Schmuck and K. M. Sheldon (eds), *Life Goals and Well-Being: Towards a Positive Psychology of Human Striving*, 182–201, Göttingen: Hogrefe and Huber.

Emerson, R. W. (1836/1982), 'Nature', in L. Ziff (ed.), *Nature and Selected Essays*, 35–82, New York: Penguin Books.

Field, N. (1996), *Breakdown and Breakthrough*, Hove, UK: Routledge.

Frankl, V. E. (1959), *Man's Search for Meaning*, London: Random House.

Fredrickson, L. M., and D. H. Anderson (1999), 'A Qualitative Exploration of the Wilderness Experience as a Source of Spiritual Inspiration', *Journal of Environmental Psychology* 19: 21–39.

Greenway, R. (2009), 'The Wilderness Experience as Therapy: We've Been Here Before', in L. Buzzell and C. Chalquist (eds), *Ecotherapy: Healing with Nature in Mind*, 132–9, San Francisco: Sierra Club Books.

Guignon, C. (2002), 'Hermeneutics, Authenticity, and the Aims of Psychology', *Journal of Theoretical and Philosophical Psychology* 22: 83–102.

Hamilton, C. (2004), *Growth Fetish*, London: Pluto Press.

Hamilton, R. (2013), 'The Frustrations of Virtue: The Myth of Moral Neutrality in Psycho- therapy', *Journal of Evaluation in Clinical Practice* 19: 485–92.

Haybron, D. M. (2008), *The Pursuit of Unhappiness: The Elusive Psychology of Well-Being*, Oxford: Oxford University Press.

Hinds, J. (2011), 'Exploring the Psychological Rewards of a Wilderness Experience: An Interpretive Phenomenological Analysis,' *The Humanistic Psychologist* 39: 189–205.

Hinds, J., and P. Sparks (2011), 'The Affective Quality of Human-Natural Environment Relationships', *Evolutionary Psychology* 9: 451–69.

Huta, V. (2013), 'Eudaimonia', in S. David, I. Boniwell and A. C. Ayers (eds), *Oxford Handbook of Happiness*, 201–13, Oxford: Oxford University Press.

Huta, V., and R. M. Ryan (2010), 'Pursuing Pleasure or Virtue: The Differential and Overlapping Well-Being Benefits of Hedonic and Eudaimonic Motives', *Journal of Happiness Studies* 11: 735–62.

Jacob, J. (1997), *New Pioneers: The Back-to-the-Land Movement and the Search for a Sustain- able Future*, University Park, PA: Penn State University Press.

Jacob, J. C., and M. B. Brinkerhoff (1999), 'Mindfulness and Subjective Well-Being in the Sustainability Movement: A Further Elaboration of Multiple Discrepancies Theory', *Social Indicators Research* 46: 341–68.

Jordan, M. (2009), 'Nature and Self: An Ambivalent Attachment?', *Ecopsychology* 1: 26–31.

Jung, C. G. (1995), *Memories, Dreams, Reflections: An Autobiography*, London: HarperCollins.

Kaplan, R., and S. Kaplan (1989), *The Experience of Nature: A Psychological Perspective*, Cambridge: Cambridge University Press.

Kasser, T. (2009), 'Psychological Need Satisfaction, Personal Well-Being, and Ecological Sustainability', *Ecopsychology* 1: 175–80.

Kellert, S. R. (1993), 'The Biological Basis for Human Values of Nature', in S. R. Kellert and E. O. Wilson (eds), *The Biophilia Hypothesis*, 42–69, Washington, DC: Island Press.

Kellert, S. R. (2002), 'Experiencing Nature: Affective, Cognitive, and Evaluative Development in Children', in P. H. Kahn Jr. and S. R. Kellert (eds), *Children and Nature: Psycho- logical, Sociocultural and Evolutionary Investigations*, 117–51, Cambridge, MA: The MIT Press.

Kirk, K. M., L. J. Eaves and N. G. Martin (1999), 'Self-Transcendence as a Measure of Spirituality in a Sample of Older Australian Twins', *Twin Research* 2: 81–7.

Kjellgren, A., and H. Buhrkall (2010), 'A Comparison of the Restorative Effect of a Natural Environment with That of a Simulated Natural Environment', *Journal of Environmental Psychology* 30: 464–72.

Koger, S. M., and D. D. Winter (2010), *The Psychology of Environmental Problems*, 3rd edn, New York: Psychology Press.

Kohut, H. (1966), 'Forms and Transformations of Narcissism', *Journal of the American Psychoanalytical Association* 14: 243–72.

Koltko-Rivera, M. E. (1998), 'Maslow's "Transhumanism": Was Transpersonal Psychology Conceived as "a Psychology Without People in It"?', *Journal of Humanistic Psychology* 38: 71–80.

Koole, S. L., and A. E. van den Berg (2005), 'Lost in the Wilderness: Terror Management, Action Orientation, and Nature Evaluation', *Journal of Personality and Social Psychology* 88: 1014–28.

Lester, J. (2004), 'Spirit, Identity, and Self in Mountaineering', *Journal of Humanistic Psychology* 44: 86–100.

MacFarlane, R. (2003), *Mountains of the Mind: A History of Fascination*, London: Granta Books.

Macy, J. (2009), 'The Greening of the Self', in L. Buzzell and C. Chalquist (eds), *Ecotherapy: Healing with Nature in Mind*, 238–45, San Francisco: Sierra Club Books.

Maller, C., M. Townsend, A. Pryor, P. Brown and L. St Leger (2005), 'Healthy Nature Healthy People: "Contact with Nature" as an Upstream Health Promotion Intervention for Populations', *Health Promotion International* 21: 45–54.

Maslow, A. H. (1956), 'Self-actualising People: A Study of Psychological Health', in C. E. Moustakas and S. R. Jayaswal (eds), *The Self: Explorations in Personal Growth*, 160–94, New York: Harper and Row.

May, R. (1969), *Love and Will*, New York: W. W. Norton.

May, R. (1981), *Freedom and Destiny*, New York: W. W. Norton.

Midgely, M. (2003), *The Myths We Live By*, London: Routledge.
Milton, K. (2002), *Loving Nature: Towards an Ecology of Emotion*, London: Routledge.
Morrison, A. L. (2009), 'Embodying Sentience', in L. Buzzell and C. Chalquist (eds), *Ecotherapy: Healing with Nature in Mind*, 104–10, San Francisco: Sierra Club Books.
Muir, J. (1966), L. M. Wolfe (ed.), *John of the Mountains: The Unpublished Journals of John Muir*, Wisconsin: The University of Wisconsin Press.
Norton, D. L. (1976), *Personal Destinies: A Philosophy of Ethical Individualism*, Princeton, NJ: Princeton University Press.
Orr, D. W. (1993), 'Love It or Lose It: The Coming Biophilia Revolution', in S. R. Kellert and E. O. Wilson (eds), *The Biophilia Hypothesis*, 415–38, Washington, DC: Island Press.
Passmore, H-A., and A. J. Howell (2014a), 'Eco-Existential Positive Psychology: Experiences in Nature, Existential Anxieties, and Well-Being', *The Humanistic Psychologist* 42: 370–88.
Pienaar, M. (2011), 'An Eco-Existential Understanding of Time and Psychological Defences: Threats to the Environment and Implications for Psychotherapy', *Ecopsychology* 3: 25–39.
Powell, A. (2018), *Conversations with the Soul: A Psychiatrist Reflects: Essays on Life, Death and Beyond*, London: Muswell Hill Press.
Reser, J. P., and L. M. Scherl (1988), 'Clear and Unambiguous Feedback: A Transactional and Motivational Analysis of Environmental Challenge and Self-Encounter', *Journal of Environmental Psychology* 8: 269–86.
Richards, D. G. (2013), 'Eudaimonia, Economics and the Environment: What Do the Hellenistic Thinkers Have to Teach Economists about 'the Good Life?', *Ethics and the Environment* 18: 33–53.
Ryff, C. D. (2013), 'Psychological Well-Being Revisited: Advances in the Science and Practice of Eudaimonia', *Psychotherapy and Psychosomatics* 83: 10–28.
Schneider, K. J. (2003), 'The Fluid Center: An Awe-Based Challenge to Humanity', *Journal of Humanistic Psychology* 43: 133–45.
Schroll, M. A., J. Rowan and O. Robinson (2011), 'Clearing up Rollo May's Views of Transpersonal Psychology and Acknowledging May as an Early Supporter of Ecopsychology', *International Journal of Transpersonal Studies* 30: 120–36.
Seligman, M. E. P., T. A. Steen, N. Park and C. Peterson (2005), 'Positive Psychology Progress: Empirical Validation of Interventions', *American Psychologist* 60: 410–21.
Shapiro, E. (1995), 'Restoring Habitats, Communities, and Souls', in T. Roszak, M. E. Gomes and A. D. Kanner (eds), *Ecopsychology: Restoring the Earth, Healing the Mind*, 224–39, San Francisco: Sierra Club Books.
Skalski, J. E., and S. A. Hardy (2013), 'Disintegration, New Consciousness, and Discontinuous Transformation: A Qualitative Investigation of Quantum Change', *The Humanistic Psychologist* 41: 159–77.
Sternberg, R. J. (1998), 'A Balance Theory of Wisdom', *Review of General Psychology* 2: 347–65.

Strasser, A., and M. Clarke (2013), 'The Challenge of Ethics and the Call to Responsibility', in E. van Deurzen and S. Iacovou (eds), *Existential Perspectives on Relationship Therapy*, 122–33, Basingstoke, UK: Palgrave Macmillan.

Tantum, D. (2014), *Emotional Well-Being and Mental Health*, London: Sage.

Totton, N. (2011), *Wild Therapy: Undomesticating Inner and Outer Worlds*, Ross-on-Wye: PCCS Books.

Trigwell, J. L., A. J. P. Francis and K. L. Bagot (2014), 'Nature Connectedness and Eudaimonic Well-Being: Spirituality as a Potential Mediator', *Ecopsychology* 6: 241–51.

van den Berg, A. E., and M. ter Heijne (2005), 'Fear Versus Fascination: An Exploration of Emotional Threats to Natural Threats', *Journal of Environmental Psychology* 25: 261–72.

van den Berg, A. E., T. Hartig and H. Staats (2007), 'Preference for Nature in Urbanised Societies: Stress, Restoration, and the Pursuit of Sustainability', *Journal of Social Issues* 63: 79–96.

van Deurzen, E. (2013), 'The Challenge of Human Relations and Relationship Therapy: To Live and to Love', in E. van Deurzen and S. Iacovou (eds), *Existential Perspectives on Relationship Therapy*, 15–31, Basingstoke, UK: Palgrave Macmillan.

van Dierendonck, D., and K. Mohan (2006), 'Some Thoughts on Spirituality and Eudaimonic Well-Being', *Mental Health, Religion and Culture* 9: 227–38.

Vernon, M. (2008), *Wellbeing*, Stocksfield, UK: Acumen.

Webber, J., J. Hinds and P. M. Camic (2015), 'The Well-Being of Allotment Gardeners: A Mixed Methodological Study', *Ecopsychology* 7: 29–37.

Weeks, G. R., and L. L'Abate (1982), *Paradoxical Psychotherapy: Theory and Practice with Individuals, Couples, and Families*, New York: Brunner/Mazel.

Weinstein, N., A. K. Przybylski and R. M. Ryan (2009), 'Can Nature Make Us More Caring? Effects of Immersion in Nature on Intrinsic Aspirations and Generosity', *Personality and Social Psychology Bulletin* 35: 1315–29.

Wiggins, B. J., J. A. Ostenson and D. C. Wendt (2013), 'The Relational Foundations of Conservation Psychology', *Ecopsychology* 4: 209–15.

Williams, K., and D. Harvey (2001), 'Transcendent Experience in Forest Environments', *Journal of Environmental Psychology* 21: 249–60.

Winnicott, D. W. (1965), *The Maturational Processes and the Facilitating Environment*, London: The Hogarth Press and the Institute of Psychoanalysis.

Woolfolk, R. L. (2002), 'The Power of Negative Thinking: Truth, Melancholia, and the Tragic Sense of Life', *Journal of Theoretical and Philosophical Psychology* 22: 19–27.

Woolfolk, R. L., and R. H. Wasserman (2005), 'Count No One Happy: Eudaimonia and Positive Psychology', *Journal of Theoretical and Philosophical Psychology* 25: 81–90.

Zelenski, J. M., and E. K. Nisbet (2014), 'Happiness and Feeling Connected: The Distinct Role of Nature Relatedness', *Environment and Behavior* 46: 3–23.

4

Ecotherapy as psychotherapy: Towards an ecopsychotherapy

Martin Jordan

Introduction

This chapter will explore the relationship between ecotherapy and therapeutic process. Starting with a review of the current ideas in ecotherapy, I then explore ecotherapy and its relationship to occupational and horticultural therapies. I then briefly outline my definition of psychotherapy and ideas that underpin the therapeutic relationship. These will include transference and countertransference with a particular emphasis on therapeutic space in relation to the ideas of Winnicott and forms of developmental vitality drawing upon Stern. Next I explore how the client-therapist-nature matrix works therapeutically looking at the different variables within this, concluding with an outline of ecopsychotherapy and therapeutic process in a natural environment.

Current understanding in the practice of ecotherapy positions contact with nature as having positive psychological benefits. There are a number of research papers and articles supporting this (See MIND 2013a, 2007; Chalquist 2009). Ecotherapy has developed along two potentially divergent and at times confusing lines. In the UK, following from the original MIND report (MIND 2007) ecotherapy developed as a form of horticultural therapy, green exercise, conservation and land management work, and finally as an amalgamation of these processes. In attempting to develop an agenda for green mental healthcare in the National Health Service (NHS), the marketing department at MIND labelled a report 'Ecotherapy' (MIND 2007) in order to communicate a diverse range of activities whose central point of convergence was some form of contact and activity within nature. The term ecotherapy in the UK has a strong association with these practices and ideas. At the same time Linda Buzzell and her colleague Craig Chalquist were developing their own definition and practice of ecotherapy and making more explicit links to both ecopsychology (Roszak, Gomes and Kanner 1995) and psychotherapy (Buzzell and Chalquist 2009). They propose ecotherapy forms a challenge to traditional ideas within psychotherapy, that locate therapy as conducted within an indoor environment abstracted from the context of nature and the outside world. 'Ecotherapy' is used as an umbrella term for nature-based methods of physical and psychological healing. Buzzell and Chalquist (2009) propose ecotherapy represents a new form of psychotherapy that acknowledges the vital role of nature and addresses the human–nature relationship. However, a recent information booklet by MIND (2013b) on ecotherapy includes the more traditional idea of therapy in its definition:

> (in its strict sense) is about building a relationship with nature, so that personal wellbeing is considered equally alongside the health of the environment. Sessions usually include some type of formal therapy such as cognitive behaviour therapy (CBT) or counselling. (MIND 2013b: 5)

However, it is clear given a review of the majority of ecotherapy projects underway in the UK that one-to-one counselling or psychotherapy doesn't happen on most programmes, with a few notable exceptions (see Linden and Grut 2002). Clinebell (1996) first coined the term ecotherapy, positing a form of 'ecological spirituality' whereby our holistic relationship with nature encompasses both nature's ability to nurture us, through our contact with natural places and spaces, and our ability to reciprocate this healing connection through our ability to nurture nature. In this sense ecotherapy has always shared a close relationship to ecopsychology (Roszak, Gomes and Kanner 1995), placing human–nature relationships within a reciprocal healing (and disconnected and destructive) relationship with nature. Clinebell (1996: pxxi) makes a distinction, preferring to use the term ecotherapy over ecopsychology, stating that ecopsychology is about the psyche and the 'greening of psychology', whereas ecotherapy focuses on the total mind-body-spirit-relationship organism. Hasbach (2012) disagrees with the notion that by just going out into nature for a walk we are engaged in ecotherapy. Hasbach defines ecotherapy as a new modality of therapy that enlarges the traditional scope of treatment to include the human–nature relationship (Hasbach 2012: 116). As a result of this confusion I want to define what I mean by psychotherapy and begin to link this to psychotherapeutic work in nature.

Defining psychotherapy

I will explore what constitutes psychotherapy in terms of knowledge, how I understand this, how it is represented in my practice and how this shifts as I take my practice outdoors into natural environments. There is no one definition of psychotherapy or psychotherapeutic process, but competing ideas based on different models of distress and understanding of how the psyche works.

The etymology of the word psychotherapy comes from the ancient Greek 'psyche' meaning soul or spirit and 'therapy' to nurse or cure. The aim of counselling and psychotherapy from this definition is healing for the soul, reflecting what it might mean to heal or cure somebody. Rogers (1957) focuses on the conditions necessary for therapeutic personality change, positing the idea of a 'core self' as central to the psyche. Freud (1912) also talks about personality change when he states 'where id was ego shall be', placing a structural model of mind that interacts and is a contributing factor in the client's difficulties. Both theories rely on modernist notions of a bounded, stable and static interiority, which exists predominantly independently of others and the contexts it exists within. While both approaches posit seeds of a relational self which is further developed in the theories of relational psychotherapy (Mitchell 1988), I believe they both still rely on modernist foundational premises which situate a core decontextualized, ahistorical self. Recent developments in the growth of Cognitive Behavioural Therapy, especially as it is positioned in the NHS, would support this idea of a rationalized, decontextualized understanding of distress, whereby mental functioning is deemed the sole domain of a person's interior psychological world, independent of any social or cultural factors.

Recent postmodern attempts to reimagine therapeutic practice have focused on a self that is dialogic and socially constructed, placing emphasis on the narrative construction of problems and distress (Brown and Scott 2007; McLeod 1997; White and Epston 1990). Postmodern therapies have also attempted to democratize the power dynamics between therapist and client by attempting to involve the client much more fully in understanding the nature of the construction of their problem (Anderson and Goolishian 1992), challenging the expert status of the therapist. There are also echoes of these ideas in Ronen Berger's work on Nature Therapy (Berger 2006: Berger and McLeod 2006) whereby nature shifts the power dynamics between therapist and client providing a more democratic space for therapy.

Counselling and psychotherapy cannot fully alleviate the symptoms unless it can treat the cause (the political and historical constellations that shape the era) and yet that cause is the exact subject psychology is not allowed to address. In this sense we can see how the critiques put forward by ecopsychology and ecotherapy, of dominant social norms which are inherently destructive to the environment and also destructive to the human race, are attempting to place counselling and psychotherapy within a wider cultural and political sphere where nature and the environment play a central role in mental health and well-being. Elsewhere I have written about the relationship between developing an ecological self and the role of psychotherapy in this (Jordan 2012). I will outline some of these ideas here and how they relate to psychotherapy.

This starting point of understanding human–nature relations leaves us with the problem of how subjective interiors and objective material exteriors come into some form of communication. The question arises as to whether it is useful to think in these terms as they set up the very binary dualisms which a psychotherapy in natural environments might seek to overcome. If we view the Cartesian self as an invention of the enlightenment which drove modernism down the very path which separated things out in order to get a better view of them, reconciling them, or finding spaces where we can view interiors and exteriors without setting up the same binary dualisms which positioned us in the first place is quite a challenge. So, to experience the therapeutic potential of a natural environment we either have to fall back on interiors, for example, in terms of how I might feel and what psychological and historical frames am I bringing in my contact with nature. Along with this understanding what symbols and metaphors resonate with my personal emotional narrative. Alternatively we can move outwards, contacting the environment through our senses, exploring how our bodies feel in this process and what visual and sensory stimulus do I encounter in this process. Inside always relates to outside or vice versa, how does the outside become the inside?

The question arises in relation to where and how to focus in psychotherapeutic work in nature. Does the therapist focus solely on the interior of the client and the normative relational dynamics such as the client's developmental history and experience of relationships in this locating distress as a predominantly internal experience? Or do they focus on this sensate experience of the natural world and what the client is experiencing in the moment of encounter with the natural world by provoking and exploring contact with the natural world? Both have different potential therapeutic effects and rely on different theoretical lineages in order to understand emotional distress.

The relational turn in psychotherapy has positioned the subjects in complex relational processes between bodies and environments. Mitchell (1988) argues that there is no 'object' in a psychologically meaningful sense without some sense of oneself in relationship to it. There is therefore no 'self' in a psychologically meaningful sense in isolation outside of a matrix of relations (1988: 33). Mitchell proposes that in developing a sense of self the human being is faced with the difficulty of the temporality and complexity of our conscious existence. Mitchell sees human consciousness as operating in time and in a continual flux, a stream of thoughts, feelings, sensations and desires; from a relational perspective the self is a temporal and spatial entity in a process of continual movement.

Key to helping bring change in these distortions of self is the relationship that can be formed with the therapist. The relational perspective draws upon a variety of ideas that are not purely related to one particular school in counselling and psychotherapy. Central tenets of the approach are the idea that psychological phenomena develop within a broad field of relationships both from the past and in the present and that experience within the therapeutic encounter is continually and mutually shaped by both participants. The approach draws upon ideas from self-psychology, psychodynamic developmental psychology and intersubjectivity theory.

There are some central components of the therapeutic relationship that manifest as a process of the therapeutic encounter. Transference was initially identified by Freud (1912) as a pattern of relating to both the therapist and others in the client's life which originates from early experience with caregivers, predominantly the child's parents. Transference issues manifest in the process of therapy in terms of how the client feels towards the therapist, their needs and conflicts. Often these issues can manifest around the frame of therapy in terms of timing of sessions, whether the client arrives late and finds it difficult to end the therapy, how the client feels about the therapist's breaks and holidays. What also emerges, as the later school of object relations develops and moves away from Freudian drive theory, is the process of counter transference. This is understood as the therapist's emotional reaction to the client's transference issues (Heimann 1950). The emotions the therapist experiences during the therapy sessions become central to understanding the emotional material of the client that is sometimes held out of awareness or is unconscious. In this sense the intersubjective space between therapist and client contains the affective material that is central to understanding and conducting counselling and psychotherapy. Gill (1982) emphasizes the importance of re-experiencing in the therapeutic process, believing that as the client's problems are caused experientially they will be transformed experientially, and cannot be reasoned away intellectually. Therefore the therapy process becomes one where the client can feel safe and held enough to re-experience some of the initial emotional difficulties that brought them to therapy in the first place. Therefore the 'space' within which therapy takes place is very important for the emotional work that occurs and it is here I turn next.

The emotional space of therapy

Winnicott (1958) outlines the importance of emotional space in early infant development. In his theory of transitional phenomena and transitional objects, he identifies the centrality of the growing relationship to interior emotional and exterior emotional spaces for the baby. This process, undertaken in relation to the mother and the outer world, is where the baby is attempting to negotiate the relationship between the 'me' and the 'not me'. Winnicott sees the transitional phenomena that the baby is using as a way of the infant making sense of objects that are not part of the infant's body, yet are not fully recognized as belonging to external reality. He introduces that idea of the 'transitional space', a space between the dyad of inner and outer. Winnicott posits this space as a kind of 'third space':

> there is the third part of the life of a human being, a part that we cannot ignore, an intermediate area of experiencing, to which inner reality and external life both contribute. It is an area which is not challenged, because no claim is made on its behalf except that

> it shall exist a resting place for the individual engaged in the perpetual human task of keeping inner and outer reality separate yet inter-related. (Winnicott 1951: 230)

By introducing the idea of the space between the objective and subjective world of the infant as a transitional space, he positions the infant as an active participant in having to negotiate this sense of the subjective and objective. He sees play as the vehicle through which the transitional space functions to both join and separate the baby and the mother. Winnicott falls back onto the interior of the infant, stating how external objects are appropriated and used in the service of emotional development, and used in the defence against anxiety and depressive states. Transitional objects in their symbolic form represent the 'external' breast – the good enough 'mother', who makes active adaptation to the infant's needs, and helps the infant to negotiate the emotional upheavals of early emotional development (Winnicott 1951).

Counselling and psychotherapy from a psychodynamic perspective have always foregrounded the holding environment as the space within which affect can be understood and contained (Bion 1970). The holding environment and containment of the client's emotional states have become synonymous with the room: the indoor, comfortable, safe and warm space. This in turn has become synonymous with safe, ethical counselling and psychotherapy practice (Casement 1992).

The importance of the transitional space that Winnicott (1951) posits, allows for the concept of emotional space which can exist between the internal and external, the subjective and objective, the mother and the infant. This helps us to start to imagine other forms of emotionality which can exist within and between geographical and relational 'spaces', and between mind and nature. The idea that space can have an emotional affect has been taken up within the field of emotional geography.

Emotional geography

In recent years geography has taken an 'emotional turn' (Smith et al. 2009; Bondi, Davidson and Smith 2005), locating the importance of emotions in relation to places and spaces and how affect positions the perceiver and place in a reciprocal feedback loop. Bondi, Davidson and Smith (2005) state that the importance of places and their symbolic importance stems from their emotional associations and the resultant feelings they inspire. Emotional geography attempts to understand emotion as experiential and conceptual, and how it is mediated and articulated in a socio-spatial way, rather than as a purely interiorized subjective mental state. Bondi, Davidson and Smith (2005) argue for a non-objectifying view of emotions as relational flows, fluxes or currents, in between people and places rather than 'things' or 'objects'; in doing this they want to position emotions 'spatially'. This relationship between affect and space is an important aspect of understanding the rationale for taking therapeutic work outdoors and why for some people specific natural spaces have a particular emotional effect. This was one aspect of what was happening therapeutically outdoors that I hoped the research might illuminate further.

Bondi and Fewell (2003) see counselling as working at a 'spatial temporal' interface which transgresses normal boundaries of care, in particular issues of confidentiality and ethical boundaries are reimagined simultaneously as being both concrete and specific, fluid and illusory. This dualism between what is real, material concrete space and what is imagined, fantasy symbolic space is played out in the counselling relationship via the contradictory positions of counsellor and client attempting to maintain what Bondi and Fewell (2003) call a non-hierarchical and relational practice, while at the same time engaging with the positioning of their clients which are neither fixed nor easy to change. In relation to boundaries, counselling attempts to offer a clearly demarcated time and space which is safe and confidential, protecting clients from relationships with the counsellor outside of the counselling relationships. In this sense Bondi and Fewell argue spatio-temporal boundaries mark a separation between 'ordinary life' and the space of counselling, in which deeply private anxieties and concerns can be addressed. One of the most prominent spatial metaphors of counselling is the space between inside and outside. In their research Bondi and Fewell argue that counsellors conceptualize the interface between client and practitioner as a dynamic space within which these exteriorizations and interiorizations can be explored, thereby redefining the space and boundary between inner and outer realities (Bondi and Fewell 2003: 540).

Case example

Micky was a trainee therapist his previous experiences of therapy had been difficult he had either experienced the therapist as too cold or distant or had felt that the therapist had 'invaded' his mind and he felt at times suffocated. This experience was mirrored in other intimate relationships with partners, where he would oscillate between feeling desperately needy or would reject people when he felt he was getting too close or the relationship was getting serious. At assessment Micky talked about his family history, his mother and father's marriage had been unstable and very argumentative, his father would regularly walk out leaving Micky with his depressed mother, he would feel overwhelmed by her despair and neediness. Micky had grown up with a poor sense of himself, quite often adapting himself to others' needs and wishes in order to be liked. Initially the therapy was very difficult and Micky would quite often cancel sessions or try and change the time of therapy, the therapist felt it was very difficult to connect with Micky and form a working therapeutic relationship. There were long pauses and silences in the subsequent sessions and Micky reported feeling very ambivalent about therapy. When the therapist suggested that the therapy wasn't working and that maybe Micky wanted to end the therapy, Micky became very angry with the therapist accusing him of being not committed to the relationship and unprofessional. Rather than reacting to this anger the therapist explored it with Micky and suggested they might meet outdoors and walk together as the sessions indoors felt so difficult and for them both and to see how this felt. They met in some woodland and walked and talked as they moved through the woods and stopped to notice things on the way. In the session Micky talked more about how he felt and the session went well, he said he found the woods containing and holding and he could relax more in the sessions. Micky also reported that he found it 'much easier' to talk without the room and the eye contact of the therapist that somehow he felt safer with the therapist whilst they were walking. In subsequent sessions they met in woodland locations and walked and talked, the therapist also found it easier to tune into Micky on an embodied level and make contact with him more easily than they had done indoors, the therapist reported in supervision that he found much easier to regulate his emotional responses to Micky. As the sessions progressed Micky was more able to be in contact with the therapist turning up on time and not cancelling sessions. He begun to be more able to stay in touch with painful feelings whilst moving and feeling contained by the trees and eventually the therapist outdoors.

Nature as a 'third' space for psychotherapy

When we traditionally think of the therapeutic relationship we think of the dyad between the therapist and client as being the central vehicle through which the therapy happens. However recent developments particularly within relational psychoanalysis have posited a third space created between therapist and client, a meeting of the two subjectivities, both conscious and conscious, which both create this shared third area (Ogden 2004). Benjamin (2009) sees this third space as an essential containing space where both therapist and client can survive the failures and ruptures inevitable in the therapeutic encounter. Benjamin (ibid.) sees the third space as providing the psychic ground for regulation of both parties and a vital space which enables both to bring this regulation into conscious awareness and to be utilized in the therapeutic dyad.

For psychotherapy in nature, I propose that nature acts as a third space for the therapeutic dyad to inhabit in a concrete and material sense, as well as both consciously and unconsciously. Research undertaken by the author (Jordan 2014a) found that a significant number of therapists who had taken their therapeutic practice outdoors into natural spaces had a long personal history of using nature as a space for affect regulation and well-being. For some, complex family dynamics in early childhood meant that they had formed a relationship with natural spaces that provided them with comfort and affect regulation, something that was much more complex and less available to access in human relationships growing up. Nature, as well as providing a space for the client to affect regulate during the therapeutic encounter outdoors, also provides a regulatory space for the therapist thus enabling them to metabolize difficult emotional material, particularly when this is in the form of projective identification and more powerful unconscious material related to abuse and trauma. The third space of nature is very important to both parties.

I have proposed elsewhere that nature is a 'vital' space (Jordan 2014b) and it is precisely this vitality in its living and vibrant qualities that is so important to the therapeutic process outdoors. Therapy expands to include both the therapeutic dyad and the third space of nature which either forms a backdrop to the therapy or situates itself in the foreground of the work, taking the form of powerful metaphors and symbols. Although discredited within contemporary scientific understanding of biology and ecology, 'Vitalism' (Driesch 1914), the idea that there is a living force in matter, has found a resurgence in social scientific thinking. Bennett (2004) has advocated a contemporary form of vitalism proposing that we can account for matter in terms of the affect it has on humans, what she terms 'thing power'. Rather than a dead material space, things acquire power in terms of their ability to hold matter and energy in the spaces between inert matter and vital energy, between animate and inanimate 'and where all things to some degree live on both sides' (Bennett 2004: 352). For psychotherapy, Stern (2010) defines vitality as a manifestation of being alive and essential to human experience, something distinct from known physical, chemical and mental forces. Drawing from the original ideas of vitalism as a dynamic teleology, a moving unfolding and relational force of becoming, vitality is positioned as a constant sense of movement which maintains our sense of being alive. Nature therefore becomes a space that gives the therapeutic encounter a different kind of vitality and aliveness aiding the therapeutic process.

Concluding comments: The therapist-client-nature matrix

The relationship between therapist, client and nature is of central importance to understanding the psychotherapeutic processes of ecotherapy. A number of interesting things emerge, not only around the relationship to nature but also the effect on the therapist–client relationship. For some the outdoors and the natural space acts as an intermediary in what some clients experience as an intense process. In this way we can see the outdoor natural space, how it allows therapist and client to walk alongside each other and not have such direct eye to eye contact, as a less threatening way of doing therapy. In this we can understand why nature acts as a 'third space' – a safer transitional space for the intensity of the therapeutic encounter. Nature can act as another form of object relation which allows both client and therapist to find ways to relate to one another. Recent research by Iantorno (2013) found that clients using nature as a therapeutic space were seeking to either regulate difficult emotions or to strengthen and revitalize themselves through contact with nature.

A central idea in emotional geography is different geographic spaces have an effect on emotions and that different outdoor locations can have an effect on feelings and on the therapeutic relationship. The idea that it is the room alone that provides a safe container for therapeutic work is challenged by utilizing nature as a therapeutic space essential for some clients to feel safe. The transitional space created outdoors, that for some clients who have difficult early experiences, can feel less threatening, allowing the client to make contact with the therapist more easily. Some clients find the intensity of contact created in a room environment difficult and need a different kind of space in order to feel safe enough in the therapeutic relationship.

Berger (2006) in his research into nature therapy discusses the idea of nature as a 'co-therapist' in the process of nature-based therapy. It is through the presence of the natural world that the therapeutic process is facilitated; nature in this sense acts as another presence which both guides and provokes therapeutic process. Within psychotherapeutic work it is important to not lose sight of the centrality of the therapeutic relationship between therapist and client, which must be part of the assemblage of relationships between therapist, client and the outdoor natural space. This is an important distinction in different approaches to ecotherapy and especially when ecotherapy becomes psychotherapy.

In this sense the client and therapist relationship is essential for processing and understanding difficult feelings. This sits alongside the importance of nature as a 'vital' space for therapy where both therapist and client can regulate their emotional responses to each other and feel held by nature as embodying and representing a transitional space. This has been under-theorized to date in ecotherapy and this chapter is an attempt to address this gap in thinking and understanding.

References

Anderson, H., and H. Goolishian (1992), 'The Client Is the Expert: A Not-Knowing Approach to Therapy', in S. McNamee and K. Bergen (eds), *Therapy as Social Construction*, Newbury Park, CA: Sage.

Benjamin, J. (2009), 'A Relational Psychoanalysis Perspective on the Necessity of Acknowledging Failure in Order to Restore the Facilitating and Containing Features of the Intersubjective Relationship (The Shared Third)', *International Journal of Psychoanalysis* 90: 441–50.

Bennett, J. (2004), 'The Force of Things: Steps toward an Ecology of Matter', *Political Theory* 32 (3): 347–72.

Berger, R. (2006), 'Beyond Words: Nature-Therapy in Action', *Journal of Critical Psychology, Counseling and Psychotherapy* 6 (4): 195–9.

Berger, R., and J. McLeod (2006), 'Incorporating Nature into Therapy: A Framework for Practice', *Journal of Systemic Therapies* 25 (2): 80–94.

Bion, W. R. (1970), *Attention and Interpretation: A Scientific Approach to Insight in Psycho-analysis and Groups*, London: Tavistock Publications.

Bondi, L., and J. Fewell (2003), '"Unlocking the cage door": The Spatiality of Counselling', *Social and Cultural Geography* 4 (4): 527–47.

Bondi, L., J. Davidson and M. Smith (2005), 'Introduction: Geography's "Emotional Turn"', in J. Davidson, L. Bondi and M. Smith (eds), *Emotional Geographies*, Aldershot: Ashgate.

Brown, C., and T. Augusta-Scott (2007), *Narrative Therapy: Making Meaning Making Lives*, London: Sage.

Buzzell, L., and C. Chalquist (2009), *Ecotherapy – Healing with Nature in Mind*, San Francisco: Sierra Club.

Casement, P. (1992), *On Learning from the Patient*, Hove: Guilford Press.

Chalquist, C. (2009), 'A Look at the Ecotherapy Research Evidence', *Ecopsychology* 1 (2): 1–10.

Ogden, T. H. (2004), 'The Analytic Third: Implications for Psychoanalytic Theory and Technique', *The Psychoanalytic Quarterly* 73 (1): 167–95.

Clinebell, H. (1996), *Ecotherapy: Healing Ourselves, Healing the Earth: A Guide to Ecologically Grounded Personality Theory, Spirituality, Therapy, and Education*, London: Fortress.

Driesch, H. (1914), *The History and Theory of Vitalism*, trans. C. K. Ogden, London: Macmillan.

Freud, S. (1912), 'Recommendations to Physicians Practising Psychoanalysis', *Standard Edition*, 12: 109–20, London: Hogarth Press.

Gill, M. (1982), *Analysis of Transference: Volume 1 Theory and Technique*, Madison: International Universities Press.

Hasbach, P. (2012), 'Ecotherapy', in P. Kahn and P. Hasbach (eds), *Ecopsychology: Science, Totems and the Technological Species*, London: MIT Press.

Heimann, P. (1950), 'On Counter-Transference', *International Journal of Psycho-Analysis* 31: 81–4.

Iantorno, R. (2013), Encounters with Nature: A Heuristic Inquiry into the Experience of Connecting with Nature through Metaphor in Integrative Psychotherapy. Unpublished MSc Thesis, The Sherwood Psychotherapy Training Institute/Coventry University.

Jordan, M. (2012), 'Did Lacan Go Camping? Psychotherapy in Search of an Ecological Self', in M. J. Rust and N. Totton (eds), *Vital Signs: Psychological Responses to the Ecological Crisis*, London: Karnac.

Jordan, M. (2014a), Taking Therapy Outside: A Narrative Inquiry into Counselling and Psychotherapy in Outdoor Natural Spaces. Unpublished PhD Thesis, University of Brighton.
Jordan, M. (2014b), *Nature and Therapy: Understanding Counselling and Psychotherapy in Outdoor Spaces*, London: Routledge.
Linden, S., and J. Grut (2002), *The Healing Fields: Working with Psychotherapy and Nature to Rebuild Shattered Lives*, London: Francis Lincoln.
MCleod, J. (1997), *Narrative and Psychotherapy*, London: Sage.
MIND (2007), *Ecotherapy: The Green Agenda for Mental Health*, London: Mind.
MIND (2013b), *Making Sense of Ecotherapy*, London: MIND.
Mitchell, S. (1988), *Relational Concepts within Psychoanalysis: An Integration*, Cambridge Mass: Harvard University Press.
Rogers, C. R. (1957), 'The Necessary and Sufficient Conditions for Therapeutic Personality Change', *Journal of Consulting Psychology* 21: 95–103.
Roszak, T., M. Gomes and A. Kanner (1995), *Ecopsychology: Restoring the Earth Healing the Mind*, London: Sierra Club.
Smith, M., J. Davidson, L. Cameron and L. Bondi (2009), *Emotion, Place and Culture*, Aldershot: Ashgate.
Stern, D. N. (2010), *Forms of Vitality: Exploring Dynamic Experience in Psychology, the Arts, Psychotherapy, and Development*, Oxford: Oxford University Press.
White, M., and D. Epston (1990), *Narrative Means to Therapeutic Ends*, New York: W. W. Norton.
Winnicott, D. (1951), 'Transitional Objects and Transitional Phenomena', in D. Winnicott (ed.), *Collected Papers: Through Paediatrics to Psycho-Analysis*, London: Tavistock.
Winnicott, D. (1958), *Collected Papers: Through Paediatrics to Psycho-Analysis*, London: Tavistock.

5

The many ecotherapies

Linda Buzzell

(Note: An earlier version of this chapter was first presented at the University of Brighton Ecotherapy and Nature Based Therapy Symposium on 20 June 2014; a subsequent updated version was published in Jordan, Martin, and Joe Hinds, eds (2016), *Ecotherapy: Theory, Research and Practice*, London UK: Macmillan/Palgrave. The chaotic years of the last decade, full of escalating planetary and social metacrises beyond our worst fears, have only deepened the urgency for the kinds of effective ecotherapeutic understandings and interventions plus practical ecoresilience guidance this new version addresses.)

Ecopsychology is the study of the relationship between the human psyche (body-mind-soul-spirit) and the rest of nature. Ecotherapy (also called applied or clinical ecopsychology) focuses on healing that dangerously dysfunctional relationship. Because of the fact that humans are an integral – and increasingly destructive – part of nature, many ecotherapists now look beyond how humans can merely 'use' nature to feel better psychologically and physically, and increasingly stress a reciprocal circle of healing that must tend to the needs of humans *and* the rest of nature. Both are hugely ambitious endeavours, especially at this make-or-break moment of human and ecological history on our home planet.

Level 1 and Level 2 ecotherapies

The terms I use to describe these different approaches to ecotherapy are Level 1 (human-focused ecotherapies and results-oriented nature-based therapies) and Level 2 (whole-systems ecotherapies). And of course it's not always clear at what level we are operating at any given moment, or where along the scale between the two that we find ourselves.

Broadly speaking, Level 1 can be described as Human-Centred Nature Therapy ('using' nature and nature-connection to improve human mental and physical health; taking one's daily 'Vitamin N' to avoid Nature Deficit Disorder, etc.). The good news at Level 1 for humans and human-tending clinicians is that a rapidly growing body of research supports the effectiveness of many Level 1 ecotherapies – enough for many nature-based therapies to qualify as 'evidence-based medicine' (Louv 2011; the University of Essex studies (Mind 2013); Bratman 2015, 2019, 2022; Goldsby 2022). This has led to an increase in the demand for trained ecotherapists and a rise in various professional training programmes and symposia. The bad news is that the history of humans 'using' the rest of nature for whatever purposes is a cautionary tale, as such usage has destroyed the life support systems and ecosystems of countless species and threatens the annihilation of our own life support systems as well.

Level 1 ecotherapy is often based on a traditional Western world-view that values humanity well above the rest of nature. This allow us to adopt a distanced, 'objective' dominator position where 'using' other living beings or inanimate 'natural resources' for whatever purposes requires no permission or thought for the effects of that usage on the 'used' – a form of colonization or slavery (Kidner 2001).

This narcissistic, human-centred world-view also includes the dysfunctional delusion that there is a human self that can be safely disconnected from both healthy culture and the rest of nature.

David Kidner's profoundly important book *Nature and Psyche: Radical Environmentalism and the Politics of Subjectivity* (Kidner 2001) guides us in exploring modern industrial culture's repressed subjective, challenging 'our taken-for-granted ontology' and describing a dissociated 'industrialized [human] psyche' that needs to relearn a 'flowing outward of the self into the world beyond, and a resonance between "self" and "world" that places a question mark over their separability' (Kidner 2001: 166). He offers a timely reminder – especially for those ecotherapists caught at Level 1 practice – that 'The task we face … is not simply to alleviate our individual discomforts, but also to recognize that these are derived from the wider ontological split [between industrialism and the natural order] that is tearing the world apart' (Kidner 2007: 137).

Kidner's work (Kidner 2001) may also encourage us to explore some of the tensions between an impersonal, seemingly objective, scientific approach to measuring the effects of various ecotherapies and a more wholistic understanding of the larger ecology of distress. So, for example, the well-known University of Essex ecotherapy research (Mind 2013) that examined the effects on mood of walks in green nature can be seen as supporting a Western empirical view of human nature-connection activity that is grounded in a positivistic scientific understanding of how this connection with non-human nature affects our emotions and how we can quantify these results – playing into a Level 1 understanding of the value of ecotherapy but failing to look more deeply at the global malaise caused by industrial growth and the effect this has on both subjectivity and the outer world.

Level 2 ecotherapies focus on a circle of reciprocal healing, a wider approach rooted in the ecologically based, whole systems understanding that there can be no true human health on a sick planet. Once we awaken from the delusionary 'big lie' that humans and the human ego are somehow magically separate from and superior to the rest of nature – and are therefore entitled to 'use' it as mere resources without considering consequences – we discover the deeper truth that we are all part of nature and embedded in the whole. This allows our perspective to widen and we can discover what John Seed calls 'the ecological self' (Seed 2005).

Psychologist Sarah A. Conn raised the critical issue of reciprocity in her essay 'When the Earth Hurts, Who Responds?' (Conn 1995: 156–71) and again, with her late husband, psychologist Lane Conn, in 'Opening to the Other' (Conn and Conn 2009: 111–15): 'Individual health … is connected to the health of other beings and to the health of the Earth as a whole … Ecological health is the larger context of human health; they go together as outside-inside. Healthy human functioning in an ecopsychological context includes sustainable and mutually-enhancing relations not just at the intrapersonal level (within humans) or the interpersonal level (among humans) but also at the level of "interbeing" (between humans and the non-human world.)' (Conn and Conn 2009: 112).

Andy Fisher's *Radical Ecopsychology, Second Edition* (Fisher 2013) also supports a second level approach. 'A straightforward question I ask in sorting through the field of ecotherapy is: In what ways and to what extent does a given practice address the roots of the ecological crisis? This is a radical question.' Fisher recommends a deeper understanding of the parent discipline of ecopsychology itself, which might lead to 'radical praxes that offer "therapy" that is as much cultural and social as personal' (Fisher 2013: 221).

So at Level 2, ecotherapy concerns itself not merely with the healing of a particular person or presenting problem or diagnosed illness, but with the larger healing of the human–nature relationship as it presents in a particular person or community or place at a particular historical moment. Level 2 ecotherapy often includes a cultivation of the sense of our extended ecological self, breaking down the artificial barriers between the health of an individual human or group and the health of the wider cultural, economic and environmental context. It involves respect, concern and even love for others and the Other (our extended ecological self, which may even include a spiritual component). The individual psyche then finds itself a seamless part of a much wider – even cosmic – whole.

With this in mind, before we ecotherapists and our clients begin to participate in any particular nature-connection healing process or activity, we might consciously choose a Level 2 approach to the interaction. Rather than rushing into one-sided, utilitarian relationships with any part of nature uncontrolled by the human ego, we could take a humbler and less narcissistic approach, as if engaging with an equal or superior being rather than an inanimate servant, slave or tool.

One simple example could involve slowing down and taking time to 'listen' to and empathize with the aspect of nature we are approaching before beginning any ecotherapeutic connection. We might also explore the ancient practice of asking permission from the particular aspect of the rest of nature we hope to connect with before barrelling into another's space and life. And we may feel called to express gratitude with gifts, reverence or reciprocal service (perhaps participating in the healing of a natural place or animal). At Level 2 we now deeply understand that what happens to the rest of nature happens to us – and vice versa. We are an integral part of nature, not separate or superior. The seeming 'other' whose presence brings healing is as worthy of care and tending as we ourselves. The boundary between self and 'nature' begins to dissolve.

One ecotherapy can be practised at multiple levels

Many ecotherapies – probably most – can be practised at either Level 1 or 2 or somewhere along the scale between them.

Let's consider *animal-assisted therapy* (AAT), an increasingly popular healing modality. At its Level 1 extreme, AAT might involve something like the capture of wild dolphins for the purpose of providing 'dolphin therapy' to paying customers, without regard for the rights or comfort of the animal in question. Thankfully, many animal-assisted therapies are now moving in the direction of further reciprocity and care – Level 2. An example of the latter might be Return to Freedom, a horse sanctuary founded by Neda DeMayo in the Santa Ynez Valley in California that rescues horses threatened with extermination and allows them to run free in natural herds in a natural habitat, interacting with each other and with humans as they choose. 'The healing effects spread beyond [DeMayo's] four-legged friends to people transformed by friendly encounters with wild horses. On the human side, the benefits have included higher self-esteem, increased trust in intuition and instinct, feeling more at home in one's body, and a sense of the spiritual arising from the natural, as during a walking meditation among a trusting herd. Something of the spirit of freedom epitomized by a galloping horse rubs off on us too' (DeMayo 2009: 149).

Perhaps the key to this effect is the fact that the animals have a real choice about who they will or won't associate with. So when a free animal chooses to make contact with a hurting or merely curious human, this is a special nature-connection moment that can be profoundly moving and even healing to the person involved. The evolving paradigm of pairing abused animals with nature-deprived or abused humans seems especially poignant and effective. Veterans with post-traumatic stress disorder (PTSD), for example, may find tending abused animals to be healing to both simultaneously (Bliss 2009a, 2009b) – the Level 2 circle of reciprocal healing at work. We might even expand AAT to include Trans-Species Psychology, which challenges ecotherapists to overcome the inherent anthropocentrism of our field and suggests that only by striving for the well-being of other animals can we ensure our own well-being (Bradshaw 2009).

Let's take a quick look at a couple of other well-known ecotherapy modalities to see how this evolution from Level 1 to Level 2 might work there as well. If we look at 'wilderness' therapy, for instance, we can see a possible trajectory from the most mundane commercial survival 'outdoor challenges' for wayward teens to the far more sophisticated offerings of The School of Lost Borders or Animas Valley Institute (Plotkin 2003), depth-oriented wilderness experiences that can even include what Bron Taylor (Taylor 2010) calls 'dark green' spiritual experiences of profound oneness with the rest of nature.

Horticultural therapies, including garden and farm therapies, can also be practised at multiple levels, from the simplest school or community garden experience, where the focus might simply be on growing food for humans to eat, to a much more integrative and profound understanding of the reciprocal nature of subjective and objective ecosystem relationships.

The difference between Level 1 and Level 2 approaches to interacting with the rest of nature in a garden became viscerally apparent to me in the 1990s when my husband and I moved to a small home with a more spacious (but sadly degraded) yard than we'd ever had in the city and then took the permaculture design course. Over the years, with careful tending and working with the rest of nature rather than against it, this tiny piece of wider nature has become a wild-looking, permaculture-style backyard food forest full of intermingling native and well-behaved immigrant plants that benefit humans, wildlife and the ecosystem as a whole. I was excited to discover that its principles and practices could be applied not only to land care but people care as well.

For example, the first permaculture principle is 'observe and interact'. Initially we applied this to garden care. Through listening to the land and observing carefully, we found ourselves breaking away from the traditional, human-and-machine-focused monocropping and 'planting in rows' and using biomimicry as we observed how nature grows her plants for maximum abundance. Quite without intending to, I also discovered how this principle could be applied to the human psyche as well. Through interacting daily with this newly restored natural environment outside our back door, now full of life and energy, I observed how spending time outside not only predictably lifted my mood but also melted away any anxiety or stress I might be feeling. This observation and interactive experience gradually transformed my psychotherapy practice into an ecotherapy practice, complete with an outdoor therapy 'office' where

I was able to share the garden's healing effects with clients as well. My gratitude for this involves a reciprocal, committed tending of the place that changed my life.

Why do nature-connection therapies work?

The robust evidence for the healing effectiveness of the various ecotherapies – at whatever level they're practised – raises the question of why almost any kind of nature-connection – even mere pictures of nature on a wall – seems to provoke a measurable therapeutic response. My theory is that what Richard Louv calls Nature-Deficit Disorder (Louv 2005, 2008, 2011) is an ongoing condition suffered by much of modern humanity in industrial cultures around the world. G. A. Bradshaw and others call this 'human zoochosis' (Bradshaw 2021) because like captive tigers born and raised in a cramped zoo cage, many of us find ourselves going crazy in industrial society but often having no idea why we're unhappy or what it is that we're really longing for. A rising percentage of today's unnaturally domesticated, 'cage-raised', cubicle-enslaved and screen-addicted humans have various symptoms equivalent to the zoo tiger's endless pacing or frustrated, depressed lethargy. Research is showing us that even the tiniest exposure and reconnection to the habitat our species evolved in and for can produce unexpected healing and profound joy in body, mind and soul. I am reminded of the popular internet videos of a herd of cows, confined for the winter to a barn and dried hay, who are allowed out in the spring onto a field of fresh, green grass. All lethargy and plodding left behind, these adult cows find themselves cavorting and prancing with calf-like joy at the sight, smell and taste of the succulent greenery, fresh air and sunlight. We too are just such animals, which is perhaps why the many online videos of released animals find such wide audiences.

But one size doesn't fit all

An important thing I learned when I began shifting my psychotherapy practice into an ecotherapy practice was that 'one size definitely doesn't fit all'. A nature-connection prescription like equine-assisted therapy that is highly effective with one person may be a complete dud with another. Taking a step back, I began to inquire more deeply into the history of my client(s)' relationships with the rest of nature. I asked, 'Have you felt a special connection with the rest of nature – including animals, plants or places – either in childhood or now?' Almost without exception, this query will open a very emotional conversation and I began to better appreciate the uniqueness of each person's connection with the wider world. For example, I once raised this question with a therapist friend, who replied: 'Oh, ecotherapy. That's not for me. I'm an urban kind of gal.' Knowing about the love she has for her companion animals, I asked 'But what about your kitties?' She sighed and replied softly. 'Oh, my babies' 'Well, that's your nature-connection ecotherapy,' I replied. 'Animal-assisted therapy'. Her cuddles with her beloved kitties have helped her through a devastating bereavement.

Experiences like this have convinced me to take more time helping clients explore and discover their preferred method of nature-connection before prescribing any ecotherapy practice at either Level 1 or Level 2. I see this as an important first step in any ecotherapy treatment. Luckily for clinicians and those who come to us for help in healing, nature-connection practices come in many shapes and colours, offering a wide enough variety that almost every client can find a way to access nature's astonishing healing powers.

Multiple ecotherapies, multiple populations, multiple methods of nature-connection – practised at multiple levels

Ecotherapy practitioners around the world are continuing to discover and develop a wide variety of creative and effective nature-connection healing practices that can be used at multiple levels to treat many different populations suffering from many different 'presenting problems'. I leave the examination of most of these to others more familiar with the modality in question and hope they will explore their possible evolution from an initial 'human use' perspective to a Level 2 reciprocal healing understanding.

One that deserves a mention here, however, is *somatic therapy*. Reconnecting with the 'wild nature' in our own bodies can be a simple Level 1 process where the focus is initially exclusively our own well-being (e.g. some of the more narcissistic Western yoga practices), but it can also – sometimes without any conscious effort on our part – begin to evolve to reciprocally connect us not only to the nature 'in here' but also to our extended body/mind 'out there'. Once we incorporate (literally) the Level 2 awareness that we too are part of nature, it becomes apparent that nature-connection healing can take place not only by going out to parks or so-called wilderness but also through deeply reconnecting with our inner nature – the parts of our bodies, minds, souls and spirits that are less under the control of our sometimes-arrogant egos (although of course those very egos are also part of nature – just a much smaller part of it than they realize!). In many cultures this idea of the body as a seamless part of wider nature is nothing new, of course. Many indigenous cultures have taught this earth-based wisdom for millennia. And for thousands of years traditional yogis have connected with their breath and the breath of the world and Chinese healers have worked with the life energy they call chi. Any practice that connects us with our wild bodies can become a true ecotherapy, even if practised indoors.

Another source of connection with uncontrolled-by-the-human-ego nature lies within the psyche itself. Ecopsychotherapeutic processes can allow us to reconnect with the 'wilderness within'. Following in the footsteps of countless indigenous cultures, Freud and Jung explored free associations and dreams for enlightenment, guidance and healing. Modern practitioners of individual and community *eco-dreamwork* like Lauren Z. Schneider (Schneider 2009) and Meredith Sabini (Sabini 2009) actively incubate dreams of and by the rest of nature, explore natural symbols and messages as they appear in dreams, and practice dream council work where 'wild mind' is allowed to speak to the collective. Ecotherapist Nick Totton's *Wild Therapy* (Totton 2011) is another great help in exploring this undomesticated, inner terrain and connecting individual psyche to wider Psyche. 'Therapy is by nature wild,' he says, 'but a lot of it at the moment is rather tame'. Totton's goal is 'to help shift the balance back towards wildness by showing how therapy can connect with ecological thinking, seeing each species, each being, each person inherently and profoundly linked to each other' (Totton 2011: 1) – definitely Level 2!

Ecotherapies that treat conditions specific to our era

I don't want to end this brief tour of the multiple ecotherapies without addressing some of the most complex and challenging modalities.

We live in perilous times. The huge, almost unprecedented historical shifts we are experiencing have many names: Joanna Macy's *The Great Unraveling* (Macy and Johnstone 2012), economist and former Harvard Business School professor David Korten's *The Great Turning* (Korton 2006), social critic James Howard Kunstler's *The Long Emergency* (Kunstler 2005), permaculture teacher Rob Hopkins' *Transition* (Hopkins 2008) and author Carolyn Baker's *Collapse* (Baker 2011). Whatever we call this era of rapid natural degradation, it is causing huge psychological trauma and distress in many humans (and other species) around the world. Some of the names ecotherapists use for the almost ubiquitous anxiety, depression, panic, heartbreak and dread (especially evident in young people worried about their future) include eco-anxiety, eco-grief, eco-trauma, solastalgia and even eco-despair.

In this critical situation we cannot afford to remain stuck at Level 1, continuing to use and abuse the rest of nature for whatever purposes. Without a collective evolution to true whole systems thinking and reciprocity, our species may not survive much longer in its present form. Ecotherapists are now faced with the daunting task of helping our clients and communities not only process the challenging information and losses of our time, but also shift consciousness towards a deeper understanding of the unity of life that will radically alter our behaviour towards the rest of nature.

Psychotherapist and ecotherapist Sarah Anne Edwards and I wrote an essay on the 'waking up syndrome' (Edwards and Buzzell 2009; Pihkala 2022) that attempts to track the various states and stages people cycle through as they awaken to the full realization of our collective jeopardy, based on thanatologist Elizabeth Kubler Ross's stages of death and dying (Kubler-Ross 1969). Our hope is that by identifying and naming the various natural emotional reactions most of us will have to the ongoing eco-trauma of Kunstler's *Long Emergency*, we and our clients can gain a compassionate understanding of our own and others' feelings and reactions, ultimately finding the personal and collective strength to go forward into constructive action and solutions.

Fortunately, the rapidly growing field of climate psychology has taken up the challenge of helping people understand the eco-emotions (Pikhala 2022; Wray 2022) and treating them when they become overwhelming. Groups like the Climate Psychology Alliance, the Climate Psychology Alliance North America, the Good Grief Network and others offer guidance both to those in distress and to the practitioners who need guidance in best therapeutic practices.

Perhaps the most challenging ecotherapies are those that directly address the possibility of total collapse. Former psychotherapist and history professor Carolyn Baker, author of *Navigating the Coming Chaos: A Handbook for Inner Transition* (Baker 2011) and many other books, offers numerous podcasts, and her practice includes 'collapse coaching' to encourage, guide and comfort those in despair over our circumstances. And for many decades, brilliant ecophilosopher and ecotherapist Joanna Macy and her colleagues have been leading 'From Despair to Empowerment' workshops that provide powerful guidance. Macy's book *Active Hope: How to Face the Mess We're in with Unexpected Resilience and Creative Power* (Macy and Johnstone 2012, 2022), co-authored with physician Chris Johnstone, offers a sensible way forward in these uniquely challenging times.

Community-based ecotherapy practices

Historically, Western psychotherapy has focused primarily on treating the individual human patient or client while ignoring not only the extended human social, cultural, economic and political context but also the environmental ground of all being. But as ecology and Level 2 ecopsychology teach us, everything is interconnected – and must be consciously reconnected in our minds by those of us who have been living under the delusion of separation.

David Kidner (Kidner 2001) is again a wise guide on this as well as many other issues. He points out that to truly heal the current, woefully dysfunctional human–nature relationship we must also heal the necessary conduit for all such interactions – modern human culture (especially Western and now global industrial culture, with its reductionistic, instrumental, extractive, materialist philosophy and practices – and dualistic, anthropocentric and domination-focused language and ideas). Facilitating the transition and recovery from nature-destroying industrial culture is a hugely ambitious ecotherapy undertaking, but one that a number of influential ecopsychology theorists and practitioners like Andy Fisher (Fisher 2013) feel is increasingly critical.

Various ecotherapies are evolving to help communities with this recovery, assisting with the practical, psychological and even spiritual healing of the ubiquitous alienation from the rest of nature and nature-based ways of living. Permaculture is one example of this and has proven to be highly attractive to young people needing a way to envision and practise a pleasurable and satisfying sustainable lifeway. Others focus on assisting in the creation of eco-villages, teaching council practice or facilitating community Transition. In fact, the Transition movement has spread around the globe and includes 'Heart & Soul of Transition' groups that address the psychological and spiritual side of The Great Turning (Macy and Johnstone 2012, 2022). Many communities now follow ecotherapist Cecile Andrews's (Andrews 2009) prescription for creating community circles with various purposes, including voluntary simplicity circles, sustainability book clubs and neighbourhood exchanges. Still others stress what ecopsychologist Craig Chalquist and I call 'cultural ecoresilience' (Buzzell and Chalquist 2023), offering specific steps towards building personal and community strength, flexibility and trauma tolerance that facilitate bioregional mitigation and adaptation in the face of escalating environmental degradation and the serial, progressive economic and ecological catastrophes our behaviour has already set in motion.

We also need to radically expand our understanding of community and diversity, actively including all human cultures as well as the rest of nature. Community environmental justice work like that being done by environmental justice activists Carl Anthony and Paloma Pavel in Oakland, California, is inspirational for many ecotherapists. Authors of the 'Breakthrough Communities' project of Earth House Center are building and modelling multi-racial leadership for regional sustainable community. Anthony has long warned against what he perceives as an 'ecopsychological blind spot in the United States, due to its Eurocentric perspective, which has been based on the dominance paradigm. The "self" that ecopsychology needs to address, is a multi-cultural self, with many voices and many perspectives'

(Anthony 1996). Excellent work in 'liberation ecotherapy' is also being done by J. Phoenix Smith, MSW, founder of The Alliance for Ecotherapy and Social Justice (Smith 2013, 2020, 2022).

Ecospirituality

Some may feel that it is not within the purview of ecopsychology or ecotherapy to address the realm of spirituality, but it is impossible to ignore the fact that every successful human culture in every era – including our own – has a sense of and reverence for what it holds to be sacred, even if that 'god' is merely money, success, 'market fundamentalism' or faith in experimental science. In practice, ecotherapists quickly discover that an ineffable sense of the sacredness of nature within ourselves and our surroundings (Jiang et al. 2024) is a key factor in both mental health and the transition towards a life-and-behaviour-changing sense of ecological selfhood that can include the wider cosmic Self (Canty 2022).

The field of ecospirituality is expanding rapidly, both among those greening up traditional religions with 'creation care' practices and those who describe themselves as 'spiritual but not religious'. In addition to perusing the work of Tielhard de Chardin, Thomas Berry and Brian Swimme, those interested may enjoy reading Bron Taylor's *Dark Green Religion: Nature Spirituality and the Planetary Future* (Taylor 2010) and Llewellyn Vaughan-Lee's anthology *Spiritual Ecology: The Cry of the Earth* (Vaughan-Lee 2013).

Cutting edges: Refining our definitions, expanding our horizons

Finally, I'd like to mention some recent books that open up new areas of discussion in the field of ecotherapy. Jungian ecotherapist Mary-Jayne Rust's important book *Towards an Ecopsychotherapy* (Rust 2020) helps us make distinctions between ecotherapy as part of a psychotherapy practice, other guided nature-connection healing practices, and what some are now calling 'natural ecotherapy' – the therapeutic effects of open-hearted nature immersion that require no professional guidance. UK ecotherapist David Key and Auckland psychotherapy professor Keith Tudor's *Ecotherapy: A Field Guide* (Key and Tudor 2023) critically explores various issues in the field, including important distinctions between therapy and therapeutic, wilderness and wild, physical and meta-physical, culture and indigeneity, and the skin-bound self and the ecological Self. Throughout their exploration, Key and Tudor privilege traditions which predate the modern interest in this subject and propose a new metatheory for ecotherapy practice that aims to bring some cohesion to the field, honour its heritage, and support its future development. They argue that more care should be taken in how ecotherapy is practised and described, as they believe that many of the terms currently being used are culturally inappropriate and therapeutically counterproductive. They also remind us that ecotherapy practice is now spreading to many more countries as clinicians, educators, guides and others receive specific training in the field, so we can expect many more changes in the field going forward.

The goal of the many ecotherapies

All of the many Level 2 ecotherapies mentioned above – different from each other as they may seem – share the same aim and dream: to facilitate the healing of the tragically pathological relationship in modern cultures between the conscious human psyche, individually and in community, and the rest of nature. We and our ecotherapy clients and students may begin with Level 1 baby steps – discovering that growing a garden or petting a dog or hiking on a leafy trail can raise our spirits and calm our anxieties – but hopefully we will also be able to advance to a deeper understanding of the indivisible unity between our bodies, minds and souls and the rest of the natural world. For it is this ancient oneness that offers the deepest healing possibilities, not only for ourselves but for our communities, cultures and the tragically wounded earth and its disappearing life forms.

This all may seem a huge undertaking for ecotherapists – and certainly we cannot heal the earth by ourselves and thankfully are part of a wider community facilitating The Great Turning. But perhaps for those of us whose calling includes psychotherapy, counselling, nature coaching and teaching, it can be the most urgent, exciting and rewarding work of our era.

References

Andrews, C. (2009), 'The Small Group as Ecotherapy: Building a Culture of Connection', in L. Buzzell and C. Chalquist (eds), *Ecotherapy: Healing with Nature in Mind*, 192–6, San Francisco: Sierra Club Books.

Anthony, C. (1996), '"Ecopsychology" with Carl Anthony.' Retrieved from http://www.noetic.org/library/audio-lectures/carl-anthony-ecopsychology/ (accessed 25 November 2024).

Baker, C. (2011), *Navigating the Coming Chaos: A Handbook for Inner Transition*, Bloomington, IN: iUniverse.

Bliss, S. (2009), 'Agrotherapy: How Farms Heal'. Retrieved from http://www.commondreams.org/view/2009/02/02-5 (accessed 25 November 2024).

Bliss, S. (2009), 'In Praise of Sweet Darkness', in L. Buzzell and C. Chalquist (eds), *Ecotherapy: Healing with Nature in Mind*, 174–84, San Francisco: Sierra Club Books.

Bradshaw, G. A. (2021), 'Enculturated Captivity, Zoochosis, and Collective Trauma', *Psychology Today*, 17 June. https://www.psychologytoday.com/us/blog/bear-in-mind/202106/enculturated-captivity-zoochosis-and-collective-trauma?

Bradshaw, G. A. (2009), 'Transformation through Service: Trans-Species Psychology and Its Implications for Ecotherapy', in L. Buzzell and C. Chalquist (eds), *Ecotherapy: Healing with Nature in Mind*, 157–65, San Francisco: Sierra Club Books.

Bratman, Gregory N., and Hector A. Olvera-Alvarez, editors (2022), 'Nature and Health: Perspectives and Pathways', *Ecopsychology* September: 133–6. http://doi.org/10.1089/eco.2022.29007.editorial Published in Volume: 14 Issue 3: 15 September 2022.

Bratman, Gregory N., J. Paul Hamilton, Kevin S. Hahn, Gretchen C. Daily and James J. Gross (2015), 'Nature Experience Reduces Rumination and Subgenual Prefrontal Cortex Activation', PNAS (Proceedings of the National Academy of Sciences of the United States of America), 14 July 2015. www.pnas.org/content/112/28/8567

Buzzell, Linda, and Craig Chalquist (2023), 'From Eco-Anxiety to Eco-Resilience: Toward a Psychology of Care', in Douglas A. Vakoch and Sam Mickey (eds), *Eco-Anxiety and Pandemic Distress: Psychological Perspectives on Resilience and Interconnectedness*, Oxford, UK: Oxford University Press.

Canty, J. M. (2022), *Returning the Self to Nature: Undoing our Collective Narcissism and Healing Our Planet*, New York: Penguin Random House.

Conn, L. K., S. A. Conn (2009), 'Opening to the Other,' in L. Buzzell and C. Chalquist (eds), *Ecotherapy: Healing with Nature in Mind*, 111–15, San Francisco: Sierra Club Books.

Conn, S. A. (1995), 'When the Earth Hurts, Who Responds?', in T. Roszak, M. Gomes and A. Kanner (eds), *Ecopsychology: Restoring the Earth, Healing the Mind*, 156–71, San Francisco: Sierra Club Books.

DeMayo, N. (2009), 'Horses, Humans, and Healing', in L. Buzzell and C. Chalquist (eds), *Ecotherapy: Healing with Nature in Mind*, 149–56, San Francisco: Sierra Club Books.

Edwards, S. A., and L. Buzzell (2009), 'The Waking Up Syndrome', in L. Buzzell and C. Chalquist (eds), *Ecotherapy: Healing with Nature in Mind*, 123–30, San Francisco: Sierra Club Books.

Fisher, A. (2013), *Radical Ecopsychology, Second Edition: Psychology in the Service of Life*, Albany, NY: State University of New York Press. Retrieved from http://books.google.com/books?id=mqa_4Nn8YfMC&pg=PA219&lpg=PA219&dq=international+association+for+ecotherapy&source=bl&ots=D3yWneb2hU&sig=iFo0jE5688wrCkKszzYr9dK3jgI&hl=en&sa=X&ei=Lr1GVPe1KKXo8QH8z4CgBA&ved=0CFUQ6AEwCQ#v=onepage&q=international%20association%20for%20ecotherapy&f=false.

Goldsby, Tamara (2022), 'Nature-Based Therapy at Work Is Linked to Reduced Stress: Nature Therapy Is Effective for Stress Reduction, According to a Recent Study, *Psychology Today*, 20 May. https://www.psychologytoday.com/ca/blog/less-stress-more-peace/202205/nature-based-therapy-work-is-linked-reduced-stress?

Hopkins, R. (2008), *The Transition Handbook: From Oil Dependency to Local Resilience*, White River Junction, VT: Chelsea Green Publishing.

Jiang, T., J. A. Hicks, W. Yuan, Y. Yin, L. Needy and M. Vess (2024), 'The Unique Nature and Psychosocial Implications of Awe', *Nature Reviews Psychology* 3: 475–88. https://doi.org/10.1038/s44159-024-00322-z.

Jordan, M., and J. Hinds (2016), *Ecotherapy: Theory, Research and Practice*, Basingstoke, UK: Palgrave MacMillan.

Key, D., and K. Tudor (2023), *Ecotherapy: A Field Guide*, Bicester, Oxfordshire, UK: Karnac Books.

Kidner, D. (2001), *Nature and Psyche: Radical Environmentalism and the Politics of Subjectivity*, Albany, NY: State University of New York Press.

Kidner, D. (2007), 'Depression and the Natural World: Towards a Critical Ecology of Psychological Distress', *International Journal of Critical Psychology* 19: 123–46.

Korten, D. C. (2006), *The Great Turning: From Empire to Earth Community*, San Francisco: Berrett-Koehler Publishers.

Kubler-Ross, E. (1969), *On Death and Dying: What the Dying Have to Teach Doctors, Nurses, Clergy and Their Own Families*, New York: Scribner.

Kunstler, J. H. (2005), *The Long Emergency: Surviving the End of Oil, Climate Change, and Other Converging Catastrophes of the Twenty-First Century*, New York: Atlantic Monthly Press.

Louv, R. (2008), *Last Child in the Woods: Saving Our Children from Nature-Deficit Disorder*, Chapel Hill, NC: Algonquin Books.

Louv, R. (2011), *The Nature Principle: Human Restoration and the End of Nature-Deficit Disorder*, Chapel Hill, NC: Algonquin Books.

Macy, J., and C. Johnstone (2012), *Active Hope: How to Face the Mess We're in with Unexpected Resilience and Creative Power*, Novato, CA: New World Library.

Mind (2013), 'Feel Better Outside, Feel Better Inside: Ecotherapy for Mental Wellbeing, Resilience and Recovery', London: Mind. Retrieved from http://www.mind.org.uk/media/336359/Feel-better-outside-feel-better-inside-report.pdf?ctaId=/about-us/policies-issues/ecotherapy/slices/read-the-report/.

Pihkala, Panu (2022), 'The Process of Eco-Anxiety and Ecological Grief: A Narrative Review and a New Proposal', Sustainability. https://www.mdpi.com/2071-1050/14/24/16628 (Note: discussion of the Edwards-Buzzell stages of 'waking up syndrome' is on p. 16).

Pikhala, Panu (2024), 'Ecological Sorrow: Types of Grief and Loss in Ecological Grief' (graphic), https://www.mdpi.com/2071-1050/16/2/849.

Plotkin, B. (2003), *Soulcraft: Crossing into the Mysteries of Nature and Psyche*, Novato, CA: New World Library.

Rust, Mary-Jayne (2020), *Towards an Ecopsychotherapy*, Woodbridge, UK: Confer.

Sabini, M. (2009), 'Dreaming a New Paradigm', in L. Buzzell and C. Chalquist (eds), *Ecotherapy: Healing with Nature in Mind*, 211–18, San Francisco: Sierra Club Books.
Schneider, L. Z. (2009), 'The Whale's Tale', in L. Buzzell and C. Chalquist (eds), *Ecotherapy: Healing with Nature in Mind*, 116–22, San Francisco: Sierra Club Books.
Seed, J. (2005), 'The Ecological Self', *EarthLight Magazine 53* 14 (4). Retrieved from http://www.earthlight.org/2005/essay53_johnseed.html.
Smith, J. Phoenix (2020), Repairing Our Relationship to Nature, *Liberation Ecotherapy*. https://therapyforblackgirls.com/2020/09/16/session-173-repairing-our-relationship-to-nature/?
Smith, J. Phoenix (2013), 'Ecopsychology: Towards a New Story of Cultural and Racial Diversity', *Ecopsychology journal* 5 (4).
Smith, J. Phoenix (2022), Ecofascism as White Climate Anxiety, *Medium*, 26 May 2022. https://medium.com/@phxcan/eco-fascism-as-white-climate-anxiety-eaa9c300721e.
Smith, J. Phoenix (2022), 'When Things Fall Apart, We Sing: Afro-Indigenous Ecotherapy Practices for Wellness', 26 May. https://medium.com/@phxcan/when-things-fall-apart-we-sing-ebd4458886f7.
Taylor, B. (2010), *Dark Green Religion: Nature Spirituality and the Planetary Future*, Berkeley, CA: University of California Press.
Totton, N. (2011), *Wild Therapy: Undomesticating Inner and Outer Worlds*, London: Karnac Books.
Vaughan-Lee, L. (2013), *Spiritual Ecology: The Cry of the Earth*, Point Reyes, CA:Golden Sufi Center.
Wray, Britt (2022), How to Have More Productive Climate conversations, *Gen Dread*, 23 March. (Interview with Renee Lertzman, Ph.D.) https://gendread.substack.com/p/how-to-have-more-productive-climate?
Wray, Britt (2022), 'Climate Emotions aren't all "negative"', *Gen Dread*, 11 February. https://gendread.substack.com/p/climate-emotions-arent-all-negative?

Part II

Research

6

Working with nature in palliative care

Deborah Kelly

Introduction

This chapter focuses on a pilot study conducted as part of doctoral research some ten years ago, exploring the experiences of working in and with the natural world within the field of palliative care. The intervening years, since the first edition of this book, have seen a continued growing concern for the plight of the Earth, and, perhaps from the years of the Covid pandemic, a deeper engagement with Nature and its therapeutic benefits (ONS 2021). As with most research, the process has hermeneutic and iterative qualities – the exploration is continuous and evolving. To use an alchemical analogy, the 'gold' from the pilot study provided the foundation or 'prima materia' for the doctoral research, and those findings engendered further exploration and reconsideration. While the findings of the original pilot study must remain unchanged in this chapter, I have included further brief commentary to reflect the passage of time and conditions.

Working with nature

My 'way in' to working in and with nature was, in part, through my childhood experiences of the natural world and the seasons: being in nature, the physical, sensory and imaginal experiences; lying in the summer grass, playing in streams, talking to trees, learning the folklore, knowing the freedom of the fields and skies. Alongside the extraordinary familiarity and sunlit security of my childhood home lands, I knew too that some landscapes and weathers can be wild and dangerous, some stories tell of the darkness of the earth, of journeys to the underworld and beyond – stories that resonated with and intrigued me.

Later, my interest developed through a sense and exploration of sacred landscapes and geometry, where land and structure, ritual and invocation amplify and deepen the experience within certain places, offering the potential of healing ourselves and the land (Dawkins 1998; Kumar 2009). Through Chinese medicine and, in particular, the Five Phases theory (Kaptchuk 1983) I learned how nature, health, the elements and the rhythm of the seasons are interlaced.

Thus, for me, working in and with the natural world is many layered, incorporating the experience of the moment, the sensuousness of the landscape, captured in reverie or through full phenomenological contact. Our relationship with nature may evoke a sense of the past, a sense of belonging, by way of personal memories and ancestral echoes of the land, felt in our bodies, or reimagined through folk law and legend. As an integrative arts psychotherapist, nature became a place of creative exploration and embodied imagination. The natural world offers a rich abundance of metaphors and poesies: of struggle and conquest, beauty and awe, life and death, stories of initiation, of journeying to other realms.

I work in landscapes of southern England, ancient woodland and rolling hills close to the sea. The landscapes evoke, for me, a benign beauty, and, yet in wild weather, the surging seas and wild winds can be both exhilarating and formidable. Our relationship with nature can be a source of inspiration, exploration and revelation, yet it is not always comfortable. Nature is not always benign. To borrow from Richard Mabey, 'I am all for nature cures, but let them be profound and mysterious and terrible at times. We will be all the better for it' (Mabey 2010: 196).

The pilot study draws on my work with palliative care groups held in natural environments, and in particular on research into the experience of practitioners in this field. This work began over twenty years ago, inspired by Dr Michael Kearney's vision of an integrated approach to palliative care, which incorporated the advantages of modern medicine and symptom control, alongside holistic approaches that might address existential pain and suffering (Kearney 1996, 2000).

A new paradigm in palliative care

Palliative medicine developed rapidly in the 1960s in response to the pioneering work of Cicely Saunders. Prior to this, medical interventions in end-of-life care were minimal. While nursing and spiritual care was available, medicine had been concerned with cure rather than palliation. As doctors became more involved with the terminally ill, a huge improvement in symptom management and pain control was seen, alongside an acknowledgement of the interrelatedness of physical, emotional and spiritual distress. In 1987, palliative care was recognized as a new medical speciality in the UK. However, as the medical influence continued to develop, there was concern among some practitioners that original 'holistic focus of (palliative care) might be lost under the weight of the biomedical model' – (Balfour Mount, in Kearney 2000: viii), and that the new specialists in palliative care would be reduced to 'symptomologists' (Kearney 1992: 41). Kearney's concern was that while the advances in medicine were addressing the physical symptoms more efficiently, the medical model had no paradigm for attending to suffering, to the spiritual or existential domain of human experience.

The challenge to palliative medicine, articulated by Dr Kearney, was a dual commitment – to improve analytical and clinical skills, while facilitating a personal experience of illness, in an intuitive way, enabling patients to 'dive down into the experience of illness in a quest for healing' (1992: 46), be it emotional or spiritual if not physical healing. This ability to facilitate experiences of depth corresponds to the skills required in depth psychology – moving from the surface experience, the abode of the ego, where language is literal and the mode of knowledge is scientific and rational, to the depth experience, where the mode of knowing is intuitive, and the language that of symbol and metaphor.

Kearney also challenged the palliative care practitioners to be committed to making a journey themselves from the surface to the deep 'to know what it means to cross these inner boundaries' (1992: 45). He argued for a new paradigm in palliative care, rooted in ancient Greece and based on a synthesis of Hippocratic medicine and Asklepian healing. There are over 100 healing centres or shrines to Asclepius, the god of healing, over the ancient world, the most famous being at Epidaurus and Kos. The temples were usually built in beautiful and significant landscapes, close to wells or springs. Here the 'invalid' was attended to through bathing, fasting, exercise, through ritual and festivals. Plays and philosophical debate were also considered therapeutic and part of the preparation for the final rite of healing: the incubation of a dream. This took place in the 'abaton', a specially designated place, often a depression in the earth, where the invalid, close to the earth and the heart of the temple, would receive a healing dream. If Asclepius himself, or his snake, the bearer of earth wisdom, appeared in the dream, this was considered particularly significant. In this way, the Asklepian rites prepared the patient for an encounter with the divine. 'This was no visit to a doctor who simply administers medicine; it was an encounter with the naked event of healing itself' (Kerenyi 1959: 34).

Kearney presents a comparison between Hippocratic medicine (our modern medicine) and the Asklepian healing. He sees Hippocratic medicine as drawing on objective evidence, and treats pain 'from without'. Asklepian healing draws on subjective evidence and is concerned with healing suffering 'from within' (Kearney 2000: 37). The Asklepian principles of attending to body, mind and soul, in preparation for healing to emerge 'from within', is an important influence on my work. The use of bodywork, imagination, reverie and ritual invites a journey into depth, into the chthonic aspects of nature, of myth, facilitating a reconnection to the potential healing within. Even in palliative care, this healing can be a remembering, a reconnection that allows the person to die in peace.

More than twenty years on, palliative care still falls short of its potential, arguably becoming even more entrenched in the medical paradigm. To acknowledge that we belong to the natural world, to community, to a social network, places dying and death in a wider interconnected context, and it is this holistic approach that welcomes nature into end-of-life care.

Nature and palliative care

Inspired by Kearney's work, I set up two projects for people living with life threatening illness. One was a weekly group held in woodland, the other a monthly 'Sanctuary day' set in locations of natural beauty. The groups are supportive and reflective rather than psychotherapeutic. However, the invitation for exploration is ever present, through reflection, meditation, ritual (e.g. walking a labyrinth, fire rituals), creative exploration, and working with stories of the seasons._Nature has many avenues into the exploration of mortality and all that this engenders. Deepening our experience and connection to the natural world opens us to a different perspective on the eternal questions of life and death, belonging and meaning. Some ways may be containing and supportive, such as the reconnection to Mother earth; some are awesome and touch on the numinous; some follow Persephone into the underworld. All are potentially transformative.

For example, the natural world offers us a sense of cyclical time, rather than the linear trajectory governed by Chronos. Life and death ebb and flow, through continual cycles of growth, decline and renewal. Nothing is lost.

When there is a sense of time running out, an experience of beauty can expand a moment into eternity. As Rollo May writes, 'Beauty is eternity born into human existence' (May 1985: 72). At the same time, a glimpse of the incalculable distance of the stars, or the age of the universe can help place our individual lives in perspective.

A sense of interconnectedness, of being 'at one' with the natural world can facilitate our search for meaning. If we can move away from Cartesian duality, we may experience becoming 'enwrapped in a world-soul' (Tacey 2009: 153). In this way nature can take us beyond ego: 'an overcoming of selfhood, an adventure beyond the eclipsing mind' (O Donoghue 2013: 31).

Nature also offers us a mirror, reflecting both beauty and ugliness, health and disease. The growth on a tree may reflect the cancer inside; the ecological damage outside can mirror the physiological or psychological damage inside. Wild winds can match our rage, cold mists our despair. Nature therapy may not always be about well-being, it also needs to resonate with our pain.

Research

One of Kearney's challenges was that while Hippocratic medicine required external knowledge and skills, an Asklepian approach calls for self-knowledge, a demand to face our own mortality, to be alongside suffering. This research hoped to contribute to the issue of psycho-spiritual care provision in palliative care settings, and the part nature may play in this.

In choosing a method of inquiry, I wanted to use a methodology that resonated with my therapeutic approach, to support the concept of fidelity, as proposed by Levitt et al. (2017: 2). Thus the research needed to encompass nature, metaphor and imagination within the process. Writers on imaginal and transpersonal research (Angelo 2005, 2010; Braud and Anderson 1998, 2011; Romanyshyn 2007) discuss an approach to research that is circular rather than linear. This process of researching, relooking and circling round a subject to view it from many perspectives and through many avenues, stands in contrast to the linear process of empirical and quantitative research, inviting a creative approach not just in the collection of data but also in the dissemination. Likewise, Marie Angelo delivers an invitation to allow images to speak in academic research: 'I wanted to establish a practitioner vision, for which the method and grounds of knowledge, the epistemology, would be as imagistic as the content' (2005: 16).

This approach to research offers an opportunity to develop a broader, deeper, more expansive exploration with imagination as an integral part of the process.

Moustakas' heuristic research (1990) presented a framework, which could address both the inquiry into experience and a creative methodology.

Moustakas identified six stages within the research process: initial engagement, immersion, incubation, illumination, explication and creative synthesis (1990: 28). The research process demands the researcher to explore their internal experience and to remain connected to, and in relationship with, the subject of inquiry. Rather than observing the subject from a distance, heuristic inquiry leads the researcher into a deepening experience (an immersion), collecting data through self-dialogue, personal journals and self-inquiry, incorporating opportunities for creative exploration. Similar to the holistic and intuitive preparation for the incubation of a healing dream, the process also follows a flow of engagement and immersion in preparation for the incubation, illumination and explication of a creative synthesis. As for the Asklepian invalid, it offers the researcher the opportunity to be 'visited by the gods'.

The research participants consisted of myself and two co-researchers, each of whom had facilitated or co-facilitated the group relevant to the inquiry. The two co-researchers were included to support validation and to address a peripheral question concerned with the qualities and training needed to do this work. One co-researcher was a specialist palliative care nurse, the other a complementary therapist. Since I had been trained in both these professions and was an arts psychotherapist, I hoped to elicit how our professional trainings might impact our experience. The question we aimed to explore was simply this: What is our experience of working in nature with palliative care groups? The method in practice involved semi-structured interviews, exploration through journal writing, creating images, reverie and being in nature.

From an initial phase of engagement with the material, several themes began to emerge and the collected data began to be arranged accordingly. Once each theme was established it was illustrated by a photographic image from nature, and checked by the research participants for its suitability and resonance. These formed the creative synthesis: twenty-four photographic images of nature, taken by me and a colleague, representing the themes, and a poem, which emerged in a form of embodied writing, in contemplation of the data.

The findings and the images were presented at an exhibition open to palliative care workers. The main themes are presented here, all of which I consider to be completely interconnected:

- Nature as healing: being 'at ease', supported
- Nature as container: physical and emotional sense of a benevolence, sheltered, coming home
- Nature as a resource: of immediate experience, of metaphors, myths, stories
- Nature holding and reflecting the cycles of life and death, seasons, rhythm
- Depth of experience: listening more clearly, hearing more, sacred space, dropping into depth, shadow lands of death, fear
- Boundaries, professional or personal, death or life

There follows an expansion of some of these themes, with examples of researchers' comments *in italics.*

Nature as healing, being at ease, supported

Being in nature was seen as a positive experience that gave a sense of being 'at ease' of 'breathing more easily', of groundedness.

'Whilst working in nature, the whole experience feels more natural. It feels easier to breathe, to relax and the words, stories, metaphors flows freely. I feel energy is coming through me, not from me, to support me'

'There is freedom. I need my shoes off! Need to feel in touch with the earth to be grounded'

'There is a sense of time slowing down, my body easing, my vision clearing'.

This was extended to include experiences of 'feeling better' once connected to nature.

'When I came here today, I felt a lot tension ... now I feel more able. Being here is like a pause between breaths, to clarify what has been going on outside of here, so I feel able to go back.'

'My eyes felt blurred yet when I heard the wind, my breath softened.'

All three participants had positive childhood experiences of being in nature, and connections were made between these and their current experiences. There was a sense of reconnection, which felt deeply benign and nurturing.

'I think it's to do with my upbringing of being in nature, of a love of being outdoors with grandpa, of loving the allotment and walks and being close to nature.'

'I've gone back in time to my childhood dancing – being barefoot. Always being barefoot. ... It's about being at one with the sounds of the woodland, and being at one with nature and therefore feeling relaxed'.

'I feel my feet on bare earth, soft, firm, delicious, dropping into memories and smells of wild childhoods, summer meadow, warm earth.'

Nature as container

This sense of being at home and at ease developed into the theme of 'container', which became another layer of therapeutic holding. Nature, the wood, the trees, the circle, seemed to amplify the sense of containment. This was experienced as not only having a supportive and positive impact on the research participants, but also that group members felt 'held' by nature, which influenced the experiences of research participants in two ways: that the therapeutic containment as facilitators was amplified, and, possibly as a consequence, that group members seemed to speak more deeply about their feelings and experiences, compared with other venues. In turn, the facilitators felt more able to be with group members in depth, because they too felt 'held' by nature.

'I feel physically very safe, secure and at ease.'

'My mother, mother earth, motherhood, nurturing and nourishing, I feel held and at home, giving and receiving. I know this place.'

Nature as a resource

From the sense of containment, to 'containing resources', nature was experienced as a huge source of therapeutic material. This seemed important and significant not just for me, who, as an art psychotherapist saw the 'resources' as an extension of my modality, but the co-facilitators drew on this resource too. This resource was experienced in two different but interconnected ways – as an opportunity to draw on the natural world as a source of creative exploration – to create poetry, to meditate, to see the metaphors of death and rebirth as a vehicle for reflection, and also as a source of ancient wisdom.

'It means I am not alone. That I have this huge resource of beauty, metaphor, of cycles of life and death, on which I can draw. It holds everything'.

'If I get stuck, or if somebody talks of unsolvable problems, there's always a metaphor from nature, or there's a moment you can just sit with, and hear the birdsong, or the wind, and ... there are stories.'

The stories were linked to a felt source of 'ancient wisdom, of knowledge'; stories of the seasons, myths and folklore and the sense of people having been here before us.

Nature isn't just trees and seasons, it's about ancestors.

Not only was there a sense of the ancestral presence, but a more literal aspect of this came in the realization that previous members of the group were also with us, literally in some cases, with their ashes scattered, but more generally through memories and rituals. The land offered an opportunity for planting trees 'in memoriam', for shared activities such as planting bulbs in the autumn, creating mandalas and celebrating the festivals of the seasons. As rituals were repeated each season, past group members came to life again in our hearts and memories, their offerings remembered, their stories retold.

'This ancient woodland, the dead are with us.'

'It helps me deal with grief and bereavement, because the people who have died are also held in memories in the mandala, the labyrinth, in the woods, so that they take their place in the present which is not overwhelming. Not denying their passage, but includes the positive aspects of loss.'

The natural resources within nature and the landscape were not only experienced as a therapeutic tool to support facilitation but were used by research participants to support themselves, a true resourcing, particularly in managing the deeper and shadow aspects of the experience, fear, death, illness, tragedy, suffering. Stories of initiation and journeys to the underworld (e.g. Persephone, Chiron) were relevant to the facilitators as well as the group members in the sense of them having to 'go deeply' into their own fears about mortality and illness, about experiencing grief.

> *'For me, this sense of nature holding both life and destruction holds me in the present. Witnessing suffering, I can draw on nature to balance me; just by listening to the wind, or looking at the blue sky, brings in other realities alongside suffering. It stops me being overwhelmed.'*

> *'I hear a robin sing, persistent, sublime … Transcendent. a silver sliver of music, like a rope cast towards us from nature's heart, to stop us from drowning. We just need to reach out and hold it.'*

Nature holding the cycles of life and death, the rhythm of the seasons

This aspect is linked to the nature's clear ability to reflect the cycle of life and death. The seasons also acted as a structure to the ongoing work, and therefore provided another sense of containment. Participants experienced this as positive and useful in the sense of their own place in the cycle of life, and the cycle of the seasons, in teaching them about rhythm, pace, and in reconnecting themselves with old rituals and festivals. There was a sense of unity in this, of shared experience with group members. However, there was also a sense of 'here we go again' as the year turned, people came and some died, and the facilitators were still here.

> *'Death a normal part of life … In a strange way supports me to feel calmer and I'm not exempt, so there is a common theme. I still have lots of questions of life and death, learning to trust the process and draw on nature … but nothing new under the sun!'*

> *'Unlike the hospice, which holds, for me, accumulated death with no processing, here, people's deaths become compost for the people left behind – teaching wisdom. Stories, adding to the material for growth'.*

> *'There is an exchange of energies, the breath breathing in ideas from nature-ripples on a pond, the flow of the waves, the wind in the trees, the sunlight and the shadow, the rain drops cleansing. The breath expelling worries, fears, concerns feeling. A natural cycle, an exchange of gases, pruning, coppicing, composting to enable new growth and blossoming'.*

Depth of experience: Listening more clearly, hearing more, sacred space, dropping into depth, shadow lands of death, fear

Research participants talked of the experience of being able to see and hear more clearly when working in nature, of entering sacred space.

'Being here, you can see them more clearly, and hear them more clearly.'

'Feels easier to see people's souls!'

'And communicating without words.'

And how people seem to drop into a deeper place more quickly

'I still feel moved by the way people tell their story and how they feel so easily here … how easy it seems in this environment for people to tell their story, to let go of their story … reflect on how they feel.'

From a sense of being grounded in nature, there was a sense of being able to 'go deeper'

'I feel grounded in nature and therefore able to go deeper with people, and hear pain more easily. Or experience it as less overwhelming as I do in the hospice, where there is no relief'.

'Listening, silences, "cueing" talking, questioning is like a dance. Daring to go further, deeper, knowing when to step back, knowing when to change direction'

'There is a challenge to hold them, so having taken them there, that you don't leave them there, that you can hold them in that place for as long as they need to be, and bring them back out again. It easier here, in nature'

'It's not just profound, its more than that it's more like going into a sacred place – and at that level you find yourself saying things and you don't know where its coming from'.

Being close to people who are dying inevitably brings us closer to shadow feelings of fear, death, loss.

'And I thought I might get hardened and build up resistance to it and that hasn't happened, and its scary, an awareness someone is an individual and precious and I want to listen attentively, and yet I get so tired'

'At times I get overwhelmed by the amount of illness and death'

'If I get cancer what <u>will</u> *I feel- not what* <u>would</u> *I feel*

Sometimes it feels safe and secure, sometimes its scary'

'We witness and share deep parts of ourselves, and that changes the relationship, travelling with people to their death, or near death. Sometimes I feel tired: the constant cycle of dying and new people coming, and loss'.

'We purposefully develop a profound relationship with people who are going to die'

'It teaches me constantly about facing death and dying and at times I want to get away from it – yet there is a place within me that knows how great a teacher death is and how the world seems so big and rich'.

'And sometimes I can feel so intensely connected to someone's story and feeling being taken into Hades, and then I remember to breathe and look at the sky, or the swaying trees and I'm pulled back to life, or perhaps can hover at the edge, seeing both ways'

Boundaries

Researchers experienced a sense of equality and reciprocity in the woods. While the hospice sets boundaries, roles, expectation, the woods provide none.

> *'something about equality, equanimity, so being in nature brings me to a more equal place. It isn't owned by anyone, it's all of ours. It belongs to us all, we belong to it, so it sets us off in a different place'.*

They experienced a change in professional boundaries.

> *'Just walking towards the labyrinth we were walking together and that felt so different, a freedom'*
>
> *'Just two souls meeting'*
>
> *'I'm aware of holding a boundary, but it's more subtle, knowing my responsibilities and holding, yet being at ease and a fellow traveller'*
>
> *'You need a higher level of self awareness and of your own boundaries'.*

And the subject of the group belongs to us all. We're all going to die.

> *'If you work with someone who has appendicitis or schizophrenia, the chances are you won't experience these things, but we will all die, so there is no difference other than the question of when death may come'.*

Their journey, not ours

The researchers recognized that as facilitators, each could travel alongside a group member, accompanying them towards their dying and death, and yet they were also separate. This required an awareness and exploration not only of their professional boundaries, but also the boundary between life and death.

> *'I suppose, working with people that are dying and then listening to their experiences and feelings, in nature, which is the medium that helps give that freedom … I feel at ease that I'm going alongside them into dying, but at the same time, I won't take that final step, not yet'.*

And the management of professional and personal boundaries changes again, allowing them to loosen at times.

> *'I see them with different eyes. No boundaries. We drop into life. And I can still contain the day. One foot in the professional world, one in theirs. One foot in life, one in death, or just standing on the threshold looking both ways, like Janus. We peer again at death and the robin sings. Someone says something amazing.'*

Discussion and summary

It became clear from the final interview of the research that nothing in the co-researchers' training (nursing and complementary therapy) had prepared them for working with nature, and at this kind of depth. Experiences outside their professional training were more relevant: their childhood love of nature, their self-awareness, their personal journeys and creative exploration plus the accumulated knowledge from the many years' experience in these particular projects and in palliative care. For myself, my experiences as a hospice nurse and my personal exploration acted as a foundation to encountering death. My psychotherapy training in the use of arts, metaphor and imagination, and in group process, helped me ground, contain and develop the work. Access to other streams of knowledge, from ancient Greek myths, Chinese Five Element theory, to Western folklore and Celtic wisdom provided structure, inspiration and vehicles for creative embodied exploration. Further study of the sacred geometry of landscapes developed my understanding of the significance of working *with* the natural world; for example, asking permission to enter certain places, acknowledging the Spirit of Place, walking the land with love. All this helped build on a natural intuitive aspiration to honour the land and take care of the earth, as our groups evolved.

Several of the themes which emerged from the research resonate with evidence from the research literature: the relationship between nature and well-being and the boundary shifts in working outside.

The positive effects on body and emotions of being in and deepening our relationship to nature are widely recognized (e.g. Grut and Linden 2002; Berger and Mcloud 2006; Mitten 2009; MHF 2021). While this is normally discussed in terms of benefits to clients, this study showed how healthcare professionals and practitioners can feel more at ease and at home in a natural environment. Symptoms of stress – 'blurred eyes, tension' were soothed by contact with nature. The positive effects go beyond this however, to include nature as a container and resource for therapeutic work. Nature provides a multiplicity of metaphors, analogies, both literal (e.g. in the turning of the seasons, the cycle of birth, death and rebirth) and in its associated folklore and myth. For these researchers, accessing this knowledge not only helped their facilitation, as extra 'tools', but also helped them reflect, contain and make meaning of their own experiences around life and death.

Nature, in its containment and holding, offered support for the practitioners, which was not so evident in hospice and clinical environments. Part of this sense of 'feeling contained' was nature's capacity to hold polarities: the light and the dark, death and renewal, health and disease, tragedy and birdsong. It also modelled collaborative diversity. Nature can be seen as a metaphor for many positive psychological concepts: the secure base, solid ground, the safe container and good mother, nurturing parent. In symbolic and literal form, being in nature was undoubtedly significant in supporting practitioners to be alongside suffering, and dropping into depth. It was a place to be re-sourced, re-rooted and nourished. There was a sense of a collaboration through the connection to the natural world. The practitioners felt they were not alone. And they had a sense of 'belonging' rather than alienation, which can be experienced in clinical environments. There was a reciprocity here too, in offering gratitude and respect for the land and the more-than-human community, which had supported and nourished the researchers.

The experience of seeing and hearing more clearly, of communicating without words assumed, at times, the nature of sacredness, of liminal space. This attunement at a deep level might be seen in terms of Eliade's sacred space, where the threshold divides the profane from the sacred. He notes that woods and trees can take on a religious meaning, in their shape and heavenward growth (Eliade 1987). To the researchers it seemed that a sense of temenos was facilitated by the woods, by the journey to the woods, and by the journey towards death, with each threshold taking the researchers and group participants into more 'sacred ground'. The ability to safely accompany another across thresholds is crucial when working with the imaginal realm. A knowledge of ritual, of entering sacred space, and, for me, my training in working with the imagination facilitates this process, and the ability to 'grade' experiences appropriately.

That therapeutic boundaries change when working outside is expected. The absence of institutional hierarchy, rules and expectations also gave a sense of mutuality and neutrality to our researchers. The sense of travelling alongside was amplified by a perception of mutual suffering (we're all going to die) and by the invitation to be alongside fear and pain, rather than to fix it. This aspect is implicit in Kearney's work, where the therapeutic holding becomes, in Jordan and Marshall's terms, more flexible (2010). Jung also echoes this when he writes: 'learn your theories well, but be prepared to put them aside when you encounter the miracle of the human soul' (1953: 4). Working at the threshold of life and death invites the facilitators to go through a death initiation themselves, a mythic journey into the dark, and back again, so that they can truly accompany another into the unknown. The positive sense of nature as grounding, a good mother, a therapeutic container and resource, may prepare the practitioners for those journeys 'into Hades', where, so the myths tell us, we may be transformed.

This pilot study provided the ground for further doctoral research into therapeutic space, specifically working with nature and embodied imagination in end-of-life care (Kelly 2019). Among the findings, the research emphasized the collaborative aspect of the work, opening to the therapeutic presence of the earth, the elements, the trees, animals, birds and insects, the ancestors, the imaginal world and even death itself. Participating in this interdependent community places psychotherapy in a new paradigm of interbeing, where 'each bumblebee that nestles in the white lilac is a grail ... opening up alternative worlds' (Strand 2022: 107), and where our individual self belongs to a much wider web of existence. As such, we, as practitioners, become part of a greater diverse and manifold fellowship of wisdom, from where we may see our living and dying, and that of the Earth, from a different, expanded perspective.

References

Angelo, M. (2005), 'Splendor Solis: Inviting the Image to Teach', *Harvest* 51 (2): 13–35.

Angelo, M. (2010), 'Re-Imagining Research', *Pre-Publication Papers* from the MA Transpersonal Arts and Practice, University of Chichester, West Sussex.

Berger, R., and J. McLeod (2006), 'Incorporating Nature into Therapy: A Framework for Practice', *Journal of Systemic Therapies* 25 (2): 80–94.

Braud, W., and R. Anderson (1998), *Transpersonal Research Methods for the Social Sciences*, London: Sage.

Braud, W., and R. Anderson (2011), *Transforming Self and Other through Research*, New York: SUNY.

Dawkins, P. (1998), *Zoence. The Science of Life*, York Beach ME: Samuel Weider.

Eliade, M. (1987), *The Sacred and Profane: The Nature of Religion*, Florida: Harcourt.

Grut, J., and S. Linden (2002), *The Healing Fields. Working with Psychotherapy and Nature to Rebuild Shattered Lives*, London: Francis Lincoln.

Hillman, J. (1989), 'Cosmology of the Soul: From Universe to Cosmos', *Sphinx: A Journal for Archetypal Psychology and the Arts* 2: 17–33.

Jordan, M., and H. Marshall (2010), 'Taking Counselling and Psychotherapy Outside: Destruction or Enrichment of the Therapeutic Frame?', *European Journal of Psychotherapy and Counselling* 12 (4): 345–59.

Jung, C. (1953), *Psychological Reflections*, New York: Pantheon.

Kaptchuck, T. J. (1983), *The Web That Has No Weaver: Understanding Chinese Medicine*, New York: Congdon & Weed.

Kearney, M. (1992), 'Palliative Medicine - Just Another Speciality?', *Palliative Medicine* 6: 39–46.

Kearney, M. (1996), *Mortally Wounded. Stories of Soul Pain, Death and Healing*, Dublin: Marino Books.

Kearney, M. (2000), *A Place of Healing: Working with Suffering in Living and Dying*, Oxford: Oxford University Press.

Kelly, D. (2019), 'An Intuitive Inquiry into Therapeutic Space', *The Humanistic Psychologist* 47 (2): 158–80.

Kerenyi, C. (1959), *Aslepios. Archetypal Image of the Physician's Existence*, New York: Pantheon.

Kumar, S. (2009), *Earth Pilgrim*, Dartington: Green Books.

Levitt, H. M., S. L. Motulsky, F. J. Wertz, S. L. Morrow and J. G. Ponterrotto (2017), 'Recommendations for Designing and Reviewing Qualitative Research in Psychology: Promoting Methodological Inquiry', *Qualitative Psychology* 4 (1): 2–22. Retrieved from http://dx.doi.org/10.1037/qup0000082.

Mental Health Foundation (2021), 'How Connecting with Nature Benefits Our Mental Health', Mental Health Awareness Report 2021. https://www.mentalhealth.org.uk/sites/default/files/2022-06/MHAW21- Nature-research-report.pdf.

Mitten, D. (2009), 'The Healing Power of Nature: The Need for Nature for Human Health Development and Well-Being', Prepared for *The Birth of 'Friluftsliv'*: 50 Year Dialogue Conference Jubilee Celebration, North Troendelag University College, Levanger, Norway 14–19 September. http://norwegianjournaloffriluftsliv.com/doc/1220.

Mabey, R. (2010), *A Brush with Nature, 25 Years of Personal Reflections on the Natural World*, BBC Books.

May, R. (1985), *My Quest for Beauty*, Dallas: Saybrook Publishing.

Moriaty, J. (2011), *Nostos*, Dublin: Lilliput Press.

Moustakas, C. (1990), *Heuristic Research: Design, Methodology and Application*, London: Sage.

O'Donoghue, B., ed. (2013), *A Moriaty Reader. Preparing for Early Spring*, Dublin: Lilliput Press.

ONS (2021), 'How Lockdown Changed Our Relationship with Nature', https://www.ons.gov.uk/economy/environmentalaccounts/articles/howhaslockdownchangedourrelationshipwithnature/2021-04-26.

Romanyshyn, R. (2007), *The Wounded Researcher: Research with Soul in Mind*, New Orleans: Spring Journal.

Strand, S. (2022), *The Flowering Wand. Rewilding the Sacred Masculine*, Vermont: Inner Traditions.

Tacey, D. (2009), *Edge of the Sacred. Jung, Psyche, Earth*, Eisiedeln: Daimon Verlagh.

7

Evidence-based design and a salutogenic approach in nature-based rehabilitation (NBR) for individuals with stress-related mental health disorders

Anna María Pálsdóttir

Introduction

This chapter is based on research conducted at Alnarp Rehabilitation Garden on nature-based rehabilitation (NBR). The core text is based on the doctoral thesis 'The Role of Nature in Nature-Based Rehabilitation for Individuals with Stress-Rrelated Mental Disorders. Alnarp Rehabilitation Garden as Supportive Environment' (Pálsdóttir 2014). The thesis aimed to increase the understanding of supportive outdoor environments, especially the role of the natural space (nature) and the essential qualities supporting the rehabilitation process. The study is based on fifty-nine interviews with former clients after twelve weeks of NBR (Pálsdóttir 2014). Alnarp Rehabilitation Garden was established in 2002 as a Living Lab in a real-life context on nature-based rehabilitation for individuals suffering from stress-related mental disorders (Pálsdóttir, Kyrö Wissler and Thorpert 2024, Stigsdotter and Grahn 2003), mainly exhaustion disorders (ICD 43.2) (Glise 2014) but also, mild to moderate depression and anxiety.

The concept of nature can be problematic (Jordan 2014), but in this context, nature-based rehabilitation is defined as a phenomenon in which the natural space is the bearing element of the rehabilitation and where it takes place. Hence, the term *nature* is used as an overall term for the natural space in the healing garden.

The healing garden in Alnarp

The 2-hectare garden was designed according to theories on nature's restorative and salutogenic effects (Stigsdotter and Grahn 2002; Tenngart Ivarsson 2011). It contains places for work, rest and contemplation and is divided into two major areas: the nature garden and the cultivation and gardening areas. In 2016, the garden was downsized to 1.5 hectares as some parts were seldom used, and the management of unused space was costly (see Figure 7.1).

These areas are further sub-divided into eight garden rooms, with different themes and qualities intended to support the client's rehabilitation process. The garden is planted with evergreen and deciduous trees and shrubs as well as a vast variety of perennials and annuals, with an emphasis on seasonal variation. To stimulate and awaken the different senses, plants' size, height, form, texture and fragrance differ. However, soft hues dominate the colour scheme, with strong hues limited to certain places in the garden (Pálsdóttir et al. 2018). Greenhouses in the garden were used interchangeably for horticultural purposes, personal relaxation and individual or group therapeutic sessions (Pálsdóttir, Kyrö-Wissler and Thorpert 2024). The garden is fenced and was closed to visitors during the NBR (Tenngart Ivarsson 2011) and offers a multi-sensory experience supporting the client's recovery process (Cerwén, Pederssen and Pálsdóttir 2016; Pálsdóttir et al. 2021).

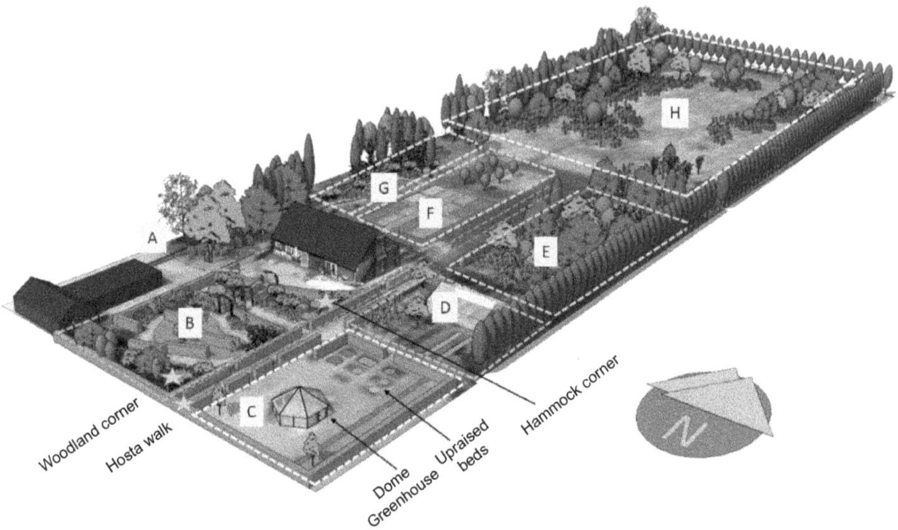

Figure 7.1 The garden is divided into eight main areas: (A) the entrance, (B) the Welcome garden, (C) hard scape room, (D) cultivation and large greenhouse, (E) forest garden, (F) cottage garden, (G) the large pond and (H) the meadow.

Original illustration: Gunnar Cerwén with modification by AM Pálsdóttir.

Nature-based rehabilitation programme

The NBR was designed as group therapy and supported by the multimodal rehabilitation team. It integrated four major therapy forms: occupational therapy, physiotherapy in the form of Rosen therapy, psychotherapy and horticultural therapy (Lavesson 2013; Grahn et al. 2010). The NBR aimed to enhance salutogenic processes to improve individuals' health and well-being with firm support from natural space (Tenngart Ivarsson 2011; Pálsdóttir, Kyrö-Wissler and Thorpert 2024).

Over one year, the NBR was divided into four rehabilitation periods (I–IV) of twelve weeks each: I, winter to spring; II, spring to summer; III, summer to fall; and IV, fall to winter. The weekly programme was managed by an occupational therapist, assisted by a horticulturist. All occupations were performed outside except when the weather was unfavourable; in such cases, they took place in one of the glass buildings/greenhouses. The programme was scheduled four days a week, each day lasting three and a half hours (Table 7.1). In the first week, the participants attended the therapy for one day, and over the following weeks increased their attendance to four days a week. Each day had the same basic structure, with four themed sessions led by an occupational therapist, assisted by a horticulturist. Sessions 1, 2 and 4 were the same on all four days, whereas the third session varied daily.

The first themed session was the morning get-together, with a cup of tea, allowing the participants to 'catch their breath' and settle down before entering the second themed

Table 7.1 The Weekly Schedule for the Nature-Based Programme in Alnarp Rehabilitation Garden* for Clients Suffering from Stress-Related Mental Illnesses

	Monday	Tuesday	Wednesday	Thursday
Session 1	Morning tea and gathering	Morning tea and gathering	Morning tea and gathering	Morning tea and gathering
Session 2	Relaxing exercise	Relaxing exercise	Relaxing exercise	Relaxing exercise
Session 3 – the main focus for the day	Creative occupations (indoors or outdoors depending on weather).	Individual meeting with the psychiatrist (30 minutes). Before and after: garden and horticultural occupations (in a group or by oneself).	Individual meeting with the physiotherapist (30 minutes). Before and after: garden and horticultural occupations (in a group or by oneself).	Garden and horticultural occupations (in a group or by oneself).
Session 4	'Closure' with light refreshments	'Closure' with light refreshments	'Closure' with light refreshments	'Closure' with light refreshments

* Sessions 1, 2 and 4 are the same for each day, but session 3 varies from day to day (light grey colour).

session, a relaxation exercise performed indoors or in the garden. The third themed session varied each day. On Mondays, it consisted of creative occupations performed either indoors or in the garden; on Tuesdays, the participants were invited to meet individually with the physiotherapist for a thirty-minute session on bodily awareness; on Wednesdays, they were invited to meet privately with the psychotherapist for a thirty-minute counselling session. Before and after these sessions on Tuesdays and Wednesdays, the participants could participate in horticultural occupations led by the occupational therapist, assisted by the horticulturist or stay in the garden, resting or enjoying the surroundings. On Thursday, the themed session included garden and horticulture occupations. The fourth and final themed session was 'closure' for the day, in which all participants gathered for light refreshments (often something harvested from the garden, fresh or preserved) before going home. Also, at this time, the participants could discuss the morning's events, reflecting on their experiences from the themed sessions (Pálsdóttir et al. 2014).

Health-promoting design

The term *salutogenic* derives from the Latin word *salus* ('health') and the Greek word *genesis* ('origins') and refers to the origin of health (Antonovsky 1979). Aaron Antonovsky introduced the *salutogenic model*, handling aspects as stress, coping and health. The model focuses on the direction towards health instead of ill health and diseases, that is, the *salutogenic* approach (Lindström and Eriksson 2009). It consists of two concepts: (i) generalized resistant resources (external and internal resources) and (ii) sense of coherence (SOC), which in turn consists of three components: meaning (subjective and a motion-driven component), comprehensibility (a cognitive component) and manageability (the ability to act and meet challenges). SOC is determined by our ability to cope and maintain good health (Lindström and Eriksson 2009; Antonovsky 2007).

The *salutogenic* approach in health design focuses on elements promoting improved mental and physical health (Souter-Brown 2015; Westlund 2010). Grahn, Ottosson and Uvnäs-Moberg (2021) argue that a supportive environment is an essential part of salutogenesis and is needed to maintain good health. The theory of supportive environment (SET) explains that people need supportive environments to develop physically (senses, muscles, locomotion) and mentally (the ability to feel and think) (Grahn et al. 2010). SET discusses that the need for supportive environments will differ depending on a person's physical and mental capacity, situation and state of mind; that is, *a scope of meaning*. This term indicates that there exists a scope in which nature, culture and people can change the meaning (comprehensibility, manageability, significance) for an individual, depending on his or her mental and physical resources at the moment (Pálsdóttir 2014; Grahn 1991). When people become ill or experience a life crisis, they need strong environmental support to regain their health and wellness. However, they often experience a change in how they perceive the environment; their scope of meaning has changed. Phenomena they previously experienced as comprehensible, manageable and meaningful (and that even provided valued support in their daily lives) can suddenly be perceived as chaotic or even threatening (Ottosson 2007). They often have great difficulty understanding and managing people, whereas physical environments – especially natural ones – are easier to understand and manage (Ottosson and Grahn 2005; Ottosson 2007; Sahlin 2014). The more a person feels pressured, insecure, and lost, the greater the need to find salutogenic environments (enriched social and physical environments) that support healing processes. This is illustrated as a pyramid of supportive environments (Pálsdóttir et al. 2014; Grahn 1991). The pyramid is divided into four levels of executive functions, the lower part symbolizing low capacity of executive functions and characterized by inward involvement and a high need for a supportive environment. Conversely, the higher levels symbolize higher capacity for executive functions and are characterized by active or outgoing involvement and less need for a supportive environment. Based on their situation, SET argues, people try to self-regulate – find environments they perceive as supportive and secure. Sensory impulses in a supportive environment can give rise to salutogenic effects regarding, for example, senses, hormones, emotions and cognition, which affect function, feelings and behaviour (Grahn, Ottosson and Uvnäs-Moberg 2021).

Three themes on the role of nature in relation to the rehabilitation process

Based on the findings, an explanatory model of nature-based rehabilitation is presented to explain and illuminate the role of the natural environments concerning three main themes: Prelude, Recuperating and Empowerment (See Table 7.2). The themes are presented in chronological order, as described by the participants (Pálsdóttir et al. 2018).

The theme *Prelude* describes the importance of settling safely into the new context before starting to notice everything around oneself. The following theme, *Recuperating*, describes the intimate and embracing interaction between the participants and nature during the rehabilitation period that supports different therapeutic processes. The third theme, *Empowerment*, describes how the garden supports the participants in controlling their health and life.

Table 7.2 The Three Main Themes on the Role of Nature in Relation to the Rehabilitation Process of Individuals Undergoing Nature-Based Rehabilitation at Alnarp Rehabilitation Garden*

Superordinate themes	Subthemes	Dimensions
Prelude	Alliance	Establishing contact
	Permissiveness	Taking armour off
Recovery	Restoration	Being in the present in nature Being one with nature Feeling peace and tranquillity in nature
	Awakening and processing	Entrusting nature Being inspired by nature
Empowerment	Moving on	Challenging oneself

* The themes are presented in the chronological order in which the participants described they occurred.

These findings partially confirm earlier findings of Grahn and colleagues (Grahn et al. 2010). However, there are some crucial differences, which apply mainly to the finding of the *Prelude* not earlier described and the theme of *Recuperating* that resembles the phases earlier described by Grahn et al. (2010), that is, the phases of Contact (with the external world and themselves), Breaking the shell (starting to re-evaluate their situation) and Opening (processing). Also, a new component of the restorative environment was identified: Social quietness, as an essential component facilitating personal and intimate engagement with the natural environments in the *Recuperating* and *Empowerment* phases (Pálsdóttir et al. 2014, 2018).

Social quietness – pre-requisite for intimate engagement with nature

The participants specifically expressed a strong need to be alone with nature, in a self-chosen supportive location in the rehabilitation garden, undisturbed by the presence of others when resting or handling all the emotions evoked in the rehabilitation. This essential quality of a supportive environment is hereby defined as *Social quietness* and is seemingly one of the crucial qualities of a supportive environment in nature-based rehabilitation. It was essential for engaging in intimate communication with the natural environment. The profound non-verbal communications with nature in the garden seem not only to be a source of restoration but also to reconciliation's complex mental processes evoked by the professional rehabilitation team. Solitary engagement with nature was negatively affected when others entered the scene because of the noise from other people and the actual presence of another person in the surroundings. The participants expressed that the possibility of acting on the emotions evoked instantly was crucial to moving on with the recovery processes and not being left with these emotions. This, the participants often repeated, was not possible in the usual healthcare facilities, and participants said that nature could meet them where they were emotionally, without words or judgement. 'To cry in despair and let go of all the tension that was inside of me; I felt bad and it felt like there was no point living with this. I didn't want to let go of these feelings in front of others, but the garden and nature could take it' (Pálsdóttir et al. 2018).

Nature supports and embraces the rehabilitation

Several areas in the garden were experienced as having strong attributes of nature and being rich in species, and were repeatedly sought out during the theme of *Recuperating*. The participants found garden rooms and supportive locations where they felt safe and were in tune with their state of mind. Participants sought the prospect of *refuge*, where one could 'see but not be seen' (Appleton 1975), where one could hide from others. The common physical features of the supportive locations are as follows: a firm and solid support from the sides and the back as well as a (canopy) roof; alternative paths ('escape exits'); varied ground cover (e.g. soft bark, gravel); sufficient distance from the user to passers-by, with the area in between planted with lush vegetation in a soft colour scheme (e.g. white, purple, blue, variations of green and grey); plants of varied textures and shapes, giving the eye a resting point; comfortable sitting facilities; and a mixture of stone, water and plants. Other important qualities were comfortable temperatures, pleasant fragrances and considerable quiet (though the sounds of nature were acceptable). Soft shapes and curves were perceived as less demanding than strict lines and hard surface structures. A balanced and coherent colour scheme, with soft colours such as lilac, pink, white and blue, was perceived as calming and did not bother tired minds. Pleasant plant fragrances and the sounds of nature, such as birds twittering and the wind sweeping softly through the leaves, were perceived as soothing (Cerwén, Pederssen and Pálsdóttir 2016; Pálsdóttir et al. 2021). Locations with a clear and firm structure and the attributes of prospect and refuge and escape routes were highly regarded as supportive environments.

The seasonal changes reminded the participants of eternity and being part of a bigger whole. It also demonstrated that nature cannot be rushed; it has its own rhythm, which the participants expressed as a peaceful and calming experience. Stones, water, plants, small animals, birds and insects – all these wonders of nature represent the origin of humans. It gave participants a strong feeling of being in tune with nature. This allowed them to get closer to their inner feelings and to stay with them without demands from their surroundings. This was in contrast to their experience of everyday life, which was more or less dominated by expectations and demands from others and, hence, even themselves (Pálsdóttir et al. 2018).

The participants explicitly expressed that a natural environment in the garden gave the impression of taking care of itself and that they did not have to take responsibility for anything other than themselves. That gave them the feeling of *just being* in the present and resting without effort. The *nature-like* and *rich of spices* attributes gave the feeling of lush greenery where the participants could be alone with nature without the disturbance of others. The *nature* dimension represents the force and power of nature – not human-made, but on nature's own terms and seems to dominate the participants' thoughts neither nor demand their *direct attention* (Pálsdóttir et al. 2018). Instead, mental recovery is facilitated through *soft fascination* (Kaplan 2001).

The participants frequently mentioned the importance of permissiveness from the surroundings and that access to the garden was vital for mental restoration and emotional processing. This was always preferred in solitude, without the disturbance to others. Social interaction demanded attention and depleted their fragile energy source, but the interaction with nature did not (Pálsdóttir et al. 2018). Further, there seems to be a positive correlation between time spent in the garden programme and return to work or studies, that is, indicating that twelve to fourteen weeks is optimal for recovery (Grahn et al. 2018).

Nature in everyday life

After nature-based rehabilitation, the participants in this study included more nature-related activities in their everyday life as both restorative and pleasurable experiences. These changes seem to have been initiated in the NBR. The participants re-engaged in or introduced new occupations into their everyday life. These occupations were characterized by enjoyment, pleasantness and creativity, all of which have been described as meaningful (Pálsdóttir et al. 2014). Nature's role as a supportive environment was extended into everyday life to maintain and improve health and well-being. This emphasizes the need for close connection to nature in everyday life and that access to everyday greenery can be a key to better mental health.

References

Antonovsky, A. (1979), *Health, Stress, and Coping*, San Francisco: Jossey-Bass.

Antonovsky, A. (2007), *Hälsans Mysterium* [*The Mystery of Health*], Stockholm: Natur och Kultur. (In Swedish).

Appleton, J. (1975), *The Experience of Landscape*, London: Wiley.

Cerwén, G., E. Pederssen and A. M. Pálsdóttir (2016), 'The Role of Soundscape in Nature-Based Rehabilitation: A Patient Perspective/Patients' Perspectives', Special Issue: *Landscape & Health, International Journal of Environmental Research and Public Health* 13: 1229. https://doi:10.3390/ijerph13121229.

Glise, K. (2014), 'Exhaustion Disorder – Identification, Characterization and Course of Illness', PhD thesis, Institute of Medicine at the Sahlgrenska Academy, University of Gothenburg, Gothenburg.

Grahn, P. (1991), 'Om Parkens Betydelse' ['On the Meaning of Parks'], Stad and Land nr 93, PhD thesis No. 93, Alnarp: Swedish University of Agricultural Sciences. (In Swedish).

Grahn, P., J. Ottosson and K. Uvnäs-Moberg (2021), 'The Oxytocinergic System as a Mediator of Anti-Stress and Instorative Effects Induced by Nature: The Calm and Connection Theory', *Frontiers in Psychology*, 12, Article 617814. https://doi.org/10.3389/fpsyg.2021.617814.

Grahn, P., A. M. Pálsdóttir, J. Ottosson and I. H. Jonsdottir (2018), 'Longer Nature-Based Rehabilitation May Contribute to a Faster Return to Work in Patients with Reactions to Severe Stress and/or Depression', *International Journal of Environmental Research and Public Health* 14 (11): 1310. https://doi:10.3390/ijerph14111310.

Grahn, P., C. Tenngart Ivarsson, U. K. Stigsdotter and I- L. Bengtsson (2010), 'Using Affordances as a Health-Promoting Tool in a Therapeutic Garden', in C. Ward Thompson, P. Aspinall and S. Bell (eds), *Innovative Approaches to Researching Landscape and Health. Open Space: People Space 2*, 116–54, New York: Routledge.

Jordan, M. (2014), *Nature and Therapy: Understanding Counselling and Psychotherapy in Outdoor Spaces*, London: Routledge.

Kaplan, S. (2001), 'Meditation, Restoration, and the Management of Mental Fatigue', *Environment and Behaviour* 33: 480–506.

Lavesson, L. (2013), 'A Pilot Study of Rosen Practitioners' Experiences Receiving a Modified Form of Rosen Method Bodywork in a Garden Setting', *Rosen Method International Journal* 6 (1): 5–16.

Lindström, B., and M. Eriksson (2009), 'The Salutogenic Approach to the Making of HiAP/ Healthy Public Policy: Illustrated by a Case Study', *Global Health Promotion* 16 (1): 17–28.

Ottosson, J. (2007), 'The Importance of Nature in Coping: Creating Increased Understanding of the Importance of Pure Experiences of Nature to Human Health', PhD thesis No. 115, Swedish University of Agricultural Sciences, Alnarp, Acta Universitatis Agriculturae Sueciae.

Ottosson, J., and P. Grahn (2005), 'Measures of Restoration in Geriatric Care Residence: The Influence of Nature on Elderly People's Power of Concentration, Blood Pressure and Pulse Rate', *Journal of Housing of the Elderly* 19 (3/4): 229–58.

Pálsdóttir, A. M. (2014), 'The Role of Nature in Rehabilitation for Individuals with Stress-Related Mental Disorders. The Alnarp Rehabilitation Garden as Supportive Environment', PhD thesis No. 45, Swedish University of Agricultural Sciences, Alnarp, Acta Universitatis Agriculturae Sueciae, http://pub.epsilon.slu.se/11218/.

Pálsdóttir, A. M., D. Persson, B. Persson and P. Grahn (2014), 'The Journey of Recovery and Empowerment Embraced by Nature – The Clients' Perspective on Nature-Based Rehabilitation in Relation to the Role of the Natural Environments', *International Journal of Environmental Research and Public Health* 11: 7094–8015.

Pálsdóttir, A. M., S. Kyrö Wissler and P. Thorpert (2024), 'An Innovative Approach in Research and Development of Clinical Nature-Based Rehabilitation in Health Care and Vocational Training: The Living Laboratory, Alnarp Rehabilitation Garden', *Landscape Architecture* 31 (5): 116–23. doi: 10.3724/j.fjyl.202404020196.

Pálsdóttir, A. M., S. Spendrup, L. Mårtensson and K. Wendin (2021), 'Garden Smellscape – Experiences of Plant Scents in Nature-Based Intervention', *Frontiers in Psychology* 12. doi: 10.3389/fpsyg.2021.667957.

Souter-Brown, G. (2015), *Landscape and Urban Design for Health and Well-Being. Using Healing, Sensory and Therapeutic Gardens*, Oxon: Routledge.

Sahlin, E. (2014), 'To Stress the Importance of Nature: Nature-Based Therapy for the Rehabilitation and Prevention of Stress-Related Disorders', PhD thesis No. 98, Swedish University of Agricultural Sciences, Alnarp, Acta Universitatis Agriculturae Sueciae,

Stigsdotter, U. A., and P. Grahn (2002), 'What Makes a Garden a Healing Garden?', *Journal of Therapeutic Horticulture* 13: 60–9.

Stigsdotter, U. A., and P. Grahn (2003), 'Experiencing a Garden: A Healing Garden for People Suffering from Burnout Diseases', *Journal of Therapeutic Horticulture* 13: 38–48.

Tenngart Ivarsson, C. (2011), 'On the Use and Experience of a Health Garden. Exploring the Design of the Alnarp Rehabilitation Garden', PhD thesis No. 89, Swedish University of Agricultural Sciences, Alnarp, Acta Universitatis Agriculturae Sueciae, http:// pub.epsilon.slu.se/8388/1/tenngartivarsson_c_111018.pdf.

Westlund, P. (2010), *Salutogen design är framtidens äldreboende* [*Salutogenic design is the future nursing home for elderly*], Solna: Fortbildning AB. (In Swedish).

8

Nature connectedness, belonging and social identity in a group-based ecotherapy programme

Matthew Adams and Martin Jordan

Introduction

This chapter recounts the findings of a unique collaboration between researchers at the University of Brighton and the Grow Project, a charitable organization providing free and low-cost nature-based interventions for groups of people who have experienced depression, anxiety and stress. The collaboration involved teaming up a research psychologist and psychotherapist from the University with coordinators, volunteers, former and current participants in an intervention. The main purpose of the collaboration was to delve into the organization's own evaluations spanning multiple years, with the aim of understanding how participants made sense of their involvement in the Grow Project, especially their mental health and well-being. We worked towards this aim by collating and thematizing the preliminary evidence already generated by those involved in Grow, devising a set of research questions with the project's co-coordinators by carrying out some additional targeted qualitative research and by contextualizing the findings in existing literature. Finally, we considered the implications of our results for mental health practitioners, policy makers and other decision-makers. In what follows we first outline literature addressing the relationship between mental health and natural settings before providing an overview of our approach, findings and discussion.

Mental health problems and associated distress are a vitally important issue in today's society. From a personal, community and social point of view struggles with mental health exacts enormous costs. Back in 2006 Layard claimed that 'in Britain mental illness has now taken over from unemployment as our greatest social problem' (Layard 2006: 1030), and since then, the problem appears to have deepened. Figures suggest that mental health problems affect an increasing number of people in the UK – in any given year around one in five children and young people (NHS, 2023), and one in four adults (Mental Health Network, 2014). An increase in the prevalence of mental health problems at a national and international level represents 'the second biggest reason for long-term disability globally' (World Health Organization, 2025), permeating human endeavours as diverse as employment, housing, relationships and physical health (Drake and Wallach 2020). In the UK this increase is occurring against a backdrop of the consequences of years of far-reaching 'reforms' and cost reductions imposed on health service and welfare provision, increased income inequality, ongoing controversy regarding both the efficacy of medication to treat psychological problems, and severely limited access to appropriate psychological therapies (Mental Health Foundation, 2021; MIND, 2014).

In this context, applications of ecopsychology have garnered increased attention as a potential adjunct or even alternative to existing treatment programmes that might be referred to as ecotherapy, outdoor therapy, nature-based interventions, and green social prescribing (Garside et al. 2020). Ecopsychology, at its simplest, is the study of the relationship between humans and nature – historically a neglected aspect of psychology (Metzner 1991). Ecopsychology is also often considered as a foundation for an advocacy of the positive benefits of this relationship and has long been associated with research exploring and evaluating how various aspects of contact with the natural world are central to psychological well-being, and the field continues to develop and diversify (e.g. Clark, Vanclay and Brymer 2023; Mintz et al. 2021; White et al. 2017). Doherty, for example, states that ecopsychology's 'mission' is 'to validate that an emotional connection to nature is normal and healthy' (Doherty 2009: 2); and a range of empirical studies in ecopsychology and beyond explore this connection in relation to various health measures further (Mayer and Frantz 2004; Kleepsies et al. 2021; Watts et al. 2022). More recent terms such as 'nature-based interventions', 'green care' and 'green social prescribing' reflect the mainstreaming of at least some of the principles of ecopsychology and ecotherapy (e.g. Menhas et al. 2024; Howarth et al. 2020; Silva, Matos and Gonçalves 2024; Taylor et al. 2022). More widespread acceptance and applications of the potential benefits of being with nature also raises critical questions around issues such as unequal access, the commodification of 'nature', sidestepping of vitally important questions relating to ecological and climate crisis (e.g. Dickinson and Gray 2022; Lee, Mai and Park 2023).

Grow, Ecominds and Mind

Via its 'Ecominds' programme, the UK national mental health charity Mind, with National Lottery support, kickstarted several funded projects in England that 'provide[d] a range of outdoors green activities for people with mental health problems' (Mind 2014), geared towards improving confidence, self-esteem and physical and mental health (Bragg, Wood and Barton 2013). This programme and the initial report (Mind 2007) turned out to be significant landmarks in what has become a burgeoning, if still chronically underfunded, landscape of ecotherapeutic and nature-based interventions. The Grow Project (hereafter Grow for short) was originally funded as one of these projects, though it now operates independently as a charitable organization. Grow is designed to support people with diverse lived experiences of mental distress to experience the significant well-being benefits of being in nature in a safe and supportive group. Each day with Grow is structured around a 'check in' session when people arrive and a 'check out' session at the end of the day. Participants are offered the choice of a range of activities to suit varying levels of mental and physical health in rural Sussex. Options include guided walks, conservation activities, green woodworking, environmental art, mindfulness, healthy lunches, fireside tea and conversation. Participants meet fortnightly for three-month 'seasons' and are welcome to attend however they feel and whether they wish to be involved in any activities. Transport to and from the site is provided, travelling together by minibus.

Each Grow season has included participants experiencing a range of difficulties often accompanied by diagnoses – including bi-polar, borderline personality disorder, schizo-affective disorder, schizophrenia, delusions, psychotic episodes, hearing voices, depression, anxiety, PTSD, eating disorders, OCD and self-harm. Trained project staff and additional volunteers offer a high level of support alongside the peer support that develops within the group. Service-user involvement has been central to the subsequent development of Grow. Previous participants have been recruited as volunteers, and a user-led development group has been integral to the project design and delivery for forthcoming seasons of Grow, including the structure of sessions, which activities are chosen, how participants are supported, volunteer roles, and the design and development of methods of monitoring and evaluation. After being part of a closed group season, people can continue on to Grow's 'drop-in' days, which also offer a wide variety of nature-based activities as well as close links to other nature-based community projects.

That the programme has had positive effects for those involved was widely acknowledged by past and present participants, volunteers and coordinators, and was reflected in the project's own measures of well-being. While there would be value in further quantifying aspects of well-being, the outcome of the project's own feedback mechanisms identified the need for more qualitative data – a requirement slowly being addressed more broadly in a field dominated by quantitative research (e.g. Djernis et al. 2023; Johansson et al. 2024; Richardson et al. 2020). As a result, the project founders and the research team were in agreement that the priority for a small-scale project of limited duration was to explore peoples' own perceptions of the positive effects of participating in Grow in more depth. To this end an initial decision was made to adopt an explorative and qualitative approach to evaluation.

Our research

The research focuses on one iteration of a Grow programme – a 'season', consisting of eight weekly day-long sessions involving a range of outdoor activities, for a closed group of ten participants identifying as suffering from moderate to severe forms of psychological distress. Data collection comprised of three elements: semi-structured interviews, open-ended questionnaires and a focus group. All participants had the option to participate in evaluation and choose the form of responding they felt most comfortable with. All ten participants responded across the three evaluation options. The group was made up of four men and six women, aged between twenty-six and sixty-five. Nine participants identified as white British, one as white Irish or gypsy. To maintain some parity across the evaluation formats, there was a parallel schedule for the focus group, interviews and questionnaires, and a sequence of eight explorative questions was posed.

Following Wilson et al.'s guidance (2011: 7–8), the questions were 'designed to be open, neutral, non-directive and free of jargon'. They were geared towards exploring participants' own perceptions of the benefits of involvement in Grow, and were broadly consistent with a phenomenological approach (Wilson et al. 2011).

The focus groups and interviews were recorded and transcribed verbatim. In approaching analysis, we adopted a version of Gordon, Holland and Lahelma's (2000) three-stage process of interpretative thematic analysis. The first stage (thematic) denotes immersion in the data for the purpose of identifying emerging themes. The second stage (interpretative) requires a return to the data to now interpret content through the themes identified in the first stage. The third stage involves the extraction of illustrations and examples of those themes. Building on the authors' previous experience, we modified these stages by cross-referencing between emerging themes to try and capture the ways in which aspects of participant's talk spoke to multiple themes simultaneously. Findings were subsequently organized around five themes: positivity, nature connectedness, autonomy, belonging and social identity (for further discussion of themes, see Adams and Morgan 2018).

Positivity and nature connectedness

A primary finding was a reiteration of what Grow's existing feedback had strongly indicated: participant's experiences of Grow were overwhelmingly couched in positive terms. In fact, most of the subsequent themes are effectively elaborations on perceived causes and detail of the positive experiences. Nonetheless something can be said about the particular qualities of this experience in general terms. Positivity cohered around related terms of gentleness, stillness, peace and calm.

> *The peaceful environment helps your mind become peaceful in contrast to the hectic city environment which seems to make your mind more hectic.*
> *Life is at a gentler pace than in the town.*
>
> *It helps my mind become more peaceful and calm.*
>
> *The positive emotions and experiences described here are often accompanied by an acknowledgment of their contrast – urban life in the above quotes, or more specifically, 'normal' mental health provision settings:*
>
> *Indoors is really claustrophobic and clinical.*
>
> *[At Grow] there are no tables which always seem like such a barrier. It's much more formal indoors.*

Other comments incorporated peace, stillness and quiet in tandem with the opportunity to focus mind or senses on nature, which leads us to our second theme, nature connectedness. Expressions of a felt sense of connection to nature were often accompanied by hesitation and uncertainty – that this was a difficult experience was put into words. Not surprisingly participants often cited feeling connected to nature as an important part of Grow:

> *Nature walks – learning about the different plants etcetera – it helps you get connected to nature.*
>
> *I really liked foraging and finding things like the wild garlic.*
>
> *The peacefulness and the quietness and the spaciousness and the birds and the sky. The quality of the air was so gorgeous.*
>
> *I just love being around the animals, hearing the birds singing and breathing in the fresh air.*

The emphasis in the final quote on a relational sense of well-being rather than a dyadic 'individual–nature' connection is elaborated in the theme of belonging. These first two themes support existing research highlighting the capacity of natural settings to reduce stress (e.g. Nguyen et al. 2023). Clearly it is possible that people may find natural settings uncomfortable or anxiety inducing, at least initially, especially if they have had little prior experience of such settings (Bixler and Flood 1997).

Autonomy

As noted above, an important element of Grow is the inclusion of service-users in the decision-making processes around how the project is run. Previous and current participants have been involved in planning and organizing Grow seasons. Participants also have the freedom to engage, or not, with the activities on offer on any given day without judgement, to be separate (while support is on hand) or together, and to discuss preferences for future activities. However, the provision of choice was not expressed as an unequivocal 'good':

> *Sometimes I like someone to tell me what to do but I did appreciate the choices given – it helped me be able to make more choices.*

> *Sometimes the choices made me a bit anxious. I was also anxious about missing out on activities if I made 'the wrong choice'.*

Nonetheless autonomy appeared to be highly valued in most participants' accounts of Grow, particularly if it was understood as genuine choice.

> *The choice whether to do an activity or not meant that negative feelings don't escalate. For example there was one exercise which we did one morning. I didn't feel like doing at all because I didn't feel great and having the choice not to do it made me feel not quite so bad and so feelings that could have escalated and got worse quickly just went away.*

> *There are several really deep messages which Grow has reminded me of and made clear to me again and again, in different states and levels of illness and wellness. One of the key messages was – 'come as you are', 'please come as you are however you are', 'please come', 'we would love to have you however you are'.*

> *It's a group out in nature doing some really nice activities but with unconditional acceptance. I was a bit confused by the choice, freedom and complete acceptance of the group to start with because it was so unusual.*

All three quotes here indicate that the positive value attributed to autonomy occurs alongside experiences of unconditional acceptance. This lack of judgement seems vital, as it embraces and encourages choice without normative expectations or interpersonal penalties. It also elides with what we consider to be a progressive recovery model advocated by the Mental Health Foundation among others (Mental Health Foundation, 2021; Adams and Morgan 2018; Wilson et al. 2010). The recovery model moves away from a focus on symptom reduction or removal towards a way of being in the world and the hope for optimal functioning given the vicissitudes of an enduring mental health problem.

Belonging

As stated at the outset, the intention in this chapter is to focus in more detail on the related but less well-understood dynamics of therapeutic green care programmes reflected in the last of our two themes, belonging and social identity. The group therapeutic element of ecotherapy is much less well documented (Smyth et al. 2022), despite the fact that group-based interventions are often advocated in supporting mental health (e.g. NICE, 2020), and are predominant in nature-based practice. Social contact is now emerging as an important dimension of people's own understandings of the benefits of ecotherapy projects they are involved in (Bragg and Atkins 2016), but less so as a central component of green care and ecotherapy provision (though see Rees and Gosling 2020). Participants frequently voiced what felt good about Grow in terms of developing attachments – a sense of belonging, acceptance, safety, that applied to the group.

> *Support from my peers has been really beneficial.*
> *Grow has helped me enjoy meeting new people and made me realise that I'm not so alone – that there are others who have been through similar things.*

> *I enjoyed being able to wander off alone and take pictures but know that I had people to come back to and have the safety of the group.*

> *Safety and security are clearly key leitmotifs, and many participants suggested that this sense of feeling 'held' was in turn a secure basis for some affirming self-reflections, for example:*

> *I used to be a sociable person but when I had my breakdown 2 or 3 years ago people stopped getting in contact with me. I was getting more and more isolated and coming to Grow has made me realise that I can form relationships with people again.*

On the other hand, it must be noted that the social contact integral to Grow was sometimes experienced as difficult:

> *I find it hard in a group sometimes but it's good to challenge yourself.*

> *Check-in and check-out is challenging sometimes.*

It is potentially significant that despite the attendant challenges, for our participants the positive value of belonging and the natural setting were often articulated as interdependent:

> *The natural environment is safer (than) consultation rooms, hospitals are a problem rich area dealing with crisis, that environment is a tricky one to visit because there are so many problems all in one place. Being in a natural environment those problems are all out so its safer there isn't the concentration (of) issues which are spread out a lot wider than it would be in a room and I think that's a big factor being outdoors.*

The ways in which positive group dynamics interweaves with experiences of natural settings take us beyond the consideration of 'social contact' as separate benefit or variable of group-oriented green care (Bragg, Wood and Barton 2013). The appreciation of belonging recounted was often entwined with expressions of feelings of acceptance and openness here aligned with the themes of nature connectedness and autonomy. It is a fascinating area for future research, and one that we address further in our concluding discussion.

Social identity

Broadly speaking, social identity refers to a person's sense of who they are based on their membership of a group (Tajfel and Turner 1979). In placing emphasis on the role of the group, it is claimed that social interactions between two or more people can be viewed as expressions of both interpersonal and intergroup dynamics (Tajfel 1981). The social cognitive origins of social identity theory have given way too many variations on the concept of social identity. Contemporary understandings of social identity tend to incorporate some of the core tenets of social constructionism, allowing for a more fluid, dynamic and situational conceptions of social identity. The challenge here is 'to replace the traditional assumption of individual selves with a vision of self as an expression of relationship' (Gergen 2009: 124). Thus, following Gergen, the term 'relational self' perhaps better captures the aspects of social identity we consider salient in the context of this study.

When asked about previous experiences of mental health service provision, participants commonly elaborated on the previous themes by talking about the kind of experience of self participation in Grow encouraged, often in contrast to the normal environments, habitually indoors, that were supposedly therapeutic.

> *I don't feel like I'm here because I've got mental health issues and so it changes the way I see myself.*

> *With indoor mental health services you are constantly reminded of mental health issues, diagnoses, labels – this isn't the case outdoors. This was a bit strange for me at first – I wanted to talk about my 'label' but now I don't.*

> *It's more about focusing on nature rather than mental health – you only start thinking about mental health issues and your problems when you get near to home again.*

> *You are also not surrounded by posters displaying a whole range of things … All these problems that people can have are there in front of you. Being in an environment where you are not bombarded with problems, there is no clock ticking, that takes way a lot of the pressure and stress.*

Participants here express the value of Grow in terms of it offering an escape from the social and cultural markers of mental ill health, often, ironically, compacted in normal (and indoor) therapeutic settings. Here we potentially broaden our understanding of the benefits of providing nature connectedness, beyond individual psychological functioning, and the supportive dynamics of the immediate group, to the 'softening' of social and cultural reference points that might normally position a person's health as problematic more 'sharply'. This finding again adds to emerging findings in ecotherapy that social contact, and more specifically, supporting and feeling supported by others, both contributes to and is an outcome of the process of reconnecting with nature (e.g. Burls 2007; Rees and Gosling 2020).

Culture, nature, identity

The natural setting of Grow, intertwined with the themes discussed above, appeared to combine to provide an alternative social environment, or set of relations, out of which to forge a sense of self. This is neither to underestimate the obdurate nature of relationship, norms and expectations outside of the setting, nor to make unfounded or exaggerated claims about the endurance of alternative configurations beyond the setting. Nonetheless, participants' own words seem to us to speak to the possibilities of an alternative identity closely tied to the relational dynamics. The informality, 'softness' and openness of the natural settings are expressed as integral to the possibility of alternative understandings of self. At the very least it seems to signify a temporary escape from the relationships, symbolism and discourses of everyday life – a social identity – that routinely 'trap' participants in a particular identity.

Simultaneously, the positive benefits of the natural setting were intertwined with the experience of a supportive group and the exercise of a degree of autonomy not routinely experienced elsewhere. This discovery combines emerging findings that social contact is vital to the process of reconnecting with nature touched upon earlier in this chapter (Bragg, Wood and Barton 2013). It also connects to developments in social theory, human geography and elsewhere that emphasize the entanglement of social and cultural dynamics in experiences of nature (e.g. Bear 2016; Rautio et al. 2020; Castree 2005). There is of course a great deal of variation in what 'social' and 'cultural' is taken to signify, and how these phenomena intersect with each other. There is also a great deal of debate about the extent to which nature is socially mediated or constructed (e.g. Crist 2004). There is not the space here to even begin to address these concerns. Our intention instead is to flag up the possibility that the value of natural settings is derived, in part, by experiencing them as antithetical to problematic everyday social and cultural contexts.

This point can perhaps be better illustrated via a brief example from an earlier study of the benefits of ecotherapy (Mind, 2007). In this study, researchers were keen to measure the health outcomes of being in nature. To this end, in one study, two groups of mental health service users went on a walk. One group walked in a shopping centre, the other in a more natural park setting. Mood and well-being was measured before and afterwards for both groups. From similar baselines, the group walking in nature reported significant improvement on a range of outcomes related to well-being compared to the group in the built environment. The latter reported deterioration on a number of indicators. The project's authors saw this as evidence of the benefits of a natural setting. While we would not dispute this finding, a shopping centre is not a neutral or non-specific exemplar of a 'built' environment in contrast to a 'natural' one. In fact, it carries a great deal of symbolic and semantic load, a place embedded in a range of sociocultural expectations and embodied in myriad of practices. This space, in turn, invokes various forms of identification, recognizing certain aspects of self or their lack. A sociological perspective here is not tangential; it helps explain the disidentification that may be experienced as discomfort in places such as shopping centres, compounding a heightened sensitivity to crowds and noise, and perhaps to the performance of the aforementioned 'preoccupation'. A shopping centre, in other words, is a place laden with normative social and cultural expectations about how to be, and that afford autonomy and choice but only if one has the requisite psychological, economic, social and cultural capital to 'belong' (Boström 2020). At stake here and in many other contemporary places of work, leisure, health and entertainment is the potentially spoiled identity of a 'flawed consumer' (Bauman 2007).

On the other hand, natural settings are less saturated with such expectations. This is not to say that how we come into natural settings is free of normative expectations, or what we experience as nature escapes such mediations. It permits, again potentially, a form of intersubjectivity less dependent on sociocultural prescriptions we may feel we have already been judged by and failed to match up to. Combine this possibility with a supportive group structure and a sense of being held, a form of intersubjective recognition and validation become plausible. Grow participants often commented on how the usual trappings of service provision often reinforced their sense of being unwell. The rich opacity of the natural setting, an abundance of metaphors, alongside the supportive group dynamics, seemed to offer a basis for engagement on a spectrum other than illness–well-being.

Conclusion

We have no hesitation in adding to the increasing calls for ecotherapy to be recognized as a clinically valid treatment for people with diverse lived experiences of mental distress. Access to natural settings and green space is a marker of health inequality nationally and globally (Geary et al. 2021; Sun et al. 2022), so it is equally important that access to these spaces is extended to more people, more of the time. This chapter is intended as another voice, however small, that contributes to the chorus proclaiming the social and psychological benefits of being in natural settings under the right conditions. A number of practices specific to Grow but potentially reproduced in other settings seem to have contributed to the Grow Project's success. If an environment can be fostered where access to the setting is made relatively easy and routinized, and where a sense of safety, love and belonging through effective interpersonal structures and practice is established, then it is likely that an effective holding environment is created. What we hope to have also suggested in this chapter is that those conditions involve social and cultural processes of belonging and identity. Accordingly, more than an individual connecting to an external 'nature' is involved in successful ecotherapy programmes. The talk of our participants articulates the importance of the complex entanglements of natural settings, psychology and the social and cultural contexts that shape identity. More specifically, our participants describe the way users of indoor National Health Service (NHS) services are situated within certain frameworks and narratives of understanding, and how, by regularly attending supportive groups and activities outdoors, alternative frames and narratives can be initiated and explored.

References

Adams, M., and J. Morgan (2018), 'Mental Health Recovery and Nature: How Social and Personal Dynamics Are Important', *Ecopsychology* 10 (1): 44–52.

Bauman, Z. (2007), 'Collateral Casualties of Consumerism', *Journal of Consumer Culture* 7 (1): 25–56.

Bear, C. (2016), 'Socio-nature', in D. Richardson, N. Castree, M. F. Goodchild, A. Kobayashi, W. Liu and R. A. Marston (eds), *International Encyclopedia of Geography: People, the Earth, Environment and Technology*, 1–5, Oxford: Wiley. https://onlinelibrary.wiley.com/doi/10.1002/9781118786352.wbieg0212

Bixler, R. D., and M. F. Flood (1997), 'Nature is Scary, Disgusting and Uncomfortable', *Environment and Behavior* 29 (4): 443–67.

Boström, M. (2020), 'The Social Life of Mass and Excess Consumption', *Environmental Sociology* 6 (3): 268–78.

Bragg, R., C. Wood and J. Barton (2013), *Ecominds Effects on Mental Wellbeing: A Report for Mind*, London: Mind. http://www.mind.org.uk/media/354166/Ecominds-effects- on-mental-wellbeing-evaluation-report.pdf.

Bragg, R., and G. Atkins (2016), 'A Review of Nature-Based Interventions for Mental Health Care', *Natural England Commissioned Reports* 204: 18.

Burls, A. (2007), 'People and Green Spaces: Promoting Public Health and Mental Well-Being through Ecotherapy', *Journal of Public Mental Health* 6 (3): 24–39.

Castree, N. (2005), *Nature*, London: Sage.

Clark, H., J. Vanclay and E. Brymer (2023), 'Forest Features and Mental Health and Wellbeing: A Scoping Review', *Journal of Environmental Psychology* 89: 102040.

Crist, E. (2004), 'Against the Social Construction of Nature and Wilderness', *Environmental Ethics* 26: 5–24.

Dickson, T. J., and T. L. Gray (2022), 'Nature-Based Solutions: Democratising the Outdoors to Be a Vaccine and a Salve for a Neoliberal and Covid-19 Impacted Society', *Journal of Adventure Education and Outdoor Learning* 22 (4): 278–97.

Djernis, D., C. M. Lundsgaard, H. Rønn-Smidt and J. Dahlgaard (2023), 'Nature-Based Mindfulness: A Qualitative Study of the Experience of Support for Self-Regulation', *Healthcare* 11 (6): 905.

Doherty, T. J. (2009), 'Editorial: A Peer Reviewed Journal for Ecopsychology', *Ecopsychology* 1 (1): 1–7.

Drake, R. E., and M. A. Wallach (2020), 'Employment Is a Critical Mental Health Intervention', *Epidemiology and Psychiatric Sciences* 29: e178.

Garside, R., N. Orr, R. Short, B. Lovell, K. Husk, R. McEachan, R. Rashid, I. Dickie, S. Preston and H. Ainsworth (2020), 'Therapeutic Nature: Nature-Based Social Prescribing for Diagnosed Mental Health Conditions in the UK', *Final Report for DEFRA*.

Geary, R. S., B. Wheeler, R. Lovell, R. Jepson, R. Hunter and S. Rodgers (2021), 'A Call to Action: Improving Urban Green Spaces to Reduce Health Inequalities Exacerbated by Covid-19', *Preventive Medicine* 145: 106425.

Gergen, K. J. (2009), *Relational Being: Beyond Self and Community*, Oxford: Oxford University Press.

Gordon, T., J. Holland and E. Lahelma (2000), 'Friends or Foes? Interpreting Relations Between Girls in Schools', in G. Walford and C. Hudson (eds), *Genders and Sexualities: Studies in Ethnography in Education*, 689–706, London: JAI.

Howarth, M., A. Griffiths, A. Da Silva and R. Green (2020), 'Social Prescribing: A 'Natural' Community-Based Solution', *British Journal of Community Nursing* 25 (6): 294–8.

Johansson, G., J. Johansson, Å. Engström and P. Juuso (2024), 'Stakeholders' Perceptions of Value of Nature-Based Interventions in Promoting Health in People with Stress-Related Illness: A Qualitative Study', *International Journal of Circumpolar Health* 83 (1): 2349330.

Kleespies, M. W., T. Braun, P. W. Dierkes and V. Wenzel (2021), 'Measuring Connection to Nature—A Illustrated Extension of the Inclusion of Nature in Self Scale', *Sustainability* 13 (4): 1761.

Layard, R. (2006), 'The Case for Psychological Treatment Centres', *British Medical Journal* 332: 1030–2.

Lee, K. O., K. M. Mai and S. Park (2023), 'Green Space Accessibility Helps Buffer Declined Mental Health During the Covid-19 Pandemic: Evidence from Big Data in the United Kingdom', *Nature Mental Health* 1 (2): 124–34.

Mayer, F. S., and C. M. Frantz (2004), 'The Connectedness to Nature Scale: A Measure of Individuals' Feeling in Community with Nature', *Journal of Environmental Psychology* 24: 503–15.

Menhas, R., L. Yang, Z. A. Saqib, M. Younas and M. M. Saeed (2024), 'Does Nature-Based Social Prescription Improve Mental Health Outcomes? A Systematic Review and Meta-Analysis', *Frontiers in Public Health* 12: 1228271.

Mintz, K. K., O. Ayalon, O. Nathan and T. Eshet (2021), 'See or Be? Contact with Nature and Well-Being during COVID-19 Lockdown', *Journal of Environmental Psychology* 78: 101714.

The Mental Health Foundation (2021), 'Recovery', http://www.mentalhealth.org.uk/help-information/mental-health-a-z/R/recovery/.

Metzner, R. (1991), 'Psychologizing Deep Ecology: A Review Essay', *ReVision* 13 (3): 147–52.

Mind (2007), 'Ecotherapy: The Green Agenda for Mental Health', http://www.ecother apy. org.uk/files/ecotherapy/home/ecotherapy.pdf.

Mind (2014), 'Ecominds', http://www.mind.org.uk/ecominds.

Nguyen, P. Y., T. Astell-Burt, H. Rahimi-Ardabili and X. Feng (2023), 'Effect of Nature Prescriptions on Cardiometabolic and Mental Health, and Physical Activity: A Systematic Review', *The Lancet Planetary Health* 7 (4): e313–28.

NHS (2023), 'Mental Health of Children and Young People in England, 2023 - Wave 4 Follow up to the 2017 Survey', https://digital.nhs.uk/data-and-information/publications/statistical/mental-health-of-children-and-young-people-in-engl and/2023-wave-4-follow-up.

NICE (National Institute for Clinical Excellence) (2020), Generalised Anxiety Disorder and Panic Disorder in Adults: Management, https://www.nice.org.uk/guidance/cg113/chapter/Recommendations#:~:text=%5B2011%5D-,1.2.,%5B2011%5D.

Rautio, P., R. Hohti, R. M. Leinonen and T. Tammi (2020), 'Reconfiguring Urban Environmental Education with "Shitgull" and a "Shop"', in B. Duhn, K. Malone and M. Tesar (eds), *Urban Nature and Childhoods*, 27–38, London: Routledge.

Reese, R. F., and M. Gosling (2020), 'The Group Ecowellness Model of Change: A Conceptual Framework for Facilitating Groups in Nature', *The Journal for Specialists in Group Work* 45 (4): 331–52.

Richardson, M., E. Richardson, J. Hallam and F. J. Ferguson (2020), 'Opening Doors to Nature: Bringing Calm and Raising Aspirations of Vulnerable Young People through Nature-Based Intervention', *The Humanistic Psychologist* 48 (3): 284.

Silva, A., M. Matos and M. Gonçalves (2024), 'Nature and Human Well-Being: A Systematic Review of Empirical Evidence from Nature-Based Interventions', *Journal of Environmental Planning and Management* 67 (14): 3397–454.

Smyth, N., L. Thorn, C. Wood, D. Hall and C. Lister (2022), 'Increased Wellbeing Following Engagement in a Group Nature-Based Programme: The Green Gym Programme Delivered by the Conservation Volunteers', *Healthcare* 10 (6): 978.

Sun, Y., S. Saha, H. Tost, X. Kong and C. Xu (2022), 'Literature Review Reveals a Global Access Inequity to Urban Green Spaces', *Sustainability* 14 (3): 1062.

Tajfel, H. (1981), *Human Groups and Social Categories*, Cambridge: Cambridge University Press.

Tajfel, H., and J. C. Turner (1979), 'An Integrative Theory of Intergroup Conflict', *The Social Psychology of Intergroup Relations* 33: 47.

Taylor, E. M., N. Robertson, C. J. Lightfoot, A. C. Smith and C. R. Jones (2022), 'Nature-Based Interventions for Psychological Wellbeing in Long-Term Conditions: A Systematic Review', *International Journal of Environmental Research and Public Health* 19 (6): 3214.

Watts, R., H. Kettner, D. Geerts, S. Gandy, L. Kartner, L. Mertens, C. Timmermann, M. M. Nour, M. Kaelen, D. Nutt and R. Carhart-Harris (2022), 'The Watts Connectedness Scale: A New Scale for Measuring a Sense of Connectedness to Self, Others, and World', *Psychopharmacology* 239 (11): 3461–83.

White, M. P., S. Pahl, B. W. Wheeler, M. H. Depledge and L. E. Fleming (2017), 'Natural Environments and Subjective Wellbeing: Different Types of Exposure Are Associated with Different Aspects of Wellbeing', *Health & Place* 45: 77–84.

Wilson, N. W., R. Jones, S. Fleming, K. Lafferty, L. Knifton, K. Catherine and H. McNish (2011), 'Branching Out: The Impact of a Mental Health Ecotherapy Program', *Ecopsychology* 3 (1): 51–7.

World Health Organisation (2025), 'Over a Billion People Living with Mental Health Conditions – Services Require Urgent Scale-Up', 2 September, https://www.who.int/news/item/02-09-2025-over-a-billion-people-living-with-mental-health-conditions-services-require-urgent-scale-up.

9

The garden, the wind and the river: Exploring unconscious and lesser-known parts of the self in nature

Claire Lamont

Introduction

This research project grew out of an intuitive yearning, mid-way through my therapy training in 2019, to do some gardening. I started volunteering weekly at an urban community garden, and one day, pausing absent-mindedly in a polytunnel, I looked at a foxglove. Sudden memories bubbled up of when I was eight years old, of foxgloves growing at the top of my childhood garden. I found some understanding in Bollas' (2009: 61) theory of the 'evocative object' – he describes how, 'the objects experienced during childhood will contain parts of the self's experience that will have been projected into the objects as mnemic containers of lived experience'. Did the foxglove contain a part of me from childhood, a lost part that loved the outdoors, the garden, nature? I started to want to get to know these unconscious parts of me more. Emerging from my initial interest and seeing a space in the available ecotherapy literature, I had found a direction for my MSc dissertation project, focussing on two questions:

1. How does being in nature help me get to know myself better, particularly unconscious and tacit aspects of myself?
2. Can I draw out broader conclusions for counselling as a profession? Are there qualitative experiences that explain or expand the power of nature for improving mental health and enabling personal growth?

Methodology

I wanted to work with a research methodology which could open up the parts of myself that are unconscious, non-verbal, or perhaps pre-verbal. The lesser-known parts of me communicate in different ways, and may need different tools. Sela-Smith (2002: 62) describes the pre-verbal nature of this knowledge, driven underground by our conscious selves: 'Changes in flawed tacit knowledge must take place through thought that is connected to pre-verbal, body-based, global experience of wholes rather than reflective reason' – the 'I-who-feels'.

In seeking to uncover some of the tacit aspects of my experience in nature, I decided to use the heuristic research method. Heuristic technique was developed by Moustakas (1990: 15) and offers, 'a way of engaging in scientific search through methods and process aimed at discovery; a way of self-inquiry and dialogue with others aimed at finding the underlying meanings of important human experiences'. This gave me a methodology through which non-verbal knowledge could emerge. Heuristic method grew out of psychotherapeutic research: Rose and Loewenthal (2006: 133) describe heuristic research as, 'a relational research method that facilitates exploration of the lived experience of psychotherapy'. It therefore also fits well with my wider aims of relating my research back to therapeutic practice.

The heuristic method has six stages: an initial engagement, followed by a period of immersion, and then an incubation where the topic is put on hold. After this there is (hopefully) an illumination around the themes and an explication of this, finishing with a creative synthesis (which, for me, was a poem – a very personal thing, and so I have not included it here) (Rose and Loewenthal: 134–5). As my introduction shows, the intuitive pull towards this subject began in an initial gut feeling that I wanted to start gardening, and then continued in the regressive elements of my experience at the garden site. For Moustakas (1990), intuitive knowledge is the bridge that allows us to open up to tacit or implicit forms of knowledge and is therefore a key focus of a heuristic search. As some form of intuitive knowledge had already emerged and guided me to the start of this research, I made it a focus of my own process.

The central immersion period of the research took place from December 2019 to mid-March 2020. While my initial plan was to undertake all of my research at the garden site, as I entered the immersion phase I realized that I was experiencing strong feelings and memories in other natural places too. Throughout the research time I therefore combined a weekly visit to the garden with regular walks on Blackheath and in Greenwich Park, and along the river Thames. I also spent a weekend in Yorkshire.

A heuristic approach has openness and methodological flexibility embedded within it: as Moustakas (1990: 22) says, 'the tacit dimension underlies and precedes intuition and guides the researcher into untapped directions and sources of meaning'. In methodological terms this meant that I attempted to follow the means that seemed to facilitate a connection with embodied knowledge, feelings, or the unknown. I decided that I would spend time at a site – anything from ten minutes to a few hours – with research being the focus of my time and energy in the space. As I formulated my method, I knew that an embodied approach would be important.

My history is of a gradual move away from an academic background towards physical and outdoor work. Van der Kolk (2015: 275) relates this to a movement back to language, reflecting my own developing process: 'People who feel safe in their bodies can begin to translate the memories that previously overwhelmed them into language.' I began to recognize that the work I was doing might involve a re-integration of language and experience, rather than language or intellectual ideas as a defence against experience or feelings.

So, I sought out therapeutic techniques to help me tune into the phenomenological experiences within my body when in the natural sites. I described this in my research journal as I began to get the feel for it, early in the process: 'A conscious letting go as I enter the space. Listen, tune into surroundings. Observe. Feel. Where things arise, let go of them. It's meditation, but active, embodied, moving, with the senses' (Research Journal, 29/12/2019). In formulating my approach I used Gendlin's (2003) and Moustakas' (1990) theories to help me try to locate and hear felt senses within my body. I also found Welwood's (2001: 335) depiction of the unfolding of experience a helpful guide: 'when we can tap into and speak from a diffusely felt sense rather than what we think about it, this allows a fresh articulation of what is true for us that was not accessible or expressible before'. When I combined Gendlin's (2003: 337) felt sense techniques with a dynamic back-and-forth with the articulation of new meanings (in language) then perhaps I could begin to let this unfolding process speak to me, with the aim of creative new discovery.

Data collection and analysis

For data collection at the sites I used a notepad and wrote immediate reflections. I focused on a reporting of my experience, with an openness to what that might mean in the moment. I was open to the spaces and if a leaf or twig spoke to me, I picked it up and got to know it. As the research unfolded, I began to hear sounds more clearly, and so started to use audio recordings on my phone as an aspect of the research.

While this research is situated in a relational milieu, it is centred on my own experience. This highlights a potential limitation of my heuristic research process, as outlined by Rose and Loewenthal (2006: 139): 'For what of [the researcher's] blind spots? What is it that they unconsciously bring to the study that may manifest in counter-transferential issues, issues that have implications for how they hear and interpret the story of the other?' Although their concern is focussed on an interview-based project unlike mine, I see the same concerns applying as I try to open up to my own blind spots and biases. They suggest a supervisor-like support through the data collection and analysis, utilizing the methods that psychotherapy has developed to guard against bias as we do when working with clients. I made use of the supervision process, attending sessions throughout the data collection where I could share work with my supervisor and peers. I also spoke to my own therapist about issues thrown up by the research process, as these had an enormous impact on me emotionally at the time.

One interesting outcome of the research process for me was my experience of the heuristic process itself. For me, there was not one discrete iteration of immersion-incubation-illumination, but it felt like many versions of this process occurred over the research period, and then more occurred during the write-up. Illumination came not as one profound insight as Moustakas (1990) describes it, but as many realizations, some feeling small, some immense. All led to a sense of broader illumination in a transformed relationship with myself, as I felt far more attuned to my feeling states and their nuances. My explication section reflects this process: I present data and analysis together, grouped by thematic clusters which corresponded to particular illuminative moments in the research. Though now organized and presented through the academic lens of discrete, understood experiences, these themes showed themselves in overlapping, messy and confusing ways throughout the research.

The garden: Containment

I have already introduced the therapeutic garden space where I remembered lost childhood memories. It is about an acre in size, a mixture of beds, a greenhouse, polytunnels, ponds and an orchard area with some older apple and pear trees. There are chickens, free to roam during sessions. I volunteered regularly on the site for about eighteen months, helping on a therapeutic horticulture project, and I often experienced it as a haven or sanctuary, separate from its urban setting.

Before I return to the memories these gardens opened up for me, I'll explain more of my history to provide the context of this project. We moved regularly with my mum's job throughout my childhood, and we moved to the house with the significant garden – the one that I remembered – when I was six years old. Then when I was ten, we moved again. I changed schools, and things got very hard. I struggled intensely with the change, and I was bullied. Things got worse when I started secondary school. I was scared most of the time and tried to keep my head down. I struggled to open up to my parents and felt very isolated. Alone and scared, I escaped into an internal world in my head. I made up elaborate stories, had imaginary friends, and lived almost entirely in this fantasy world. This went on in earnest for several years when I was a teenager. I knew that things were very wrong, but I always maintained the illusion that I was functioning. I went to school, I ate, and I slept. But I felt that I was barely alive.

Winnicott's (2005: 36) definition of fantasying is of, 'an isolated phenomenon, absorbing energy but not contributing-in either to dreaming or to living'. The inaccessibility of the inner life forms a dissociative process rather than one of repression. I suspect that this experience shaped my inner life deeply, and I have felt aspects of fantasy in many of my adult relationships – a sense of not being in contact with real feelings and of powerless repetition at times. I think the omnipotence and control I could maintain in my childhood fantasying state remained an important defence in my life, preventing me from feeling able to get close to anyone or anything 'real' – probably because close, emotionally open relationships felt too frightening.

Gardens therefore played an important role for me in reconnecting with the child that I had lost touch with, from before that dissociated time as a teenager. Reflecting in the Rose Garden in Greenwich Park one day, I made this connection:

> *needing to contain myself, so after work I came here. And I ate chocolate honeycomb, like I did when I was 8, from the market. I realised then – ah, she is here. I found a way to comfort and contain myself, the child part of me, unconsciously ... [before I went to the garden] I felt it but didn't let myself feel the pain of it – too deep perhaps. (Research Journal, 23/12/2019)*

I was beginning at this point to recognize the power of gardens as a containing space for me, a space where I can access a childlike part of myself. Brazier (2016: 42) describes how nature holds us: 'The earth is found to be trustworthy and solid ... Connecting with the wild, people discover intrinsic reliability of life and of the earth.'

I wonder about the containing role that the garden played for my eight-year-old self. Before I started therapy I really didn't remember much from before I was ten or eleven years old; reconnecting with my child self has been a cornerstone of my growth, and that moment with the foxglove opened up a wealth of memories. I reflected on this as I took notes in the therapeutic garden early in my research process: 'How do I change this? How do I take the power I need, to feel like my adult self? Is this where I was in the garden ... as a child? I want to cry. Is the garden holding me right now?' (Research Journal, 9/1/2020). At times this feels like a direct plea for Winnicott's (2005: 6) 'holding environment' provided by the mother to the infant. Early parts of my research are littered with this yearning to be contained by the landscape and reflect findings by Schweitzer, Glab and Brymer (2018) that for many people nature can play the role of attachment figure or 'secure base'.

But the garden (and nature more broadly) can also be a place where feelings can be avoided and (perhaps necessarily) denied. Escapism rules, through defences of projection, or a sense of merging. I think of the powerful book *The Peregrine* by Baker

(2017), with its overwhelming sense that Baker seeks (and to some extent achieves) a degree of merging with the birds he so loves over time, what Foster (2016: 6) sees as the explicit pursuit of the annihilation of self and the fantasy of purification that might follow. I know that these elements are front and centre of my experience in nature – perhaps they describe my escape into playful fantasy that I enacted aged eight, or aged eleven to fifteen when I lived to some extent in a fantasy world (I can remember playing out fantasy scenarios when I was in natural spaces). But I had a clear and different intention in this research: It was to be with myself rather than escape, to be curious about what might happen if I let my defences down just a little and see what comes. Solnit (2017: 165) describes this distinction while exploring the human tendency to map terrains, to want to know (and control) the great unknown expanses outside of us, perhaps to fool ourselves into thinking that we know the expanses within us: 'To imagine that you know, to populate the unknown with projections, is very different from knowing that you don't.' I was wrestling with this tension throughout this project, which is, after all, partly about widening understanding.

For me gardens are powerful spaces as they can hold both these elements: A need to control, but also an ability to let go and meet openly what comes. They are places where wildness is always present – weeds grow, borders overrun, snails eat the lettuces – but there is a constant effort at human control and mastery. These tensions are inherent in therapeutic work, and Doherty (2016: 25) highlights the abilities of ecotherapy to hold the tensions of dichotomies between wild and tame, built and natural, inner and outer. For me, there is that most deep tension between wanting to be held and needing to feel free, not overwhelmed, which gardens seem to meet. Bollas (2009: 63) describes this pull towards wild spaces to feel free: 'each person senses something of his or her own unique idiom of being as he or she moves freely through space'. For me gardens are places where I can experience my yearning for containment but also freedom. And that seems to allow me to let down my defences, to let in new experiences and memories.

Playing in the wilds

Visiting ancient woods in south London early in the research, I walked along a path that was fenced on one side and dense with growth on the other. I experienced a strong sense of being trapped in place. I felt suffocated and deeply frustrated. Then the path opened and I escaped into the woods, where I felt like a child, deliberately going 'off the beaten track' and into the undergrowth. I climbed over logs and into hollows. On the bus home, I reflected in my research journal about the experience: 'In the woods, I think I played … Off the track, into brush and hidden paths. Under and over – beneath logs, tracks, mud (so muddy). Messy and not fenced-in' (Research

Journal, 29/12/2019). Back in the therapy room, Meares (2001: 762) describes a sense of spontaneity that can arise when feeling, recognizing and acting on, 'the entrapment imposed by the patient's form of relating' and I wonder if there is an alignment in that clinical experience with my personal experience in the woods. For Meares (ibid: 766), 'the therapist's leap to freedom is often an attempt to maintain his or her own sense of "aliveness" – his or her own self, or personal being, which is stifled by a constrictive intersubjective field'. Was I connecting with my own sense of aliveness through play – not in a therapist's office, but in the woods?

Winnicott's (2005: 72) theory of play describes a creative space outside the individual, but not exactly the outside world; it sits between inner and outer worlds, like the 'potential space' between mother and baby. Psychotherapy is a space for adult play, where one can be creative and perhaps discover different parts of the self. Meares (2001: 759–60) describes the fundamental nature of play in therapeutic technique: 'The kind of activity manifest in symbolic play is the foundation of the sense of "myself". It is this experience toward which therapy is directed.' He relates this to a child's discovery of a 'stream of consciousness' aged four or five – interesting in the context of my attempt at stream of consciousness in my research notes.

It was a powerful part of the research process for me to feel the need to play and be free. Instead of shutting this down I tried to acknowledge it, and to respond by letting myself go, if that impulse struck me. One day in the garden I saw dew on grass and responded to my deep urge to touch it. I reflected in my notes: 'Pick one blade: Hold it, run it through my fingers. Wet, real, tough, soft.' The word 'real' jumps out at me now – this is not the realm of dissociative fantasy. I was, perhaps, relating to this grass in a different, less defended way. A moment later I noted a playful impulse – the salad leaves in the bed I was near looked like a jungle: 'Imagine being tiny, exploring this vast forest' (Research Journal, 23/1/2020). There was a flow in my notes from a sensate experience with the grass, to a spontaneous childlike wonder and playfulness, perhaps linked to the permission I gave myself to touch and explore. This playfulness feels different from my teenage fantasy state. Does it flow from my relationship with the 'real' grass in that moment, seeking connection rather than escape? Maybe the moment of touch awakened an implicit memory of childhood games in the grass.

The wind: Anger

Growing up, my anger felt linked with a Christian moral system – it was a sin. In the past, I simply could not connect with anger easily, creating situations where I would let others take advantage of me, or have sudden outbursts of resentment at people which felt disconnected – like they came from a different person. As my relationship with my therapist developed during my training I started to experience moments of intense feeling during sessions. Often this would show itself as a sense of knowing that I felt a huge amount, but feeling cut off from it. It felt like a ball of rage and sadness, deep in the bottom of my belly. It was there, but I couldn't reach it somehow.

Midway through the research process, I travelled to Yorkshire for a weekend. That weekend was wild, with high winds and grey skies. One day I walked along the raised bank of the River Nidd, battered constantly by 45 mph gusts. I had woken up feeling ambivalent about going out and meeting my feelings, as the research asked of me, but I'd made the trip and I wanted to see the river and fields. I sat on a style at the start of the walk and reflected: 'I understand something of the force of this wind. It has shaped the trees, bushes and landscape … I feel a frustration familiar to me: I don't feel present somehow. The wind says, "come! Feel me. I am real". But some part of me is withdrawn still' (Research Journal, 1/2/2020).

Projecting onto the wind, I was acknowledging a form of the disconnection from my sense of deeper feelings, like the disconnection I had felt in my therapists' office many times. But I walked on, and as I walked along the river I was constantly buffeted by a violent wind that seemed to want to force me off the narrow raised-earth bank. And in meeting that wind, I began to connect with my feelings:

> *The wind asked me again and again: 'Who are you? Where are you? Can you face this – this new place you're in?' I met my silent, furious, sorrowful child. I felt blocked again – the trees, the rage, none of it can come, it gets stuck somewhere in my belly. Then I feel more frustrated … I felt some of the anger. The wind, like that, strong enough to push you over – a natural adversary … Until I walked to meet it, didn't let it push me to the edge of the bank. And then I felt strong, like I could access some power, resilience … And I reached out to that young part of me, felt kind, gentle to her. The wind felt less aggressive, I found a different place. (Research Journal, 1/2/2020)*

The connection I was able to make with my anger on that windy walk allowed me to consciously acknowledge the deep sense of rage I felt, and the profound frustration at my disconnection from myself. And then, through the process of walking, opening up, noticing and responding to the environment around me, I made the connection, and was able to find a softness towards the part of me I named in that moment as my 'furious, sorrowful child'.

This is a therapeutic process – Gill's (1982) re-experiencing of feelings in a new environment – but occurring through relationship with the landscape, rather than in relationship with another person. Marshall (2016: 149) comments on the capacity for nature to 'both aid the process of affect regulation (soothing) … and facilitate an expansion of internal space for reflection on and assimilation of emerging experience'. On this walk by the river, were powerful tacit feelings and memories becoming more conscious? Kelly (2016: 87) suggests how 'wild winds can match our rage; cold mists, our despair. Nature therapy may not always be about wellbeing; it needs also to resonate with our pain'. I'd argue that all forms of therapy are effective only when we can be with a person in their pain, as that landscape was for me that day.

I recognized Jordan's (2016: 65) case study of a client who found eye contact overwhelming, but felt able to open up in the woods walking alongside the therapist (p. 65); he remarks that 'nature can act as another form of object relation'. The natural landscape gave me a space that felt safe enough to access those feelings. What could the wind do in the face of my fury? I knew it would keep blowing, regardless, and that was no judgement or reflection on me. It has left me wondering about the potential for this kind of work with clients for whom human relationships feel very unsafe.

I feel that this inner rage is a part of my wild self that I set out to encounter (Totton 2011). In his famous book about living by Walden Pond, Thoreau (2016: 205) describes his own relationship with the wild:

> We are conscious of an animal in us, which awakens in proportion as our higher nature slumbers. It is reptile and sensual, and perhaps cannot be wholly expelled; like the worms which, even in life and health, occupy our bodies. Possibly we may withdraw from it, but never change its nature. I fear that it may enjoy a certain health of its own; that we may be well, yet not pure.

Thoreau's (Victorian) ambivalence reflects my own fear about letting go and meeting these wilder feelings. Perhaps once I chose no longer to withdraw, and acknowledged my fear, I was able to connect.

Alongside a connection with rage, came connection with sadness, and a sense of mourning which ran through all the research period. Part of my time at the garden was spent mourning for the place, as I knew that I would leave at the end of the research process. The containment of natural spaces suited me: 'I can bear it, can cry. Can cry in those places even when it is hard in front of people' (Research Journal, 28/12/2020). My time in the garden was a safe place for those feelings of grief and sorrow to come to the surface.

Water: Fluid experiences

Thoreau (2016: 175) said of Walden Pond 'it is earth's eye; looking into which the beholder measures the depth of his own nature'. It was on a dark winter's evening walk beside my local river, the Thames, that I had a frightening experience:

> *I went to the river and I walked along it ... and halfway along the walk ... I had a sudden panic that I am not real, was not there, that I could not locate myself in that moment. This terrifies me. At the end of the walk I reached out and gripped the black railings, wet with the dampness of the air tonight, and cold. The metal was solid, reassuring. The*

> *dampness sat on my palms and I rubbed my hands together to remind myself that I am real, am there.* (*Research Journal, 22/1/2020*)

Reading this moment back again still feels frightening – the sense of dislocation from myself, a moment that I am still struggling to describe in words. My switch to the present tense – 'this terrifies me' – perhaps captures some of the immediacy of feelings. The notion of feeling 'real' – or not – had come up again.

Making sense of it now, I turn to transpersonal therapeutic theory – as Clarkson (2003: 189) admits, often the place for the experiences that we simply don't have words for. Hinds (2016: 49) discusses the potential for emotional and spiritual transcendental experiences in nature. I feel uncertain writing about it now – my grasping for theoretical explanations and short sentences perhaps illustrate my sense of being without a clear answer or path. I can suggest theoretical concepts for something that I know was fundamental, but that I still feel more able to describe through the metaphors offered to me by the river – of fluidity, flow, merging, melting, all descriptions of my emotional state that night. In the experiences of water in my research there is a particular sense of merging and fluidity, as if its presence allows for the breaking down of defined affective patterns, my (consciously) known ways of thinking and experiencing. This is profoundly unsettling, but Hinds (2016: 50) describes the potential in these moments: 'Direct contact with nature may lead to a non-dualistic identification which is sometimes a confusing and paradoxical place where opposing emotions can co-occur and there is a blurring of "self" and "other".'

Shepherd (2011: 29) describes freezing as the process wherein water's strength is, 'held and punished'. Reading back through this part of the research, I thought of trauma theory and the nervous system's options under threat of flight, fight – or freeze. Now recognized as a fundamental trauma response in the body, van der Kolk (2015: 72) describes how unresolved threat responses are split off from experience leading to dissociation: 'Blank stares and absent minds, the outward manifestation of the biological freeze reaction.' Merleau-Ponty (2012) saw this experience of 'time standing still' as a defining factor of trauma, as our world becomes frozen by a fear of going into the ambiguity of relating, which feels catastrophically unsafe (Orange 2010: 73).

Responding to Shepherd's (2011) words as I read them at the time, I noted down my own sense of un-freezing as I went into my experience and encountered feelings I felt deeply unfamiliar with – from a state of dissociative withdrawal, to learning how to live again in those feelings. From freezing to that sense of melting and fluidity that described my experience by the Thames that night. Shepherd (2011: 13) describes a transcendent experience of her own standing in remarkably clear water in a loch: 'There was nothing that seemed worth saying. My spirit was as naked as my body. It was one of the most defenceless moments of my life.' Reflecting on Stern's (2010) idea of vitality, Jordan (2016: 66) suggests that it is a 'dynamic teleology, a moving unfolding and relational force of becoming … a constant sense of movement which maintains our sense of being alive'. This dynamic unfolding speaks to me of water, the flow of a mighty ancient river like the Thames. Perhaps paradoxically, this intense and frightening moment of questioning my own reality may have been a formative experience in my own growing sense of vitality.

Relating to and in nature

From the beginning of this research, I have asked myself whether I was undertaking a process that was actually a form of withdrawal. I entered therapy because of my problems with human relationships. But in choosing a heuristic project based on my relationship to nature (and to myself in natural spaces), was I unconsciously withdrawing from human relationships again, a familiar pattern of 'coping by myself'? Over the research process, I realized that something more nuanced was going on. For a start, my research was filled with people. Fellow volunteers and service-users in the garden asked how it was going and reflected on their own experiences in nature. I regularly stayed for lunch after my research time there, and there was a common pattern in my research journal where, following the intense emotional experience of my research process, I would see or meet another person or people and my mood would shift again. I emerge from a place of intense feeling and am almost surprised to find that the people around me now provide some of that holding, the simple interest in me and my well-being. I was letting people in.

The shift in how I related to nature through the research process can also be seen in the voices I let in – like the angry power of the wind that day by the river. As I understand them, my childhood and teenage ways of being involved a highly defended state of maintained fantasy where projection defined my intimate relationships. Growing out of this state involves both the safety of relationships in which to grow alongside the risk of letting people, and the world, in.

The day after my river walk in Yorkshire, I walked around the field next to where I was staying, also bounded by the river. The day was markedly different: It had rained overnight and the sky was overcast, but the world had that sense of freshness, calm after a storm. The wind had gone completely. I felt at peace after my experience the day before and a good night's sleep. On my walk, I encountered a cormorant, sitting elegantly on the top of a huge tree branch: 'Striking, I catch my breath. The beauty of the moment is in its stillness, the muted winter colours, the calm, damp air, the water gently burbling and gurgling. I walk gently closer. Eventually she takes off, powerful wings, down the river. I'm left with a sense of her as I go past the bare tree' (Research Journal, 2/2/2020). The cormorant shifts my feeling state again, and I let in a sense of awe. I unconsciously give her a female power; perhaps this relates to my own sense of self after the day before.

Foster (2016: 206) has similar reflections following his own experimental experience of living as various animals for some time – a fox, a badger, an otter. He links his experience with animals to Buber's (2013) I and Thou:

> I've lived and I live with the fox in an embodied, sensual world of wood and earth and bone and semen and cold. We met and we meet in a real place, and there I've started to use the words 'I and thou'. The 'I' has grown in the encounters, I can tell you. If the 'I' has grown, why not the 'thou'?

Foster (ibid: 209) describes his excitement at the sense that he can, 'know and be known!', both by foxes and by people.

Buber (2013) described how, when we allow the other to speak to us, we are both changed – and as Orange (2010: 21) points out, this involves letting go into uncertainty, allowing for risk, loss and loneliness. We need a partner in this work – since we cannot be unpredictable to ourselves – so we find that in other people, but also sometimes animals and nature. As with people, often this relationship will be based on I–It dynamics; but where we can enter into it with our 'whole being' there is the possibility for genuine meeting and empathy (Orange 2010: 25). I think this was starting to happen for me. Similarly, Shepherd (2011: 107–8) described her years-long relationship with the Cairngorm mountains and how it changed:

> I was not interested in the mountain for itself, but its effect upon me … but as I grew older and less self-sufficient, I began to discover the mountain in itself. Everything became good to me, its contours, its colours, its waters and rock, flowers and birds … And I have discovered that man's experience of them enlarges rock, flower and bird, the thing to be known grows with the knowing.

For Totton (2011: 159), this is the difference between nature being a commodity for us to use (even in therapeutic or healing work), and another stance, 'letting the other-than-human itself perform the therapy'. On occasion, perhaps I was achieving this in my ongoing natural relationships: In my moment with the cormorant, by the river Thames, and with the heath I lived beside. Embodied responses form the basis of my research process, an attempt to attune to presence in the world while healing from the absence of dissociation (Orange 2010: 63). Merleau-Ponty (2012) described this embodied sense of self as, 'a phenomenology of lived experience' where our perceptions of the world are always, necessarily, situated in a wider context. There is a breakdown of the dualism of inner and outer experience. The world is revealed as relational, a state where emotions unfold between us. Macfarlane's introduction to Shepherd (2011: xxiv-xxv) links this to experiences of nature: 'The first law of ecology is that everything is connected to everything else … the world will not fall into divisible realms, as an apple may be sliced, but is instead an unmappable web of interrelations.' I was finding that I could let in experiences, senses, and my relationships with the landscapes around me.

Conclusion

Re-reading and editing this research, four years on, has been an interesting and moving experience. I'm now a full-time indoor and outdoor therapist, with an increasing part of my client work taking place in nature. As I reached the end of my research period in 2020, a contradiction was already opening up within me. I felt increasingly more at home in myself and my landscapes; but at the same time, I also recognized that I felt ready for change. I felt my perceptions widen – in the garden one day, I noticed the view of south London beyond the fence from one aspect: 'There is a wooded hill in the distance, to the west … But I want both: to leave be free, find new adventures – pastures new. And to belong, to find home … I'm ready to leave home again' (Research Journal, 1/3/2020). Perhaps there is something again of the tension of freedom and containment, the strong urge to both belong and to be autonomous, and the profound difficulty in finding a balance. One day I described the sense as 'perspective shift, everything is more complex, beautiful' (Research Journal, 20/2/2020).

Coming back from Yorkshire during the research process, my south London heath felt frustratingly urban and domestic; I wanted more wilderness, hills and fields. A year after finishing the research project, I followed the intuitive pull started by this work and moved to Edinburgh in search of wilder horizons. I followed Nan Shepherd into the mountains of the Highlands, now a regular part of my life here. I am also lucky to live in a city with its own smaller mountains, and I have some clients here who find nothing more therapeutic than a walk along Salisbury Crags.

References

Baker, J. A. (2017), *The Peregrine*, London: HarperCollins Publishers.

Bollas, C. (2009), *The Evocative Object World*, London: Routledge.

Brazier, C. (2016), 'Nature-based Practice: A Buddhist Psychotherapy Perspective', in M. Jordan and J. Hinds (eds), *Ecotherapy: Theory, Research & Practice*, 32–44, London: Palgrave.

Buber, M. (2013), *I and Thou*, London: Bloomsbury Academic.

Clarkson, P. (2003), *The Therapeutic Relationship*, 2nd edn, London: Whurr.

Doherty, T. J. (2016), 'Theoretical and Empirical Foundations for Ecotherapy', in M. Jordan and J. Hinds (eds), *Ecotherapy: Theory, Research & Practice*, 12–31, London: Palgrave.

Foster, C. (2016), *Being a Beast: An Intimate and Radical Look at Nature*, London: Profile Books.

Gendlin, E. (2003), *Focusing: How to Gain Direct Access to Your Body's Knowledge*, London: Ebury Press.

Gill, M. M. (1982), *Analysis of Transference, Volume 1: Theory and Technique*, Madison, CT: International Universities Press.

Hinds, J. (2016), 'Eudemonic Philosophy and Human(istic)-nature Relationships', in M. Jordan and J. Hinds (eds), *Ecotherapy: Theory, Research & Practice*, 45–57, London: Palgrave.

Jordan, M. (2016), Ecotherapy as Psychotherapy – Towards an Ecopsychotherapy', in M. Jordan and J. Hinds (eds), *Ecotherapy: Theory, Research & Practice*, 58–69, London: Palgrave.

Kelly, D. (2016), 'Working with Nature in Palliative Care', in M. Jordan and J. Hinds (eds), *Ecotherapy: Theory, Research & Practice*, 84–97, London: Palgrave.

Marshall, H. (2016), 'A Vital Protocol – Embodied-Relational Depth in Nature-Based Psychotherapy,' in M. Jordan and J. Hinds (eds), *Ecotherapy: Theory, Research & Practice*, 70–82, London: Palgrave.

Meares, R. (2001), 'What Happens Next? A Developmental Model of Therapeutic Spontaneity: Commentary on Paper by Philip A. Ringstrom,' *Psychoanalytic Dialogues* 11: 755–69. doi: 10.1080/10481881109348641.

Merleau-Ponty, M. (2012), *Phenomenology of Perception*, London: Routledge.

Moustakas, C. (1990), *Heuristic Research: Design, Methodology, and Applications*, London: Sage Publications.

Orange, D. M. (2010), *Thinking for Clinicians: Philosophical Resources for Contemporary Psychoanalysis and the Humanistic Psychotherapies*, London: Routledge.

Rose, T., and D. Loewenthal (2006), 'Heuristic Research', in D. Loewenthal and D. Winter (eds), *What is Psychotherapeutic Research?*, 133–44, London: Karnac Books.

Schweitzer, R. D., H. Glab and E. Brymer (2018), 'The Human–Nature Experience: A Phenomenological-Psychoanalytic Perspective', *Frontiers in Psychology* 9: 1–12. doi: 10.3389/fpsyg.2018.00969.

Sela-Smith, A. (2002), 'Heuristic Research: A Review and Critique of Moustakas's Method', *Journal of Humanistic Psychology* 42: 52–88.

Shepherd, N. (2011), *The Living Mountain*, Edinburgh: Canongate Books.

Solnit, R. (2017), *A Field Guide to Getting Lost*, Edinburgh: Canongate Books.

Thoreau, H. D. (2016), *Walden*, London: Penguin Books.

Totton, N. (2011), *Wild Therapy: Undomesticating Inner and Outer Worlds*, Ross-on-Wye, UK: PCCS Books.

Van der Kolk, B. (2015), *The Body Keeps the Score: Mind, Brain and Body in the Transformation of Trauma*, London: Penguin Books.

Welwood, J. (2001), 'The Unfolding of Experience,' in K. J. Schneider, J. F. T. Bugental and J. F. Pierson (eds), *The Handbook of Humanistic Psychology*, London: Sage Publications.

Winnicott, D. (2005), *Playing and Reality*, London: Routledge.

Part III

Practice

10

A vital protocol: Embodied-relational depth in ecopsychotherapy

Hayley Marshall

Introduction

I knew I would become an ecopsychotherapist when, with the sea on one side, and the mountains on the other, the wilderness immersion group I was a member of began to reflect on the powerful happenings from the previous two hours. We had just experienced a turbulent journey by canoe around a headland where the sea had become a bit rougher than anticipated; and although there was a lot of anxiety and anger being expressed in the group about the practicalities concerning this, people were also directly in touch with some very profound personal issues. At the time, I was in contact with a sense of my own physical inadequacy and vulnerability in the world in a way I'd never quite managed to access in the many years of personal therapy I'd undertaken by this point. I was both disturbed and amazed at the immediacy of this process.

As I write this, I realize just how much I assimilated the learning from this experience within my body. Essentially, I think this was because of the group's live focus on physical engagement with the land *and* the resultant group process. This seemed to offer a direct route into what I would view as the fundamental aspects of my sense of self. I am also conscious of how much I associate this life-changing experience with the landscape it took place in – the landforms leaning into the embodied learning happening for me at the time.

My decision to go on the immersion trip was prompted by a desire to breathe new life into my work. After many years as an indoor Transactional Analysis psychotherapist, I was struggling with the sedentary nature of the work – I knew I wanted to get moving. There were also aspects to the therapeutic process that felt frustrating to me, specifically in terms of helping clients access and transform what I would term the deeper aspects of their personal process – their intrinsic 'ways of being' in the world. I wanted to develop a deeper, more relationally active approach.

The experience I had on that trip laid firm foundations for my subsequent outdoor clinical focus, following two strands. Firstly, an interest in the way we organize our personal experience in the somatic (of the body) non-conscious domain, and how these aspects may be evoked and worked within outdoor ecopsychotherapy through an emphasis on movement and vitality. And secondly, the dynamics that come alive in the relational matrix when working with other living beings – who David Abram (1996) terms 'the more-than-human' – who in therapeutic terms, I would name as the *living third* (Jordan and Marshall 2010). Both aspects relate to the notion of embodiment in therapy, more generally, that is, giving a new living shape or form to personal experience.

In this chapter, I follow the first of these two interweaving paths and attempt to shine a light on the process of outdoor ecopsychotherapy as viewed through an embodied-relational lens. Referring to some of the subtleties and intimacies from an actual ecopsychotherapy process, I explore how embedding therapy within the more-than-human offers the potential to evoke early relational experiences and traumas through the sensory impact on the body–mind and the increased physical movement within the therapeutic relationship. In addition, I link findings from environmental psychology concerning our innate responses to nature with how the living third can both aid the process of affect regulation (soothing) in therapy and facilitate an expansion of internal space for reflection on and assimilation of emerging experience.

The outdoor therapeutic place – setting the scene

Over the past eighteen years following the formative experience described in the introduction, I have developed an outdoor ecological psychotherapeutic practice – ecopsychotherapy for short! (For nomenclature of the many different types of ecotherapeutic practice see Key and Tudor 2023). I work with individuals for ecopsychotherapy and eco-supervision outside with my local land. I also facilitate an extensive range of outdoor training courses and groups for therapists and other human relations practitioners who want to develop their ecological practice in both urban spaces and places that have a less obvious human presence.

With clients and supervisees, my work nests in a large patch of open access (to the public) countryside on the edge of the town in northern England where I live. Having developed a close, intimate relationship with this land, the place offers me, among many other things, important holding in my clinical work (Marshall 2014, 2023). This land (see Figure 10.1) comprises large tracts of mixed woodland incorporating very old beech trees, some flatter ground with tracks and paths, streams and waterfalls, a nature reserve with ponds, and then steeper climbs up to wilder open moorland and rocky edges, affording wide-ranging views across a wider landscape. There are people walking their dogs and running here (they too, as part of nature, become part of the therapy!), but there are also plenty of more secluded areas in which to gain privacy.

Most of my work is conducted on the move; there is some sitting and standing, but usually we are walking and talking, interacting with the landscape and the happenings around us. The place described in bald terms here certainly flows in and out of the human-to-human therapeutic conversation in an explicit sense. However, I also understand it to be part of the implicit (non-conscious and wordless) dialogue that is going on in ecopsychotherapy all the time (Marshall 2016, 2021a). Therefore, although the place forms a discrete obvious relational element in some aspects of my work, its vibrancy and intelligence infuses the therapy throughout.

This psycho-physiological process has important implications, inevitably calling for a rich, developed attention to the somatic domain of the therapeutic process. A significant theme has been how some clients connect physically with key, profound, emotional experiences in relation to the place and to me, the human therapist. These appear to be intensified by interaction with the dynamic processes of the more-than-human, often experienced with a sense of immediacy.

Figure 10.1 My outdoor therapeutic place.

An ecopsychotherapy where considerable therapeutic potency was gained through attending to these somatic, non-conscious processes was with my client Fiona.

Fiona struggled in her adult life with generally feeling worthless and physically 'useless'. She had strong feelings about her body, feeling that it was 'ugly and lets me down'. She described feeling emotionally and physically vulnerable around others. She reported that although she often felt 'closed down', she had a 'strong spiritual connection to nature', it being the one place she felt 'vaguely okay' about herself.

Fiona – sensory awakenings

It's mid-spring and in a session early in the work, we are walking up the track. Fiona is commenting on how happy she is that there are so many trees and how loudly the birds are singing. She is feeling really excited by the noisy cascading water that is in evidence, owing to recent heavy rainfall. She says she feels that she 'is opened up and alive' when she's out here. She feels more alive in this therapy than she has before, comparing it to some previous indoor therapy. I am noticing how excited I feel about being here with her today, even though I've just had a session with another client, in this same place, where I'd felt rather flat. I note that I too am feeling very tuned in to the vigour present in the environment. She also notices this, smiling as she says to me at one point, 'You really *seem to like it out here!' As well as listening to her, I am also aware of her style of movement. She seems eager to keep up with me, yet at the same time not quite certain of where to place herself. She keeps trying to turn sideways and adjust her pace to match mine. I begin to experience a sense of unease and awkwardness in my own body and feel unsure about whether to keep my own pace or try to match hers. As a result, our walk up the path, although enthusiastic, is also somewhat stilted!*

Vitality

In the traditional therapy room, there is a limited range of movement, textures, colours, sounds and smells to focus on. This facilitates a particular type of relational attention necessary for some clients helping them to connect with and hold their internal experience. By contrast, in outdoor ecological work the physical 'container' for the therapy is a range of dynamic and living processes, brimming with motion and vitality. This setting calls for a sharpening of the senses – an organismic 'switching on' – involving a more active level of engagement for both therapist and client. Like Fiona, many clients report a sense of 'coming alive', particularly in the early stages of the work, as they relate with the world around them through increased sensory interaction and awareness. The example illustrates that this also happens for the therapist too. My experience has been that working outside in a place full of the more-than-human supports my aliveness within the therapeutic process. This, then, is therapy in a vitalizing space, where I think that the participants are effectively being 'tuned up' to hone in on movement and process.

In his writing about forms of vitality, Stern (2010) elegantly portrays how we relate to and make meaning of the world surrounding us through the cross-modal (multisensory) languages of movement. In foregrounding the primacy of movement in our basic sense of who we are, Stern argues that vitality forms provide the fundamentals of our felt experience. They are the 'how' or 'style' (not content specific) of what happens as we think, feel, speak, move and relate. This is part of our non-conscious sensing of others and the world around us, the way we know the movement essence of others and reveal ours to them. He describes our experience of vitality as 'a fundamental dynamic pentad'. This consists of *movement*, bringing with it a perception of *force(s)*, then a sense of *space* in which the movement happens, also, a sense of *time* profile, and finally, a *direction or intentionality* (going somewhere).

The case vignette illustrates the early stages of a vital bond with the place – the living third. Although Stern does not discuss our connection with the more-than-human through vitality forms, he does ponder briefly on the fact that they do probably 'correspond with realities in nature that may not exist independent of the mind', positing that we do tend to see all dynamic events in these terms. As the place (with its myriad of interconnecting elements) is already on the move, the therapeutic dyad is certainly surrounded by many different forms of vitality. There is therefore much to attune to, as both other human and more-than-human forms of life layer their way into our minds and bodies. This vital resonance is a significant part of building what I term the *vibrant alliance* between client, therapist and the place in ecopsychotherapy (Marshall 2016, 2021a). With Fiona, I also think it was important that I experienced the work as full of excitement and vigour as she did, as it proved to be a way of forming the human-to-human aspect of the ecological therapeutic alliance.

The important consideration in the forging of a vibrant alliance, though, is that it seems to root both therapist and client more firmly in their bodies, offering instant access to the immediacy of bodily experience. Returning to Stern's ideas concerning vitality forms, this potentially places the therapist in a position of being able to really feel and understand the live 'movement signature' of the client they are working with, and all that can offer. With Fiona, through feeling the vitality in the place I also felt a heightened sense of her physical style as we walked. As a result, I began to catch her movement process through observing her awkwardness and feeling a resonance with this in my own body. My hunch was that this seemed to reflect part of an issue she came to therapy with, namely her relational vulnerability. I view all this as an enlivening of my somatic countertransference through sensory contact with the place, an opening of a powerful channel for really 'knowing' my client.

The vitality in an outdoor space full of the more-than-human invites a dynamic resonance that has the power to evoke all kinds of important experiences. Through this process a therapeutic portal is opened to the implicit, non-conscious layers of experience for both client and therapist.

Non-conscious, implicit 'knowings'

The implicit memory system is the realm in which our earliest experiences of the world are processed and organized. It contains sensorimotor, sub-symbolic (Bucci 1997) and emotional processes, essentially forms of 'knowing', such as implicit relational knowing (Lyons-Ruth 1998). Allen (2009) describes these early organizing mental processes as 'prerepresentational protonarratives, relational knowings involving self-with-others which may later be expressed in sensations, feelings, and interpersonal behaviours, but the person involved has no sense that he or she is remembering' (Allen 2009: 187).

These non-conscious, somatic, non-verbal ways of organizing experience continue throughout life and are experienced with immediacy in the here and now. They coexist with the later developed explicit memory systems. The latter forms the basis for our conscious factual, autobiographical and verbalizable perspectives on our world, which bring with them an internal sense of something being recalled.

The implicit aspect of our functioning, although out of awareness, is systemic and organized, and provides important channels of learning, sensing and being that continue to develop throughout life, forming a significant aspect of everyday functioning. However, non-conscious experience also contains kernels of past experiences that are more fixed, unprocessed and dissociated. These are the elements that are often the most influential in terms of problems we bring to therapy and typically out of awareness, are the most difficult to access and transform. Known in Transactional Analysis theory as the protocol, they correlate to the repressed dynamic unconscious.

Fiona – 'hostile' stirrings

On a chilly autumn day, Fiona and I are sitting on a rock by the side of one of the streams. We are both engrossed in her story about something that has happened for her recently. However, I suddenly become aware of how cold I feel, and then, with a jolt, I realize that she doesn't have a coat on! I feel a bit appalled that I hadn't noticed this until now and start wondering about the significance of this 'ignoring' of the situation. I notice how she's pulling her cardigan gradually tighter and tighter around her and ask her how she's doing with the temperature out here. She smiles, saying that she's fine and that she doesn't feel the cold. She flatly refuses the tentative offer of my scarf! As we continue to sit, my discomfort grows as she seems to be 'holding herself together' against the increasingly inclement weather. Soon it begins to drizzle, and I suggest we go back and sit in one of the cars as I am concerned that she will get too cold.

Back in her car, Fiona describes how after trying to ignore things, she had eventually begun to connect with just how cold she was feeling and reported experiencing a strong sense of the 'hostility' of the environment. She cries as she realizes it felt like being 'under attack'. She also reported that she felt she couldn't admit to me that she needed to get warm. It was like it wouldn't be okay to do this as I might also 'turn on her', even though I'd seemed concerned about how she was doing. She says that what is powerful for her right now is the fact that she was in touch with all of this through her body.

In relation to the weather, Fiona began to connect on a felt level with a sense of being attacked by others. This, it transpired, was something that she'd not ever fully accounted for before. There was a clear link with her early history, that is, being in a family where bullying was the relational norm.

The protocol concept

Eric Berne (1972), writing about the unconscious organization of early childhood experiences, described 'primal protocols' evocatively as 'echoes of the original situation'. I understand protocol as an unconscious aspect of non-conscious experience reflecting traces and shadows of problematic past encounters with self, others (human and more-than-human) and the material physical environment. I relate this to Cornell's (2010) thinking that protocol represents an 'incorporation of the environment that the child grows up in'. Providing the essence for the later-formed life script (Erskine 2009), these experiences are deeply held within our sub-symbolic (nonverbal), body–mindscapes. They profoundly influence our everyday functioning, as well as offering invaluable information about the relational atmosphere of our earliest times.

Fiona's experience on this level was the beginning of an understanding within her body of early relational trauma – a 'somatic knowing' (Allen 2003) – a felt sense of *how things are in the world*. I view this process as the unearthing of a deeply embedded way of being on a protocol level. In our session, she had a lived experience of 'needing' (and the associated 'ignoring' of this by both her and me) amid a 'hostile' environment (the weather). In essence, she was gaining a physical glimpse of the relational environment of her childhood.

In my work outside, I have noticed that access to protocol experiences generally appears to occur more readily and spontaneously because of the impact of a more dynamic environment on the human body–mind (Marshall 2014). Direct encounter with self-willed, more-than-human others invites an increased sense of immediacy, offering the therapeutic dyad a potential new pathway into the world of the client's protocol. Therefore, a vital access is gained to the sensory shapes of these protocol experiences as they begin to reveal themselves from a stimulated non-conscious layer in an intensified form. In Fiona's case this manifested as her sense of being 'under attack'.

Due to it being part of the implicit memory system, our experience of protocol is present centred; so as happened with Fiona, this is a living process rather than something just talked about, although this may well happen too. Bringing protocol alive involves activation, and an opportunity to work with what Bucci (2008, 2021) calls 'the affective core' of the internal relational world, through sensory and bodily experience.

Interaction

There are also implications for ecopsychotherapeutic work at the protocol level once the therapist is involved in an even more active physical process with the client. In my experience and that of other practitioners (Holland 2010; Jordan and Marshall 2010; Ray 2010), there is further potential for an increase in immediacy once this occurs, as the therapy is now an active process – therapist and client out in the world.

It seems that moving together in a terrain where the body is already highly stimulated by the immediate context puts us in a prime position to access more of our somatic experience. A huge amount of 'information' is now available both to the client and the therapist in the form of a vast range of somato-sensory phenomena – our breathing, muscle tone, pulse, skin colour, mucous membranes, viscera, facial expressions, smells, pulse and style of movement, bodily tension, and so on. Although clearly also evident in the therapy room, once moving within a vital living place, both client and therapist's 'somatic infrastructure' (Cornell 2003) are revealed in an intensified active form, and so here again I think that there is ample potential space for exploration of protocol experience.

Returning to Stern, I find the vitality forms concept useful in understanding the 'language' of protocol, particularly when working on the move outside. With reference to the work of the Boston Change Process Study Group (2010), Stern elaborates on the role of vitality dynamics in how we internalize and identify with the 'other' involved in an experience, clarifying that what we take in are dynamic forms of vitality (the movement styles, shapes and essences) from an interactive experience. So, this includes how others were when around us, reflected through behaviour, feelings and attitudes; and as can be seen in the next case example, how they have made us feel in response. This is the *felt shape* of relating. Stern views dynamic forms of vitality as pathways to access non-conscious experience and therefore as an important way of opening the past. Following the trail of a facial expression, breathing style, bodily gait and emphasis through speech or hand gesture can open a whole landscape of past experience. Traces of these past vitality forms are held in our implicit memory system, so 'the sharing of another's vitality forms is probably the earliest, easiest, and most direct path into another's subjective experience' (Stern 2010: 43).

In ecopsychotherapy, therapists have golden opportunities to explore a somatic immersion in the dynamic experiences of their clients, consequently finding out more about the lived physical reality of their past and present worlds.

Fiona – 'the runt of the litter'

Throughout our work to this point, we had explored Fiona's relationship with her own body, which she felt to be letting her down much of the time. In a winter session several months into our work, Fiona and I are walking a narrow path up the hill; she is talking about events in her week. However, what stands out for me is my sense of her straining her body to keep up, even though we are moving slowly. I begin to feel tightness in my stomach, as she seems to be trying to shove her body forward alongside mine. I am suddenly aware that I feel very physically capable and powerful. I muse on the significance of all this happening in my body as she continues to talk, and I notice that I am also beginning to feel some level of irritation with her and, interestingly, an urge to push her!

I reflect aloud about some of my experience with her. There is a moment of silence in which she appears to flush, and I wonder if this has been too much, too soon. However, she seems to take my lead and begins to recount her experience of her body, especially in relation to mine. She says that she experiences mine as a strong, competent body capable of walking with ease up the hill, and hers as a useless body that lets her down at every juncture. She says, 'I'm letting you down, because I can't even walk up this hill properly.'

We stop, as she begins to feel 'shaky and nervous' about sharing these feelings with me. We stand together as I invite her to stay with what's happening, and then she cries, expressing frustration and hatred of her body that 'won't do what it's meant to' and how she feels 'useless'. In this moment, she connects to being what she eventually describes as 'the runt of the litter' in her large family and to her physical sensations of being violently rejected: 'It's like I'm no good ... the others are always after me,' she says.

For Fiona, this is a fuller expression of her protocol level. Through her manner of moving her body (the straining and shoving) as a way of keeping up with me, I seemed to sense something powerful from her. Pursuing this path led to her connecting with an early way of being in the world in relation to other more domineering members of her family.

As described in the previous examples, Fiona's protocol was present in embryonic form in the early sessions (as we first walked up the track) and gradually became more and more embodied throughout the therapy. At this point in the work, her sense of worthlessness, physical weakness and vulnerability in relation to others is captured with greater physical intensity during our walk up the hill.

In terms of my somatic countertransference, I think both my feeling a level of aggression towards Fiona within my body and my external reflection upon this were significant in her accessing her protocol experience. This demonstrates the potential increased capacity of the therapist to 'know' the client through moving around in an outdoor natural context. As we walked up the hill, I connected with a clear sense of how Fiona functioned with others in the world, influenced by her protocol. So, the therapist can use his or her own moving and enlivened body to help make sense of what's happening for the client on a protocol level. This involves working in what is effectively an intensification of the somatic transferences between therapist and client.

If Fiona and I had been working in a room, we may well have come to this same point, but I believe we arrived there more quickly via a direct physical route outside, and in a way that was hugely powerful for this client's therapy, as significantly, her story was about living in a physically threatening world.

A place for regulation and reflection

One of the important implications of working outdoors with protocol in the manner explored in this chapter involves thinking about how to support clients to regulate and assimilate (through linking cognitively) their previously dissociated experiences (Marshall 2021b, 2023) Although the relationship with the psychotherapist is, of course, important in this, the more-than-human world as well as offering green potency in evoking these depth processes, can also provide some assistance in managing what Bucci (2008, 2021) refers to as the *referential process*.

Research evidence, much of it from the field of environmental psychology (Pham and Sanocki 2024; Berman and Schertz 2019; Herzog et al. 1997; Kaplan 1995; Heerwagen and Orians 1993; Wilson 1993; Kaplan and Kaplan 1989; Ulrich 1983), demonstrates that part of the sensory engagement we experience in relation to more-than-human spaces seems to happen for us as innate restorative responses to the variety of natural stimulus presented. We are naturally equipped to function and to 'survive' in these settings, so we are predisposed to focus on living processes (Wilson 1993). This in turn restores our brain functioning and physiology (Kaplan and Kaplan 1989; Ulrich 1983), readying us for effective responses to the immediate demands of our environment. From this ever-growing body of research, there are two key concepts that I find useful in relation to ecopsychotherapy, as they provide some clue as to how the more-than-human world may help us to self-regulate in relation to our traumatic experiences and offer a new 'way of being with' our protocol.

Firstly, Ulrich's (1983) psychophysiological stress recovery theory highlights the genetic ability we possess to affect a swift recovery from the fight-or-flight response to threat. Involving the limbic system of the brain, natural settings, or even pictures or sounds from nature have been shown to lower heart rate, reduce blood pressure, lower anxiety and increase feelings of well-being. I view this process as relevant in regulating affect (Marshall 2021, 2013; Jordan 2009; Allen 2003; Fonagy et al. 2002) while in a state of arousal, happening when protocol processes are surfacing. Although this regulatory process is ongoing throughout ecopsychotherapy on the implicit level, there are times when a more specific explicit focus on the client's connection with the place can also be beneficial (Marshall 2021b).

Fiona – supportive 'other'

It's a warm summer day, and Fiona and I are standing on the side of a hill. She is expressing some sadness about the losses connected with living in such a hostile family environment. She seems to be holding her body rather tensely. Thinking that she may need more support, I offer her the opportunity to sit down in the bracken surrounding us. We both sit down, and as Fiona decides to lie further back in the bracken, she moves more deeply into what she's feeling.

Later she reports that she felt she could really let go and feel what she needed to, knowing both that I was there, and that the place was supporting her.

The second significant concept is 'soft fascination', developed by Kaplan and Kaplan (1989), whereby the natural environment is found to offer the optimum conditions for attentional recovery within the brain (occurring in the frontal cortex) and for clearing the mind, thus providing increased internal space for absorption of and reflection upon emerging experience. This is important, as our natural response to being in direct contact with the more-than-human world can then facilitate the potential to bring a more conscious and new symbolic processing to protocol experience.

Fiona – an overview

In summer, towards the end of our sessions, Fiona and I decide to walk halfway up the hill. As we look out together over the landscape, she reflects on where she's been, both physically and emotionally. She points out the places we've done our work, especially places associated with things feeling 'almost unbearable' and comments on what happened and what's changed for her as result. She reflects on how she can still revisit 'these places' but that she can also 'get up high and gain perspective' thereby responding differently to others and to herself.

Bringing all this together, I find the work of Allen (2009) useful here in his thinking about different therapeutic emphases relating to three different neural networks in the brain. He considers that the greatest psychological growth occurs through 'simultaneous activation' and integration of limbic (subserving attachment, emotion and safety), neocortical (for cognition), and medial pre-frontal (concerned with response-ability, intuition, mentalizing, mindfulness, introspection and autobiographical processes) networks. As we facilitate the opening of the protected landscapes of protocol to a new kind of 'knowing', the more-than-human offers a significant positive impact on the process of integration. It appears that the qualities and processes contained within the external spaces of the more-than-human can help promote an expansion of an *internal space* that incorporates both self-reflective processes and an internal ability to regulate internal states (Marshall 2014, 2021b). This allows for a new kind of relating, initially, to self, as the natural setting may help facilitate clients to find a more fluid response to the trauma of their protocol experience. The person is then also opened anew to the wider world (both human and more-than-human).

Transformation at protocol level

Moving around out in the world seems to bring the protocol aspect of our psyche alive. As the elements of our protocol tumble their way out of our internal landscape, they are played out within the external landscape – reflected though our bodies and in our style of relating with the place and the therapist. As demonstrated in the work with Fiona, my experience has been that working outside can help facilitate clients to inhabit the shape – the dynamic vitality – of their protocol, felt within their body. I see the nature of ecopsychotherapy at this level as an exploration of clients' process, that is, of how things 'happen' for them, as well as a provision of a space for them to develop a new kind of 'knowing' of themselves, others and the world around them. Cornell and Landaiche (2006) state that protocol can 'be brought into awareness, understood and lived within', and as a result, opened 'to new experience and action'. In this sense, then, change at protocol level is a form of reorganization on a sub-symbolic implicit level.

Fiona – changes

In a final session, as we move around the place saying our goodbyes, Fiona reflects on how she's developed a stronger connection with her own body. This means both a realization of how she's been treating it and how she's begun to take care of herself better. For her this has simply 'started to happen', as she's gradually felt better about herself. She's also feeling 'slightly stronger' in her relationships with others, more able to ask for what she needs and feel okay about doing that. For her, these changes are not so much conscious behavioural ones but seem to arise from a more 'solid place' inside of her. She comments on how important the relationship with me has been in this process, but that also she feels very physically connected to the place we've worked in and that this is something she will also be holding inside her as she leaves therapy.

An important element in this final vignette is the significance of the place in the reorganization process for Fiona, and how it seems that this vibrant 'other' has now become part of a new embodied sense of her 'self-in-the-world'.

Conclusion

Introducing the more-than-human into the therapeutic encounter can provide for some powerful possibilities, especially at the depth level of personal transformation. An unseating of protocol evoked by walking from the therapy room out to the natural world, potentially enables the therapeutic dyad to engage with the robust direct experience of living.

Our innate responses to being outside can elicit somatic knowing not always easily accessible in the more static environment of the therapy room. This, coupled with a more physically active therapeutic experience, can offer up an increased sense of immediacy and vitality within the process. In ecopsychotherapy, clients are prompted to open themselves to new experience – to begin to breathe the flow of life into their halting self-limiting processes. Out in the world 'anything can happen'; so, both the creative ways in which they hold the world at bay *and* new prospects can be clearly felt and explored.

The perpetual relationality in the living context effectively moves the therapy into a process-oriented mode, enabling a richly embodied ecological intelligence to be brought to the work.

References

Abram, D. (1996), *The Spell of the Sensuous: Perception and Language in a More-Than-Human World*, New York: Vintage Books.

Allen, J. R. (2003), 'Concepts, Competencies, and Interpretative Communities', *Transactional Analysis Journal* 33: 126–47.

Allen, J. R. (2009), 'Constructivist and Neuroconstructivist Transactional Analysis', *Transactional Analysis Journal* 39: 181–92.

Berman, M. G., and K. E. Schertz (2019), 'Understanding Nature and Its Cognitive Benefits', *Current Directions in Psychological Science* 28 (5): 496–502.

Berne, E. (1972), *What Do You Say After You Say Hello?*, London: Corgi Books.

The Boston Process Change Study Group (2010), *Change in Psychotherapy: A Unifying Paradigm*, New York: Norton.

Bucci, W. (1997), *Psychoanalysis and Cognitive Science: A Multiple Code Theory*, New York: Guildford Press.

Bucci, W. (2008), 'The Role of Bodily Experience in Emotional Organisation: New Perspectives on the Multiple Code Theory', in F. Sommer Anderson (ed.), *Bodies in Treatment: The Unspoken Dimension*, 51–76, New York: Analytic Press.

Bucci, W. (ed.), and W. F. Cornell (2021), *Emotional Communication and Therapeutic Change*, New York: Routledge.

Cornell, W. F. (2003), 'Babies, Brains and Bodies: Somatic Foundations of the Child Ego State', in C. Sills and H. Hargaden (eds), *Ego States* (*Key Concepts in Transactional Analysis Contemporary Views*, 28–54, London: Worth.

Cornell, W. F. (22 June 2010), 'Protocol', Workshop presentation in Mobberley, Cheshire, UK.

Cornell, W. F., and M. Landaiche III (2006), 'Impasse and Intimacy: Applying Berne's Concept of Script Protocol', *Transactional Analysis Journal* 36 (3): 196–213.

Erskine, R. (2009), 'Life Scripts and Attachment Patterns: Theoretical Integration and Therapeutic Involvement', *Transactional Analysis Journal* 39 (3): 207–18.

Fonagy, P., G. Gergely, E. L. Jurist and M. Target (2002), *Affect Regulation, Mentalization, and the Development of the Self*, New York: Other Press.

Heerwagen, J. H., and G. H. Orians (1993), 'Humans, Habitats and Aesthetics', in S. R. Kellert and E. O. Wilson (eds), *The Biophilia Hypothesis*, 138–72, Washington: Island Press.

Herzog, T. R., A. M. Black, K. A. Fountaine and D. J. Knotts (1997), 'Reflection and Attentional Recovery as Distinctive Benefits of Restorative Environments', *Journal of Environmental Psychology* 17: 165–70.

Holland, H. (2010), Personal Communication, 22 February.

Jordan, M. (2009), 'Nature and Self – An Ambivalent Attachment?', *Ecopsychology* 1 (1): 1–6.

Jordan, M., and H. Marshall (2010), 'Taking Counselling and Psychotherapy Outside: Destruction or Enrichment of the Therapeutic Frame?', *European Journal of Psychotherapy & Counselling* 12 (4): 345–59.

Key, D., and K. Tudor (2023), *Ecotherapy: A Field Guide*, Bicester: Phoenix.

Kaplan, R., and S. Kaplan (1989), *The Experience of Nature: A Psychological Perspective*, Cambridge: Cambridge University Press.

Kaplan, S. (1995), 'The Restorative Benefits of Nature: Toward an Integrative Framework', *Journal of Environmental Psychology* 15 (3): 169–82.

Lyons-Ruth, K. (1998), 'Implicit Relational Knowing: Its Role in Development and Psycho-Analytic Treatment', *Infant Mental Health Journal* 19 (3): 282–9.

Marshall, H. (2013), 'The View from Here – Greening the Adult Ego State', *The Transactional Analyst* 4 (1): 37.

Marshall, H. (2014), 'The View from Here – A Vital protocol', *The Transactional Analyst* 4 (2): 26.

Marshall, H. (2014), 'The View from Here – A Sustaining Transaction', *The Transactional Analyst* 4 (3): 40.

Marshall, H. (2016), 'Taking Therapy Outside: Reaching for a Vital Connection' [Online Module]), Eco-psychotherapy: Synthesising Ecology and Psychotherapy in Practice and Theory. http:// www.confer.uk.com/module-ecopsychotherapy.html.

Marshall, H. (2021a), 'Ecological Transactional Analysis: Allowing the Leopards into the Temple', *The Transactional Analyst* 11 (2): 31.

Marshall, H. (2021b), 'An Elemental Relationship: Nature-Based Trauma Therapy', in A. Chesner and S. Lykou (eds), *Trauma in the Creative and Embodied Therapies: When Words Are Not Enough*, 128–40, Abingdon: Routledge.

Marshall, H. (2023), 'A Place for the Ecological Third: Eco-TA in Therapeutic Practice', *Transactional Analysis Journal* 53 (1): 93–108. doi: 10.1080/03621537.2023.2152567.

Pham, T. P., and T. Sanocki (2024), 'Human Restoration, Flow, and Creativity: A Conceptual Integration', *Journal of Imaging* 10 (4): 83. doi: 10.3390/jimaging10040083.

Ray, N. (2010), Personal Communication, 10 May.

Stern, D. (2010), *Forms of Vitality: Exploring Dynamic Experience in Psychology, the Arts, Psychotherapy, and Development*, Oxford: Oxford University Press.

Ulrich, R. (1983), 'Aesthetic and Affective Responses to the Natural Environment', in I. Altman and J. F. Wohlwill (eds), *Behaviour and the Natural Environment*, 85–125, New York: Plenum.

Wilson, E. O. (1993), 'Biophilia and the Conservation Ethic', in S. R. Kellert and E. O. Wilson (eds), *The Biophilia Hypothesis*, 31–41, Washington: Island Press.

11

Renewed by nature: Nature Therapy as a framework to help people deal with crises, trauma and loss

Ronen Berger

Introduction

Nature Therapy is a creative and integrative therapeutic method that takes place in nature and functions through direct contact with it. Derived from an eco-psychological perspective, Nature Therapy acknowledges the healing that exists in the relationship between mankind and nature, while at the same time integrating elements from rituals and expressive art therapy – a method to be used in therapy. The chapter will present the basic concepts and methods of Nature Therapy, highlighting ways in which it can be used to aid adults and children cope with crises, trauma and loss and to develop from them.

Nature Therapy – A theoretical and applied framework

Nature Therapy, as developed and conceptualized by the author of this chapter, is a creative therapeutic method that takes place in nature while perceiving nature as a partner in constructing a therapeutic setting and process (Berger 2014, 2008, 2009; Berger and McLeod 2006). It correlates with other nature-based therapeutic approaches, such as Nature-guided Therapy and Ecotherapy (Burns 1998; Clinebell

1996), but develops unique concepts and methods. These concepts and methods are based on the author's therapeutic experience doing, teaching and researching Nature Therapy and on concepts and methods from shamanism and drama therapy which were integrated into the creation of Nature Therapy.

Nature Therapy creates a theory, practical models and an ethical code which can help therapists to work in nature, integrating nature in the process. Like other postmodern approaches which have developed social theories in order to explain the expansion of psychological distress such as depression, anxiety and trauma (West 2000; McLeod 1997; Gergen 1991), Nature Therapy developed a theory which views human suffering, illness and healing from a psycho-eco-social perspective. This perspective stems from a perceived connection between mankind's estrangement from nature and the decline of community and spiritual ways of living, leading to the spread of psycho-social distress and manifestations such as loss of meaning, depression, anxiety, loneliness and alienation. In response to these processes, Nature Therapy focuses on methods that attempt to strengthen the body–mind connection, the connection to the inner child and the creative self, as well as interpersonal relationships, self-inclusion and normalization abilities via the strengthening of the connection with nature (Berger 2014, 2008, 2009; Berger and Lahad 2011).

At the heart of Nature Therapy, and in accordance with eco-psychological ideas such as 'the ecological self' (Totton 2003; Roszak 2001; Roszak, Gomes and Kanner 1995), stands the term 'Touching Nature'. This term implies that direct contact with and a connection to nature can deepen a person's sense of his or her basic nature: to feel authenticity and to develop important personal elements and a way of life that might have been difficult to achieve in the intensity of modern life (Berger 2005). This concept highlights the importance of nature within Nature Therapy.

Related to this term, the second of Nature Therapy's basic concepts was developed: the triangular relationship, that is, therapist–client-nature. This concept seeks to broaden the classical therapeutic relationship between therapist and client by bringing in a third partner – nature. Like the artistic process and the artistic product, which can be addressed as the third element in art therapy (Berger 2014), the term 'triangular relationship' is conceptualized in the unique context of Nature Therapy. It is intended to aid the therapist in relating to nature as an active partner in the process, affecting not only the design of the therapeutic setting but also the therapeutic process itself. In this way it is different from the perception of the artistic product as a third medium in art therapy, since in Nature Therapy nature plays an active role, having an intrinsic value with a life and dynamic of its own. In art therapy, by contrast, the medium is under the complete control of the therapist or client or both (Berger 2014).

The triangular relationship is intended to support the development of a working approach which gives the therapist greater movement and flexibility in the therapeutic relationship: to take a central role in the relationship and in the interaction with the client and to be assisted by nature as a backdrop or as a supplier of materials. Alternatively, to take a secondary, background role and to serve as a mediator between the client and nature, or as a witness to a process occurring directly with nature. In general, it can be said that when the client or group is involved in investigating processes connected with relationships and 'communication', for example, examining questions of trust and control, the therapist can focus on interpersonal interaction and relate to nature as a background or as a supplier of material for a creative exploration. On the other hand, when the client is concerned with comprehensive questions of identity and meaning, the therapist can invite him or her to interact directly with nature, its cyclicality and its perennial sequences, as she or he remains a witness, seeking to intensify the significance that the individual receives from the encounter with nature. Clearly, in many cases, with changes in the dynamics and the issues being examined, the position of the therapist can (and should) change. A change in position and attitude which may occur several times during the same meeting also enables the client to move along the axis between the interpersonal and the transpersonal, broadening the framework and perspectives regarding the issues being investigated (Berger 2009, 2008).

In this chapter, I would like to expand the perception of the triangular relationship to a hexagonal one, made up of two identical triangles in the form of a six-pointed star. At the vortexes of one triangle are the three formerly mentioned terms: therapist, client and nature, and on the three other vortexes are the group (when working in a group), art (and the creative-artistic process) and the spiritual dimension – the relationship with the universe and what is greater than oneself. At the centre of the hexagon, composed of the meeting of all parts, is the process. Maintaining the structure of the two triangles and the movement between them and their vortexes enables the therapist to choose the axis on which to focus at the various stages of the process and how to advance the process.

The healing forest – resilience, loss and trauma

The Nature Therapy method has been used for some years and in that time it has gained extensive experience working with people and communities that have been exposed to trauma, ongoing stress and loss. It has acquired specific methods and protocols that can help people connect with their strengths, develop coping mechanisms and resilience, as well as to deal with, recover and emerge from traumatic experiences and loss. From the research that accompanied this work it emerges that there are a number of elements in Nature Therapy that support this process in particular (Berger and Lahad 2011, 2009). The first one relates to the way Nature Therapy refers to nature as a partner in the process and to its independent dynamic and the element of uncertainty and unpredictability in particular. This, occurring alongside the cycles present in nature, can help people develop their flexibility and coping abilities while normalizing, and also give a broader meaning and perspective to difficult stories. A second element present in nature relates to the way nature awakens our senses, inviting us to be present in the moment. This can help people to connect with the 'here and now' and be present in the moment, as opposed to holding on to past experiences and fears. Another contribution of this element relates to the way nature calls for playfulness and creative being: to play children's games, to build castles in the sand and to get involved in physical activities. This connection to the inner child and to the creative self has a therapeutic impact (Berger and Lahad 2011). It helps people connect to their inner strength, releases difficult feelings and fosters hope. It also allows people to forsake familiar patterns and ways of being and behaving in their everyday environment while exploring and experiencing new modes of behaviour. Spending time in nature and the direct encounter with it, connecting to the feelings and sights afforded by nature, can help the individual to bypass cognitive defence mechanisms and broaden perspectives, both important elements in therapy in general and in the process of recovery from trauma and loss in particular (Berger and Lahad 2011).

In the context of this chapter it is important to stress the intimate relationship between Nature Therapy and the resilience and strength of the BasicPh model (Lahad 1992). According to this model, which was developed in relation to people's coping mechanisms and the ways they deal and recover from trauma and stress, a person is born with six languages or coping channels: Belief, Affect (feeling), Social, Imagination, Cognition and Physical. Being in contact with these six channels, expressing oneself through them, in addition to the ability to move between them and to integrate them, enables the individual to function better in the world, to deal with and overcome crises. Parallel to technological-scientific development, modern life has emphasized the development of cognitive channels, while other channels have been neglected or even ridiculed and have consequently been overlooked. Treatment in the spirit of BasicPh and, similarly, in the spirit of Nature Therapy, does not necessarily focus on developing insight or a psychological conflict solution, but rather, centres on the creation of a setting which will encourage remembrance and renewed accessibility to the languages of resilience and the development of a flexibility which will enable movement and integration (Berger and Lahad 2011; Lahad 1992).

These elements emphasize the outlook of Nature Therapy, recognizing the independent healing powers of nature, and the important contribution of being in direct and creative contact with it. From research that followed Nature Therapy programmes with children, adults and families who were exposed to trauma and stress, it would appear that these are the main elements that supported recovery and healing. It is important to say that these programmes were helpful not only in cases dealing with trauma caused by war, terror or natural catastrophes, but also in cases dealing with sickness or loss.

From theory to practice – examples from therapy

This unit will include two examples from practice followed by a conceptualization engaging the practice with the theory. The first story will demonstrate ways in which Nature Therapy can be used in individual therapy with people dealing with loss. The second will show ways it can be used with groups of young children who have been exposed to large-scale trauma.

With the river's flow – Example # 1

Sharon, a woman in her forties and mother of two children, contacted me after her husband died, asking me to help her process his death. She said that since he died six months earlier she felt depressed and found it hard to function, to work and take care of the children. She told me that she and her husband used to do most things together and now she had stopped doing many of them. 'Every day we used to go for a walk on the river bank near our home and every weekend we went there as a family. Going there alone now is too painful as the memories flood me. Every tree and rock remind me of him and the longing is too painful. For this reason I have also stopped seeing mutual friends and talking to people about him. I know he is gone. Yet, I am waiting for his return.'

During this telephone conversation Sharon said she wanted to do Nature Therapy as she felt that with the loss of her husband she had also lost her connection to nature and to the landscape she loves so much. She also said that she feels very sad inside but can't find words to describe her sadness, and perhaps the non-verbal and creative ways nature can offer will help her express her feelings. When I asked her where she would like us to hold our first encounter she said, 'Let's meet on the path to the river, near the graveyard. My husband is buried there.' This statement made by Sharon in our first telephone conversation told me much about the future of our work and process.

The first three sessions took place on a cliff near the path to the river. Overlooking the landscape of the river, the landscape of her life, Sharon told the story of her marriage and family. Telling me about her love of the river she unfolded her love, memories and longing for her husband. Using the landscape as a metaphor and container of stories and memories, a process of intake began. Sharon would point to a specific place and would tell me a personal story related to it. Slowly, we formed a basic contract, defining the aims of the work and establishing a safe place from which to start.

Following this process, Sharon asked me to join her for a visit at her husband's grave. I agreed and we held the next session in the graveyard. After we watered the flowers she and her children had planted around the grave we sat near it in silence for a long time. Leaving the graveyard, she thanked me for the quiet way I joined her and said, 'It's the first time since he died that I can be here and see the beauty of this place. It's the first time that I can be here in peace and see this beauty without being overcome by sadness and depression.'

The next sessions took place at the same location. After watering the flowers Sharon collected stones and mud from the flowerbed around the grave and began to create something. At first it was not clear what she was creating; she just enjoyed playful doing and the physical encounter with the natural elements. Later she realized that she was creating a monument. As she placed the last stones on the top of her creation she said, 'I know that I was physically involved in the planning of his gravestone but only today, after creating this memorial myself, I feel I have made my first steps of saying goodbye.' Hearing this, I asked Sharon if I could offer her some homework to do until our next encounter. She agreed and I asked her to visit the grave again later in the week, and, after watering the flowers to write a letter to her husband and perhaps, reversing the roles, write a letter in his name to her.

At the beginning of the next session Sharon said, 'Writing the letters I realized it's time to rise up from the grave and step out of the graveyard … I was there for too long. Can we go to the river today?' We made our way to the river quietly. Arriving at a big tree near the water Sharon stopped. 'This is where he kissed me for the first time,' she said silently. Then she took off her shoes and went into the water. Crying and washing her face she stood there for a few long minutes. 'I missed this place; the trees, the water, myself. Can we come here again?' she asked.

In this way each place on the river revealed stories and memories relating to Sharon's life and the life she had with her husband, allowing her to voice these memories and work through the process of mourning. As the stories were being told it seemed that the memory of Sharon's husband gained a different perspective, as did Sharon's perspective of her current and future life. A small waterfall and a pond, a place that they used to visit daily became our meeting place for the next three sessions. Using flowers she had collected Sharon created a sculpture symbolizing their family relationship. The sculpture included rocks in the water connected by four sticks with a flower on top of them. Looking at the sculpture made Sharon happy. 'This is us, my family – my husband, the kids and me. This is our home,' she said. Arriving at the same location the week after and seeing the sculpture made Sharon very sad. All the elements of the sculpture were there but the flowers had dried out and died. 'This is what happened to me. This is the story of my family.' Silently we sat there together, our legs touching the water, throwing stones into it. After a while Sharon stood up and said, ‘Look how the water keeps flowing, finding a way around the rocks. This also is my story. It is time to move on.’

The example above illustrates the way in which basic Nature Therapy concepts can be integrated into practice, supporting people on their journey to process and recover from loss. It shows how important the location, that is, the physical places in nature are in the process, and the way that the therapist takes into account the choice of location and its possible impact as part of the planning of the intervention. This was highlighted throughout the story, from the first choice of the meeting place to the way that different places and landscapes were used to evoke different memories and then to process them. It also showed how the connection to nature and the observation of phenomena in nature, for example, the flow of the water and the dying of the flowers, gave the client meaning and broadened her perspective. It connected her to a sense of continuity in her life and to the cycle of life and death, which is larger than the self. These issues relate to the concepts of ‘touching nature’ and ‘the three way relationship’ as well as to another concept called ‘choosing the right space’ (Berger 2014). Another element that the example illustrates relates to the way that the independent dynamics of nature can be integrated into the process: Sharon confronting the flowers that had died in the sculpture she created. This encounter connected her with a parallel process within her, giving it a wide and holistic meaning which changed Sharon’s perspective. The example also touched on the issues of the way Nature Therapy relates to rituals and to the way it supports their spontaneous creation. This relates to the ‘art as therapy’ orientation of Nature Therapy and to the ways this approach relates to the creative process as healing activity (Berger 2014). Lastly, Sharon’s story shows the soft ‘joining and leading’ therapeutic approach that Nature Therapy promotes, inviting the therapist to join the client as a witness and supporter on his or her journey to self-recovery and healing in nature.

A safe place – Nature Therapy assists children to deal with a traumatic experience – Example # 2

In 2006, after the Second Lebanon war in Israel, it was clear that there was an urgent need for a wide and systemic, national therapeutic programme to help the thousands of children who were exposed to the war to deal with and heal from emotional stress. To meet this need The Nature Therapy Center together with the Israeli Community Stress Prevention Center designed the programme ‘A Safe Place’, which aimed to develop resilience and coping resources in young children. The programme was based on the metaphoric relationship between the damage caused to the forests as a result of the fires during the war and their recovery afterwards.

This process paralleled the experiences the children went through in their communities. The programme was built on the outline story of the hero's journey, using healing metaphors from the story to empower the children and support their recovery and development. The story tells of the forest watchmen who cared for the forest, its plants and animals. One day a big fire broke out and burnt down the forest. Although the forest watchmen did all they could to extinguish the fire, many animals ran away, some got injured and a few even died. Slowly the fire was put out and the animals started to return. Some came back injured, and some did not return at all. The forest watchmen were very happy to meet the animals again and did all they could to help them feel safe. It took time until winter came and it rained again, and until the plants and the forest recovered. The forest watchmen took care again of the forest and its animals and the plants they loved. They played with the animals and the animals loved them in return.

Relating to the Drama Therapy basic concept of distancing (Jennings 1998; Landy 1996) and via role play techniques, the programme allowed the children to tell their stories in an indirect and safe manner. Using healing metaphors from the story (the forest watchmen as authority and protecting figures, the power and the ability to help the trees and animals) while playing and acting characters and situations from the story, the programme assisted the children to regain their strength and rebuild a sense of safety. The connection to the universal story about how trees and animals also dealing with natural catastrophes coped helped them to normalize their stories and get in touch with a wider perspective and meaning (Berger and Lahad 2011).

The programme begins in a classroom, by reading the story to the children and inviting them to choose one of the characters and to draw it. Then, through ritual, make-up and other accessories, the children enter the characters of the forest watchmen as they leave the classroom and go outside into the surrounding nature. In the next nine to ten encounters they build the forest protectors' camp, prepare power symbols and conduct activities which enable them to tell their stories and to link up with their strengths. Afterwards, in line with the outline stories – after the fire has been extinguished and when the forest becomes secure again, including the animals which had left – the children plant trees, build and set up feeding stations for birds and, if possible, nesting boxes. In this way, the children do not just connect with their strengths via metaphors and forest protector's role play, but also give of their strength to others, helping nature and the environment. Thus, the ecological, social activity aids them in creating a link to the sense of cyclicality, meaningfulness and value of attachment to the community and to nature.

'A Safe Place' is a Nature Therapy recognized programme, which has been in operation since 2006, involving more than 12,000 kindergarten and school children in both normal and special educational frameworks, in Jewish, Arab and Druze schools in the north of Israel. It has been awarded recognition by the

Ministry of Education; it has received a recommendation from the Educational Psychological Services and has won prizes for its contribution to helping traumatized children (Berger and Lahad 2010). Since the programme is based on the components of drama therapy mentioned above, we can also relate to it as a drama therapy programme existing in nature, and thus it constitutes an example of Nature Therapy as a model for drama therapy (Berger 2014). It is important to stress that in this protocol programme independent dynamics in nature are not emphasized, rather, the approach relates to nature more as a backdrop or a stage for a story which has been written in advance. In this context, there is less flexibility and movement in the 'triangular relationship' and less reference to spontaneous events which nature makes available. The side of the 'active partner' of the three-way relationship is hardly related to in this example. A more flexible approach which integrates the dynamics of nature in the process and the aspect of nature as an active partner can be seen in the previous example. It, too, raises the possibility of approaching Nature Therapy as a model and an extension of drama therapy and other creative-expressive therapy, combining various aspects of art in nature-based work (Berger 2014).

Conclusion

This chapter presented the basic, theoretical cornerstones and central concepts of Nature Therapy, and delineated a number of possibilities of using it in therapy with people dealing with loss and trauma. It shows how this concept could assist the therapist not only to enable creative therapy in nature while relating to nature as both a setting and as a stage for work, but also how it integrates nature as a partner into the therapeutic process and in this way, advances and broadens it.

The chapter elucidates Nature Therapy's outlook towards health and illness, emphasizing the connection to imagination and creativity as a basis for well-being, happiness and development. It also highlights the focus it puts on strengthening people's connection with nature and the possibilities for self-healing and development. It shows the specific contribution that Nature Therapy can make to these processes and in connection with the cycles of nature, the normalizing of complex stories. By doing so the chapter showed the uniqueness of the method in general and in work with people dealing with loss and trauma in particular.

Considering the self-healing value of nature, and terms such as ritual, fantastic space and distancing, the chapter presented the relationship between Nature Therapy and the perceptions of art as therapy. In addition, it presented the possibility of relating to Nature Therapy as a method in drama therapy and other methods of art-based therapy, broadening them to the realm of nature.

References

Berger, R. (2005), 'To Be in Nature – Nature Therapy with the Elderly', *Dorot* 80: 36–41. (In Hebrew).

Berger, R. (2008), 'Building a Home in Nature: An Innovative Framework for Practice', *Journal of Humanistic Psychology* 48 (2): 264–79.

Berger, R. (2009), 'Nature Therapy – Developing a Framework for Practice', A PhD thesis, University of Abertay, Dundee: School of Health and Social Sciences.

Berger, R. (2014), 'Nature Therapy – Integrating Nature in Therapy', in R. Berger (ed.), *Arts – The Heart of Therapy*, 411–43, Kiryat Byalik: Ach Publication. (In Hebrew).

Berger, R., and M. Lahad (2010), 'Safe Place. Ways in Which Nature, Play and Creativity Can Help Children Cope with Stress and Crisis: Establishing the Kindergarten as a Safe Haven Where Children Can Develop Resiliency', *Early Child Development and Care* 180 (7): 889–900.

Berger, R., and M. Lahad (2011), *The Healing Forest – Nature Therapy and the Integration of Arts for the Care of Children after Crisis*, Kiryat Tivon: Akh Publications. (In Hebrew).

Berger, R., and G. McLoed (2006), 'Nature Therapy – A Theoretical and Practical Framework', *Social Work Journal* 46: 22–31. (In Hebrew).

Burns, G. A. (1998), *Nature-Guided Therapy: Brief Intervention Strategies for Health and Well-Being*, London: Taylor and Francis.

Clinebell, H. (1996), *Ecotherapy – Healing Ourselves – Healing the Earth*, New York: Routledge.

Davis, J. (1998), 'The Transpersonal Dimensions of Eco-Psychology: Nature, Non-Duality, and Spiritual Practice', *The Humanistic Psychologist* 26 (1–3): 60–100.

Gergen, K. J. (1991), *The Shattered Self: Dilemmas of Identity in Modern Life*, New York: Basic.

Jennings, S. (1998), *Introduction to Drama Therapy*, London: Jessica Kingsley.

Landy, R. J. (1996), *Essays in Drama Therapy*, London: Jessica Kingsley Publishers.

McLeod, J. (1997), *Narrative and Psychotherapy*, London: Sage.

Roszak, T. (2001), *The Voice of the Earth*, Grand Rapids: Phanes Press.

Roszak, T., M. E. Gomes and A. D. Kanner (1995), *Ecopsychology: Restoring the Mind, Healing the Earth*, San Francisco, CA: Sierra Club Books.

Totton, N. (2003), 'The Ecological Self: Introducing Eco-Psychology', *Counselling and Psychotherapy Journal* 14: 14–17.

West, W. (2000), *Psychotherapy & Spirituality: Crossing the Line between Therapy and Religion*, London: Sage.

12

Equine-assisted therapy: Developing theoretical context

Joe Hinds and Louise Ranger

This chapter remains largely true to the original version contained within the first edition of this volume. There are additional text relating to the second author's personal reflections about their experience of and with horses in the time since the first writing. These have helped deepen the phenomenology of these experiences and indeed how, mirroring therapeutic relationships, they were able to use horses to 'see' and break old detrimental unconscious relational patterns. We begin by discussing equine-assisted therapy (EAT) as an element of ecotherapy by briefly reviewing animal-assisted therapies (AAT) in which it is embedded, and then address the often overlooked or under-theorized epistemological aspect of these approaches by proposing pre-therapy (Prouty 2001) as a theoretical guide to further elucidate the widely reported outcomes within the broad AAT literature generally and EAT specifically. Secondly, we note the specific qualities of EAT that differentiate it from other animal-based therapies by proposing the concept of *awe* as fundamental consideration. We situate these conceptual and theoretical ideas within a phenomenological, experiential and relational frame using a heuristic case study to support their inclusion in a contemporary understanding of EAT.

Introduction

Despite the large body of writing on AAT and its variants (e.g. Pet Therapy; Animal-Assisted Interventions; Equine-Facilitated Psychotherapy; see Kruger and Serpell 2006), which have much details of the therapeutic benefits to be gained from utilizing the services of animals (e.g. Chandler 2012; Fine 2006), AAT has been largely absent from *Ecotherapy*, albeit with some notable exceptions (e.g. DeMayo 2009). We wish to therefore make this connection explicit and to summarize here the body of literature to date, as best we can, and to build on the theoretical understanding for the efficaciousness of these interventions.

Many animals provide comfort at a simple psychological and physiological level as 'companions' (e.g. Friedmann and Tsai 2006) while other animal-based interventions are targeted to alleviate deeper psychological trauma (e.g. Dietz, Davis and Pennings 2012). Moreover, there appears to be a spectrum on which animals lay in this regard: small and domesticated through to large and wild. This range elicits very different relational qualities and experiences (Siporin 2012); compare, for instance, being in the company of a whale (DeMares and Krycka 1998) or goldfish (Cole and Gawlinski 2000). Typically, pet animals such as birds (Holcomb et al. 1997), cats (Noonan 2008), guinea pigs (Kršková, Talarovičová and Olexová 2010) and, in particular, dogs (Dietz, Davis and Pennings 2012) have been utilized for a range of psychological interventions such as loneliness (Banks and Banks 2002) and general well-being (O'Haire 2010).

Despite a small number of informed and theoretically based exceptions (e.g. Karole 2007), there is only cursory coverage of the theoretical reasons *why* these interventions may work (Kruger and Serpell 2006). In some cases biomedical models of stress have been used to explain how dogs reduce anxiety in a clinical setting (Lang et al. 2010). Others have drawn on traditional therapeutic philosophies. For instance, Dietz, Davis and Pennings (2012) refer, in a person-centred sense, to dogs providing unconditional love and engendering an environment of warmth, acceptance, security and empathy. Psychodynamic approaches, particularly with children, have conceived animals as unthreatening and can therefore be viewed as transitional objects and as a focus of projection (Karole 2007; Melson and Fine 2006; Noonan 2008), and attachment theories have been used to explain how animals provide a secure base (Geist 2011; Zilcha-Mano, Mikulincer and Shaver 2011).

In addition, the evidence for these therapeutic interventions, consisting of a variety of anecdotal and empirical sources, remains disparate. To add to a growing complexity, these various approaches may be summative in determining positive outcome (e.g. developing secure attachment *and* lowering heart rate), and may only be appropriate to certain people at certain times. With that in mind, we wish to draw on our respective strengths and experience here to restrict our discussion specifically to EAT and set in motion a more informed consideration of the theoretical underpinnings of EAT using heuristic case study material in which to ground our epistemological claims. Although others have made implicit reference to the importance of non-verbal communication, drawing for instance, on pre-verbal ideas to explain the utility of horses within a psychotherapeutic environment (e.g. Siporin 2012), we wish to make explicit the links between EAT and pre-therapy

(Prouty 2001). Moreover, we wish to show that the horse is able to elicit awe-like experiences which may explain and underpin some of the theoretical frameworks suggested above.

Heuristic enquiry

Moustakas's (1990) heuristic process requires the researcher to explore their internal experience while being in relationship with the topic of inquiry. This requires an immersion in the subjective experience to deepen understanding by collecting data through self-dialogue, personal journals and developing a broadening of horizons by engaging in creative exploration. From a relatively unique position, the primary researcher is both a humanistic therapist and an experienced horse handler and therefore is able to be personally involved in the 'search for qualities, conditions, and relationships that underlie a fundamental question, issue or concern' (Moustakas 1990: 11). Alongside this personal reflexivity, an open discussion with the co-researcher was utilized to further elucidate those musings as well as drawing on the primary researcher's own client accounts of their experience of EAT. Due to word limit restrictions only part of this body of data will be presented here; the process of insight and discovery is still ongoing.

Pre-therapy: The non-verbal world

Pre-therapy (Prouty 2001, 2008) was conceived within a phenomenological and person-centred tradition and was devised for those people deemed to be outside of normal psychological contact such as for those with dementia and schizophrenia (Dekeyser, Prouty and Elliot 2008). Contact within pre-therapy may be divided into three types: reality contact is awareness of people, places, things and events; affective contact is awareness of distinct moods, feelings and emotions, and communicative contact is the symbolization of reality contact and affective contact to others (Dekeyser, Prouty and Elliot 2008; see also Solomon 2010). In particular we are concerned here with the non-verbal contacts (e.g. body and face: Prouty 2001) provided by the 'horse-as-mirror' (Vidrine, Owen-Smith and Faulkner 2002) and the subsequent emotive and symbolic insights that develop from this. This is not to say that we do not acknowledge the important function of the therapist in the triad and their role to verbally reflect, communicate and facilitate sense-making, rather we wish to attend to and focus on the specific qualities that the horse is able to engender in EAT.

There is increasing evidence to indicate that animals in AAT are able to serve as a 'clinical bridge' (Barker and Dawson 1998) for people who are typically viewed as being beyond 'talking' therapy such as childhood sexual trauma (Dietz, Davis and Pennings 2012), autism (Solomon 2012), schizophrenics (Lang et al. 2010), and people with dementia (Filan and Llewellyn-Jones 2006). This has also been an important consideration for EAT interventions (Ewing et al. 2007; Schultz, Remick-Barlow and Robbins 2007).

The horse has, through evolutionary necessity, developed high sensitivity and responsiveness to body language including humans' (Johansen et al. 2014). Equally, the human response to a large animal will be attuned to its movements and may, through the tactile, embodied and physical quality of the animal encounter, enhance important affect expression and build relational aspects of the self that have been thwarted or under-developed (Myers and Russell 2003; Solomon 2010; Yorke 2010). These encounters can provide a 'bodily experience … in an expressive gesturing landscape, in a world that *speaks*' (Abram 1996: 81; see also Totton 2011).

Sanders (2003) emphasizes the importance of the richness of human–animal relationships to provide a non-linguistic cooperative interpretative process, such as through mutual gaze to define 'self' in relationship with 'other'. Some have gone further suggesting 'animals are critical contributors to the construct of human identity and a "relational self" ' and that people tend to view animals as they view themselves (Kalof 2003: 161). There is an importance implicit here for personal engagement with the 'more-than-rational' world to develop a sense of self within a community of inter-subjectivities (Garcia 2010: 86). Social communications are made up of non-linguistic and embodied signals which may be more important to certain people, such as those with autism, at certain times and contexts (Solomon 2010). It seems that the strengths of autistics' experiencing (e.g. visual imagery) may make it easier to connect to the non-verbal world of the animal and in turn foster the development of empathy and self-expressiveness (Grandin 1995; cited in Barrett-Lennard 2013; see also DeMayo 2009). This process can benefit many; borrowing from Buber, Leontiev (2013) suggests that open, authentic and mutual relationships may be represented by non-verbal dialogue and this seems to manifest in human–horse encounters:

> *I feel much happier being round animals at the moment, there seems to be something so much more real and present and calming for me about the nonhuman world. Human communication is so bloody complicated!*

> *There is this moment where I stand with my horse and we are together in meaningful silence. He stoops his head down, lip slightly protruding and his whole body sinks down in a relaxed state. I rest my hand on his shoulder and feel utterly content, both of us looking out into the horizon. I know, with absolute certainty, he is enjoying my company and me his. He is standing next to me freely, no head collar or rope restraining him he could walk away at any point. Often these moments only last for several minutes, and occasionally up to half an hour. I feel a sense of relief I don't have to talk, there are no expectations. He doesn't need or want anything from me at this point in time … It is*

strange, when I think about it I do not have this type of interaction with people, and I cannot explain in words why this is so.

[since childhood] I had spent time in relationships, become close friends with people I didn't particularly like and done countless numbers of favours in martyr like fashion, all to avoid causing (seeing) someone else's disappointment. Somehow, just the simple act of the horses standing and looking at me I was able to access this sudden realisation. It sounds inconceivable this could cause such an insight, but it is true. The horses had inspired within me a perfect moment of non-directive therapy.

Jung speaks of the mystery of this encounter: 'the eyes of the animal … are full of woe and beauty because they contain the truth of life', an experience that is 'most bewildering', and that is recommended for all people in order to 'find again the connection with the nature within, with one's own nature' (Sabini 2008: 171–2). The horse acts as an embodied non-talking 'catalyst' and 'metaphor' (Klontz et al. 2007), which allows a deeper level of relating:

I feel like I'm starting to 'see' Sparkle a bit more, or taking him in more somehow. He is gradually changing from just 'horse' to a personality and a more detailed physical presence. When I think about him now I can picture the texture of his coat and his mane, and the shape of his hooves, and the look in his eye. It feels like a long time since I've seen beyond just horse and felt that sense of actually getting to know and connecting with one.

The horse encourages the client to act and behave in a way consistent with actual thoughts and feelings, which could potentially be missed within a therapists counselling room environment (Lentini and Knox 2009). The horse responds with blatant honesty and without opinion or hidden agenda (Weiss 2009) reacting to the internal world of the person, regardless of their efforts to conceal it, either consciously or unconsciously (Lentini and Knox 2009); in essence the horses are 'truth sensers' (Totton 2011). And, indeed, much of the literature on horse–human interaction acknowledges that horses act congruently, responding immediately, clearly and non-verbally (Karol 2007). This here-and-now immediacy is also transmitted to the person in contact with the horse:

With a horse you can't reflect on challenging behaviour, you need to react to it immediately. And I think this is something that I really need to learn, to have the confidence to act straightaway on my intuition. With people and with horses, because unfortunately if I don't, not only does the difficult behaviour often escalate but my lack of response means that I feel unheard, and I then end up ruminating on what I actually should have done, and how upset and wronged I feel, for far longer than is good for me!

Direct experiences with a wild animal can produce a deep sense of perceived mutual understanding – an ineffable feeling state (Myers and Russell 2003). In essence, there is a substitution of verbal cognitive communication for a symbolic, basic or primal motivational drive that dictates behaviour and communication, something that is evident in autistic children (Solomon 2012). Direct (in-the-moment) tacit knowledge brought about through therapeutic animal encounters, engenders an embodied and metaphorical experiential 'felt shift or change' equating to the idea of focusing (Bohart 2011: 258). Bringing cognitions together with bodily involvement can elicit important change during therapy outdoors (Corazon, Schilhab and Stigsdotter 2011) and can illicit authentic moments in the human experience of them: '*Actions speak louder than words*' (Sanders 2003).

> *I realised I had been supressing sadness all day. My horse wandered over to connect with me, rubbed his head on my shoulder, and searched through my pockets for treats. A wash of emotions rose from the depths, and I let the sadness be.*
>
> *My horse continues to be a teacher to me, and as long as I listen, as long as I'm clear about my intentions, we get on just fine. If I am not in touch with my emotions, he doesn't want me around, and certainly not on his back. He is not perfect and neither am I. We both have days when either one of us is grumpy or bad tempered, or simply wants to be left alone. That's ok, it makes our relationship authentic.*

Awe

Awe is a transpersonal concept that represents deeply meaningful, evocative and ineffable experiences (Bonner and Friedman 2011) and may be an emotional moment of self-reconfiguration (Schneider 2011). Furthermore, awe has been defined as 'the thrill and anxiety of living … the cultivation of the capacity for humility and boldness, reverence and wonder' (Schneider 2003: 135). Wild animal encounters have elicited emotionally profound and intense experiences including deeply relational and harmonious moments (DeMares and Krycka 1998; Smith, Ham and Weiler 2011). Similar therapeutic experiences have been reported with horses (Garcia 2010). Being with horses has been described as 'indescribably healing' and 'profound and emotional, almost mystical' (DeMayo 2009). Moreover, 'being carried on the back of a 1,200 pound vulnerable giant can certainly provide access to core personal issues' (Weiss 2009: 227).

> *A horse can cause significant damage to a person in an instant, and yet mostly they choose (and even seem to enjoy) being around us peacefully. In the few cases where I have been next to a dangerous horse, it has been absolutely terrifying, and sharply reminded me of my own mortality. Awe in this case is about being in the presence of an animal who chooses not to kill you when it so easily could. There is a real moment when a horse leaves the herd and walks over to say hello (regardless of whether this is simply because they think you might have food), that feels very special. In this case, the awe for me is rooted in the fact that I am significant enough to a different species. At times I do literally feel awestruck by this, much more so than with a small pet like a cat or dog … So the awe doesn't always come from the size of the animal, but from the choice it has just made to leave its safe base to be with me.*

It is possibly the sense of awe that triggers regression to development periods that reflect similar relational experiences during childhood. To revert to a childlike propensity in order to resolve and work through issues does not necessarily require two persons; pre-psychological interaction (contact) may initially involve objects and non-human beings (Dekeyser, Prouty and Elliot 2008). This is perhaps why the horse may be deemed the 'ideal' therapist for the transferential relationship (Vidrine, Owen-Smith and Faulkner 2002) – a mixed sense of love and fear (awe) whereby the horse is enriched as a powerful but trusted transitional object. We are in agreement here with others (e.g. Kruger and Serpell 2006) that once imbued with metaphorical significance and meaning the horse acts as transitional object to facilitate movement from one pattern of human relating and behaviour to another rather than horse being seen as a substitute attachment figure. Observing the spontaneity and playfulness of horses, in a carefree childlike manner, can return the person to past and unresolved parts of themselves:

> *This morning ... they galloped round and round the field together playing racing games. Then they would screech to a halt, stop and eat taking huge mouthfuls of grass, then suddenly start racing again with the grass still half hanging out their mouths. Watching them like this reminded me of being a child, and I wondered at what age I had stopped playing, I had stopped running, and when I had stopped doing things spontaneously just for the hell of it. Their simple love of life lifted my mood ... This brief but joyous moment with the horses had set off a whole host of thoughts in my head, remembering happy times from my childhood I had long forgotten. Having recently lost my Mum, these thoughts were welcome, as I had become bogged down in a myriad of grief and sadness, with repetitive thoughts about her death and the difficult months following ... this was helpful, not to dispel the necessary grief, but as a reminder that I can still have moments of happiness within the grieving process.*

> *I'm still slightly amazed when Sparkle does anything that I'm asking him to, and feel rather like an insignificant weightless bubble that he can nudge around to his heart's content. And that reminds me of another really long-term theme for me that I am invisible somehow, not really seen or heard. Which I guess links in to the theme of authority, I'd like to get to a place where I naturally walk more upright and hold myself with a stronger internal energy that horses and people respond to.*

The horse–human relationship could be observed and experienced as an indication of attachment issues (Siporin 2012). There is something about working with horses which seems to replicate our family scripts. The way the person is around horses, and the way they respond to the horse, seems to mirror the position or role within their family of origin and present relationships. On a basic level the person is 'acting out' a script which the horse then reacts to, particularly with people who refer to the horse as 'difficult' or 'naughty' or 'deliberately not doing what I say'. The horse does not have a concept of these terms, and is simply responding to an unhealthy psychological communication. Once worked through, these experiences can be applied in other aspects of their lives:

I had spent the majority of my life being invisible in the world. Sparkle taught me I couldn't be invisible around him, he needed me to be heard. And crucially, I needed to hear him too. I was ignoring his body language, and then getting angry when he didn't do as I asked. The anger often overwhelmed me, and I would find myself shouting at him with pure frustration, then immediately breaking down in floods of tears which I couldn't stem. I had to face up to the big question, who was I actually angry with? Was it really him? Or was it my family, partner, best friend, work colleagues? Almost every day I would turn up with something on my mind, and transferred these problems straight onto our relationship.

When I feel like they're going down a familiar route that I know is not for the best. Sometimes I can catch myself and do something different, sometimes I can't. But I'm finding having the visual memories of the work with Sparkle really helps me to behave differently in situations.

The reflections that follow give some indication about how the horse–human relationship can so clearly put a spotlight on unconscious and unhealthy relationship patterns that are repeated *until* there is an awakening. The horse maybe mirroring the insecure attachment and codependency behaviour that existed before we knew who we are.

Relationships

As somebody who identified as neuro-diverse later in life, I can look back now and see as a young person how I connected with animals but struggled significantly with people, who I mostly did not understand. Being outdoors with horses was my safe space, I belonged in the herd and I could truly be me. Interactions with horses became even more important during a period in my life where I become involved in toxic and co-dependent romantic relationships, which were extremely damaging. I started therapy at this time and the counsellor introduced me to the concept of insecure attachment. On exploration I started to understand times in my life where I had felt abandoned and feared death, I had chronic separation anxiety. Practically this manifested itself in rescuing animals, and in particular horses who had been abused or abandoned by others. I prided myself on being 'the one' who the horses learnt to trust where others had failed; it felt like I had saved their lives. With each new rescue I would experience a surge of validation and purpose, and that alone felt ok. But problems arose where I clung on to these damaged horses where I did not have the emotional bandwidth, knowledge, or finances to care for them in the way they needed. Ultimately these were not fulfilling horse-human relationships, they were fraught with pain and anxiety. Through therapy and on finding myself in a loving and secure partnership, I recognised that this need to rescue horses had in fact been a desire to rescue and heal me and my relationships. The horses were a mirror for my anxiety and co-dependency, without me realising it they were showing me the way out of the negative cycle. It's fascinating to me today that I have no wish to rescue horses anymore. Instead the interactions with my one remaining horse are joyful and our time together is therapeutic for both of us. An added gift is that in looking after him, I am brought close to nature every day, and I love that.

Summary

EAT is not necessarily for everyone – *horses for courses* (e.g. Berget et al. 2007). There may be cases where a client simply does not like horses, may be scared of such a big animal, or cannot see any benefit to working with them. Sometimes the thoughts and emotions horses instil can be so strong and immediate that it can feel extremely uncomfortable and uncontained. Moreover, in counterpoint to much literature regarding animals as representing an unconditional acceptance, the primary researcher's experience of working with equines has been at times contrary to this proposition – horses are a challenge. Much like person-to-person interaction, the relationship between person and horse can be unique and often complex. However, '*pets communicate something about the owner and how they want to be regarded and so are as revealing as dreams may be*' (Noonan 2008: 396; emphasis added). If mistreated, overworked or not listened to, horses can become 'shut-down' and unresponsive engendering countertransference from the client, for example, 'No-one ever listens to me'. With the aid of an accomplished and intuitive therapist this important 'difficult' or 'resistance' information can be better understood.

We do not intend to underestimate either the important role of the natural environment or of the therapist here. Our focus has been on the therapeutic nature or quality of the horse while leaving implicit both the role of the therapist as an important facilitator or 'go-between' in this triadic relationship and the natural environment in which equine-based therapy takes place. Although we have drawn attention to both pre-therapy (animal therapy generally) and awe (large animals [horses] specifically) as elements for theoretical consideration, and how these relate to other theories, we wish this chapter to be a springboard for greater attention to, and development of, the epistemological foundations of both EAT and AAT practice within an ecotherapy frame.

References

Abram, D. (1996), *The Spell of the Sensuous*, New York: Vintage.

Banks, M. R., and W. A. Banks (2002), 'The Effects of Animal-Assisted Therapy on Loneliness in an Elderly Population in Long-Term Care Facilities', *The Journal of Gerontology* 57: 428–32.

Barker, S. B., and K. S. Dawson (1998), 'The Effects of Animal-Assisted Therapy on Anxiety Ratings of Hospitalized Psychiatric Patients', *Psychiatric Services* 49: 797–802.

Barrett-Lennard, G. T. (2013), *The Relationship Paradigm: Human Being beyond Individualism*, Basingstoke, UK: Palgrave Macmillan.

Berget, B., I. Skarsaune, O. Ekeberg and B. O. Braastad (2007), 'Humans with Mental Disorders Working with Farm Animals', *Occupational Therapy in Mental Health* 23: 101–17.

Bohart, A. C. (2011), 'A Meditation on the Nature of Self-Healing and Personality Change in Psychotherapy Based on Gendlin's Theory of Experiencing', *The Humanistic Psychologist* 29: 249–79.

Bonner, E. T., and H. L. Friedman (2011), 'A Conceptual Clarification of the Experience of Awe: An Interpretative Phenomenological Analysis', *The Humanistic Psychologist* 39: 222–35.

Chandler, C. K. (2012), *Animal Assisted Therapy in Counselling*, New York: Routledge.

Cole, K. M., and A. Gawlinski (2000), 'Animal-Assisted Therapy: The Human-Animal Bond', *AACN Advanced Critical Care* 11: 139–49.

Corazon, S. S., T. S. Schilhab and U. K. Stigsdotter (2011), 'Developing the Therapeutic Potential of Embodied Cognition and Metaphors in Nature-Based Therapy: Lessons from Theory to Practice', *Journal of Adventure Education & Outdoor Learning* 11 (2): 161–71.

Dekeyser, M., G. Prouty and R. Elliot (2008), 'Pre-Therapy Process and Outcome: A Review of Research Instruments and Findings', *Person-Centered and Experiential Psychotherapies* 7: 37–55.

DeMares, R., and K. Krycka (1998), 'Wild-Animal-Triggered Peak Experiences: Transpersonal Aspects', *The Journal of Transpersonal Psychology* 30: 161–77.

DeMayo, N. (2009), 'Horses, Humans and Healing', in L. Buzzell and C. Chalquist (eds), *Ecotherapy: Healing with Nature in Mind*, 149–56, San Francisco, CA: Sierra Club Books.

Dietz, T. J., D. Davis and J. Pennings (2012), 'Evaluating Animal-Assisted Therapy in Group Treatment for Child Sexual Abuse', Journal of Child Sexual Abuse 21: 665–83.

Ewing, C. A., P. M. MacDonald, M. Taylor and M. J. Bowers (2007), 'Equine-Facilitated Learning for Youths with Severe Emotional Disorders: A Quantitative and Qualitative Study', *Child Youth Care Forum* 36: 59–72.

Filan, S. L., and R. H. Llewellyn-Jones (2006), 'Animal-Assisted Therapy for Dementia: A Review of the Literature', *International Psychogeriatrics* 18: 597–611.

Fine, A. H. (2006), *Handbook on Animal-Assisted Therapy: Theoretical Foundations and Guidelines for Practice*, San Diego, California: Elsevier.

Friedmann, E., and C-C. Tsai (2006), 'The Animal-Human Bond: Health and Wellness', in A. H. Fine (ed.), *Handbook on Animal-Assisted Therapy: Theoretical Foundations and Guidelines for Practice*, 95–117, San Diego, California: Elsevier.

Garcia, D. M. (2010), 'Of Equines and Humans: Toward a New Ecology', *Ecopsychology* 2: 85–9.

Geist, T. S. (2011), 'Conceptual Framework for Animal Assisted Therapy', *Child and Adolescent Social Work Journal* 28: 243–56.

Holcomb, R., C. Jendro, B. Weber and U. Nahan (1997), 'Use of an Aviary to Relieve Depression in Elderly Males', *Anthrozoos* 10: 32–6.

Johansen, S. G., C. E. A. Wang, P-E. Binder and U. F. Malt (2014), 'Equine-Facilitated Body and Emotion-Oriented Psychotherapy Designed for Adolescents and Adults Not Responding to Mainstream Treatment: A Structured Program', *Journal of Psychotherapy Integration* 24: 323–35.

Kalof, L. (2003), 'The Human Self and the Animal Other: Exploring Borderline Identities', in S. Clayton and S. Opotow (eds), *Identity and the Natural Environment: The Psychological Significance of Nature*, 161–78, Cambridge, MA: MIT Press.

Karol, J. (2007), 'Applying a Traditional Individual Psychotherapy Model to Equine-Facilitated Psychotherapy (Efp): Theory and Method', *Clinical Child Psychology and Psychiatry* 12: 77–90.

Klontz, B. T., A. Bivens, D. Leinart and T. Klontz (2007), 'The Effectiveness of Equine-Assisted Experiential Therapy: Results of an Open Clinical Trial', *Society and Animals* 15: 257–67.

Kršková, A., L. Talarovičová and A. Olexová (2010), 'Guinea Pigs: The "Small Great" Therapist for Autistic Children, or: Do Guinea Pigs Have Positive Effects on Autistic Child Social Behavior?', *Society and Animals* 18: 139–51.

Kruger, K. A., and J. A. Serpell (2006), 'Animal-Assisted Interventions in Mental Health: Definitions and Theoretical Foundations', in A. H. Fine (ed.), *Handbook on Animal-Assisted Therapy: Theoretical Foundations and Guidelines for Practice*, 58–95, San Diego, California: Elsevier.

Lang, U. E., J. B. Jansen, F. Wertenauer, J. Gallinat and M. A. Rapp (2010), 'Reduced Anxiety during Dog Assisted Interviews in Acute Schizophrenic Patients', *European Journal of Integrative Medicine* 2: 123–7.

Lentini, J., and M. Knox (2009), 'A Qualitative and Quantitative Review of Equine Facilitated Psychotherapy (EFP) with Children and Adolescents', *The Open Complementary Medicine Journal* 1: 51–7.

Leontiev, D. (2013), 'The Challenge of Otherness: Relationships, Meaning and Dialogue', in E. van Deurzen and S. Iacovou (eds), *Existential Perspectives on Relationship Therapy*, 32–43, Basingstoke, UK: Palgrave Macmillan.

Melson, G. F., and A. H. Fine (2006), 'Animals in the Lives of Children', in A. H. Fine (ed.), *Handbook on Animal-Assisted Therapy: Theoretical Foundations and Guidelines for Practice*, 207–26, San Diego, California: Elsevier.

Moustakas, C. (1990), *Heuristic Research: Design, Methodology, and Applications*, Sage: London.

Myers, G., and A. Russell (2003), 'Human Identity in Relation to Wild Black Bears: A Natural-Social Ecology of Subjective Creatures', in S. Clayton and S. Opotow (eds), *Identity and the Natural Environment: The Psychological Significance of Nature*, 67–90, Cambridge, MA: MIT Press.

Noonan, E. (2008), 'People and Pets', *Psychodynamic Practice* 14: 395–407.

O'Haire, M. (2010), 'Companion Animals and Human Health: Benefits, Challenges, and the Road Ahead', *Journal of Veterinary Behavior* 5: 226–34.

Prouty, G. (ed.) (2008), *Emerging Developments in Pre-Therapy: A Pre-Therapy Reader*, Ross-on-Wye, UK: PCCS Books.

Prouty, G. F. (2001), 'The Practice of Pre-Therapy', *Journal of Contemporary Psychotherapy* 31: 31–40.

Sabini, M. (2008), *C. G. Jung on Nature, Technology, & Modern Life*, Berkley, California: North Atlantic Books.

Sanders, C. R. (2003), 'Actions Speak Louder Than Words: Close Relationships between Humans and Nonhuman Animals', *Symbolic Interactions* 26: 405–26.

Schneider, K. J. (2003), 'The Fluid Center: An Awe-Based Challenge to Humanity', *Journal of Humanistic Psychology* 43: 133–45.

Schneider, K. J. (2011), 'Awakening to an Awe-Based Psychology', *The Humanistic Psychologist* 39: 247–52.

Schultz, P. N., G. A. Remick-Barlow and L. Robbins (2007), 'Equine-Assisted Psychotherapy: A Mental Health Promotion/Intervention Modality for Children Who Have Experienced Intra-Family Violence', *Health and Social Care in the Community* 15: 265–71.

Siporin, S. (2012), 'Talking Horses: Equine Psychotherapy and Intersubjectivity', *Psychodynamic Practice: Individuals, Groups and Organisations* 18: 457–64.

Smith, L. D. G., S. H. Ham and B. V. Weiler (2011), 'The Impacts of Profound Wildlife Experiences', *AnthroZoös* 24: 51–64.

Solomon, O. (2010), 'What a Dog Can Do: Children with Autism and Therapy Dogs in Social Interaction', *Ethos* 38: 143–66.

Solomon, O. (2012), 'Doing, Being and Becoming: The Sociality of Children with Autism in Activities with Therapy Dogs and Other People', *Cambridge Anthropology* 30: 109–26.

Totton, N. (2011), *Wild Therapy*, Ross-on-Wye, UK: PCCS Books.

Vidrine, M., P. Owen-Smith and P. Faulkner (2002), 'Equine-Facilitated Group Psychotherapy: Applications for Therapeutic Vaulting', *Issues in Mental Health Nursing* 23: 587–603.

Weiss, D. (2009), 'Equine Assisted Therapy and Theraplay', in E. Munns (ed.), *Applications of Family and Group Theraplay*, 225–36, Lanham, Maryland: Jason Aronson.

Yorke, J. (2010), 'The Significance of Human–Animal Relationships as Modulators of Trauma Effects in Children: A Developmental Neurobiological Perspective', *Early Child Development and Care* 180: 559–70.

Zilcha-Mano, S., M. Mikulincer and P. R. Shaver (2011), 'Pet in the Therapy Room: An Attachment Perspective on Animal-Assisted Therapy', *Attachment and Human Development* 13: 541–61.

13

Exploring a spirituality of the earth in therapy

Elaine Thélier

Introduction

It is mid-summer. I am invited by our group supervisor to spend some time alone before meeting with the group in the space that has been our outdoor supervision location for several years. As I walk up the wet, grassy path alongside a small stream, brown with mineral elements, I notice cheek high grass stalks hanging heavy with rain and early seedheads. I wonder at the wonderful flexibility of a grass stalk, each one standing alone and yet together with the same perfect arc as they bow earthward. I love their capacity to yield to the rain yet stay upright just enough to retain their seed-load, there is so much beauty here, and intelligence. As I walk, I let my eyes wonder back and forth across the scene in front of me. Slender grass stalks silhouetted against the sky nodding in unison, responding to a slight breeze. I sway with them, feeling their rhythmic dance. I observe more stalks upright with their tighter seedheads and thicker stems resisting the downward pull of the earth. Others still, with their splayed cupped flowerheads, netting rainwater in purpose-built 'sinks' made from the tiniest of watertight petals. The grasses bob and bow, each stalk foregrounded by the expansive sky, my vision and consciousness aware of both.

This is how we approach each supervision session. A time to connect, meet the space and to be with it. What meets me is what might come later in the work. Flexibility, yielding, secure containers, tenderness, resistance, a rhythmic dance between therapist and client, moving from smallness to expansiveness might all feature in today's supervision conversations in one form or another. The emphasis initially is to allow an embodied engagement and connection and to receive what is offered there and for this to be a part of the process. Or not. For me it is an essential and implicit spiritual component of the work. As Thomas Berry states, 'The Divine communicates primarily through the language of the natural world, not to hear the natural world is not to hear the Divine' (2009)

This chapter introduces the idea that working therapeutically outdoors can be an opportunity to explore spirituality with whatever form or language that might evoke. It discusses how ecotherapy can promote the discovery and expression of a, perhaps long-forgotten, part of ourselves and in doing so may be one way of responding to, and possibly reversing, the ecological devastation we all currently face. A bold statement perhaps, but there are many, some cited here, who have convinced me of this possibility.

The ideas for this piece have emerged from engaging in a range of processes and practices over the spring, summer and autumn seasons of this year. It has involved hours of indoor and outdoor silent meditations, walking alone and with others along the edges of shorelines, rivers and canals, sitting in fields, on moors, and in woods, seeking permission to enter and then listening deeply to the more-than-human world, much talking, moving, listening and reflecting with my outdoor practitioner colleagues and friends in the ancient Derbyshire woodlands and the spaciousness of the Suffolk landscape, reading and listening to poetry and music, reading and listening to a vast number of authors at my desk, on the beach, on the train, in bed, in the car, constructing passages and themes and reading these aloud to the birds, the trees and the incoming and outgoing tides on Findhorn beach in the north of Scotland. It has been an embodied, exhilarating, moving, frustrating, despairing and profound process as creative endeavours can often be. So not exactly 'a walk in the park', you might say.

It is a familiar alchemic pattern, one that involves many parts of myself, my life and work. I cannot even say that there has been a consistent, linear, goal orientated pathway for my life or this work. I think it has been, what Parker J. Palmer describes as a calling at a deepest level, and, in his words, 'something I cannot not do, for reasons I am unable to explain to anyone and don't fully understand myself but that are nonetheless compelling' (Palmer 2000: 25)

My spiritual practice has always been an important part of my life, less obviously to my work but nonetheless influential to it. Having worked outdoors with groups and individuals for almost twenty years I was curious when my outdoor therapeutic work and spiritual life began to converge in ways I had not anticipated or planned for, even though I knew deep in my heart both were inextricably connected. I did not express this explicitly within each community. In my spiritual community I did not speak of my connection with nature and in my therapeutic community, I did not openly describe my spiritual practice or inner life. Now, I am finding that I can do both. And with each book I read, each climate statistic I absorb, each encounter I have with the natural community, including us humans, I find that I *must* do both.

I would describe myself as a seeker and an 'edge walker', to borrow a term from Terry Tempest Williams (2005, cited in B. Taylor) occupying a thin space between groups, ideas and faiths, not always entering fully into a movement, a system or community. As a consequence of this and perhaps also a reflection of the original failure of 'the family', I have experienced a deep need to belong, to be affiliated with a group, a movement, anything that would tell me who I am meant to be, where I am meant to be and what I am meant to be doing. I have now found, through a combination of my spiritual life and practice, my outdoor therapeutic practice community, and the times in which we live, that I have a greater sense of belonging and a much clearer idea of what I need to be doing in the world.

The field

We know from the increasing numbers of therapists taking their therapy practice outdoors, evidenced here in this edition, and more and more people accessing activities such as forest bathing, outdoor mindfulness, art and nature-based therapies, that there is a renewal for more encounters with nature, not just for horticultural pleasure and necessity, but to develop a more meaningful, beneficial relationship. As we encounter this natural world, we are tentatively also being invited to consider the notion that nature is not a resource to be exploited or consumed, but a living breathing, and some would say, sacred entity. One that is at risk. And those of us who choose to work outdoors, are in direct relationship with this risk be it conscious or unconscious. How do we respond to this? What is our role?

Working outdoors or being 'in nature' is often described as a beneficial, health focused activity, one that helps us humans feel good, alive and well; however, David Tacey sees these encounters with nature not as a romantic, wholesome movement which can often accompany the descriptions of these experiences, but as a spiritual, political and social movement. (2004). He believes there is a renewed interest in spirituality, and this is manifesting as 'engaged spirituality' where there is a concern for the welfare of the world, and an awakening in us, particularly in the Western world, of the sacredness of our endangered world. As different people also enter this field – theologians philosophers, artists, poets, mystics, pagans, shamans, Indigenous peoples – and engage in different conversations generating new and different stories, we are being potentially invited into what Bill Plotkin says is the 'largest story we're capable of living, serving something bigger than ourselves' (2008). Perhaps, as Tacey laments, 'just in the nick of time' (Tacey: 182). These ideas coincide with a growing disenchantment with our materialistic and technological world, as well as an increasing number of nature aesthetic writings that have come from deep ecological practice. There is now a genuine concern for the welfare of the world highlighted on our screens and through news reports where we witness determined action to alert others to the environmental devastation. Joanna Macy's work has for many years made the significant connection between the environmental destruction and loss and a deeper part of our human psyche and states 'that unless you have some roots in a spiritual practice that holds life as sacred and encourages joyful communion with all your fellow beings, facing the enormous challenges ahead becomes nearly impossible' (Vaughan-Lee 2016).

Conversations in the field

How, and when in our work, do we have these conversations? What is our own spiritual story as we practise activities like 'walk and talk' sessions? Is it climate anxiety? An existential crisis? A religious or spiritual crisis? In a recent supervision session, Anne and I were discussing spirituality in the context of her work with clients. We were reflecting on the possibility of disclosing our own spiritual or religious beliefs with clients and wondering about the ethics of this, the impact on clients, on ourselves and the work. 'There is always a hesitancy about this' says Anne. 'It's a relational edge I never seem to be able to navigate. How do I make this explicit, do I even want to? Do I ask permission, seek consent to have conversations that include the spiritual?' 'When is the most appropriate time to do it? What does it mean to speak of presence? But' a tone of exasperation enters her voice, 'this is where I believe am most potent!'

We both laugh but feel equally bemused, confused, and insist that this needs more discussion. It also begs the question of why would we speak of this? What would be the purpose or how would this be of service to the work itself or, to be bold, the earth? Both of us have long-standing spiritual practices, we talk about how these practices support our personal lives as well as our work. However, Anne is right to highlight the level of hesitancy with clients and with other therapists. Although the term spirituality is used more frequently these days, not everyone understands what each of us mean by this term. Sometimes people refer to spirituality as their religious faith, sometimes to their specific grounding practice, sometimes to someone's personal qualities, a yoga practice, mindful practice or even the feeling they get from a beautiful view or scene they regularly visit. These can all be true. Spirituality for me is a physical, embodied momentary or extended experience, not an abstract idea, feeling, theory, ideology or movement of some kind. It is a personally lived reality. A consistent, constant, engaged practice. For me it is a reminder of how I connect to the energy and wonder of life, a practice of self-reflection and a form of service.

Being invited by William Bloom, director of The Spiritual Companion's Trust to 'do what works best for you' (Bloom 2011: 39), in relation to what helped me connect with the wonder and energy of life, put my years of floundering around on the edges of one religious or spiritual tradition or another into perspective and something inside me sighed a huge sigh of relief. What? Anything? Yes. Just know it about yourself. Become conscious and intimate with that part of you, then do it as often and whenever you can. And, if you can, make it a ritual or a practice so that you connect regularly, daily if possible. It was an invitation, as Bloom suggests, to recognize and know what activities, situations, environments helped me to soften and open my heart, melt my boundaries, open my awareness and enter into a deep and sacred consciousness.

So here are some of the ways in which I most easily connect in no specific order or level of importance.

Swimming. Noticing a point in a pottery class when everyone is quiet and totally involved in their clay work. Listening to the sounds of bread-making and people chatting in my local café bakery. Watching my granddaughter as she wriggles her way into the sea. Lying down under a tree. Silent meditation with a candle. Listening to music. Enjoying a good joke. Stillness. Cooking for people who are coming around to eat. Listening to my sons (now in their thirties) in their Tolkien-speak. Lying underneath a sandbank full of the tiny holes from which sand martins emerge and fly over me. Drawing. Being in the presence of someone who is troubled or suffering. Praying.

We know at some point in our practice as counsellors, supervisors and therapists we will encounter those who may want to speak of their faith, spiritual needs, religious influences, and indeed we may have our own ideas, value systems and faiths. How do we provide a setting that enables a client to explore the deeper aspects of self-awareness and self-determination? For the most part I have kept this part of my life separate from my clinical practice until relatively recently. I often felt uncomfortable describing my spiritual experiences to others, worrying I am sounding a bit sanctimonious or getting into 'airy-fairy stardust' stuff, (practices, e.g., that might just be about escapism rather than insight and service sometimes attributed to New Ageism) but how many of us feel competent in this area? How many of us had training that included this subject with any depth? We do have a responsibility to support and understand clients as they explore these issues for themselves as part of working within a diversity model, but how do we do this if spiritual or religious practices or experiences are not part of our language or behaviour? The language used in these areas is also somewhat problematical, many shunning terms that may have emotional, political or personal associations. So how do our own religious or spiritual-but-not-religious affiliations and experiences shape our responses? How do our own practices, if any, support our work?

Approaching these themes in our work can be challenging but in working outdoors I have discovered there is a natural opportunity to cultivate a more nuanced, less human, more spiritual approach in our work. Once habituated with working outdoors, the natural world itself becomes part of the process – if we let it. If we listen and allow whatever comes into the field to be our guide or in some way inform the therapeutic process, if we let go of the need to be the 'all-knowing ones' and bring information or 'messages' from the field then we are naturally engaging with our earth community and thus beginning to 'think with' rather than 'think about' nature as Donna Haraway suggests (Haraway 2016, cited in Duncan R., p. 20). And she is by no means alone, there are many others in this field, other than obvious but still not heard Indigenous communities, encouraging us to 'think with' nature, such as Kimmerer, Abrams, Berry, Plotkin.

Most people I encounter in the field of outdoor work, without fail, speak of their spiritual experiences as they engage with clients, groups or themselves. Or at least, in speaking about the context of outdoor experiences, they shift into using terms and expressions that might be associated with spirituality. Working outdoors can unlock, unravel or remind us of a different part of ourselves. With more nature encounters we are discovering for ourselves the fascinating, the intricate, the poetic, the beautiful, the wild, the predictable, the unpredictable, the awesome and, as Karen Armstrong (2022) suggests, the sacred. This in turn, she says, exposes us to the sacredness within ourselves, which for many, in our Western mainly secular culture, is a novel experience. As we engage with the natural world, whether through knowledge acquisition, environmental interest or deep concern for the natural world we are, more and more, discovering our place within it, understanding our relationship to ourselves, to each other as well as to the natural world and in doing so we are, as Tacey suggests, asking nature 'to tell us who we are' (Tacey 2004: 182). As outdoor practitioners we are coming into direct contact with a sacred part of our selves whether we consciously know it, acknowledge it, or even desire it. This part has been described by Merton as 'the True Self', by Jung as 'the Anima/Animus' and by Martin Shaw as 'our Wild Twin'. Jung also reminds us 'called or not called, God will be there'.

Knowing the ground

In their recent book, *Ecotherapy, A Field Guide*, David Key and Keith Tudor (2023) set out several key theories around ecotherapy and the implications for practice with a question aimed at those of us therapists who work outdoors and choose to call ourselves ecotherapists. In their meta-analysis they suggest that in working outdoors, we are, consciously or unconsciously, expressing something about how we view ourselves in relation to the natural world. They offer a challenge to the ecotherapy world, not that of finding 'philosophical congruence or a common language for this field, but to fearlessly find ways to stop retreating [as eco-practitioners], from matters of spirit' (Key and Tudor 2023: 110). The idea that humans are not separate from the natural world, that we are part of the natural world is a key component of what Key and Tudor term the 'line of ecological contradiction'. Some might challenge a Western, human-centric and possible patriarchal bias but it offers us as practitioners an opportunity to explore our place in the earth community and how this affects our work as therapists. They state that if we are to call ourselves ecotherapists, we are situating ourselves as reciprocal and ecocentric, that is, humans are nature, and nature is therapist. Which is opposite to the anthropocentric, extractive position, that is, human as therapist and nature as resource. This, they suggest, would be an alignment with some of the more consumerist, exploitative behaviours of this position. By situating ourselves as relationally ecocentric and reciprocal we are potentially opening the possibility of developing a sacred relationship with ourselves and the natural world.

Armstrong reminds us that there are many ancient traditions and practices; Confucians and Daoists, Hindus and Buddhists, Greeks and Sufis for example, who have cultivated a reverence for the natural world and our part in it for centuries. Indigenous communities for millennia experienced themselves as partners in nature and are bewildered by the idea of humans being separate from the natural world. Interestingly, two First Nation women in response to Tudor and Key's metatheory, point out their difficulty in responding to the Westernized concepts and definitions of ecotherapy as it represents a 'two-dimensional concept for a place, a space that is a non-linear, timeless, physical and spiritual' (O'Neill, Stawiarski cited in Key, Tudor p. 87). An ecocentric approach demands that as a therapist I relate to the more-than-human world in a way that aligns with these values and that means going in deeper, spending time longer, engaging in a way that respects and assumes an intelligence and a sacredness of the earth community.

What are the conditions that best support the development of spirituality in this work? How might we make this more explicit and, a I suggested earlier, should we? I believe, having worked outdoors for many years now, that working as an ecotherapist we are best placed for this to happen naturally within this approach. This, of course, can be an implicit part of one's soul or self-care practice, but what I am proposing here is that that as outdoor practitioners this can become more explicit, intentional and shared. Below are some examples of the ways in which we can make this more explicit. There have been many occasions in my work, training and supervision practices where we have been, to my mind, developing a spiritual competency albeit, implicitly. The following example where a supervision group member volunteers to lead a task that identifies a spiritual approach, shows how this can be achieved more explicitly.

The wild nature of nature

In our seasonal supervision meetings, our supervisor supports us in collating ideas for a shared agenda over the course of the weekend. In this autumnal session Martha brings her interest in exploring spirituality and the group agrees they would like to explore this too. Martha takes time to prepare her session which comes on the last morning of the weekend – Sunday. Her instructions and invitations are simple. No long explanations of what to expect, think about, experience, or focus on, no rationale or theoretical principles to digest en route. We are simply invited to walk silently together to a familiar place in the woods. When we reach the space, we will give time to fully encounter ourselves there and to allow whatever expressions, movements, thoughts, gestures to be received and expressed, after which we will return silently together to the original meeting place.

This is often the way we might encounter these woods where we regularly meet for supervision, and silence is part of the process. It allows us to attune, be with, attend to, notice, listen, be heard, receive each other, and to connect with, the 'more-than-human other' to use a David Abram's phrase (1996). Silence is part of traditional contemplative practices of many faiths and religions. Silence also helps, I believe, to develop a psychological and spiritual literacy crucial to this work.

> *The task starts as soon as we pick up our backpacks. We go through the initial practical adjustments, fiddling with our bags , clothing, sticks, water bottles. There is, it seems to me, a collective sigh from the trees and birds, as we head out. The woods 'know, respond and notice' us as we move, birds instantly fly off or send out their territory calls, creatures scatter underfoot. Martha determines the pace and leads us, silently, along the uneven forest path. As we walk, we fall into a steady manageable rhythm. This can change depending on the weather, time of day, season, temperature, the terrain underfoot, the path we have chosen and so on. Today we negotiate a few fallen branches, some muddy patches, hold spikey brambles aside for each other, silently step over boulders, climb up small slopes, watch as each one of us negotiates a zig-zag path designed to keep out trail bikes, wait while those of us who are slower, older, catch up. It is companionable and comforting. I am reminded of witnessing a large flock of geese seen on a river recently, each one stepping up onto the bank in turn, then walking slowly in single file. As I walk, I notice my breathing slow down and deepen. I feel my body soften, become less tense, open to what is here. I feel very welcome in this space. It 'knows' we are considerate, respectful. There is an ease I have become accustomed to in this setting, with this group, as I step into our rhythm, our movement, our togetherness. I feel a sense of belonging. We arrive at the* bowl-like *,womb-like opening in the trees. With another invitation to allow ourselves to receive or to move to whatever we feel drawn to, we silently shed our bags and look around. Here is an invitation to find personal thresholds of where we might be drawn, inviting the sensuous body to intuit what we might need at that moment or for the space to call to us.*

In her book *Church of the Wild*, Victoria Loorz (2021) suggests that entering into the natural world quietly, pausing at a threshold, waiting to be invited in, asking permission, waiting in silence for that permission begins to invoke a sense of the sacred in us. We are paying attention to the wild nature of nature and in doing so might be awakening our own wild sacred self. Our wild twin. We are also letting go of the inner 'is this right?' or 'what am I supposed to be doing?' which can often beset us as we therapists step out of our subject comfort zones or even the consulting room into a different therapeutic frame. This slow, intentional, attuned approach is the start of developing reverence. We might be brought to tears, experience a quickened heart rate, notice a softening within our bodies, experience awe. Clients I have worked with have often spoken of this in ways that are sometimes surprising and illuminate a 'true' part of themselves. As O'Donohue suggests, 'reverence bestows dignity, and it is only in the light of dignity that the beauty and mystery of a person will become visible' (O'Donohue 2005: 31).

> *I watch as each member of our group quietly settle into their own space. Some stay standing, others curl themselves into fern-lined nooks, or perch on boulders alongside the fast-flowing stream, wrap arms around the girth of a tree or across a boulder softened by moss or gently rest their back and head against the base of a tree. As I watch, I have the sensation within me of enchantment, devotion, intimacy, love. It was not dissimilar to the sensation I experienced as a young and unconfirmed member of the Anglican congregation, watching each person walk their way to the alter to receive the Christian ritual of the Communion. Each person, very much grounded in the physicality of their experience and, to my young and impressionable mind, experiencing what I thought might be observable joy. In the woods now I decide to stand, closing my eyes for many minutes. I become the tree, the water, the ground. I also become aware of the stillness as well as the movement around me.*

David Whyte reminds us that to practise the 'ecstasy of silence' and 'to stand stock still and allow the astonishing moveability of the world to instruct us in the way we belong to qualities and powers much larger than our own, can help us to get to a place of joy' (Whyte 2024).

> *After poems, words, personal expressions, we are invited to attend to our closing and leaving of the space, do whatever needs to be done to embody, celebrate the experience and to thank the space. We walk back to our meeting spot, in silence and then with flasks of tea, biscuits, and cake (always cake) we speak of our feelings and insights. We thank Martha for providing us with a simple but deeply enriching time. Everyone without exception using terms that define a spiritual experience.*

This experiential approach both models and provides us with an example of how explicit spiritual literacy and skills can be acquired through contact, intentional engagement, solitude and silence in and with nature.

Wild mind

I generally work outdoors, but because many of my supervisees are situated around the country, I also work online. I endeavour to bring my 'wild mind' and a spiritual approach to the online sessions. This calls for intention, connection and a willingness to surrender to the mystery as well a degree of creativity. Below is a description of how I might include this approach in the work.

Stella opens our online supervision session looking strained with slumped shoulders and a tired look on her face. She tells me about her difficult month. She looks pained as she describes her partner's long spell in hospital following a recent life-changing diagnosis and the effect this has on her personal and professional life. She describes the return of her stepson from university who was now installed in his old room – her online consulting room of late – and the tricky negotiations of having him vacate the room minutes before meeting her clients online.

We talk about options. Negotiating earlier room vacation, a rota, timetable? Won't that just be read and forgotten about? She says. Renting a therapy space? Expensive and conflicts with her new caring role. A shed in the garden? Mmm … a possibility. There is a shed, she says, as a memory of the reasons why this shed was installed many years ago stirs for her, mainly as a sanctuary from a new step-parenting situation. Ideas flow. Interest mounts. I suggest a break and invite Stella to wonder into the garden to view this new possibility.

I take my tea into my garden space. I go out with intention. 'What would you have me receive?' I say to the distant hills. This is my way of greeting and an intention to be receptive to what, in the field, might be useful here. I scan the horizon but notice a scuffling much closer to me. I see buzzard lift its feathered speckled weight easily from the ground and watch yellow clawed feet alight and loosely hang, immobile, like aircraft wheels. Buzzard takes flight and to my delight is followed by another. They ascend directly, assisted by the found thermals. I watch in familiar awe, then am taken by more scuffling and watch as another buzzard from the same spot takes flight. Pairs of buzzards I had seen before but not three. Was this usual? Was it a young one? Too early in the season perhaps. But why three together? Were they feasting on a caught prey? The third buzzard joined the two others, though not quite in their path, seeming to fly out to the side then back in their circle-line over and over. Much like a child on a walk, coming and going, always a parent within its range. It occurred me that this grouping might represent Stella's situation. Her partner, and stepson, together, apart, negotiating space. I felt a sense of hope rise in me. A feeling of evolving families struggling but ultimately ascending. I remember the ideas of what buzzard sightings might represent to those who want to gain clarity of meaning. For some they represent resourcefulness, the seizing of opportunities, freedom, rebirth. The three buzzards soon become dots high up above me and I venture back inside to the online space with Stella. I felt transformed. Hopeful.

After hearing Stella's excitement and plans to clear, sort and clean the shed I ask if I might share my experience of the break. I tell her of the sighting of the three buzzards being careful not to give too much of my interpretation of the scene. But Stella has already her own meaning. To her it was the three of them, winding around each other, getting to grips with their new environment and grappling over how to negotiate the space, who needed to be resourceful, who needed support right now, who needed to be allowed to come and go for a while. It gave us both a more nuanced approach to the situation.

It was a psychological shift and, I believe, a spiritual experience. Why so? What makes this spiritual? It may not differ from other supervision sessions where imagery, metaphor, dreams, feelings, intentions, interpretations often support the supervision process. Here though, there is the intention to be open to mystery, to a non-human wisdom and a 'thinking with' nature rather than 'thinking about' nature to use Haraway's earlier terminology. If we chose to include the earth community, we are potentially including so much more than we humans can bring. David Abram (1996) observed that the human body has evolved in conjunction with Earth: 'Our bodies have formed themselves in delicate reciprocity with the manifold textures, sounds, and shapes of an animate earth … to shut ourselves off from these other voices … is to rob our own senses of their integrity' (p. 22), and, in my experience, the messages and signals we receive in that space can often be transformative.

Leaning in, naturally

As part of my learning on the Spiritual Companions Trust's diploma and now as a tutor myself on the programme, we invite reflection as a way of developing a spiritual literacy and practice through a specific exercise of group listening. The structure is not unlike the Quaker clearing committee format, a group process that enables one person to explore something that might be a specific daily life challenge or a particular dilemma that they cannot see clearly to resolve by themselves. It consists of three rounds. In the first round the Focus Person shares the growth edge or challenge, next each group member is invited to ask one question to better understand the situation, to clarify something or for the Focus Person to reflect on at a different time, finally, each group member is invited to share insights, not to offer advice, but to share what they might have learned about that person and their particular challenge.

The major benefits of a session such as this come from participants experiencing an extended amount of time of careful holding and listening. The spiritual dimension comes from a sustained period of compassionate engagement and listening and aligns with many spiritual or religious traditions of compassionate presence as in 'when two or more are gathered' (Satsang). The idea is to enable and develop whole body listening within a safe holding space. In an ecospiritual context this includes the ecological earth body. Being with and among nature provides us with an added dimension that may support, illuminate or generate action.

> *Amy brought a personal issue that she felt was permeating all areas of her personal and professional life. As our facilitator helped us explore the options of how we as a group might support Amy, I noticed a 'nudging' from the cliffs behind me. There was the usual holding I felt there, but also something more. I felt as if I was being gently told to 'step up'. I looked towards the immediate environment, saw scattered leaves, freshly emerging*

> *bracken in the rock crevasses, then towards the distant swaying trees. There was a hushedness, and a sort of 'leaning in' of all those elements. An attentiveness. A waiting to hear. Even though I felt slightly under prepared but emboldened by the 'nudging' I found myself offering the focus-group style structure as a way of allowing Amy to explore her issue. I explained the process to the group and our facilitator and Amy agreed to go ahead. As our facilitator stepped back into the cliffs and trees so that I could lead the session, I asked Amy what she would like to share and she began slowly, tentatively, to describe her situation. Although I was attentive to Amy's sharing, I noticed that I was also aware of the human and other-than human group. I noticed small creatures busying themselves around us, a regular robin hopping from rock to stone to branch, and still that sense of 'leaning in' as everything remained silent, hushed, expectant. The afternoon sky began to darken, reflecting perhaps the depth and darkness of the inner place Amy was experiencing. A dark and lonely place. A longing that might not happen for her in her lifetime that was painful to contemplate for her at that time. Someone tended the fire, and I noticed it brought light and a fierce glow to Amy's face and body as she finished speaking, an energetic lighting up. At the end of the process, we thanked her for her courage to access her deepest thoughts and share these with us. It was, for me, a profoundly moving experience, literally moving us all.*

When Amy reflected on this several months later, she commented to me that the session was transformational for her. It was very much about feeling heard and seen in her experience of her then struggle with life. She said it was hugely supportive, and that it helped her let go of some difficult emotions and blocks that may have been getting in the way of her own seeing and being seen in the world and acknowledged that for her, things had worked out positively following that experience. For me the woodland context for this was hugely important, a vital life force that energized each of us in that moment and that had something to say, something to give.

Natural service

I began this chapter with an admission that often in my life I have felt unsure of what I am meant to be doing and where I belong. Working outdoors and shifting my spiritual practice to encompass this has helped me establish a sense of belonging which I hope this piece has illustrated to some extent. I belong to the earth community. What I am meant to be doing feels trickier. I am not by nature an activist. I have never stood side by side with others to protest in the hope for change and I admire those who do. I have worked in community settings to facilitate community gardens and allotment growing and volunteered for many similar projects, but it had not felt, back then, like activism nor an act of service, more an imperative, urgent, enthusiastic impetus to get people 'into nature'.

Service at this point in my life feels different. How do I serve others? And I include the more-than-human other in this quest. My spiritual life is important, but I found myself smiling when I heard Joanna Macy declare in a recent podcast, that sitting serenely in a spiritual 'haze' is not enough right now. Ecospirituality is not about just seeking bliss, joy and internal personal transcendence in the natural world. Strong, fierce love is what is needed right now in the world says Macy. And love in the face of despair. As a spiritual companion my role is to be a loving and benevolent presence with suffering. The earth is suffering. How can I be the loving, benevolent presence with the earth? How do I do this?

My recent participation in a one-day pilgrimage with the River Dart Wild Church in Devon, in association with the British Pilgrimage Trust, helped me to define this a little. It was created and led by Rev Sam Wernham, who developed one of the first contemporary wild churches, with its sea to source pilgrimage route, over ten years ago. Their Sunday service is conducted alongside the River Dart, their mission being 'an invitation to re-member Sundays as whole and holy time, re-visit local sacred spaces, returning to the community of all beings through walking out into nature for elemental celebration, sinking into deep silence and opening to the spirit of the wild' (https://www.riverdartwildchurch.com/).

The practice was akin to Martha's simple invitation in the woods. To walk alongside the river with others, in silence, with reverence and intention. As a group we gathered outside in the church grounds in preparation for our walk. We were encouraged to focus on 'edges', consider what the marginal means to us, an interesting coincidence for me given my earlier description. For five hours we walked, picnicked, and celebrated the edge of the river silently together. It was punctuated from time to time with information from Sam about the fragile state of the salt marshes and the depleted numbers of spawning salmon returning to the river. Being immersed in the place and hearing these facts, as opposed to acquiring the information from news reports, books or TV, offered a close-up experience of environmental devastation and for me, generated, a different sensation of grief. On receiving this information, I was filled with despair about our world. I felt my heart break. Wordlessly I apologized to the scene in front of me, expressed sorrow to the river, the egrets, geese and gulls wading at the water's edge, asked for forgiveness from the tiniest of salt-tolerant plants clinging to the unstable, barely discernible salt-marsh edge and expressed my immense gratitude to the enormous oak tree against which I was leaning.

I was in touch with the beauty and fragility of our world and experiencing this essentially alone but also with others. It really was a moment of 're-membering' me back into this natural community in quite a profound way. Macy's work on environmental destruction and the associated despair calls for just this approach. Her encouragement to engage with others in this despair is what marks a different approach. Instead of reeling from the intensity of facts and statistics, I was confronted with the effects at the water's edge and held them within me within the silence.

Although I have worked therapeutically outdoors for almost twenty years, with clients, individuals and for my own well-being, this recent intense encounter did something different. It generated within me a fierce form of love. As David Hinton proclaims, 'before intention and choice, before ideas and understanding and everything we think about ourselves – we love this world around us' (Hinton 2022: 3). Hinton reminds us that to love nature we need to love it and of itself, not because it is useful to us, nor even like us. He suggests the way to love it is to 'weave our consciousness' back into the landscape, into nature so that we might value it for itself and therefore care for it. When I work, think with, or allow myself to be with nature I am essentially weaving myself and, indirectly, the people with whom I work, back into the landscape, and nature. I am not suggesting for one moment, that during our therapeutic work sessions we bombard our clients with environmental statistics, people can find those for themselves, or not, but we are uniquely positioned as ecotherapists to simultaneously serve our earth community as well as our clients – a fact I have increasingly become aware of over my many years of working outdoors and feel a great deal of gratitude to nature for teaching this to me.

References

Abram, D. (2017), *The Spell of the Sensuous. Perception and Language in a More-than-Human World*, New York: Vintage Books.

Armstrong, K. (2022), *Sacred Nature: How We Can Recover Our Bond with the Natural World*, UK: Penguin Random House.

Berry, T. (2009), *The Sacred Universe, Earth Spirituality and Religion in the Twenty First Century*, New York: Columbia University Press.

Bloom, W. (2011), *The Power of Modern Spirituality*, London, UK: Piatkus.

O'Donohue, J. (2005), *Beauty: The Invisible Embrace*, [Audio book] Audible.

Haraway, D. (2016), 'Staying with the Trouble: Making Kin in the Chthulucene', in L. Aspey, C. Jackson and D. Parker (eds), *Holding the Hope*, PCCS Books.

Hinton, D. (2022), *Wild Mind, Wild Earth*, Colorado: Shambala Publications.

Key, D., and K. Tudor (2023), *Ecotherapy: A Field Guide*, Bicester, Oxfordshire, UK: Phoenix Publishing House.

Kimmerer, R. W. (2015), *Braiding Sweetgrass*, Minneapolis, MN: Milkweed Editions.

Loorz, V. (2021), *Church of the Wild: How Nature Invites Us into the Sacred*, Minnesota: Broadleaf Books.

Palmer, P. J. (2000), *Let Your Life Speak: Listening to the Voice of Vocation*, Jossey Bass.

Plotkin, B. (2008), *Nature and the Human Soul: Cultivating Wholeness and Community in a Fragmented World*, [Audio Book] Audible

Tacey, D. (2004), *The Spirituality Revolution. The Emergence of Contemporary Spirituality*, Hove, Sussex, UK: Routledge.

Tempest Williams, T. (2005), *Encyclopaedia of Religion and Nature*, ed. B Taylor, London: Continuum.
Vaughan-Lee, L. (2016), *Spiritual Ecology: The Cry of the Earth*, Second edition, CA, USA: The Golden Sufi Centre.
Whyte, D. (2024), 'Three Sundays': Intimacy [Webinar] (Accessed 22 September 2024)

14

Rewilding therapy, the therapeutic ecosystem and imagin-action

Chiara Fortina Santin

Introduction

This chapter will offer some ecosystemic ideas about working therapeutically in nature, including a case example. As a systemic thinker and therapist, I consider the importance of multiple identities and relationships and the multilayered contexts, including nature, the climate emergency and the cosmos. I will describe my own personal and professional journey towards rewilding therapy and how to make sense of the therapeutic process using an ecosystemic map for working in nature. I will conclude with some reflections on therapeutic activism and the urgency to come together to imagine new landscapes for mental health services that promote the benefits of spending time in nature for our ecological well-being as well as looking after the planet through *imagin-action*, that is, becoming visionaries, therapists or activists through daily actions.

My ecological self or selves and systemic thinking

I am a middle-age white woman from the south of Europe. My husband and I came to the UK in 1998 as economic migrants in search for jobs and a better life. I had the privilege to develop a bond with nature since I was a child, through the landscape surrounding the small village where I grew up, its woods and hills, streams and mountains. I strongly identify my roots in the Italian Alps as they have shaped my inner landscapes (Fortina Santin 2024). Another big influence has been my grandmother's indigenous knowledge and her wisdom rooted in living alongside nature in everyday life through looking after her garden, full of flowers and vegetables, and animals, for example, chickens, rabbits, turkeys in addition to cats and dogs.

In the last eight years my ecosystemic practice has evolved through my personal and professional journey of *homecoming*, that is, reconnecting, adapting and rekindling my bond with nature in a different landscape, weather and smells in Sussex (UK). This has led to rewilding my systemic practice, that is, transferring my therapeutic skills to practising in nature with individuals, couples, families and groups (Santin 2021).

The idea of an ecological self (Næss 1987) has been helpful in considering my identity within an ecological framework across cultures and landscapes. In line with systemic thinking, I also like to regard ourselves as an ecology of selves (Bateson 2016) or a community of selves (O' Sullivan 2021) to reflect the multiplicity and relational aspects of our identities across all dimensions of difference (called the social Graces by Burnham 1992, 1993 and Roper-Hall 1998). These include ability, geography and place, north and south, culture, race and ethnicity, gender and sexual orientation, class, economics and employment, whether visible or invisible, voiced or unvoiced (Burnham 2012) and their intersectionality (Crenshaw 1989; Butler 2015).

Systemic thinking and practice represent a relational and contextual approach to individual and family problems. It focuses on how key relationships shape our beliefs and narratives about ourselves, others and the world and how people in a system inevitably influence each other. It follows that even when working individually, therapy considers individuals as embodied and embedded (Hardham 1996) in the multiple identities and sociocultural political contexts they are part of, with a consistent focus on relationships and context. It is, therefore, imperative that we include the ecological context in all therapeutic conversations, whether we practice outdoors or indoors.

The wider ecological context

Bendell (2018, 2023), Macey (2014) and Greta Thunberg are some of the most powerful public voices in recent years who have highlighted the severity of the ecological crisis and the threat of the survival of our planet, including social collapse. In spite of a collective denial and apathy, a sense of despair and overwhelm about the climate emergency, there is the progressive acknowledgement of eco-anxiety and eco-grief as emotional responses to the crisis (see Clayton 2020; Cunsolo et al. 2020; Macy 1983; Oliveira 2023; Pihkala 2020, 2021, to name a few).

Kearney (2013, 2021, 2024), family therapist and climate activist in Ireland, strongly challenges the state of denial of the climate emergency in which we are both perpetrators and victims. He claims that this process is advanced and escalating and its full impact on us and the new generations is described as an emotional and psychological tsunami that cannot be ignored and demand action.

The biophilia hypothesis (Wilson 1984: 1) has highlighted that, as biological beings, we have an innate desire to connect with nature, an attraction to 'life and lifelike processes'. The disconnection from the natural world, rooted in anthropocentric Western cultures, has led to the disconnection from ourselves and others, a progressive deterioration of our mental health and increased social isolation (Rust 2020). Therefore, a fundamental therapeutic aim of ecotherapy is to help people reconnect with nature, as a living and healing space in which we can recognize our biological roots and restore our physical and mental health. However, as Buzzell (2016) claims, this is not enough as this first level ecotherapy may reinforce an anthropocentric view based on the dominance of humans over nature for their own needs. Second level ecotherapy acknowledges the need to protect and look after the environment to reflect the reciprocity between nature and humans and our responsibility towards mutual healing and restoration.

Koziol (2022) suggests that there is a third-level ecotherapy, that is, a nature-based community approach towards a collective commitment to serve other communities of life, and other social-ecological communities.

As systemic therapists we cannot ignore the ecological context in which we are all living. The panmorphic crisis (Simon 2021) is affecting all areas of our lives, that is, the economic, the social, the political, the local and the global contexts. Moreover, it is an ethical call to respond as human beings as well as therapists through rewilding our lives and our practices by engaging in activism.

Rewilding psychotherapy

In line with systemic thinking, we can consider various definitions of rewilding in order to embrace multiple perspectives that are inclusive of personal, professional experiences across therapy modalities, psychological theories and indigenous knowledge and practices. I will include a few here.

In the field of ecology and environmental sciences rewilding has become a popular word to describe how nature can regenerate through little human intervention while promoting biodiversity. Tree (2018: 9), leading a rewilding project at Knepp Castel Estate in West Sussex (UK), writes:

> Rewilding – giving nature the space and opportunity to express itself – is largely a leap of faith. It involves surrendering all preconceptions, and simply sitting back and

> observing what happens. Rewilding Knepp is full of surprises, and the unexpected outcomes are changing what we thought we knew about some of our native species' behaviour and habitats – indeed it is changing the science of ecology. And it is also teaching us something about ourselves, and the hubris that has led us to our current predicament.

In the field of psychotherapy, Totton (2011, 2021), who first introduced the idea of *Wild therapy*, invites us to challenge traditional therapy against a progressive domestication of our lives, urging us to consider the more-than-human world and the socio-political and historical contexts. He emphasizes our need to connect with the wild mind to rewild our inner and outer worlds.

Plotkin (2008, 2013) also advocates for rewilding psychology through re-visioning ourselves towards a holistic and integral ecology of the human psyche, reclaiming our indigenous human nature and wild mind. Plotkin writes (2013: 2): 'We must reclaim and embody our original wholeness, our indigenous human nature granted to us by nature itself.'

Rewilding starts from us as therapists. As a way of rewilding my systemic practice (Santin 2021) I have been actively looking for opportunities to increase wildness in my personal and professional life, to remain open to the many possibilities of practising alongside nature as a co-therapist rather than following prescribed ways of being a therapist.

From my experience, human rewilding and rewilding therapeutic practices can be summarized as follows:

1. Returning, reconnecting with nature.
2. Acknowledging our biological blueprint, that is, biophilia hypothesis (Wilson 1984) and the innate attraction to nature.
3. Reclaiming our relationship with nature as fundamental to our physical, emotional and mental well-being.
4. Recognizing, experiencing and believing in the healing power of nature for ourselves as therapists and for clients.
5. Re-discovering reciprocity and intimacy with the natural world and our responsibility to look after the planet.

Inner and outer landscapes through mirroring

Rewilding therapy (Santin 2021; Fortina Santin, 2024) relies on our ongoing commitment to self-reflexivity (Burnham 1993, 2005, 2012; Simon 2023). It leads to becoming explorers of the wildest edges of our inner landscapes through the mirror of nature. If we pose that nature is us and we are nature, when we connect with the outer landscapes in a meaningful way, nature reflects back an image that it is not an exact copy of who we are or who we think we are. In fact, nature is not a passive, objective mirror. It offers a different perspective on ourselves, a glimpse of our true human nature, an expanded sense of our ecological self (Næss 1987) as intricately woven into the mystery of the cosmos and natural ecosystems in which we are embedded and entangled with as one matter. As Barad (2007: 383) claims: 'The very nature of materiality is an entanglement. Matter itself is always open to, or rather entangled with, the "Other"'.

An example of this relational process of mirroring in nature between inner and outer landscapes is provided by Jordan (2012: 142), one of the pioneers in taking therapy outdoors in the UK. He describes the self 'as relational process, folding and unfolding in spatial temporal locations, which are both interior and exterior'.

The more we become familiar with our inner landscapes as therapists, the more we are able to help clients become co-explorers of unchartered territories and painful inner landscapes. Therefore, I believe that key aspects of becoming ecotherapists can be summarized as follows:

1. Exploring our inner landscapes, for example, the wild edges of our ecological self.
2. Tuning into our innate wildness in our personal and professional lives.
3. Deepening our relationship with nature.
4. Believing that ecotherapy is key to healing human–nature disconnection.
5. Developing intimacy and familiarity with nature as co-therapist.
6. Engaging in *Imagin*-action (Fortina Santin 2024).

These ideas are expanded in the following sections.

Ecosystemic therapy: An ecosystemic map

Theoretically, my ecosystemic practice in nature has evolved out of my core training in systemic and family psychotherapy but I have been integrating different theoretical ideas from family attachments (especially Byng-Hall 2008) and trauma (particularly Dana 2018) as well as environmental art (e.g. Siddons Heginworth and Nash 2020), movement and embodiment (Frizzell 2023).

By practising in nature, I have realized that I can be more present to my ecological self, that is, I can access the whole of myself, all the knowledges, skills, my own bond with nature, and my life experiences as therapeutic resources. I can also feel more aligned with my professional value base, that is, my commitment to collaborative and creative practice, decolonizing and social justice (Fortina Santin, 2024) which are key in systemic thinking and practice.

An ecosystemic theoretical framework has its roots in Gregory Bateson's work, an anthropologist, biologist, philosopher who based his interdisciplinary understanding of human mind on observations of nature. He greatly influenced the emerging field of family therapy in the 1960s and throughout its development in the 1980s and 1990s in different countries, for example, Italy, Ireland, the UK, Canada and Australia. However, Palmer (2024) argues that his ecological legacy has been dismissed in the systemic field and should be reclaimed.

Bateson (1972, 1979) highlighted that *everything is connected* through patterns that connect and a web of relationships, including our relationship with nature. Furthermore, the concept of '*The map is not the territory*' (taken from Alfred Korzybski 1933) is particularly relevant for ecotherapy. It can be used as a metaphor to describe how we, as therapists, have a map to orient our ways of practising with clients, for example, our preferred theories, techniques or specific plans for a session. However, when we practice, we often discover a different terrain, that is, what clients bring on the day and what emerges as we connect and interact within a complex web of relationships in the therapeutic process.

Similarly to when we go hiking, we may have a map to guide us but our experience of the landscape, the natural paths, the weather, the level of fitness or difficulty can be very different from what we expected or prepared for. Therefore, when we practise in nature, the therapeutic landscape is unveiling as we walk alongside our clients.

We may find ourselves responding to something unexpected, we may have to let go of our plans, ideas and clinical formulations as tentative *hypotheses* which may or may not be useful for clients (Selvini Palazzoli et al. 1980). Clients, whether they are individuals or couples or families, become *co-explorers* of the territory which is likely to be different from the original map. The map is not the territory!

Barry Mason (2005) invites therapists to engage in relational risk-taking to be open to what he called, 'safe uncertainty' (Mason 1993, 2019) and what is emerging in the therapeutic process. 'Safe uncertainty' is described as 'never fixed. It is always evolving. It is a place where doubt, uncertainty, unhelpful difference, can be safely, if at times uncomfortably, explored as part of developing and maintaining emotional intimacy and more constructive, safer relationships' (Mason 2019: 347).

When working in nature, this potential for the emerging, the unexpected, the unpredictable is enhanced by the therapist's not-knowing position (Anderson and Goolishian 1992) and a stance of neutrality and curiosity. Cecchin (1987: 405) explains: 'Curiosity leads to exploration and invention of alternative views and moves, and different moves and views breed curiosity. In this recursive fashion, neutrality and curiosity contextualize one another in a commitment to evolving differences, with a concomitant non-attachment to any particular position.'

Through systemic curiosity, we are naturally engaging in deep listening of what is emergent, a different level of consciousness which is key to entering the imaginal world (Duncan 2018, 2021). These ideas fit well with the therapist being an explorer rather than an expert and nature as the expert of our lives.

A case example

This example from my ecotherapy practice will highlight some of the key principles and ideas described in this chapter. I will use the present tense to invite the reader to become part of the therapeutic scenario.

I have been working with my co-explorer Kirsty for a couple of years. She and her partner Karen have adopted Frankie as a baby and he is now seven. Looking after him is very intense, challenging and emotionally demanding. Frankie has been showing some neurodiversity, early developmental trauma and attachment difficulties. I have been working mainly with Kirsty, being the main carer, but trying to include her partner and Frankie whenever possible.

It has been a long five-week gap since the last ecotherapy session with Kirsty. At the beginning of the session, as we enter the woodland, our usual venue, we both acknowledge that this feels like a long gap. As a way of saying hello to nature and each other, I stop and notice all the different shades of green around us. All has changed in this gap. New growth, new leaves, new shoots in this spring. Kirsty says that if she were to be a month, she would choose May. It was September in previous conversations. In my inner conversation (Rober 1999) I am thinking: 'Maybe a sign of change in her inner landscape as reflected in the outer landscape and the seasons?'

No specific agenda or topic today. I try to stay curious, avoiding any assumption of how things have been for Kirsty, inviting her own curiosity. As we gently walk into the woods, I ask 'How is your body right now?' She replies: 'Tense'. I ask another question: 'How has the hypochondria voice been in these past weeks?' She says 'Loud, very loud. It's big. It's obsessive. I have to do something to reassure me and my body that I am ok so many times in a day. It's exhausting'. I am trying to relate the problem to nature as a co-therapist so I continue: 'Is there anything around here that reminds you of hypochondria and how big it is?'

Kirsty says: 'This is it. It's this big tree covered in dead ivy'. Then she notices another tree which is standing next to the big tree and how the ivy has become one with the tree. She says: 'There is a part of me that wants it off, and a part of me that thinks that it should be there. Maybe I could cut the roots right down.'

A memory resurfaces. Kirsty shares a sad story about a holly tree in her garden which was covered with ivy and when the neighbour cut the ivy roots, the holly tree also died. Kirsty says that she doesn't want to do that and turns back to the big tree. It's huge and has a solid trunk and many big branches reaching out to the sky, all covered with dead ivy. The tree looks so majestic, heathy and full of new growth and leaves though. There is a point where the ivy has been cut and the ivy is so intricate and entangled that nobody has ever tried to get it off the tree.

I can see that Kirsty is determined to free the tree from the dead ivy. The first attempts are very successful as she pulls off the lower branches with ease. A big piece of entangled ivy comes off like a carved piece of wood. She says: 'Now I am proud! Gosh, it feels quite emotional.'

I am just taking an observing position, curious as to what is unfolding. I say: 'What are you going to do with it?' She replies: 'Burn it!' I add: 'Is there anything you want to say?'. Looking at the ivy she replies: 'I kind of want to say, "Thank you but you are not needed any more"'. I ask her to repeat this statement again. It sounds even more powerful this time. Her mission, however, is not accomplished yet. Kirsty cannot reach the higher branches where there is more ivy to unpick. She says: 'I wish I were taller'. I am amazed at Kirsty's determination and comment: 'You are not giving up. You never give up!'

Kirsty keeps going, she is totally absorbed in her task, trying to find ways to reach higher and higher. I feel like I am in a witnessing position, now wondering in my inner conversation (Rober 1999) 'When is she going to stop?'. I am reminded of previous conversations about her determination and resilience in life. It is getting more and more challenging now. She gets hold of some long sticks, and she is now using them hoping more ivy branches will fall off. At different points she stops as if she were to give up; just for a moment but then she is trying again, with more energy and new strategies and alternative sturdy sticks. Eventually Kirsty says: 'I'm going to try one last time'. I smile and comment: 'You don't give up easily, do you?'

I am thinking that she has used all the possible resources. In that moment Kirsty declares: 'I am ok with it now'. I am now trying to engage in a meaning-making process, mindful of nature as a co-therapist and ask: 'How does the tree feel?' She replies: 'It can breathe!' and adds: 'It's like I can see myself now!' At this point Kirsty gently puts her head against the trunk as if she needed some rest and touching the bark, says 'Hello!'. I ask again 'How does it feel?' She becomes emotional: 'Like coming home. This is how I want my partner to see me.' This is a way for Kirsty to think relationally and bring her partner into the therapeutic space.

I am aware that the session is coming to an end and want to create an opportunity for Kirsty to savour (Bryant and Veroff 2007) these therapeutic moments of connection to herself, nature and myself. As she looks at the first big piece of ivy fallen off, I ask 'What do you want to do with this?' She says 'Burn it. Actually, I would like to make a bonfire like my dad used to do. It was very exciting.' Another interesting relational connection where Kirsty's dad is brought into the conversation.

I suggest the next move: 'Well, there is a pile of green rubbish and wood nearby. Let's go there.' We walk for a few minutes, and she throws the ivy on top of the pile. She looks pleased about where it landed, right on top of everything. I say: 'Let's imagine lighting the fire'. At this point Kirsty starts dancing around the bonfire like a happy child.

Right in that moment I notice a bird, a red kite, just flying over us and point it to Kirsty. I ask her: 'What does it say?' She replies: 'Fly like a bird'. An example of the *Wild Reflecting Team* (Santin 2021; Fortina Santin 2024) in action, a voice from the wild becoming part of the therapeutic process! This will be expanded later in this chapter.

We slowly walk back to where we started. I ask: 'How loud is the hypochondria voice now?' She says: 'It's been almost silent and I feel safe and relaxed in my body now. Like the ivy is part of me but I can take it off sometimes. Maybe I can feel lighter like the Red Kite'.

Nature as a co-therapist

Many authors have described how nature becomes part of the therapeutic process, for example, as a co-therapist (Burls 2008; Pfeifer 2017), the therapeutic partner (Duffin 2023); a presence and active participant (Berger 2016), a 'tripartite relationship' (Hegarty 2010: 66) or a 'triadic constellation' between nature, therapist and clients (Bodnar 2023: 207) or the relational third (Marshall 2016a, 2023).

In my ecotherapy practice, as highlighted in the case example, I experience nature as both a context and a co-therapist, that is, becoming a living participant in the therapeutic process, in the following ways:

1. Nature as a safe container, that is, the background and the context in which therapy takes place, for example, the familiarity of the woods as a therapy venue for me and for Kirsty.
2. Nature as a green canvas, that is, a creative space where co-explorers can enter the freedom to express themselves through natural art, movement and metaphors, for example, Kirsty identifying with trees and dancing around the bonfire.
3. Nature as a *Wild Reflecting* Team, a wise presence, the expert of our lives, for example, Kirsty receiving a message from the natural world through the trees, the ivy, the bird.
4. Nature as a healing space where natural metaphors can promote new meanings, for example, hypochondria being associated with ivy that can be there and can be taken off with determination and resilience.

All of these elements form the *Therapeutic Ecosystem*. This way of conceptualizing the therapeutic process is similar to the representation of ecological therapeutic relating and the ecological third by Marshall (2016a, 2023) who highlights the intermingling of the human and non-human world in a relational way. The ecological space represents a container where client, therapist and nature interact in an emergent flow of body–mind connection with the place, the terrain and the more-than-human world. She (2023:104), writes 'our bodymind process arising from our relationship with a broad matrix of living organisms, including the non-human world of trees, rocks, animals … This is a state of receiving – catching the drift – where anything potentially has meaning.'

Similarly, my way of visualizing the therapeutic process is to represent it as an ecosystem and a web of relationships as shown in Figure 14.1.

In systemic therapy, we often work with more than one client, hence multiple co-explorers. The therapeutic process becomes fluid and open (hence the dotted boundaries around and between the circles) to join imaginary conversations happening within nature all the time, for example, between birds and trees, water and rocks, fungi and the ground, air and fire, clouds and rain which are interacting with each other as part of the ecosystem. This can be regarded as the *Wild Reflecting Team* (Santin 2021; Fortina Santin 2024), that is, multiple voices from the more-than-human world becoming part of the therapeutic process, in the case example through the trees, the ivy and a bird.

The circles are shown as having permeable boundaries to show the interaction in the space between people, the natural objects (matter) and the living natural

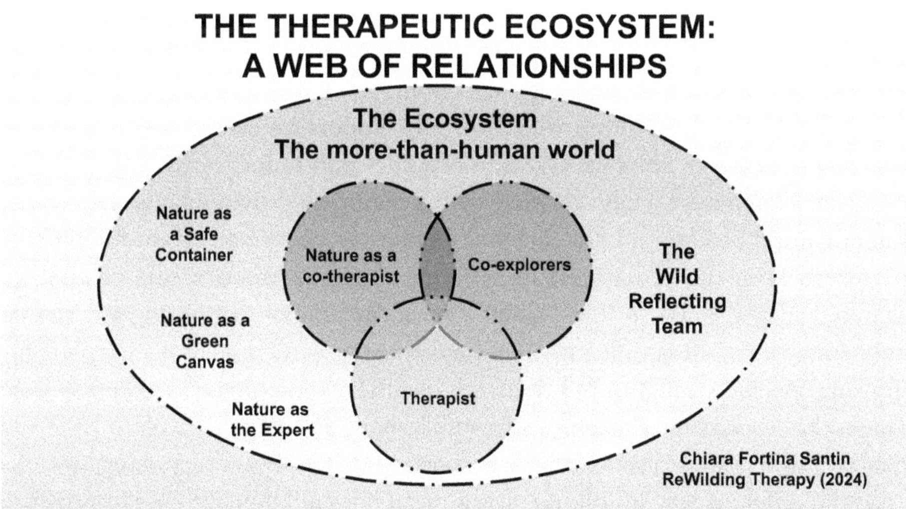

Figure 14.1 The therapeutic ecosystem: A web of relationships. Chiara Fortina Santin (2024), *Rewilding Therapy*.

world, the more-than-human world that are entangled with each other. The way they intersect becomes the liminal space where new insights into inner landscapes, new patterns of connections, relationships and meanings can emerge.

In line with an ecocentric approach, an ecosystemic framework regards clients and therapists as guests and nature becomes a host, hence the idea of dual hospitality (Fortina Santin 2024). It is a paradigm shift as it challenges the persistent Western egocentric view based on a sense of entitlement and dominance of humans over the natural environment. It helps reduce the power imbalance and promotes more equality in the web of relationships within the therapeutic ecosystem, including the more-than-human world.

The Wild Reflecting Team

The *Wild Reflecting Team* is based on a team approach (Andersen 1987, 1991; White 2000) used in systemic and family therapy. In addition to the conversation between the therapist and clients, team members listen (either behind a screen or in a corner of the room) and at some point, share their reflections. Clients and therapist listen before resuming their conversation. This approach promotes multiple voices and perspectives, and allows different positions, for example, listening, talking, observing and witnessing into the therapeutic process.

Similarly, when working in nature, an animal, or the weather or a tree can be regarded as the *Wild Reflecting Team*, becoming a presence and part of the therapeutic process. These occurrences are like voices or messages from the wild, always providing a relevant and meaningful insight. In practice, it means welcoming unexpected interruptions from the wild into our therapeutic conversations in nature. Even when working indoors we can intentionally bring nature, for example, animals, places, metaphors into indoors conversations. For example, I often start a conversation with a family by providing a wooden bowl full of natural objects and ask each one of them to choose an object for another person to keep the process relational. Often many memories surface and are shared. I may also ask to think about a favourite animal or to bring a desirable animal's quality into a difficult situation. Or using gardening as a metaphor for growing specific strengths and desirable qualities. Sometimes, I create a *Nature Pause*, that is, asking co-explorers to think about an image or a place from the natural world that connects with the current topic. It is always surprising how this creates a different way of talking, using metaphorical language based on nature and promoting useful reflections on the therapeutic conversations taking place indoors.

Therapeutic positioning in working outdoors

Some have described how nature can be in the background or can be foregrounded. Jordan and Hinds (2016: 66) write: 'Therapy expands to include both the therapeutic dyad and the third space of nature, which either forms the backdrop to the therapy or situates itself in the foreground of the work, taking the form of powerful metaphors and symbols.'

It is useful to use positioning theory (Harré and Langenhove 1990) to focus on the therapeutic positioning of the therapist while working outdoors. Using a continuum, we can have on the one end, nature in the background and, on the other end, nature in the foreground. If we consider these two positions as equally valid rather than mutually exclusive, we can embrace a *both and* approach to encourage more flexibility in our thinking and movement beyond polarised positions as shown in Figure 14.2.

With different co-explorers or at different points in a session, we might move along, between the two positions. Some of my co-explorers might prefer to have a therapeutic conversation outdoors as if they were indoors, hence nature in the background. Therefore, at the beginning of a therapy session I might ask: 'Is there any particular spot where you wish to sit and talk today?' I might also direct them to the *Wild therapy room* (Santin 2021), a designated space I have created with some

WAYS OF WORKING IN NATURE

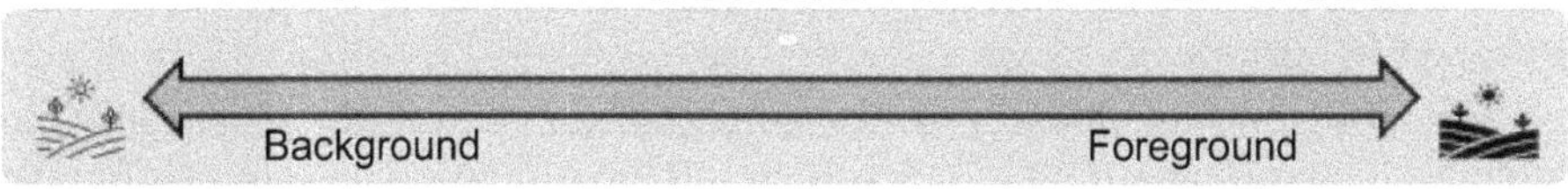

Working in/within the Natural environment	Working alongside Nature
Nature is providing the context for therapy	Nature mutually recognised as a co-therapist
Using a therapy room in nature	Engaging with Nature directly and finding language & meanings to express
Focus on conversations as if it were in a clinical room	Nature as a metaphor for life
Nature as a container	Nature in the foreground
Nature as a calming context	Nature as an active co-therapist – dialogical conversational partner
Nature as an invisible co-therapist/observer	Clients and therapist as explorers
Nature in the background	Listen to Nature
Talking to Nature/Therapist	

Chiara Fortina Santin
ReWilding Therapy (2024)

Figure 14.2 Ways of working in nature. Chiara Fortina Santin (2024), *Rewilding Therapy.*

logs in a circle to sit on in a more secluded part of the woodland. The main focus will be on the conversation. However, I might notice something in nature and decide to bring it into the conversation. Or sometimes clients are noticing and paying attention to the voices from the wild. In this example, I am moving along the continuum, starting from nature being in the background and moving towards nature being in the foreground at some point during the session.

For some other co-explorers, like Kirsty in the case example, the main focus is on interacting with nature as they have familiarity with being outdoors, may have a strong bond with nature, are open and comfortable with the natural environment and its elements. Nature is foregrounded and becomes the principal therapist by taking a prominent role in the therapeutic process.

First-, second- and third- order positioning

Berger (2017: 50) suggests that 'the therapist can take a secondary position as a mediator between the clients and nature by being a witness to a process occurring directly with nature'. Witnessing is an ethically desirable position that happens in my ecotherapy practice when I can step back as a facilitator of the therapeutic process while the co-explorers are fully immersed and interacting with nature in a meaningful way (like in the case example).

If we hold a firm belief in nature as co-therapist and expert, a paradigm shift is likely to happen in our practice as we naturally take a decentred position as a facilitator, becoming more like an observer or witness within the therapeutic ecosystem. This also means sharing our power with nature and trust that nature will provide, for example, will intervene into the therapeutic process with a message, a voice from the wild or an insight into inner landscapes.

In my experience, nature invites us therapists to move freely between different therapeutic positions. I have identified three key positions, that is,

1. a leading facilitator, directive (first order).
2. an observer, a participant and witness from a meta-perspective (second order).
3. a decentred facilitator, trusting the healing power of nature as the expert, in which we all become immersed (third order).

This could be represented by three circles as shown in Figure 14.3.

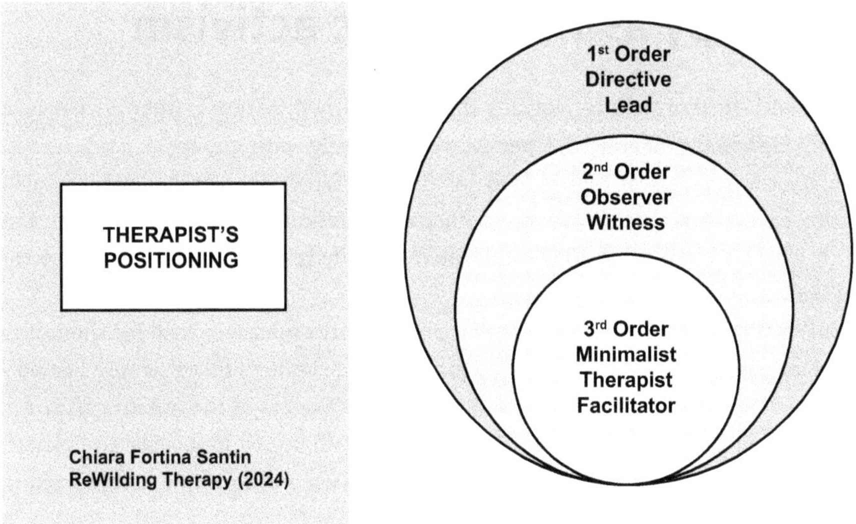

Figure 14.3 Therapist's positioning. Chiara Fortina Santin (2024), *Rewilding Therapy*.

In my practice, these three main positions are not mutually exclusive and are influenced by the complex interplay of different factors, for example, my existing therapeutic relationship with clients, their relationship with nature, my understanding of their needs and preferences, and whether I am working with an individual, a couple or a family. Our therapeutic position can also change within a session as shown in the case example, that is, Kirsty taking initiative about which tree to engage with, was initially guided by my questions (first order). Then I progressively became more decentred (second and third order), and then leading again towards the end.

If I am leading a nature-connection activity with a family and a more structured approach is needed (first order), I can later become a quiet presence as they become immersed in the task, observing and witnessing what is emerging, sharing a comment, or reflecting back (second order).

In the third-order position I am a facilitator of the therapeutic process by standing back, while nature becomes the principal therapist and regard myself as a *minimalist therapist*. This position is about holding the therapeutic space lightly and it is more likely when I have a strong therapeutic relationship that allows more relational risk taking and when clients have a meaningful relationship with nature and are open to the unexpected (as Kirsty did). This position and therapeutic intention also allow co-explorers to feel part of a wider ecological context and experience nature as a healing space as well as an opportunity to reconnect with our sense of belonging to the earth and shared stewardship of the planet.

Ecotherapy as therapeutic activism

My desire and commitment to working therapeutically in nature is not only because it allows a different and much richer way of engaging with clients as explorers in the therapeutic process as highlighted in this chapter. I strongly believe it is also about promoting stewardship of our greenspaces and kinship with the non-human world in which we are embedded, embodied (Hardham 1006) and entangled with (Barad 2007).

I think that the current ecological crisis and climate emergency call for therapists to be actively and intentionally including the ecological context into therapy (Lazloffy and Twist 2019; Lazloffy 2024). This will increase awareness of the role of nature for our mental well-being as well as the ethical responsibility to look after the planet, and a commitment to social justice and decolonizing ways of thinking and practising which perpetuate oppressive systems.

Ecotherapy, therefore, can lead psychotherapists to a necessary shift of personal and professional boundaries, a redefinition of therapy within the wider context and its aims to include social justice and activism as emphasized by many for example, Reynolds 2012; Kearney 2013, 2021, 2024; Waldegrave et al. 2003, to name a few within the systemic field. Darrigo-Patric et al. (2017: 580) defines *therapeutic activism* as 'intentionally seeking to attend to and disrupt oppressive sociopolitical contexts and processes'. McCarthy (2001: 159) claims: 'To privilege the lives of those who live on the margins of our societies within therapy cannot but be a political activity'. Therapy then becomes a political act towards social change (Cooper 2019).

Burls (2005, 2007) advocates for a paradigm shift in public mental health through ecotherapy at micro level, that is, individual health, as well as macro level, that is, the wider community through care of green spaces and the need for targeted training for health professionals, environment agencies' staff and the voluntary sectors (Burls and Ashton 2021). Similarly, Mellor et al. (2022: 541) advocate for a nature-based health care, stating:

> Cultivating a sense of kinship with the natural world unlocks further mental health benefits and promotes a deep sense of meaning and vitality. Widespread restoration of nature, combined with the equitable reconnection of people to these restored environments, must become one of the most important aspects of public health in this century.

Health systems are fast becoming unsustainable within a context of likely climate crisis and social collapse. In a world of increased polarization and chaos, the Fifth Province approach (McCarthy 2001, 2004, 2021) offers a way to imagine the space in between conflicting positions, a liminal space where complexity and polarities are held, dualistic thinking and contradictions can coexist. This opens up possibilities for embracing the old and the new, the known and the unknown where unexpected synergies between the past and the future can emerge. It also allows the exploration of ourselves and our inner worlds as inter-beings, connected to our indigenous knowledge including nature-based and spiritual practices. By engaging in liminal spaces where we put the heart at the centre, we can allow healing and hope to emerge from the unknown, the seemingly irreconcilable polarities and the uncertainty of our times (McCarthy and Duncan 2023).

A fundamental change in the way we see the world is needed, considering the human as well as the non-human world, animals, vegetable, mineral and matter as interconnected and entangled (Barad 2007). Salter and Simon (2019, 2024: 190) call this transmaterial worlding, 'a process of becoming through learning. It takes place in and between human and non-human activity motivated by a concern for ecological survival and "social justice" where social is reframed to include a consideration of all peoples and ecosystems.' Therefore, mental health would not be seen as a privilege for some and an individual problem for others but a shared concern for equality and everybody's ecological well-being.

Ecological well-being for all through rewilding and imagin-action

If we were to reframe mental health as ecological well-being, it follows that we cannot leave nature outside clinical rooms or health services, public and private. We may well take therapy outside clinics! Let's engage in *Imagin-action*. Let's be brave, creative and irreverent (Cecchin, Lane and Ray 1992). Let's come together in rewilding our practices, reimagining and revisioning the landscape of mental health services as interdisciplinary and integrated towards a natural mental health system rooted in nature's healing power, health equality and community building (Fortina Santin 2024).

Rewilding requires being irreverent (Cecchin, Lane and Ray 1992) towards dominant, oppressive ways of being in the world and a radical departure from colonizing thinking and practices, drawing from indigenous cultures and the wisdom embedded in nature. In particular, Jude (2024) encourages us to be brave enough to challenge Western European knowledge-based frames and embrace other ways of knowing and practising as valid and valuable, more inclusive of multicultural perspectives and indigenous traditions.

Rewilding will also require a rethink of our psychotherapy training programmes to reflect this epistemological shift as Moore and Cove (2024) recommend in their research. They conducted a Delphi survey with 'experts' in the systemic field. There was significant consensus about key ecosystemic ideas and practices that should be reflected in training programmes. The findings strongly emphasize the urgency and the ethical call to attend to the ecological crisis and the climate emergency that have been marginalized within the systemic field.

We can often become overwhelmed by the scale of the problems we face, thinking about the sea change, the 'quantum shift' (Kearney 2024: 111) that is required. Realistically, we may not be able to avoid catastrophe and social collapse (Cernev 2022). However, we may foster active hope (Macy and Johnstone 2012, 2022) by coming together, engaging in small, yet meaningful actions, every day, in every location, in all communities including the psychotherapy community through *Imagin-action*! (Fortina Santin 2024).

A special thanks to Imelda McCarthy, Hugh Palmer and the editors who have reviewed this chapter and have made useful suggestions.

References

Anderson, H., and H. Goolishian (1992), 'The Client Is the Expert: A Not-Knowing Approach to Therapy', in S. McNamee and K. J. Gergen (eds), *Therapy as Social Construction*, London: Sage Publications.

Andersen, T. (1987), 'The Reflecting Team: Dialogue and Meta-Dialogue in Clinical Work', *Family Process* 26: 415–28. https://doi.org/10.1177/1066480709332713.

Andersen, T., ed. (1991), *The Reflecting Team*, New York: W. W. Norton.

Barad, K. (2007), *Meeting the Universe Halfway*, Durham NC: Duke University Press.

Bateson, G. (1972), *Steps to an Ecology of Mind*, San Francisco, CA: Chandler Pub.

Bateson, G. (1979), *Mind and Nature: A Necessary Unity*, New York: EP Dutton.

Bateson, N. (2016), *Small Arcs of Bigger Circles*, Axminster: Triarchy Press.

Bendell, J. (2018), 'Deep Adaptation: A Map for Navigating Climate Tragedy', Unpublished paper. https://mahb.stanford.edu/library-item/deep-adaptation-map-navigating-climate-tragedy/

Bendell, J. (2023), *Breaking Together. A Freedom-Loving Response to Collapse*, Bristol: Good works.

Berger, R. (2016), 'Renewed by Nature: Nature Therapy as a Framework to Help People Deal with Crisis, Trauma and Loss', in M. Jordan and J. Hinde (eds), *Ecotherapy: Theory, Research and Practice*, London and New York: Palgrave.

Berger, R. (2017), 'Nature Therapy: Highlighting Steps for Professional Development', in A. Kopytin and M. Rugh (eds), *Environmental Expressive Therapies: Nature-Assisted Theory and Practice*, New York: Routledge.

Byng-Hall, J. (2008), 'The Crucial Roles of Attachment in Family Therapy', *Journal of Family Therapy* 30 (2): 129–46. https://doi.org/10.1111/j.1467-6427.2008.00422.x.

Bodnar, S. (2023), 'Introduction to the Special Issue: A Collaborative Definition of Ecotherapy', *Ecopsychology* 15 (3): 206–13. https://doi.org:10.1089/eco.2023.0022.

Bryant, F. B., and J. Veroff (2007), *Savoring: A New Model of Positive Experience*, Mahwah, NJ: Lawrence Erlbaum Associates Publishers.
Burls, A. (2005), 'New Landscapes for Mental Health', *Mental Health Review Journal* 10 (1): 26–9. https://doi.org/10.1108/13619322200500006.
Burls, A. (2007), 'People and Green Spaces: Promoting Public Health and Mental Well-Being through Ecotherapy', *Journal of Public Mental Health* 6 (3): 24–39. https://doi.org/10.1108/17465729200700018.
Burls, A. (2008), 'Seeking Nature: A Contemporary Therapeutic Environment', *Therapeutic Communities* 29 (3): 228–44. https://www.academia.edu/5265026/Seeking_Nature_A_Contemporary_Therapeutic_Environment.
Burls, A., and J. Ashton (2021), 'Public Mental Health and Nature: A Paradigm Shift', *Journal of Mental health* 20 (3): 221–8. https://doi.org/10.1108/JPMH-03-2021-0040.
Burnham, J. (1992), 'Approach-Method-Technique: Making Distinctions and Creating Connections', *Human Systems: Journal of Systemic Consultation and Management* 3 (1): 3–26.
Burnham, J. (1993), 'Systemic Supervision: The Evolution of Reflexivity in the Context of the Supervisory Relationship', *Human Systems: Journal of Systemic Consultation and Management* 4: 349–81.
Burnham, J. (2005), 'Relational Reflexivity: A Tool for Social Constructing Therapeutic Relationships', in C. Flaskas, B. Mason and A. Perlesz (eds), *The Space Between: Experience, Context and Process in the Therapeutic Relationship*, London: Karnac Books.
Burnham, J. (2012), 'Developments in Social GGRRAAACCEEESSS: Visible-Invisible, Voiced-Unvoiced', in Inga-Britt Krause (ed.), *Cultural Reflexivity*, London: Karnac.
Butler, C. (2015), 'Intersectionality in Family Therapy Training: Inviting Students to Embrace the Complexities of Lived Experience', *Journal of Family Therapy* 37 (4): 583–9. https://doi.org/10.1111/1467-6427.12090.
Buzzell, L. (2016), 'The Many Ecotherapies', in M. Jordan and J. Hinds (eds), *Ecotherapy: Theory, Research and Practice*, London: Palgrave Macmillan.
Cecchin, G. (1987), 'Hypothesising Circularity and Neutrality Revisited: An Invitation to Curiosity', *Family Process* 26 (4): 405–13. https://doi.org/10.1111/j.1545-5300.1987.00405.x.
Cecchin, G., G. Lane and W. A. Ray (1992), *Irreverence: A Strategy for Therapist's Survival*, London: Karnac Books.
Cernev, T. (2022), 'Global Catastrophic Risk and Planetary Boundaries: The Relationship to Global Targets and Disaster Risk Reduction', Geneva: United Nations Office for Disaster Risk Reduction.
Clayton, S. (2020), 'Climate Anxiety: Psychological Responses to Climate Change', *Journal of Anxiety Disorders* 74: 102263. http://doi.org/10.1016/j.janxdis.2020.102263.
Cooper, M. (2019), *Integrating Counselling & Psychotherapy: Directionality, Synergy and Social Change*, London: Sage Publications.
Crenshaw, K. (1989), 'Demarginalizing the Intersection of Race and Sex: A Black Feminist Critique of Antidiscrimination Doctrine, Feminist Theory and Antiracist

Politics', *University of Chicago Legal Forum* 14: 538–54. http://chicagounbound.uchicago.edu/uclf/vol1989/iss1/8.

Cunsolo, A., S. L. Harper, K. Minor, K. Hayes, K. G. Williams and C. Howard (2020), 'Ecological Grief and Anxiety: The Start of a Healthy Response to Climate Change?', *The Lancet Planetary Health* 4 (7): 261–3. http://doi.org/10.1016/S2542-5196(20)30144-3.

Dana, D. (2018), *The Polyvagal Theory in Therapy: Engaging the Rhythm of Regulation*, London: Norton Series on Interpersonal Neurobiology.

Darrigo-Patric, J., C. Hoff, C. Knudson-Martin and A. Tuttle (2017), 'Navigating Critical Theory and Postmodernism: Social Justice and Therapist Power in Family Therapy', *Family Process* 56 (3): 574–88.

Duncan, R. (2018), *Nature in Mind: Systemic Thinking and Imagination in Ecopsychology and Mental Health*, Oxford: Routledge.

Duncan, R. (2021), 'Deep Donkey and Dadirri: Asking Creatura Out to Play', *Murmurations: Journal of Transformative Systemic Practice* 4 (1): 32–47. https://doi.org/10.28963/4.1.4.

Duffin, K. (2023), 'Nature: The Therapeutic Partner', *Ecopsychology* 15: 222–30. https://doi.org/10.1089/eco.2022.0096.

Fortina Santin, C. (2024), *Rewilding Therapy. Ecosystemic Theory and Practice*, Farnhill: Everything is Connected Press.

Frizzell, C. (2023), *Posthuman Possibilities of Dance Movement Psychotherapy*, London: Routledge.

Hardham, V. (1996), 'Embedded and Embodied in the Therapeutic Relationship: Understanding the Therapist's Use of Self Systemically', in C. Flaskas, A. Perlesz, E. S. Wertheim, D. Campbell and R. Draper (eds), *The Therapeutic Relationship in Systemic Therapy*, London: Imprint Routledge. https://doi.org/10.4324/9780429483431.

Harré, R., and V. L. Langenhove, eds (1990), *Positioning Theory*, Oxford: Blackwell.

Hegarty, J. R. (2010), 'Out of the Consulting Room and into the Woods? Experiences of Nature Connectedness and Self-Healing', *European Journal of Ecopsychology* 1: 64–84. https://doi.org/10.1007/s10447-017-9294-y.

Jordan, M. (2012), 'Did Lacan Go Camping? Psychotherapy in Search of an Ecological Self', in M. J. Rust and N. Totton (eds), *Vital Signs: Psychological Responses to the Ecological Crisis*, London: Karnac.

Jordan, M., and J. Hinds (2016), *Ecotherapy. Theory, Research and Practice*, London: Palgrave.

Jude, J. (2024), 'African Indigenous Oral Tradition Endarkened Feminist Practice: Indigenous Knowledge and New Materialism', in H. Palmer and L. Edwards (eds), *The EcoSystemic Return. Collected Papers*, Farnhill: Everything is Connected Press.

Kearney, P. (2013), 'The Systemic Crisis of Climate Change: Clinical and Political Reflections', *Feedback Journal of the Family Therapy Association of Ireland* 1: 42–50.

Kearney, P. (2021), 'The EcoSystemic Return: Clinical and Political Implications', *Murmurations: Journal of Transformative Systemic Practice* 4 (1): 102–18. https://doi.org/10.28963/4.1.8.

Kearney, P. (2024), 'The Systemic Crisis of Climate Change: Clinical and Political Reflections', in H. Palmer and L. Edwards (eds), *The EcoSystemic Return. Collected Papers*, Farnhill: Everything is Connected Press.

Korzybski, A. (1933), 'Science and Sanity. An Introduction to Non-Aristotelian Systems and General Semantics', The International non-Aristotelian Library Pub. Co: 747–61. https://archive.org/details/sciencesanityint00korz.

Koziol, C. A. (2022), 'Community Ecopsychology: Widening Connections to Catalyse Change', *Ecopsychology*, Mar 2022: 1–7. https://doi.org/10.1089/eco.2021.0026.

Lazloffy, T. A. (2024), 'Foreword', in H. Palmer and L. Edwards (eds), *The EcoSystemic Return. Collected Papers*, Farnhill: Everything is Connected Press.

Laszloffy, T. A., and M. L. C. Twist (eds) (2019), *Eco-Informed Practice: Family Therapy in an Age of Ecological Peril*, Cham, Switzerland: Springer.

Macy, J. R. (1983), *Despair and Personal Power in the Nuclear Age*, Philadelphia: New Society Publishers.

Macy, J. R., and C. Johnstone (2012), *Active Hope*, California: Novato.

Macy, J. R., and M. Y. Brown (2014), *Coming Back to Life*, Canada: New Society Publisher.

Marshall, H. (2016a), 'Taking Therapy Outside: Reaching for a Vital Connection' [Online module]), Eco-Psychotherapy: Synthesising Ecology and Psychotherapy in Practice and Theory. http://www.confer.uk.com/module-ecopsychotherapy.html

Marshall, H. (2016b), 'A Vital Protocol: Working at Embodied Relational Depth in Nature-Based Psychotherapy', in M. Jordan and J. Hinds (eds), *Ecotherapy: Theory Research and Practice*, London, NY: Palgrave Macmillan.

Marshall, H. (2023), 'A Place for the Ecological Third: Eco-TA in Therapeutic Practice', *Transactional Analysis Journal* 53 (1): 93–108. https://DOI.org/10.1080/03621537.2023.2152567.

Mason, B. (1993), 'Towards Positions of Safe Uncertainty', *Human Systems* 4 (3–4): 189–200.

Mason, B. (2005), 'Relational Risk-Taking and the Therapeutic Relationship', in C. Flaskas, B. Mason, A. Perlesz, J. Byng-Hall, D. Campbell and R. Draper (eds), *The Space Between*, London: Imprint Routledge. https://doi.org/10.4324/9780429483295.

Mason, B. (2019), 'Re-Visiting Safe Uncertainty: Six Perspectives for Clinical Practice and the Assessment of Risk', *Journal of Family Therapy* 41 (3): 343–56. https://doi.org/10.1111/1467-6427.12258.

Mellor, C., S. Botchway, N. Barnes and S. Gandy (2022), 'Seeding Hope: Restoring Nature to Restore Ourselves. Nature Restoration as an Essential Mental Health Intervention', *International Review of Psychiatry* 34 (5): 541–5. https://doi.org/10.1080/09540261.2022.2092391.

McCarthy, I. (2001), 'Fifth Province Re-versings: The Social Construction of Women Lone Parents' Inequality and Poverty', *Journal of Family Therapy* 23 (3): 253–77. https://doi.org/10.1111/1467-6427.00183.

McCarthy, I. (2004), 'The Fifth Province and Spirituality: Co-Creating a Sacred Space of Love in Therapy Conversations', in S. Madigan (ed.), *Therapy from the Inside Out*, Vancouver: Yaletown Family Therapy Press.

McCarthy, I. (2021), 'Re-Membering and Naturing My Life and Work in a Fifth Province', *Murmurations: Journal of Transformative Systemic Practice* 4 (1): 74–86. https://doi.org/10.28963/4.1.6.

McCarthy, I., and R. Duncan (2023), 'Imagining Liminal Spaces: Handrails of Hope, Videotaped Conversation in Metalogos', *Systemic Therapy Journal* 44, October 2023. https://metalogos-systemic-therapy-journal.eu/en/issue/article/44-06.

Moore, R., and J. Cove (2024), 'Reconnecting Systemic Family Therapy: How Family Therapy Training Can Attend to the Ecosystem and Climate Emergency, Recommendations from a Delphi Survey', *Journal of Family Therapy* 46 (3): 281–305. https://doi.org/10.1111/1467-6427.12461

Naess, A. (1987), 'Self-realization: An Ecological Approach to Being in the World', *The Trumpeter* 4 (3). Retrieved from https://trumpeter.athabascau.ca/index.php/trumpet/article/view/623.

O'Sullivan, B. (2021), *Working with a Metaphor. Creating a Relationship with Self as a Community of Selves*, Dublin: Orpen Press.

Oliveira, P. (2023), 'Breaking the Silence: An Integrative Psychotherapy Model for Working with Eco-Anxiety', in L. Aspey, C. Jackson and D. Parker (eds), *Holding the Hope. Reviving Psychological and Spiritual Agency in the Face of Climate Change*, Monmouth: PCCS Books.

Palmer, H. (2024), 'Where Did the Eco Go in Systemic Practice?', in H. Palmer and L. Edwards (eds), *The EcoSystemic Return. Collected Papers*, Farnhill: Everything is Connected Press.

Pfeifer, E. (2017), 'Music-Nature-Therapy: Outdoor Music Therapy and Other Nature Related Approaches in Music Therapy', in A. Kopytin and M. Rugh (eds), *Environmental Expressive Therapies: Nature-Assisted Theory and Practice*, New York and Oxford: Routledge.

Plotkin, B. (2008), *Nature and the Human Soul. Cultivating Wholeness in a Fragmented World*, Novato: New World Library.

Plotkin, B. (2013), *Wild Mind. A Field Guide to the Human Psyche*, Novato: New World Library.

Pihkala, P. (2020), 'Anxiety and the Ecological Crisis: An Analysis of Eco-Anxiety and Climate Anxiety', *Sustainability* 12: 7836. https://doi.org/10.3390/su12197836.

Pihkala, P. (2021), 'Towards a Taxonomy of Climate Emotions', *Frontiers in Climate* 3. https://doi.org/10.3389/fclim.2021.738154.

Reynolds, V. (2012), 'An Ethical Stance for Justice-Doing in Community Work and Therapy', *Journal of Systemic Therapies*, 31 (4): 18–33. https://guilfordjournals.com/doi/pdf/10.1521/jsyt.2012.31.4.18.

Rober, P. (1999), 'The Therapist's Inner Conversation in Family Therapy Practice: Some Ideas about the Self of the Therapist, Therapeutic Impasse, and the Process of Reflection', *Family Process* 38 (2): 209–28. https://doi.org/10.1111/j.1545-5300.1999.00209.x.

Roper-Hall, A. (1998), 'Working Systemically with Older People and Their Families Who Have "Come to Grief"', in P. Sutcliffe, G. Tufnell and U. Cornish (eds), *Working with the Dying and Bereaved: Systemic Approaches to Therapeutic Work*, London: Macmillan.

Rust, M. J. (2020), *Towards an Ecopsychotherapy*, London: Confer Books.

Salter, L. K., and G. Simon (2019), 'Transmaterial Worlding. Beyond Human Systems', *Murmurations: Journal of Transformative Systemic Practice* 2 (2): 1–17. https://doi.org/10.28963/2.2.2.

Salter, L., and G. Simon (2024), 'Transmaterial Worlding. Beyond Human Systems', in H. Palmer and L. Edwards (eds), *The EcoSystemic Return. Collected Papers*, Farnhill: Everything is Connected Press.

Santin, C. (2021), 'Rewilding Systemic Practice', *Murmurations: Journal of Transformative Systemic Practice* 4 (1): 13–31. https://doi.org/10.28963/4.1.3.

Selvini Palazzoli, M., L. Boscolo, G. Cecchin and G. Prata (1980), 'Hypothesising - Circularity - Neutrality: Three Guidelines for the Conductor of the Session', *Family Process* 19 (1): 3–12. https://doi.org/10.1111/j.1545-5300.1980.00003.

Siddons Heginworth, I., and G. Nash (eds) (2020), *Environmental Arts Therapy. The Wild Frontiers of the Heart*, London: Routledge.

Simon, G. (2021), 'Panmorphic Crisis: Cultural Rupture and Systemic Change', *Murmurations: Journal of Transformative Systemic Practice* 4 (1): 87–101. https://doi.org/10.28963/4.1.7.

Simon, G. (2023), 'Reflexivity 3. Breaking Out the Reflexive Loop to Decolonise Practice', *Murmurations: Journal of Transformative Systemic Practice* 6 (2): 53–71. https://doi.org/10.28963/6.2.4.

Tree, I. (2018), *Wilding*, Dublin: Picador.

Totton, N. (2011), *Wild Therapy. Undomesticating Inner and Outer Worlds*, Ross-on-Wye: PCCS Books.

Totton, N. (2021), *Wild Therapy. Rewilding Inner and Outer Worlds*, Second edition, Ross-on-Wye: PCCS Books.

Waldegrave, C., K. Tamasese, F. Tuhaka and W. Campbell (eds) (2003), *Just Therapy – A Journey: A Collection of Papers from the Just Therapy Team*, New Zealand: Dulwich Centre Publications.

Wilson, E. O. (1984), *Biophilia*, Cambridge, MA and London: Harvard University Press.

White, M. (2000), 'Reflecting Teamwork as Definitional Ceremony Revisited', in M. White (ed.), *Reflections on Narrative Practice: Essays and Interview*, Adelaide: Dulwich Centre Publications.

Part IV

Education

15

Education as ecotherapy: Paying attention to the world

Alan Bainbridge

Introduction

This chapter will draw on a wide range of theoretical disciplines, and at times go off, for some readers on unexpected tangents that might disorientate. In recent years I could introduce myself at social gatherings as a lecturer in education and also a psychoanalytic psychotherapist. Typically eyes would roll, questions would be asked how these two areas even went together and then people would act nervously in case I had magical powers and, as we spoke, was analysing the deepest recesses of their soul. The combination of education and psychotherapy made perfect sense to me then and continues to do so now. To help avoid losing readers on the way, the central message can be made clear from the outset: It will be argued the theory and practice of ecotherapy and education are founded on and supported by similar principles.

Equally, I should clarify what this thing called 'education' is, and how, in its widest sense, I shall refer to it in this chapter. Education, I shall argue, includes those everyday formal, informal and non-formal everyday acts that involve teaching and learning, where the educative act is a purposeful moment when a more experienced other (teacher) directs the attention of a novice (learner) towards something that requires their response. This of course could also be reframed as what happens during parent–child, coach–player, or artisan–apprentice relationship.

I will also position education as a 'long-life' (as defined in the section 'Long-life education: the search for something lost') ecological evolutionary response that supports the chances of human thriving and survival through attempts to modify and control, or tame, the wild external world. Paradoxically, these attempts to make a world that meets the needs of humans will also be shown to disrupt ecological balance, damaging planetary health, increasing the likelihood of general anxiety and mental ill-health.

The 'eco' of ecotherapy shall be presented, not as a return to nature, or a need to be '*in*' nature, rather it represents the need to rekindle an awareness '*of*' the wilder, less defended, aspects of the human condition (the distinction between '*in*' and '*of*' is important and will be made clear later; see the section 'Ecotherapy: wilding the tame human').

An argument I shall also develop is that ecotherapy and education are both motivated by anxiety: For example, educational acts have their origins in the anxiety and discomfort of not knowing, or not being able to make sense of the external world. Ecotherapy similarly locates the source of human anxiety within a dysfunctional human or more-than-human relationship (note: to help the writing flow, I shall use terms like 'more-than-human', 'other-than-human', 'non-human' and 'external world' interchangeably).

Education and ecotherapy can both be argued to be motivated by anxiety rooted in the dynamic, if failing, relationship between the human and more-than-human, it would appear logical that attempts to ameliorate anxiety should centre on educational or ecotherapeutic processes that consider the dynamics of this relationship.

I shall argue that relationships that are able to contain anxiety, manage complexity and possibilities of not-knowing, will provide opportunities to disrupt current thinking leading to new imaginative and transformative possibilities. These are the sites of 'good' education and ecotherapy. I shall also present them as 'wild' ways of being human in a world that has become increasingly 'tamed' through the dominance of ideologies that seek to identify simplistic patterns of cause and effect that can be used to audit, control and manage human behaviour.

The 'Background' section, just covered, is intended to provide boundaries and help guide our thinking as the chapter becomes more expansive exploring the synergies between education and ecotherapy. The next section asks difficult questions that cannot be avoided but answers to which will clarify the functionality of the education–ecotherapy synergy.

A proposition: Asking educational questions of ecotherapy and ecotherapeutic questions of education

If the central premise of this chapter is that the theory and practice of ecotherapy and education are founded on and supported by similar principles, then an exploration of the following questions will help explore what these synergies might be, and how they support each other.

The substantive educational question is – *What is the motive for humans to engage in everyday education practices?*

The substantive ecotherapeutic question is – *What is the motive for humans to seek out therapeutic interventions, including ecotherapy?*

Combining these two, might well lead to the overarching question – W*hat does it mean to live well with the world?*

While acknowledging that education is not psychotherapy and psychotherapy is not education, it will be suggested that both seek to find answers about what it means to live well in the world: 'Good education' will share features of psychotherapeutic practice when teaching and learning moments are able to contain anxiety enabling new understanding to emerge. In this context ecotherapy will involve acts of education when new understandings of the relationship between the self and non-human other are engaged to support personal and ecological flourishing.

Both processes have a semantically focused central aim that requires individuals to sit with the anxiety associated with complexity and uncertainty, to pay attention to their world and to value diversity while seeking to engage with multiple world views. In the next section I shall suggest that educational acts can be reimagined through ecological metaphors thus serving as both an educational and ecotherapeutic encounter.

Long-life education: The search for something lost

A consideration of an evolutionary distant past will now be presented, to allow ecologically focussed questions to be asked of how it is that everyday educational acts might help make sense of what it means to be human. Drawing on Vujaković (2013), I refer to this as a 'long-life' learning perspective, deliberately inverting the better known 'life-long' view of education, as this enables an understanding of the human condition and planetary health to be viewed through ecological events from deep history to current experience.

It might sound counter-intuitive but I wish to start this section with a provocative suggestion that I am not overly interested in learning. All species learn and respond to their external world: Sometimes this will involve simple and rapid responses such as the single-celled amoeba moving away from bright light. In another context, this might be the transmission of cultural knowledge in chimpanzee groups through observing how to use a twig to 'fish' for ants. That all species respond to the ecological niche that supports their survival is not up for debate. What is up for debate, and indeed, we shall find is more troubling from a planetary and mental health perspective, is – *Why is it that humans educate?*

The educative act can be distinguished from learning, as it is a purposeful agentic moment where a more experienced other (teacher) directs the attention of a novice (learner) towards something that requires their response. This is not the mechanistic response of behaviourism, nor the opportunistic observation and copying of certain behaviours. From the context of the current history of the planet, while being aware of accusations of essentialist thinking, there is something particular about the human process(es) and outcomes of informal, non-formal and formal education.

The view that will be provided deliberately draws on the 'modern' human. It does not do so from a position of superiority, but from an acceptance that the influence of a minority of wealthy, industrialized people, although representing only 20 per cent of the planet's population (United Nations, 2011), is responsible for widespread ecological, social and (it will be argued later) psychological damage. The events in the distant past that led to the motive for humans to educate are largely open to conjecture, but first drawing on Berger and Luckmann's seminal *Social Construction of Reality* book (1966), and then social anthropologist Harvey Whitehouse's (2021) study on the continuous role of ritual in human society, will provide some possible ontological roots for the development of education.

A distant past

Berger and Luckmann's (1966) influential thesis on the social construction of knowledge and practice, attempted to account for why it was that human behaviour led to a continual modification of their external world. They noted how all other organisms are born into a world that is ready for their kind – using the term 'closed-world'. For example, lions are born into a 'lion world' that supports being a lion. This is not some fantasy where lions do not die from starvation, are not affected by human disturbance, or sudden climatic changes. Lions will struggle to survive just as their ancestors did, but crucially, these are within the normal ecological cycles of lion-life that will be continuing alongside births and deaths.

Berger and Luckmann suggested that the world humans were being born into was not '*closed*' but '*open*', noting humans have to continually modify their external world, as paradoxically this world never satisfies, or meets human ecological needs. Their reasoning is that humans are born into a world that is not ready for them. Therefore, for humans to survive, they must continually manage and control the external world. Yet, human attempts to design what ecologist would call a supportive niche, can never successfully recreate the complex ecological interrelationships to support thriving.

Being human is therefore a paradox: despite human attempts to make a world to support their thriving, such actions will never be fully successful, and may indeed be damaging to both the human and non-human world. I have argued in Bainbridge (2019) that the experience of 'open-world' living provides the 'long-life' motive to educate (in its widest sense), particularly to promote and support shared values and epistemological understandings of the external world. In the next section I will make the case that this represents a 'long-life' ancient need for social cohesion, maintained by rituals supporting shared epistemologies, that may be the ontological genealogy of the giving and receiving of knowledge and skills we now call education. I will also suggest that archives of this past are still influential in the human–non-human relationship.

Something lost

Education has been shown to be about the more experienced sharing existing knowledge and skills with less experienced others. The aspect of agency of both giver and receiver is important, as what motivates the ecological acts of giving and receiving are of particular interest in the ontology of education (Bainbridge 2019). From an evolutionary perspective the decision for individuals or societies to use valuable time and resources to teach (to gift) an 'other' who may, or may not, accept the gift, asks questions of how such a potentially unequal and risky educational exchange has, and continues to evolve. The answer may lie deep within the human psyche, alongside arguments of what it means to be human and live well in a world.

Berger and Luckmann's notion of a closed-world can guide us through some potentially difficult, and perhaps, unsettling thinking. For species experiencing a closed-world, the external world is assumed to meet their needs and the needs of other species in their particular ecological niche. This does not mean that life is lived in a fantasy where lions lie down with lambs and 'nasty things' do not happen. The exact opposite is the case. Life is messy, unpredictable and continually in balance. But this is the life of, say, a shrew, lion, buttercup or an orangutan.

The ecosystems they are part of are not static, they are dynamic. Continual and subtle changes allow the whole system to be maintained in equilibrium as a resilient place of flourishing that can respond to and manage, the sudden loss of a shrew, the kill of a lion, buttercup dying in a drought, or the nightly nest-making activity of orangutans.

Using Berger and Luckmann's closed-world as an accessible point of departure, the open-world that they suggest defines the human condition, requires more imagination. The step in the argument I am about to make is not an easy one and finding the right language is difficult. In an earlier piece of writing (Bainbridge 2022) I explored the idea of the human condition being experienced as one on the 'edge of a precipice', a place of continual physical and existential threat.

For reasons that may never be known, the ecology of our ancient ancestors changed in such a way that could not directly support them (there is of course the equal possibility that a genetic mutation emerged leading to a new way of interacting with the world). Species survival therefore required active attempts to modify and manage the open-world experience, for example, the shift suggested by Whitehouse (2021) from hunter and gatherers to farmer and herders. The question remains as to why the actions of our ancestors did not fix the precarious open-world and create a closed-world environment that could support flourishing. Two answers will be suggested and both will lead us towards thinking about education in its broadest sense.

One: In *The Sacred Canopy – Elements of a Sociological Theory of Religion*, Berger (1967) discusses how human physical and psychological products have an 'internal logic' that conflicts with and disrupts the external ecological world, including human flourishing. Berger uses the example of the plough, that although designed to make the job of cultivation easier, the 'logic' of the plough disrupts previous agricultural lifestyles as human activity now conforms to the logic and efficiency of the plough and ploughing. This process of attempting to build a world to support human flourishing, but ultimately failing, will continue into the distant future (Bainbridge 2020).

Unlike most species where learning to respond to environmental changes requires simple stimulus/response actions or imitation over longer-time frames, humans live in a comparatively rapidly ever-changing and precarious world. Very early in human evolution, stimulus and response and informal familial learning would have been sufficient to support most aspects of human life. But, over geologically long periods of time, despite the creation of increasingly complex cultural and technological worlds, such responses continued to be insufficient to meet the ecological demands of living in an open-world.

Therefore, a particular response is required to support the continual development of the creative and novel behaviours necessary to meet the demands of open-world living. It is this response that can be recognized as 'education'; a process where more knowledgeable, or experienced others, take time to share existing knowledge and experience with novices. All the time directing their attention to the external world with the expectation (or hope) that a better world can be imagined and built.

Two: The motive to educate has been positioned within an evolutionary response to imagine and build new worlds. The second response to the question why our ancestors have failed to modify the precarious open-world into a predictable and supportive closed-world, and indeed why modern humans continue to fail to do so, shall move this chapter into a more psychological arena. I shall draw on sociologist and psychoanalyst Erich Fromm (1968), a philosopher who tried to make sense of the relationship between the human and more-than-human.

In the context of humans as the unsuccessful, yet persistent architects, of a world that continues to unsettle, Fromm (1994) provides a succinct and evocative summary of the human–open-world problem:

> the nature of man is a contradiction rooted in the conditions of human existence that requires a search for solutions, which in their turn create new contradictions and now the need for answers. (p. 100)

The human condition is presented here as one of continual turmoil, where contradictions only lead to further contradictions.

The persistent drive to imagine and design solutions has been argued to be fuelled by 'brute' evolutionary ecological forces, and yet Fromm hints towards something more numinous – an existential crisis, perhaps. Something that comes from within, seeking for a life that is balanced, harmonious even, with the external world. Although Fromm may not have used this language, we can ask 'is this what a closed-world experience *feels* like?' Where the 'educational search for solutions' is a search for existential meaning.

A return to Fromm (1968) who provides more concrete, less abstract language where he notes that humans seek to replace the principles of instinct with the principles of action. A rewriting within the context of this chapter could become: that humans compensate for the loss of a distant-past experience of a dynamically balanced relationship within a closed-world, through an educationally driven solution-focussed striving to annul the experience of an anxiety riven open-world. As such, education is both the cause and solution for the alienation between the human and more-than-human world. Equally, education is both motivated by and the cause of anxiety.

Education: Coda

> Education pays attention to the world.
> Education is a response to crises, and yet causes disruption.
> Education is a response to, and cause of anxiety.
> Education is unpredictable and complex.
> Education allows new things to emerge.
> Education is about learning to live well in the world.

The ecotherapeutic turn: Being '*in*' and '*of*' the world

As the chapter reaches the half way stage it is time to move from viewing education through an ecological lens, and to explore how therapeutic knowledge and practices might help make sense of education and what it means to live well with the planet.

By the end of the previous section the case was made that the human experience is one of being cast adrift in a world that could be 'home', but unfortunately is not experienced as a place to provide the physical or psychological attributes to support flourishing. Paradoxically, it is the human attempt to control and manage the external world to provide the experience of 'home' that continues to disrupt and alienate humans from the world they live.

Sharp's (1988) evocative description about the incursion of Canadian white colonial settlers whose intention was to exploit and regulate the natural world might help make sense of this predicament, noting that:

> It talks too loudly, its posturing is wrong, its movement harsh, and graceless ... Its presence brings a stunning confusion heard deafeningly in a growing circle of silence created by a confused and disoriented animate universe. (p.144)

Here, human ways of interacting with the more-than-human are awkward and blundering as the 'modern' human desire to control only succeeds in confusing and disorientating the world they enter. It is this notion of the blundering human that provides the chapter with the context to step into a more ecotherapeutic territory to understand what it might mean to be human, and how this relates to education and ecotherapy.

When considering the synergies between ecotherapy and education it is important to consider the nature of the human and more-than-human relationship in the third millennium, particularly in relation to discussions around interconnectivity. The case will be made that the dilemma modern humans face is not one of connection, or not, with nature. The recent COVID-19 pandemic makes clear the intimate connection between humans and the more-than-human, when the microscopic SARS-CoV-2 virus led to the potential collapse of economic, social and educational systems. It is not that humans are no longer connected to the natural world, although immediate and everyday contact for many is much reduced; humans are nature, they are 'in' and 'of' the natural world.

The principle concern here is focussed on a lack of awareness, or sensitivity towards the non-human world. One might refer to this situation as an experience of alienation – of not feeling at home in a place that should be home. The role of education, and therefore ecologically informed psychotherapy is not to 're-connect' but to re-engage an awareness of the non-human other and a sensitivity towards their needs. How human actions have led to their own alienation and the detrimental effect this has on planetary health and human well-being will be discussed next

Alienation: Strangers at 'home'

I shall start by repeating the premise that humans are nature. Despite millennia of attempts to modify and control all that is non-human, and irrespective of contested definitions such as 'global majority or global minority, or Western or non-Western', human activity to a lesser or greater extent is influenced by and influences the non-human world. The human condition is both in and of nature and as such, humans are an integral part of interconnected earth systems. Being careful to avoid essentialist and anthropomorphic assumptions, questions on 'what sets humans apart', or 'what has led to the alienation of humans from the non-human' will require a focus on epistemology.

To explore how epistemological assumptions might explain the human experience of alienation, I shall return to the human desire to dominate and control the non-human other. In the section 'Something lost', I alluded to Whitehouse's (2021) suggestion that the change from hunter or gatherer to farmer or herder required an epistemic shift, supported by ritualized behaviours that favoured social cohesion and the sharing of ancestral knowledge. Although this shift can be argued to represent the beginning (if that can ever be identified) of alienation – or the transition from living a closed-world to open-world existence – a more dramatic epistemic and ultimately consequential change can be aligned to the Enlightenment period.

Enlightenment thinking advanced ideas of empirical science and rationalism representing a move away from faith, religion and the assumption that existing knowledge could simply be accepted. Ideas and actions had to be tested in the fire of instrumental reason. The rapid development of scientific and technological discoveries have been fuelled by an epistemic shift that views the non-human as a distant object to be exploited, leading to the Industrial Revolution (including the industrialization of agriculture) and the comparatively recent clamour for Artificial Intelligence. It is this psychological distancing, or 'taming', that removes from awareness a sense (and knowledge) of interconnectedness with the non-human other. What is unseen but left to percolate in the unconscious is the internal drama where the external desire to dominate the non-human, inevitably serves to dominate our own 'natural or wild' selves.

Drawing on Winnicott's (1960) identification of the 'true self ' and 'false self', the true-self can be aligned to the natural or wild experience of being human – one not contaminated by Enlightenment thinking. The true-self represents a sense of the ancient, more wild, ways of being human; for example, being more attuned to the natural world, living with unpredictability and disruptions, and alive to other possibilities. The corollary is a false-self, a self 'tamed' by the expectations of others and the fantasy that science and technology will eventually assuage the modern feeling of alienation and dislocation.

These assumptions can only be conjecture but the regularly reported increases in mental ill-health and debilitating anxiety would suggest widespread false-self psychic discomfort. It could be that humans are caught in a dilemma they cannot escape, as an event in the distant past has led to false-self epistemologies replacing true-self epistemologies. Yet the past has not been eliminated, and vestiges of an ancient wild (true) self are still alive and active in the unconscious, representing primal desires to be attuned to nature once again. The modern world though is increasingly dominated by false-self epistemologies where empiricism represses 'the call of the wild' promising that a taming of the unknown and unpredictable will bring happiness, safety and security.

Moving on, it has been argued that the contemporary modern human has been born into an open-world dominated by false-self epistemologies that seek to tame a vibrant planet through the hopeful construction of an external world that can be experienced as 'home'. This, of course, is never achieved.

For the contemporary open-world modern human experience, closed-world epistemologies continue to influence unconscious processes representing a primal urge to be attuned to the wild unpredictability of the non-human other. This, of course, is never achieved.

The ecotherapeutic act therefore revolves around the tension to dominate, or be attuned and attentive to the non-human world.

Ecotherapy: Wilding the tame human

My bold and provocative statement to open this section is that ecotherapy is not necessarily about physical connections with the wildness of nature. Rather ecotherapy is equivalent to an educational act that seeks to encounter and disrupt the dominant epistemologies that have tamed the mind, leading to fantasy thinking, that the domination and control of nature will mitigate feelings of planetary alienation. Ecotherapy will enable the voice of a wild, ancient and vibrant true-self to surface to awareness. Additionally, I make the claim that due to the ecological, economic, political and social polycrisis, largely due to human actions, there is an ethical obligation to give voice to a wild true-self. Thus, re-establishing a reciprocal relationship of awareness with the non-human other is both the focus of education and ecotherapy.

The ecotherapeutic act, and therefore educational endeavour, has as its prime objective to provoke an awareness of what it means to be 'of' and not necessarily 'in' the natural world. In the context of outdoor education, Skea and Fulford (2021) make the distinction between being 'in' or 'of' the outdoors; contrasting being physically present '*in*', as opposed to psychological ways '*of being*' attuned to and paying attention to the world. In other words an epistemological redirection from the desires of the egoistic self to the needs of the ecological other.

This does not suggest that in everyday life, or even the safe space of the therapeutic relationship, that being human and *of* the world requires to constantly think about how each direct action may influence another – say, a shrew, lion, buttercup, or an orangutan. No, it is a recalibration, as such, from tame enlightenment thinking that favours, control, patterns of cause and effect, and predictability. To a return to wild thinking that can work with uncertainty, not-knowing, complexity, and be open to spontaneity and creativity.

It is worth repeating. The suggestion is not a literal, or even fantastical, return to the wild. The premise being made is that good mental health *and* good education must be grounded in what it means to be human. Yet, the long-life educational taming of the human condition has led to the denudement of the vitality of wild ways of being (Bainbridge 2024).

Humans are not disconnected from nature, they are still intimately connected but processes of taming are extinguishing the possibility of an attuned awareness to ecological, wild, ways of being. The battle between wild and tame epistemologies is an unconscious one, where in a desire to control and manage the external world, ancient survival and existential anxieties may have led to a dominant super-ego repressing feelings of attunement and awareness – of being in and with an ecological other. Consequently, the desire to dominate nature also involves a domination of the wilder aspects of what it means to be human.

Conclusion: A case for education as ecotherapy

The chapter started with the title: 'Education as ecotherapy: Paying attention to the world'. It could equally have been 'Ecotherapy as education: Paying attention to the world.' I make no claim on the importance of one over the other. My non-negotiable is that education and ecotherapy are about paying attention to the world. In particular, paying attention to why and how humans have come to dominate the planet, and the consequence this has on planetary and mental health. The premise has been offered, that for reasons unlikely to ever fully be known, human actions interfere and disrupt the human–more-than-human relationship. Hence humans are complicit in their alienation from potentially supportive and nurturing external worlds, accordingly leading to an 'edge of the precipice' experience of continual (if unconscious) existential dread. The ritual for formalized education further contributes to this crisis, while also paradoxically seeking to quell the anxiety of alienation. As such, it has been suggested that education and ecotherapy informed by wild epistemologies that are *of* the world can provide the necessary resources to respond to the needs of the self and planet, while mitigating further existential angst and environmental degradation.

A manifesto for education and ecotherapy

Ecotherapy and good education should be supported by and encourage a return to wild ways *of* being. For example:

Accepting and working with an understanding that anxiety is a feature of the human condition. Anxiety is the motive for ecotherapy and good education. But also, ecotherapy and education will cause anxiety.

Good education and ecotherapy are a response to disruption and will be disruptive.

Ecotherapeutic and good educational places are holding environments where anxiety can be contained.

Good educational and ecotherapeutic spaces are transitional spaces where creativity can flourish and lead to novel and radical thinking.

Good education and ecotherapy does not avoid difficult thinking.

Ecotherapy and good education will respond to natural rhythms of knowing and not-knowing, and not externally imposed goal setting and targets.

Ecotherapy and good education are transformational.

The ecological and educational are fundamental to the human condition and will not go away. It is time to (re)discover our educational and therapeutic wild within!

References

Bainbridge, A. (2019), 'Education Then and Now: Making the Case for *Ecol-Agogy*', *Pedagogy, Culture & Society* 27 (3): 4232–440. https://doi.org/10.1080/14681366.2018.1517130.

Bainbridge, A. (2020), 'Digging Our Own Grave: A Marxian Consideration of Formal Education as a Destructive Enterprise', *International Review of Education* 66: 737–53. https://doi.org/10.1007/s11159-020-09866-7.

Bainbridge, A. (2022), 'Adult Learning on the Edge of a Precipice: An Ecology of Living and Learning', *Dyskursy Młodych Andragogów/Adult Education Discourses* 23: 9–24. doi.org/10.34768/dma.vi23.648.

Bainbridge, A. (2024), 'Wilding Higher Education: From Monoculture to Messy Margins', in A. Bainbridge and N. Kemp (eds), *Good Education in a Fragile World: The Value of a Collaborative and Contextualised Approach to Sustainability in Higher Education*, 141–50, London: Routledge.

Berger, P. L. (1967), *The Sacred Canopy: Elements of a Sociological Theory of Religion*, New York: Anchor Books.

Berger, P. L., and T. Luckmann (1966), *The Social Construction of Reality: A Treatise in the Sociology of Knowledge*, London: Penguin.

Fromm, E. (1968), *The Revolution of Hope: Toward a Humanized Technology*, New York: Harper & Row.

Fromm, E. (1994), *On Being Human*, ed. R. Funk, London: Bloomsbury.

Sharp, H. (1988), *The Transformation of Bigfoot: Madness, Power and Belief among the Chipewyan*, Washington, DC: Smithsonian Institution Press.

Skea, C., and A. Fulford (2021), 'Releasing Education into the Wild: An Education in, and of, the Outdoors', *Ethics and Education* 16 (1): 74–90. doi: 10.1080/17449642.2020.1822612.

United Nations, Department of Economic and Social Affairs, Population Division (2011), World Population Prospects: The 2010 Revision, Volume I: Comprehensive Tables. ST/ESA/SER.A/313. Retrieved 31 October 2024 from https://www.un.org/en/development/desa/population/publications/pdf/urbanization/WUP2011_Report.pdf.

Vujaković, P. (2013), 'Phytobiography: An Approach to "Tree Time" and "Long-Life Learning"', *Arboricultural Journal* 35 (3): 134–46. https://doi.org/10.1080/03071375.2013.852363.

Whitehouse, H. (2021), *The Ritual Animal: Imitation and Cohesion in the Evolution of Social Complexity*, Oxford: Oxford University Press.

Winnicott, D. (1960), *The Maturational Process and the Facilitating Environment: Studies in the Theory of Emotional Development*, New York City: International Universities Press.

16

Becoming ecological: Education with the earth in mind

Giles Barrow and Hayley Marshall

In this chapter we present an extended case study featuring an educational programme – Becoming Ecological – focused on developing ecological sensibilities and approaches for human relations practitioners. We believe that the programme offers a distinctive method that combines experiential opportunities, direct application of theory and what might best be termed as an embodied education in ecological practice.

Unlike in Indigenous cultures, which we loosely define as those peoples living close to their earth, many traditional Western philosophies, theories and methodologies of human relations work (such as in psychotherapy and education), do not explicitly refer to our relationship with the earth as fundamental to our ways of being. Furthermore, in our view, traditional models such as psychoanalysis and humanistic psychodynamic approaches, do not put the earth at the centre of the educative endeavour, and we regard this as a profound, almost deafening, absence. The omission has essential and urgent relevance for the current polycrisis (Morin and Kern 1999), where many are asking how we in Western cultures can support ourselves living through the late stages of modernity (Machado de Oliveria 2021) and develop a different relationship with the earth that will result in new ways of being together among our more-than-human kin (Plotkin 2003). Unless we offer a provocation to the pre-existing 'indoor mind' (Barrow and Marshall 2023), then 'business as usual' will continue with traditional trainings supporting a particular kind of practitioner, who continues to prioritize the human domain while excluding the wider living system. An ecological training needs to birth and support a new kind of practitioner, fit to meet the current demands of a Western system in crisis. Therefore, we view educating from the 'earth-up-through-the-body-mind' as central to the enlivening of the contemporary practitioner's responsiveness to the developing needs of their clients and students. In line with this developing paradigm, we discovered that participants were looking for a different kind of educative space, one where they could gain support for more embodied ways of listening, seeing, feeling and responding. They were also searching for an opportunity to learn in a way that would be congruent with a changing practice, one rooted in the more-than-human world.

Places – where we and the work are located

As is customary in our practice, we will first honour the places in which we work. The Becoming Ecological programme grew out of two very significant places in the UK that the authors have close, intimate connections with. One is a large wild public woodland in Derbyshire and the other an ecological sensitively managed smallholding in Suffolk. Both these places are going-on-being as themselves before we happened upon them. In approaching them we are mindful of the respect that this summons. This ecological reality fundamentally underpins and guides our work specifically through the principle of ecological hygiene, an important principle we discuss later, in matters such as the asking of permission to practice and expressing gratitude.

These places offer their potent self-agency as contrasting, complementary settings for our group meetings, with the woods situated in an upland gritstone landscape and the farm on rolling lowland grazing parkland, our participants leaning into them in different ways.

The atmospheres, weatherings, contours, animals, plant life, rocks, waters, quirks and characters of these generous places have fundamentally influenced how we think and practice as educators. They have informed many co-facilitatory conversations as to how the programme is to be shaped, guiding the process, breathing their unique spirit into what happens along the way.

Our position – who we are as educators

As programme facilitators, both of us have personal histories of positive and dynamic early experiences of being outdoors, having been raised in agricultural landscape and engaged in outdoor education or pursuits from an early age. We are mindful that we benefit from the privileges of both being able-bodied and, as both white and born in the UK, are advantaged in our respective familiarities with the English landscape, factors that are not always in common with those with whom we work.

Both of us are also long time experienced ecological practitioners in our respective fields (education and psychotherapy), and have been co-facilitating groups and writing about our work together for six years. Although both trained as transactional analysts, we incorporate many other influences in our work, significantly, ecological movement work (Reeve 2011), and storytelling practices (see for example, Shaw 2011). We have many years' experience of facilitating different kinds of groups both indoors and outside, teaching through the embodied experiential, tending to live process, and working with a multifactorial mix. This makes us well placed to work in such a dynamic educative group space although still find it challenging.

The groups we work with include participants from a range of disciplines, including psychotherapy, coaching, consultancy and education. These people bring varying levels of experience in their practice as well as in outdoor working, meaning that the groups have a rich alchemy of beginner and more experienced minds. The Becoming Ecological programme has been running for four years, takes place seasonally, that is, four times a year, for three days and is residential. The latter we have found to be very important for deepening the sense of 'community-in-place', which affords the group a solid place-centric container as well as a human–human crucible for exploring key themes.

We intend to present a coherent account of the work and have found it necessary to integrate theory and illustrative material from the experience in such a way as to be far more systematic than what occurred in practice! As will be clear, emergent process was a core principle of the work and rarely presented itself in the neat and tidy manner of the following presentation. In some respects, this point highlights a fundamental flaw in trying to write about working within the ecological domain; it simply does not lend itself to the form and function of a written guide.

We begin with outlining the educational philosophy of the programme followed by a discussion of its key working principles. We appreciate that readers may be most interested in knowing more about what it looked like in practice, and we have a series of vignettes of the exercises we experimented with, connecting these with the different landscapes in our programme. Finally, we offer reflections about our process – the learnings and thoughts on refining the approach as the programme develops.

Educational philosophy: Beyond training, towards education

Perhaps the most distinctive feature of the Becoming Ecological programme has been a philosophical stance which has been emphatically about education, as opposed to training. To engage in training involves embarking on a path through which the trainee benefits from learning more about a field of practice – outdoor practice in this instance – through increased knowledge and understanding and improved competence. Training requires the trainer to have clear teaching and learning objectives, a high level of expertise in the given field and capacity to teach it well but, most importantly, will already know the destination of the programme. Trainees, in response, expect clarity from the trainer, a structured curriculum and a contained learning environment. Often the trainer–trainee dynamic is 'held' within a wider context of expectation, perhaps in relation to professional regulation or credentialing arrangements, which in turn informs the agenda of what happens in terms of professional development. Fundamentally, though, training is about becoming competent in order to learn to 'do something', or to 'improve performance'. There is, in other words, a 'product' at the end of the process and this is typical of most education models. Whether it is the task of realizing human potential, emancipation from oppression or learning about 'stuff' in order to become accredited, the direction of much professional development is what can be referred to as 'product-orientated'.

The Becoming Ecological programme developed into a different sort of educational experience. As educators we became less sure of what the objectives were for us as teachers, or for the participants as learners. The curriculum was opaque, often rising into view as the work unfolded. Our previous expertise was only relevant before we each recognized that this too was an expanding part of the educational dynamic. It was not so much that we lacked expertise, but that our prior experience enabled us to effectively know how to build the track as the train came behind us! Our participants on the other hand needed to practise a high order of agency (including holding their own personal intention for their process) and presence amidst an emergent structure and learned much about managing ambiguity. To some readers familiar with mainstream professional development this may appear incoherent, potentially unsafe and, at worst, irresponsible on our behalf as educators. We might be criticized for not knowing what we were doing or making it up as we went along and there would be a grain of truth in both charges. Developing a relationship with ambiguity comes with this approach to work, a theme picked up later when we explore our facilitation partnership. However, to properly understand the method it is necessary to appreciate the concept of ecological educational encounter.

Ecological educational encounter

In educational philosophy the notion of 'encounter' is a specific term and refers to a moment or episode in which the student experiences a sense of arrival. It involves the individual being called into the world differently from that to which they have been familiar, often instigated by the educator. In doing so, the student has a sense of their subjectivity, in other words, they are called by this arrival experience to act by choosing, how to exist in relation to the world. Frequently the world might show up in a way that does not align or is desired by the individual and they nevertheless have to choose how to be in it (and even not choosing is a choice). Existential education is a quite different idea from the conventional educational models with which we might be most familiar drawn from schooling, college or professional training institutes. It is a profoundly challenging vision of what education can be, for both educators and students, and this is one of the core philosophical tenets of our programme.

A second philosophical aspect is that the educational encounter is of the 'ecological' domain. In other words, the abstract notion of the student arriving into the world becomes much more real when the work is undertaken outdoors, quite literally 'into the world' of the more-than-human, the myriad connections held in the biosphere, and the circles and cycles of sensate, somatic and movement phenomenon. When understood in this context it is impossible for the educator to fully know what they are doing or indeed be able to be sure quite what does happen next. Ecological educational encounters are by definition organic, continually embryonic and unpredictable. We may be able to cultivate the conditions by which such encounters arise, but it is counterproductive to second guess, over-plan or force the educational ground to yield. This emergent quality has a particular emphasis in the context of place. Agency is held as much in the more-than-human environment as that of the human, so in this respect it becomes part of facilitating the educational experience. In pedagogical terms the immediate environment takes on the role of 'educational object', (Barrow 2024). In addition to the student and teacher dyad, the educational 'third' exists, unable to answer for itself, yet its presence generates possible interaction between it, and across, the teacher–student dynamic.

Natality

Following on from the idea of an ecological encounter, is a third important philosophical position which is that of natality. An unfamiliar term, but essential to understanding the significance of the becoming ecological process, natality refers to birth and becoming. Based in the works of Arendt (1958) and Jantzen (1998), natality has been presented respectively as a radically different way of framing social dynamics and spirituality. A natal lens draws attention to features often overlooked or discounted in the more established and culturally embedded notion of mortality. In other words, it is the fact of our birth that gives rise to the inevitability of death. While mortality has an emphasis on the individual – many will die alone – natality emerges out of relationship; no-one is born without another, or more specifically, a mother, which leads to a further feature. Natality is associated with the power of the feminine – to date we have all been born out of a woman. In contrast to notions of mind, body, spirit divisions, natality draws attention to our embodiment – we arrive bodily into the world with all the physical demands that the newborn makes upon it. Beauty and risk also become important to the natal moment. Despite best efforts there is danger in the birthing process, sometimes there is death sitting right alongside birth. And there's beauty in the miraculous appearance of life's longing for itself. To consider natality as an existential alternative to mortality is to seek out a world that is sufficient to nurture and sustain itself and one where flourishing and renewal are fundamental to both the human and more than human survival.

What this means in more specific terms to the programme is that 'becoming' is a symbolic motif at several levels. As the group gathers for the first time it begins the process of becoming while individuals are also arriving as 'becomings' in their own right. We are also 'becoming' as educators into the space, as is the programme content. In other words, emersion is the point of movement for the programme, a recurrent uncurling of what has not been yet visible or known beforehand. So, we have found that natality forms a potent and natural philosophical anchor for Becoming Ecological, as well as providing a congruence between course content, intention and process. However, while acknowledging these philosophical assumptions, there are principles which we discovered as especially useful.

Becoming ecological: Working principles

The ground

As mentioned above, 'place before people' is our fundamental position. When we meet, we do so primarily because there's an environment in which to do so. It was there before the people turned up, existing in its own complex and beautiful manner. Indigenous peoples and cultures who live closer to the earth know this far better than we do, often greeting one another by reference to the place from which they came. This principle, therefore, means more than simply noticing the place of the work but seeking explicit connection with it.

In the programme we typically meet at the fire pit at the start time and within a couple of minutes participants go into the woods, fields or garden to receive welcome, offer libation and settle into the energetic atmosphere before returning to the fire circle to check in more directly to the human domain. This principle is a constant reference point throughout the work, with participants invited to consider the influence and relevance of 'here' on a particular exercise or conversation. It consistently draws our group attention to the biological reality of an ecological self (Ness 2008) embedded in what Nora Bateson names as our broader symmathesy, (2016).

Linked with this is our foregrounding of embodiment in the process of the group. We emphasize the significance of the moving-body-in-place as a fundamental implicit 'glue' (Abram 1996) – a guide to forms of knowing that lie beyond a more dominant (in our Western-northern hemispherical cultures) emphasis on the human verbal. We view the body process as an important language of its own that moves us into direct communication with the more-than-human – it is, therefore, an essential part of the work we do.

Working from this fundamental premise means that we will often travel with key themes through setting up non-stylized movement explorations, moving as a group (for example in group sculpts) within different places, or inviting individuals to explore a more intimate sensory relationship with small areas of land. The latter, which we refer to as niching, invites participants to develop eco-relational skills through relating with a small place or 'niche', via sensory and movement practices. It has become a core practice in our work. Originating from ecological movement teachings (Reeve 2011), we have developed this into a full-blown practice for supporting practitioners in becoming ecologically embedded. We also offer participants time to metabolize the happenings of the group though movement, viewing this as an important aspect of assimilating (sometimes troubling) material.

The vessel

We have found that offering structure is vital for steadying both us and the group as we engage in an emergent educational process. There is a dynamic tension between offering enough of this and keeping the space open for the ecological encounter. The rites of passage arc (Van Gennep 1909; Turner 1969) continues to be an invaluable frame of reference for our work. Setting intention and working with phases of severance (breaking away from the familiar), threshold (engaging with the liminal), return (to the once-familiar place) and gift (new insights) have been an explicit structure for holding the overall direction of travel, and land-marking the gradual unfolding of the programme in an overall cycle of transformation. Other times it has implicitly informed our sense of group development and thinking of when to position specific exercises. This rite of passage structure has also influenced our practice in specific points of practice, for example at each workshop, we hold a threshold ritual to open and close the session, a practice that we see as critical to good ethical ecological practice.

To offer a further holding structure for the programme, we use a medicine wheel based on the 'four shields' work of Stephen Foster and Meredith Little (1998). Their development of this medicine wheel (originally taught to them by a Cheyenne elder, the model has come to us via a close colleague who had trained at the School of Lost Borders, where Foster and Little were based), is based on years of running vision quests as a mechanism of psychological change. The wheel is based on an ancient cross-cultural symbol of the circle reflecting cycles of the seasonal, of living and dying, of becoming and being, of journeys of transition. Foster and Little also drew upon rites of passage work, which fits well with the idea of this wheel as an initiatory structure reflecting nature's perpetual cycles of 'changing-ness'.

Our work with the wheel involves working within an embodied metaphorical structure where the points of the compass are used to hold aspects of 'human-in-nature'.

In practice we use the wheel in directional walking exercises (Jordan 2015) to explore themes and questions. In these the structure cleaves us to the land – through us being a manifestation of nature, it can be our mirror, drawing us back close in to this wisdom.

We also associate each direction with a holding lens for each workshop, for example, South – Embodiment, West – Embeddedness, North – Engagement (Activism), East – Ethereality.

Another key conceptual frame guiding us in our work is Wilma Bucci's Multiple Code theory (1997). Her work, based in cognitive psychology and neuropsychology, offers a psychological framework for understanding and working with human emotional processing systems. Outlining three distinct areas of 'processing' – our meaning and sense-making capacities – she refers to the sub-symbolic (nonverbal and body based), the nonverbal symbolic (image and metaphor), and verbal symbolic levels (words). Bucci describes the referential process as the important linking of these different organizing principles of our experience. Bucci's model has offered an invaluable structure to plot the development of exercises and address specific themes, including analysing the murmurations of our group process. Most significantly it has helped us to track how the group are regulating the impact of the work, especially in accounting for the implicit nature of much of what we are doing, such as in body and movement practices and myth and story work.

The emergent process

This leads us more fully into the issue of regulating the intensity of such a fluid educational process. Working outdoors can easily become chaotic, overly risky and above all, uncontainable, in contrast to indoor practice. A multilayered holding process, based on ecological ethics, is called for and we have identified several points where good habits can help keep the work respectful, safe enough, effective and structured.

Early on in the life of our groups, in our contracting sessions, we share the twinned central tenets 'dosing' and 'resourcing'. Taken from the field of relational trauma therapy (Brantbjerg 2015), these principles invite participants to build and respect their own inner authority and that of others. This is about paying attention to nervous systems of all kinds, titrating contact with the more-than-human, and the human, including bodies, hearts and minds. In this we tune the group's attention to the integrity of a nuanced relating process including bringing care to all involved. These principles help regulate the life of the group, so that the work we are doing can be thought about and assimilated.

Following on from the reference to 'thresholding' above, ecological hygiene is one of our key working principles. This refers to the way we encourage the group to attend to the process of relating, most notably, but not exclusively, concerning the impact on our more-than-human kin. An important example is the introduction of the threshold ceremony early in the opening of the workspace. This is crucial in demarcating the work itself, not dissimilar from opening the door of a consulting room at the beginning of the session and its closure at the end. It is therefore a ritual of vessel building where a set apart – sacred – 'space' is treated as a spiritual, psychological and physical entity. This act supports the group's experience of being 'held-in-place' whereby holding is understood as a place for 'gathering in' the human in all their wholeness (Ogden 2004). Returning to our relating with place again – the threshold is also part of a ritualized statement marking that we are in a certain kind of relationship – one where nature is not just for the taking. This also manifests in matters such as the asking of permission and expressing gratitude before the ceremony, marking that we are in a reciprocal relationship with the more-than-human (Wall Kimmerer 2020).

Planning time is different in outdoor work and a useful habit that creates good hygiene is to remember that time, task and movement combine in such a way as to always extend what might be a briefer exercise if undertaken indoors. We found it helpful to remind ourselves that 'everything is the workshop', so that even the journeying between sites, or walking from a clearing in the woods to open grassland, was incorporated as part of the practice. There's an efficiency to this, as it informs a teaching point as to how to hold spaces outdoors without 'sliding out' of them – helping us all be clear when are we in and when are we out. More importantly, this also offers further opportunity to attend more thoughtfully to the significance of movement in relation to place.

Sufficiency is also a consideration in terms of monitoring how much of the educative space is taken up with human–human business. A particularly noticeable example of this was managing group check-ins at the beginning of workshops. We had noticed how the indoor practice of lengthy group check-ins was replicated around the fire circle, comprised of uneven sharing of time among individuals. We began to reflect on the possibility that check-in group process paralleled the relationship between people and planet. To be more direct, some individuals might bring their sense of scarcity of resource (available time) and either be overly responsible, mindful of not wanting take too much, or on the other hand, being mind-less about how much time they took, or acting with entitlement to the group space. We addressed this through introducing the concept of sufficiency – asking 'just how much needs to be brought into the circle?' – and then initiating the ritual of a talking stick. This involved passing the object around the circle with each person opening with, 'I am X……' and finishing with 'I have spoken'.

Another aspect of good hygiene practice was remembering to refer to the value of fractal thinking. This is an extension of the familiar group processing method whereby the facilitator might point out a pattern that is going on within the group membership, for example, scapegoating of an individual, or sibling pairing or some other transferential dynamic. In our work we would be interested to expand the perspective by being curious as to what people–planet dynamic was being played out. A frequent example of this was the tendency of the group to move swiftly into intellectualizing a process point as a way of disassociating from the grief about the violation of the world in some way. This would be indicated by the emphasis on human-to-human dialogue and the absence of including the perspective of the place in which we worked.

Principles to practice

In our experience we have had to continually grapple with the core principles from session to session. In each workshop the principles would be skittish, like wild creatures, sometimes hard to grasp, or elusive, and required constant vigilance in terms of group facilitation and leadership.

The principle, place before people, for example, seems straightforward enough, however, tracking this in practice becomes problematic. It can be an apparently simple technique to move from the group circle and out into the immediate environment in order to 'meet' the place. We have realized that this in itself does not prioritize place if individuals have not gathered themselves, are still occupied with their internal process, and experiencing dissonance in their state of arrival. To put place first is to have assumed that the person is sufficiently readied to do so and so we have to find ways of attending to the self without remaining caught within it. In this section, therefore, we want to offer accounts from the field of practice, not so much as case studies in 'how to do it', but to breathe some life into how we have addressed the task of living the principles into practice.

Working with embodiment

The movement and body work practices we introduce to the group are in general about supporting bodies to 'move among' – embodying human embeddedness in our broader more-than-human symmathesy. As we move around the place, we pay attention to how we move, our pace, our rhythm – the impact of our bodies on the place and vice versa. This is a vitalized regulatory process involving many possible focal points of attention. We base much of the body work on our personal ecological practice, the work of non-stylized movement practitioners (see Bloom, Galanter and Reeve 2014), and relational trauma therapist Merete Holm Brantbjerg (2008). In terms of practice though, what we actually do is generated anew each time the group meets, and often in the moment as a new encounter will call for a new embodied response.

Case example

It is the final morning of our meeting, and we are on the top moorland, which is often where we go in order to help the group begin to crystallize their work before leaving later in the day. The place is glistening in the winter sun; it is bright but extremely cold.

We have been working with the intensity of very low temperatures (some of the coldest we've ever worked in) alongside some challenging group dynamics about staying connected and regulated as we encounter our bodies in relation with the harsh weather and the resultant internal material. We decide to help the group regulate though teaching an impromptu 'resourcing' exercise – this, quite literally made up on the spot, builds on a pre-existing ideas in relational trauma therapy. Our aim is to resource individuals and to help them get grounded to think about what's been happening but also to support them in leaving a space where intense encounters have taken place. It will also offer them a skill that can be used in other contexts, specifically in practice with clients or students.

We decide to invite people to connect with an element of the more-than-human, dosing the amount of contact they want to have, for example, with a rock or a tree or the earth. We invite them to notice just how much or how little pressure is needed to hit a sensation 'sweet spot' of support in their body. We ask them to name the sensation and then to name the resource this may offer them. Then once this is found, a human partner joins the chain and the whole process begins again. The group works with the question 'how do I (can I?) stay in contact with my body, the more-than-human, as I come into contact with you?' The whole exercise is about nuanced contact, guided by the body – the aim is to build inner or outer authority through connection with both human and beyond. It is an invitation to be in charge of contact – to experiment with this – to bring it into human–human relating, but most importantly to ask a central ecological question, 'If I have contact with this rock or tree, for example, what will this mean for our human relating?'

Working with encounter

We have been aware that referring to 'encounter' can be a little abstract, or even off-putting for practitioners; it sounds an important idea but can be difficult to concretize. It has been something worth struggling with during the programme. Such encounters give rise to a 'becoming', a natal moment in which the individual experiences themselves anew in some way. Often encounter is understood as a happening between people and through the course we have wanted to encourage envisioning the possibility of this occurring within the more-than-human domain.

Case example

We chose one of the workshops in the middle of the programme to introduce a series of exercises by which to create the conditions whereby encounter might be explored and possibly emerge. On this occasion we were based at in the woods in Derbyshire. The landscape is formed of a steep and stepped woodland which forms the edge of open moorland. At its lowest point there is a large lake, heavily overshadowed by the trees and near vertical slopes, forming a cold, dark and primeval atmosphere. It was here that Hayley shared with the group a personal account of an encounter with an alligator while travelling in Cancun, Mexico. Amidst the cacophony of mega-cruise liners, hyper-tourism and extreme commercial exploitation of the habitat, a remarkable thing happened – an alligator appeared on the deck of the bunkhouse. It was just there, stock still, with its mighty jaws open, as if to say, 'What the fuck are you all doing? I have been here for thousands of years, and I am not going anywhere.' The impact of meeting an entity so prehistoric was palpable for us as we sat close to the banks of the primordial lake deep down in the woods; the encounter gave rise to a further encounter.

Following this first exercise we 'travelled' upwards, taking muddy tracks further into the tree line where eventually the ground gave way to open clearings among the birch and oak, the ground thickly covered with leaf mould. Blue sky occasionally broke through the canopy and we settled down into the ground, up alongside mossy trunks or leaning on fallen trees or hunkered into the pitted earth itself. This time Giles read a journal account written in a previous summer beginning with observations about life in the margins of farmland and a particular experience of niching in an irrigation ditch at the edge of a field to escape the heat of the day. He had waited and fell into a reverie recalling relationships with two women. After a while he was startled at a distant sound which became ever louder and closer. Within moment two female deer crashed through the undergrowth and stood before him. They caught his gaze and, he theirs, before they turned and galloped away. Again, the reading of the encounter cultivated the conditions for another as the group also fell into their own half-waking state, held within the closeness of the ground.

Each of these accounts were intentionally situated, in part to carry an echo of the original place, but also to prepare the group for finally setting out over the top of the ridge and onto open land. There was a shift at this point to a more conventional conversation about encounters with the more-than-human domain. We had wanted to carry the material from the ancient, primitive and instinctual symbolism of the statued alligator up and into the rich potential of the marginal territories before returning to the familiar uplands of the conscious world of the socialized self. This is in part an example of what we mean when we refer to 'travelling with' material and also in curating the possibility for encounter. However, more importantly this is an illustration of how the landscape itself impacts on the emergent process. At the outset of the workshop, we had not envisaged either the accounts of the crocodile or that of the marginal experience. The topography of the woodland location lent itself to our conjuring of a process that spoke to the theme of activism, which we had been considering important to the group. The dark waters of the lake intimated a reptilian force, a sharply ascending muddy path spiralled to the leaf moulded edge of the cliff edge before breaking out to open moorland. In many respects the shape of the land yielded to the tentative theme and, in turn, gifted us a narrative on which the group process emerged.

Working with story and myth

It took a couple of years before we properly realized the contribution of story and myth to the programme drawing on the approach developed by Martin Shaw (2011). So often the stories helped us speak into the intimate relations we have with others, or internal dilemmas, and, most importantly, the old tales tie us back into relationship with the earth, the seasonal cycles, the 'marriage' between ourselves and the land. This is an approach to storytelling best understood as a version of eco-activism. One example we share is that of Red Bead Woman, a powerful tale that opens with the desire of an old woman – a crone – who lives far apart from the centre of the kingdom. For us, the story speaks to the importance of reconnecting the village with the wild wood so that culture can thrive. It also touches on self-delusion and betrayal, falling for fake news and having our identities stolen. The heartbeat of the tale is the enduring wisdom of the old woman who, despite her own flaws, and because of her rootedness, steers a community towards renewal.

We tell the story in two parts, pausing at a point of utmost desolation and deceit, which some may find is an indictment of our own culture's position in relation to the planet. It is a dangerous place from which to send people out into the place, often to find external demons and internal ghosts running amok with the psyche. 'Taking the story out' involves bringing the individual internal dialogue into conversation with the external environment out of which the tale originated. In other words, there is a re-enactment by which the human and more-than-human relations are mediated by story.

It is in the second part of Red Bead Woman that we hear of the Crow King and the necessary 'bucket work' required to make a life worth having, the importance of forgiveness and the simple medicine of kindness. Though this might appear as a glib platitude, there's an extraordinary punch to how the story culminates in a wedding where the spilling of red bead truths brings a community back to life. Likewise, the invocation for the group is to discern for themselves what red bead truths they have to share about reconnection and the relationship between themselves and the more-than-human world which support renewal. In bringing the story to the group our interest is in cultivating an activist energy, highlighting the significance of each participant finding their own red bead speech that gives shape to their respective commitment and passion for the interconnected world.

Reflections on learning for us as facilitators

In this work we have been very aware that we are learning alongside our participants. After all, we are Western white people, so by definition we too have much to learn about living within a wider symmathesy. This does not come automatically or readily to a person living within modernity, so it has to be exercised, learnt through engaged participation, and this is as much true for us as our participants. This stance challenges us to bring a certain kind of humility to the ecological endeavour, while not losing our leadership authority.

We have found several dynamic tensions and ambiguities (all fractals of the ecological issues of our time) that we continue to engage with as group facilitators.

- Structure and emergence – certain and unknown
- Ego and ecocentric practice – human and more-than
- Experience of time – the necessity of spaciousness and slowness of the work versus the expectation of outcome and performativity

These have been present in varying degrees in some key areas:

Group container

We have referred to the challenges of holding the group in a nonlinear, multilayered process – it is not for the faint hearted! The group including ourselves as leaders, tottered on the edge of an ontic void at times, because the work inherently challenges participants to fall upon their own inner structures, which in turn can then surface personal trouble, stimulating what in transactional analysis (TA) would be called protocol material (see Marshall, this volume). We have realized that attending to group process is key but have consistently struggled with how to do this without becoming overly human focussed and egocentric. We have at times, lost our keel through not attending to the group enough by gathering them in. Our indecision has become confusing, leading to a sense of destabilization in the group, and we experienced some issues with people opting out of group processing spaces. We now know that the human domain must be attended to in a certain way – not for its own sake, but for the wider symmathesy. This is where the idea of fractal working comes in and it is a key aspect of what we are teaching.

Following Bucci (1997), we have also understood the importance of the referential process in helping the individual and the group-as-a-whole to regulate stimulated material. Offering time for explicit scaffolding of where emotional experience can be storied up through the social and into the ecological layering is steadying for each individual in the group, the group-as-a-whole's nervous system becoming better regulated as a result. However, what is also important here is that this structuring is not used to move away from the aliveness of the inherent uncertainty in the work – that we continue to hold space for the invisible or the unknown.

As we move forward, our more developed understanding of the importance of attending to the human group container brings a stronger sense of protection into the work. Experience has shown the importance of contracting, spending plenty of layered up experiential and discussion time on this. We also increasingly pay attention to the pacing and rhythm of our overall process offering lots of time for digestion and crystallization.

Leadership

We noticed that at times working with such a live process can also inevitably stimulate our own familiar difficulties and proclivities around such issues as responsibility and authority. While we recognize personal patterns in relation to leadership, it has been important to connect this with the systemic challenge of taking charge in ecological work, as if that is even possible. In other words, our individual and partnership dilemmas about power and authority are a fractal of the wider contemporary puzzle about how to lead in the face of climate collapse and ecological rupture. An example was our joint slump into passivity, self-doubt and haplessness when one of our groups began to struggle with attendance. One major learning here was that we needed to attend to our joint leadership space. We gave much more time to being and talking together in the place, in advance of the group appearing on that occasion. This is now something we make part of our educational leadership practice.

Live process

An important learning has been to build even more faith in the live emergent process, viewing it as a 'sovereign presence'. This can be understood as the land having a prior authority of its own to which we are subject. This means we have had to guard against any tendencies to force the ecological world into any kind of pre-existing theoretical realm – a form of Procrustean bed. Working to allow the voice of the earth to emerge is to be led by the emergent, with a mind of its own; it will have its way with us!

This involves monitoring and working with several domains at once, for example (not in any particular order)

- the process (pre-existing, ongoing) in the place
- our ecological and personal process, for example, our own ecological practice, our own Dreamings, our own embodied countertransference
- the process between us as facilitators
- the process between us and the places
- the process between us as leadership, and the group
- the process within the group
- the process between the group and the places

A limitation of separating out these components (typical of our Western tendencies!) is that this does not reflect the live phenomenon which is one of interconnected wholeness. Unlike indoor practice, live process work requires attention to the human–human dynamics in addition to those of the place. It is the kind of work that takes us to the edge of the familiar terrain of the Western indoor mind experience.

Concluding remarks

One of the challenges in writing this chapter has been that the work is not only emergent in practice but is also constantly shape-shifting. Just when we have thought we might have reached a point of comprehension about working in the field, its direction changes and we are set on a new course; it can shift with the wind. Consequently, we know that whatever is described in this chapter is both a culmination of a process on the move and won't reflect what we are doing by the time this is being read. However, there are some enduring truths we can see connected with this work.

First, the power of this particular approach to ecological practice to impact individuals and groups is not to be taken lightly. Beyond the superficial claims that being in nature does us all good, we have found that to be engaged, seriously, with the more-than-human domain comes with risk, upset and disorientation. It can make things happen which we cannot fully understand nor articulate. Second, that being in the outdoor realm is not about retreat or escape of some sort – this work is intended to 'wake us up'. Third, we have become increasingly intentional in the activist energy of the programme. A sense of urgency has developed for us and participants over the years. A combination of global disputes, further evidence of climate collapse, dramatic changes in favour of anti-environmental political agendas have heightened the threat that comes with the unsustainability of capitalist, patriarchal neocolonialism. In the closeness of this work, we can both feel the world burn, the need to grieve its passing and find a way to live in right relationship with it in the meantime.

References

Abrams, D. (1996), *The Spell of the Sensuous: Perception and Language in the More-Than-Human World*, New York: Vintage Books.

Arendt, H. (1958), *The Human Condition*, Chicago: Chicago Press.

Barrow, G. (2024), *Encountering Education through Existential Challenges and Community: Re-connection and Renewal for an Ecologically based Future*, Abingdon: Routledge.

Barrow G., and H. Marshall (2023), 'Revisiting Ecological Transactional Analysis: Emerging Perspectives', *Transactional Analysis Journal* 53 (1): 7–20.

Bateson, N. (2016), *Small Arcs of Larger Circles: Framing through Other Patterns*, Axminster: Triarchy Press.

Bloom, K., M. Galanter and S. Reeve (2014), *Embodied Lives – Reflections on the Influence of Suprapto Suryodarmo and Amerta Movement*, Axminster: Triarchy Press.

Brantbjerg, M. H. (2008), Resource-Oriented Skill Training as a Psychotherapeutic Method. Retrieved from http://moaiku.dk/moaikuenglish/englishlitterature/articles_pdf/a4/ROST_BP_2.2_A4.pdf.

Brantbjerg, M. H. (2015), 'About Survival Reactions – In Relational Trauma Therapy', Retrieved from http://moaiku.dk/moaikuenglish/englishlitterature/articles_pdf/a4/aboutsurvivalreactions_a4.pdf.

Bucci, W. (1997), *Psychoanalysis and Cognitive Science: A Multiple Code Theory*, New York: Guilford.

Foster, S., and M. Little (1998), *The Four Shields; The Initiatory Seasons of Human Nature*, Big Pine: Lost Borders Press.

Jantzen, G. (1998), *Becoming Divine: Towards a Feminist Philosophy of Religion*, Manchester: Manchester University Press.

Jordan, M. (2015), *Nature and Therapy - Understanding Counselling and Psychotherapy in Natural Spaces*, Hove: Routledge.

Machado de Oliveira, V. (2021), *Hospicing Modernity: Facing Humanity's Wrongs and the Implications for Social Activism*, Berkeley: North Atlantic Books.

Morin, E., and A. B. Kern (1999), *Homeland Earth: A Manifesto for the New Millennium*, New York: Hampton Press.

Naess, A. (2008), *The Ecology of Wisdom*, Berkeley: Penguin Books.
Ogden, T. H. (2004), 'On Holding and Containing, Being and Dreaming', *International Journal of Psychoanalysis* 85: 1349–64.
Plotkin, B. (2003), *Soulcraft*, Novato: New World Publishing.
Reeve, S. (2011), *Nine Ways of Seeing a Body*, Axminster: Triarchy Press.
Shaw, M. (2011), *A Branch from the Lightning Tree: Ecstatic Myth and the Grace of Wildness*, Ashland: White Cloud Press.
Turner, V. W. (1969), *The Ritual Process*, London: Penguin.
Van Gennep, A. (1909), *Les rites de passage*, Paris: Emile Nourry.
Wall Kimmerer, R. (2020), *Braiding Sweetgrass: Indigenous Wisdom, Scientific Knowledge and the Teachings of Plants*, UK: Penguin Books.

17

Breathing vitality into supervision: A creative and expansive ecological practice

Natasha Sephton

Introduction

As I write, I sit in the landscape where I work and have known well for over two decades, sharing it with family and friends. The land here is largely hilly and undulating, steep in places (to vertical) and flat in others. It is a mixed native woodland, a SSSI (Site of Special Scientific Interest) due to its flora and fauna, and which could be considered large in modern day England at just under 200 acres, but in medieval times was part of an expansive forest that stretched far across the broader Derbyshire landscape. There are areas of low gritstone cliffs, housing a number of exogene caves (shallow cave openings), and evidence of small open cast mines from the early industrialization era, now reclaimed by nature. There is a fluctuating but constant flow of water that descends as a brook through low waterfalls to an old, small reservoir, creating a watery glade in the heart of the woods. Here, it rests briefly before making its way on to where it merges into a river at the lower eastern side.

Thin tracks, made by humans and other animals, crisscross through this ancient forest, and in most places it's possible to move deeper into the woodland to find seclusion and privacy. This is a public place with open access and you may come across people with their dogs and groups engaging in activities such as forest school, and so on. Beyond the northern brow of the wooded hill, there is an open area of expansive land scattered with rocks and boulders where Scots pines, birch and fern grow. In the spring, it is a meadow with wild flowers and sky larks and, although it's not quite high enough to be considered a moorland, it can have a similar exposed feel to it during winter months. You can also wander freely (around small herds of cattle and sheep who, at times, graze on this land) and when you turn to face north, your eyes can stretch across a scooped shaped valley to the hills beyond.

I am describing this place partly by way of introducing my outdoor practice locale, but also to offer a sense that it is a place of itself: a rich and complex living system formed by a wide array of interspecies' relationships that interweave between each other. I have a particular interest in how developing an intentional relational engagement with the more-than-human-world (Abram 2017) offers potential for both supervisee and supervisor to enter into a state of vital aliveness and an ecological mind (Barrow and Marshall 2023). I see these ontological states of being, among others, as key features of nature-relatedness, which I suggest, supports clinical reflection, processing, gaining new understandings and transformation. In exploring the phenomenology of nature-based supervision I invite us to consider how we make meaning from environmental encounters. The living world is a dynamic and fluid relational place which, when engaged with, invites us into an embodied relationship. I describe what I call an *expansive* supervision which aligns with working creatively, and discuss nature as co-supervisor alongside William's Four Roles model (1995).

About me

I have been working as a dramatherapist and a lifespan integration therapist, with groups and individuals for over twenty years both indoors and outside. During my therapy training I was keen to retain the outdoor element of my previous role as an outdoor instructor or development trainer and youth worker. I was fortunate in my first clinical role in a Child and Adolescent Mental Health Service (CAMHS) team that my lead consultant was supportive of my wish to take therapy outdoors and I began running groups for adolescents in local woods. Some years later in private practice, trained as a creative supervisor, and having had some years working solely indoors, I began yearning to work outside again. Having attended Hayley Marshall's Taking Therapy Outdoors training with The Centre of Natural Reflection in 2018, I returned to working outside and then, when COVID-19 interrupted our lives, I closed my therapy studio and have been working online and outdoors since.

One of the first times my own relationship with nature was particularly enlivened in me as a child, was when our family lived outside for extended periods of time in France, while we built a family home. I grew up within a relatively large family for the 1970s in the fenlands of East Anglia, UK. My father, who regarded himself as a free-thinking intellectual, worked in languages and as a piano tutor, as well as home educating his children. He exerted dominance over his young family with his wilfully unconventional and nonconformist ways, maintaining control of 'life on his terms' through covert narcissism and his own particular humour. Unsatisfied with life in the UK, he bought a small plot of land in a relatively remote part of France with a view to build a house and relocate his family.

I was eleven years old, and over the following three years our family spent six months per year camping on the plot of land, engaged in the task of building our own home, albeit amateurishly. Being the oldest daughter, I was charged with looking after the younger siblings and cooking for the family on a camping stove and wood fire, when I wasn't brick laying or mixing cement. Living close to the earth and working together to create our future home felt exciting at times. However, living on a building site with no amenities, no car, no phone, and no friends, coupled with our parent's relationship breaking down, my psyche and soul began to suffer.

Whenever I could, I took myself off into the woods and spent time sat by a nearby lake or lying in the branches of a befriended tree, my body held by its solid structure. Once, on my way to the lake, I came across a snake curled up in the grass. I stopped abruptly and it lifted its patterned head to take me in. Naturally, I had been warned about snakes and the potential danger ran through my mind, but something else took over and I lowered myself onto my haunches and spoke appreciative words to this little creature. In turn, he or she eyed me and smelled the air between us through a slim pink tongue.

We stayed together for a while until the snake turned and made its way through the dry grass. This exchange offered something significant for my adolescent self – I experienced a part of me I hadn't known before, brought alive through being seen by this astonishing creature, who was also new to my eyes. I felt the thrill of this new encounter, and realized I wasn't alone. My engagement with the more-than-human and living outdoors during this time took the form of a vital relationship for my survival and my development.

Being in and among the living world

On occasions when I've been away from the woods where I work for any significant period of time, on my return I notice my heart feels wide open and I have a more-than-usual enlivened, embodied experience which feels to me like some sort of greeting is occurring. In these moments, I feel myself functioning from a more embodied place and notice my thinking, cognitive mind operating in a more coherent, joined up and integrated way. It could be said that whether the life here is communicating with me is neither here nor there, as the transformational impact on my whole body–mind system is notably profound, and therefore advantageous to my well-being as an individual. However, the recognition of reciprocity of the relationship has significance and goes much further than solely benefiting the well-being of my functioning. My body–mind system does not exist on its own, but is located within a much larger system that is relationally impacted by, and upon, the living system within which I am also a part. As Wall Kimmerer reminds us, living organisms are not an 'it' but our kin (Wall Kimmerer 2013).

Drawing from traditional indigenous wisdoms and the fields of ecopsychology and eco-philosophy, it is recognized that reciprocal relationships occur between all living organisms, including us humans. Chief Oren Lyons wrote that 'what happens to you and what happened to the earth happened to us as well, so we all have common interests' (2016: 15). This speaks to the perspective that for mental health – well or ill – we are all interlinked through the web of life (Capra 1996), illuminating the importance of considering the mental health of those we work with (and indeed ourselves) in context with the rest of the natural world.

Supervision outdoors

Many of the supervisees I work with outdoors comment that upon arrival in the woodland, a deeper breath is taken and a visceral transition is felt. Being under a green canopy, inhaling oxygenated air, taking in organic shapes and manoeuvring across uneven ground provides a particular experience for supervision that is multisensory, dynamic and engaging for our body–mind systems. In this way, supervisees are greeted by nature before they are greeted by me. By giving space for this, I am intentionally inviting the possibility of another relationship for the supervisee. One that for me, I acknowledge as a co-supervisor.

At the start of sessions, I often ask 'Where are we headed today?' The supervisee is invited to lead the way, being drawn to a location or a direction to walk. This can be influenced by the supervisory material they are bringing as well as a more fluid response to their environment. Outdoor supervision greatly supports a mutuality, in part as the place belongs to neither the supervisor or supervisee, and that there is a mutuality that occurs between all life that grows together, co-creating experiences fostering a 'meeting of minds' (Aron 1996, cited in Jordan and Marshall 2010: 350).

When on the move, there are moments when we may pause in our tracks. The supervisee may need to 'chew' over a particular aspect of their supervisory material. Asking questions such as 'I notice we have paused, what is happening for you in this place?' prompts the supervisee to further 'arrive' in the landscape and encourages their relationship with the living world to be present in their reflections. On a practical level, a sit mat and suitable clothing (most often waterproofs for the UK) enables us to sit comfortably in most places. When responding creatively to an enquiry the supervisee might be drawn to an area to work in to support externalization and exploration of the inter- or intra-personal dynamics of client work, organizational issues, the supervisee's personal material, theoretical or professional development.

At times, to maintain confidentiality, we might step aside from the path to move away from passing others. How we manage this is given consideration at the contracting stage of working together. Perhaps it goes without saying, that humans are also nature and when people are encountered our experience with them can be just as much a part of our dance as with the rest of the environment. Moving through the landscape, being drawn towards, or away from a place is an opportunity to take our supervisory question on the move. Sensing into our interior as well as exterior landscapes and, through working intentionally within an ecopsychological lens, we can bring the ecological whole into conscious awareness.

An ecological and creative spark in supervision

Supervision offers a pause to the rhythms of work to explore, reflect, get support, learn new perspectives and transform (Hawkins and Shohet 2010). Creative approaches to supervision invite the supervisee to pose enquiring edges for their session by framing a supervisory question which is then explored through creative means (Chesner and Zografou 2014). Depending on the level of the supervisee (Stoltenberg and McNeill 2010), either the supervisor facilitates a creative process, or holds witness to the supervisee self-facilitating, while maintaining the frame of the enquiry for the supervisee throughout their exploration. This process is particularly non-linear and could be seen to take the form of a more multidimensional exploration in which the supervision *expands* (through creative exploration and curiosity of conscious and unconscious material) and *gathers-in* making sense of their discoveries in light of their supervisory enquiry.

In regards to a dramatherapy model of supervision, Tselikas-Portmann states that 'the processes of insight, change and growth begin in and with the body' (1999: 23). Chesner (Chesner and Zografou 2014: 32) writes that the 'interventions used in creative supervision speak, to a significant extent, to the right brain hemisphere'. Working in a non-linear, right-brained way aligns with a nature-based model of supervision: the embodied state, activated by being on the move within a sensory and dynamic natural environment, fosters this same expansion-outwards and gathering-inwards intra-personal pattern. Siegel writes 'we take in the incoming stream of signals from the outer world-through sight, hearing, taste, smell, and touch – while also receiving input from the inner world of the body' (2012: 19–6). Working in this way is richly textural, rhythmical, and invites a spaciousness-of-being into the work.

O'Driscoll writes that the 'environment and/or place is engaged with in a way that perceives it as living and as a body in flux that is in dialogue at all times with the changing bodies of both supervisee and supervisor' (2015: 8). Marshall states that 'we work from the position of humans being among all kinds of others rather than being at the center of things, working not just in or from but through an ecological space' (2023: 95). This kind of ecological attunement has a bearing on the supervisor–supervisee relationship, the relationship with themselves, and the supervisee's relationship with their client.

A co-created group eco-supervision

> *Once, in a session of an outdoor supervision group I attend as a supervisee, we co-created a way in which we could listen and respond to a group member's case. The supervisee stood in a chosen spot, and the group placed themselves around and listened to them sharing the story of their client. It was agreed that we (as receivers of the story) would simultaneously move in response to what we were hearing, as and when we felt the impulse to move. It was a very touching experience through which it felt like the supervisee, and their client, were being honoured and respected in the story of the client's trauma. As we listened, we moved quietly, sometimes positioning ourselves to be closer to the supervisee, at others placing distance between us and the story being told; some gathered sticks and leaves and created a circle around the supervisee; we held positions, like sculptures, alongside the storyteller, cliff walls, boulders and trees, giving shape to what we heard and felt in our listening. There was an intensity to this experience that felt, to me, heightened by the aliveness of the place. The next time we met as a group, the supervisee shared that a significant shift in the work with this client had occurred after this experience. Interventions that take place within supervision can positively impact the client's therapeutic process without them having to be physically present.*

When we are engaged in right brain hemisphere functioning our consciousness alters to think in more visual ways where symbolism and sensory metaphor are activated. Our aesthetic expression through music, song or sound, poetry, story, dance or movement, character portrayal (acting 'as if'), sculpture and visual arts are meaningful acts that are embodied through our sensory perception. Working creatively in supervision can require, at times, some warming up and this can be aided by enquiring how they wish me to be involved, either practically (e.g. gathering found objects for a sculptural creation), spending solo time attuning to their environment, or discussing how they wish to be witnessed (including proximity). Inviting an engagement with ritual, rites of passage and thresholds brings a potential space to the work that cyrstalizes focus, purpose and honours the client, supervisee and the place. As a fundamental aspect of a Rites of Passage (Van Gennep 1960 / Turner 1969), a threshold is a boundary in which we cross from one place or state to another. A rite has three stages 'severance, transition [or liminal] and incorporation' (Plotkin 2003: 47). Bringing *severance* from a 'current role … or way of understanding' (Plotkin 2003: 47) into the liminal (in-between) offers a unique space for experiencing, sensing into, receiving and gifting gratitude. This is a creative state where expansion can occur within a supervisory enquiry. To enter *incorporation* we once more step back through the threshold taking with us our creative process into new learning, new positions and perspectives. The giving of thanks to the living world for accommodating us is an important aspect of the rite and can be viewed as a third stage to the expansion, gathering-in process, where gratitude is extended out to the more-than-human-world we are among.

Enrica

Enrica was curious about her role as a clinical lead and wanted to consider the relational boundaries within the team she headed. As we walked towards the woodland reservoir we talked about her current position and the difficulties she was experiencing. I invited Enrica to allow herself to be drawn to a threshold that would be our 'doorway' through to the liminal initiation stage. Making her way around the pool she came across a naturally formed archway between two holly trees. Pausing to focus our attention on her supervisory enquiry and to offer gratitude to the life and habitat of the holly, we took turns to step through the dark green spikey arch. On the other side, we began to move slowly together in silence, allowing Enrica's sensory curiosity to lead us. At the base of a horse chestnut, she came across its double seed (conker), still in its spikey green case and attached to its stalk. Holding the stalk and turning it between her fingers, Enrica began to see it take an animated form: to her eyes, it transformed into a small feisty bird with green spikey hair, big eyes and a pointy beak. She began to give voice and movement to this impromptu puppet and soon found a particular bird character was forming who was unabashedly swearing, 'Fuck eet! Fuck eet!'.

This new form offered Enrica possibilities to engage with her clinical role difficulties. I asked the puppet questions regarding Enrica's enquiry and she answered from her bird character. From here, Enrica was able to access a bolder part of her that wasn't afraid of being experienced as spikey by others. Ready to bring her enquiry to a close, we de-roled the puppet: a process of consciously and psychologically removing the role assigned to the conkers, and in working ecologically, offered appreciation for the horse chestnut's conkers and the place. We returned to the holly archway and, pausing to tend to the moment, we stepped through. On our walk back up through the wooded hill, we gave space for incorporation of the supervision process. Enrica reflected on new perspectives and the embodied experiences she gained through encountering the bird puppet.

The threshold boundaries within the ritual assisted Enrica in entering into a creative process from which she began forming firmer boundaries within her team relationships. The light hearted and humorous dramatic play became an important supervisory feature for her as it has been memorably imprinted as a psychodramatic and psychogeographic memory.

Supporting an emergent ecological relatedness for supervision

In relationship, we invest our attention, opening ourselves to the potential space of the in-between, sharing energy and information. All life forms exist in relationship with their own and other species, seeking to survive and thrive through processes of connection and protection, even down to single cell organisms. Hence, the relational space can be an unpredictable one, as it is in constant flux. We can feel rewarded with the bonding that comes from safe connection, inviting us to 'lean in' to the other, and we can experience moments when interruptions to a relational flow occurs with the potential to cause rupture, generating more protective, or defensive forces, creating valuable opportunities to learn.

As practitioners develop their capacity to work within an ecological frame, as with any learning, a pendulation process can occur. In this case it's between what I'm calling a human-world-mindset, where (for the supervisee) the relational field is reductive in that there is no inclusion of place or life other than humans, and a more expansive and inclusive nature mindset, or 'ecological mind' (Barrow and Marshall 2023: 13).

I am basing this definition of a human-world-mindset on a Western industrialized world-view which differs from indigenous cultures which hold earth, plant, animal, rock, air, fire and water in kinship and as community (Wall Kimmerer 2013). I further describe a human-world-mindset as a non-conscious, human-centric state supporting a world-view that solely holds the interests of our species in mind. This mindset can be experienced fleetingly, or more rigidly throughout life, and indeed throughout whole societies. Behaviours that can encourage this mindset include being over-reliant on the convenience and shelter of indoor settings and an absence of awareness of how the way we live impacts nature, creating a divorced mentality in which interpersonal dynamics are bound solely within what happens between humans.

As a supervisee within my own outdoor supervision, I have also known this reductive, non-conscious dynamic. On occasions over the years, I have been supported by some 'nudges' from my outdoor supervisor to bring the natural environment we are among back into my awareness. On being alerted to the place I am in, my sensory awareness expands in multidimensional directions, instantly bringing me back into relationship with the natural world I am among. This matters, because when I step outdoors for my supervision and then 'forget' where I am (perhaps cognitively wrapped up in the human world of my client), I am relationally divorcing myself from my more embodied experience and awareness of nature. The action of repeatedly returning our attention to include the more-than-human-world in our relational process, is in itself, a practice of nature-relatedness that holds an important role for the outdoor practitioner.

I see an ecological mind as a process that expands our thinking and sensing-being in a way that can be considered significantly different to a human-world-mindset. Barrow and Marshall describe an ecological mind as having the following features,

> It is outside of us …,
> This is paralleled by a fluid outdoor-indoor process ….
> It is inwardly opening out (Schroeder 2008)
> Associated with emergent process, valuing
> A vitalized body/mind flow
> Whereby the implicit other-than-verbal is key.
> The world is perceived from movement rather than stasis.
> The mind is of the earth, located in the more-than-human world and, therefore, is more complete' (Barrow and Marshall 2023: 14)

In describing her model, The Living Third, Marshall writes that 'working within the relational complexities of a living third offers us an ecological psychology where internal matters concerning the human soul intertwine with this broader field of concern' (2023: 96). In her model (see Figure 17.1) she offers a 'framework to show that nature is constantly influencing the human elements all the time' (Marshall 2021: 37), most often without conscious awareness.

Marshall explains that the participants each have their own 'explicit relationship' with nature whereby they project into, or experience encounters in their own particular way. The central overlap 'at the heart of [The Living Third] Figure 1 resides some of the intense magic of the outdoor encounter. This involves an evocative alchemy in which all relational elements interpermeate, resulting in an intense enrichment of the embodied attentional states [of the participants]' (Marshall 2023: 96).

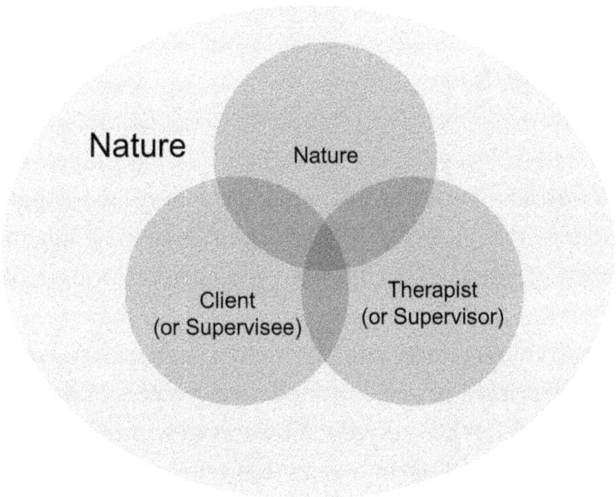

Figure 17.1 The living third – adapted from Hayley Marshall (2021).

The practice of including an ecological mind and the ecological third involves holding a sensory awareness of the ever-changing dynamic life we are among. This might look like hearing your supervisee's voice among other voices, such as a Raven's gronk, wind rustling through leaves, or a human calling their unwilling hound, while also observing the way in which your supervisee gestures or moves relatable to their supervisory material. At the same time, we also need to pay attention to what this in-flux environment is doing in us, as supervisor, on an embodied level. Arguably, we could assume this multi-functioning would split one's attention, and this can be the case especially for the practitioner new to nature-based working. However, through attending to an intentional ecological practice the spread of attention can come to feel more like a chorus or a dance ensemble where there are many players contributing to the whole.

The nature-relatedness needs of supervisees who themselves work ecologically, hold greater significance within eco-supervision as they are working both explicitly and implicitly within the living third (Marshall 2023) in their own practice. Therapies which hold particular elements as central to its focus (such as the arts therapies) require the therapist to maintain their own relationship with the form. For the outdoor practitioner, this necessitates attendance to their own nature-relatedness, which for many is experienced as deeply spiritual and creatively expressive. I deliver immersive workshops, Into the Heartwood-intentional nature experiencing, which have a specific focus on developing a personal ecological practice for the outdoor practitioner. This was also founded as a response to the ecological breakdown occurring in our time. I see the inclusion of the ecological in any area of clinical or human relations work as a political act as it is holding a stance that broadcasts that our relationship with our earth needs urgent attention.

The four roles

Williams (1995) stated that 'supervisors meet their … [supervisees] from a variety of roles' (p. 30) and developed a model which proposes four roles of supervision: *teacher, consultant, facilitator and evaluator*. Supervision is not simply instructing the supervisee how to respond to their clients or patients following a 'logical chain of command down the line' (Williams 1995: 30) – although there are occasions where this directive approach has its place. William's model has been a supportive theoretical frame within my supervision practice in moderating balance between these roles – and in eco-supervision, it has been an adaptable model within which I include nature as co-supervisor. To illuminate the four roles in brief:

- The *supervisor as teacher* brings attention to theory and offers 'challenge to provide rationales for their interventions' (Williams 1995: 30). The teacher draws upon the supervisor's own clinical experience, and welcomes the opportunity for learning to arise from mistakes made.
- The *supervisor as facilitator* supports personal development and related emotional experiences of the supervisee. The process of learning can provoke vulnerable feelings, such as 'inadequacy, inferiority, shame, and fear' (Williams 1995: 55). Supervising from facilitator offers a container for personal process that impacts the professional.
- The role of the *supervisor as consultant* holds in mind the relationships between the client and the supervisee, and between the supervisee and the supervisor. This includes conscious and unconscious processes and the 'therapy system' (Williams 1995: 79) as a whole.
- The *supervisor as evaluator* acknowledges a responsibility towards their supervisee's development, and the monitoring of their therapy work. The evaluator 'maintain[s] clinical standards' and holds a responsibility that 'relates directly to their … [supervisees] and indirectly to … [their] clients' (Williams 1995: 94).

The supervisor flows between these roles and may engage with more than one at a time.

When we contextualize William's model within an ecological frame, we can see how the four roles can influence the supervision process through the human supervisor *and* the more-than-human supervisor. Inviting nature into the work allows us to receive teachings, emotional holding, be supported in process focusing and have material mirrored through and by nature. In this more pluralistic, expansive and ecological version of the four roles, it would look thus: human and nature co-supervisors as *teachers*, *facilitators*, *consultants* and *evaluators*.

My supervision

A few years ago in my own nature-based supervision, I stood with my supervisor on the side of a grassy hill on a bright and warm summers day, amongst a smattering of pine trees. We were a short distance away from a tree lined clough, a stream that over many years has carved its way through the land leaving a steep sided gulley. I was exploring my career development and trajectory, and with quite a lot happening for me personally at the time, it felt like there was a narrow margin available to me going forward and I was feeling somewhat apprehensive about my future. In this moment, I became very aware of the sound of the moving water of the brook and I paused to listen. I felt drawn towards it, but I was also aware of how foreboding it looked with the shade of the trees providing a stark, almost impenetrable contrast to the bright sunlit areas around it. Curious though,

> *I led us towards it, taking my supervisory content with me and discovered, of course, that being there in the shade it all looked very different. I stood taking it in ... the light dancing on the ferns and grasses, the insects hovering and darting in thickly scented air, the sounds of the descending water. I let sensations, associations and memories emerge of places and times in my past that bathed my being in more pleasant and containing sensations. My supervisor wondered out loud how this place was meeting me? I replied that I felt very different: I was feeling spacious, interconnected and much more resilient in considering my next steps. I then led us down the sides of the clough and standing in the cold moving water, I raised my arms mirroring the shape of the clough's steep V shaped bank. I felt awake, alert and alive.*

The process that occurred for me in this supervision was shaped through a co-creation between myself, my supervisor, the place, and both our relationships with the life there. My supervisor recognized that my experience with the natural environment was offering me an embodied and sensory 'way in' to a transformational experience and *gave way* to nature as her co-facilitator to 'step in'. Nature, as supervisor, met me through William's supervisor roles as *teacher, evaluator* and *facilitator.* I experienced this as providing a container for a process, supporting alternative conceptualizations which altered my emotional and sensory state, and taught me some things about moving towards perceived fears. Some years on, this session continues to support me as the vibrancy and vitality of the transformational learning experience has imprinted its teachings into my psychogeographical memory and ongoing professional life.

Encounters in outdoor supervision

I have experienced supervision in a variety of settings both as supervisee and supervisor (outdoors, indoors, online indoors and online outdoors) and there are recognizable differences in terms of how the location impacts the work and what is encountered. Supervision arranged in indoor settings happens for a variety of reasons, such as the need for confidentiality, control of environment (convenience), having creative and theoretical materials to hand and requirements for a more linear and cognitive process. When we take supervision outdoors, there are encounters that we experience that are beyond our control. Outdoor settings such as the one I work from, is a home to a wide variety of plant life and animals. If you're lucky you will see oshawk adeptly flying through the trees, bats flitting at dusk and toads among the leaf litter after rainfall. The aliveness that comes from being among other wild creatures living their own lives brings us into contact with our own animal selves which is profoundly impactful to how we go about clinical reflection.

Carol

It was late Autumn and Carol and I set out walking at a fair pace side by side through the woods. She was sharing with me how she was trying to keep pace with her busy life, and acknowledging how rushing through life inhibits what is felt, experienced and encountered. Slowing in her pace and settling into her session she spoke of wanting to make the most of her contact with ground and pay attention to her inner and outer landscape. As I listened, I became aware of the presence of animals around us … small scuttling ones, large flying ones … and (unusually for me) I was noticing them out loud. This brought my supervisee's attention to their existence and, perhaps more importantly, to her not seeing them.

Curving around the head of the hill along a narrower path within the woods, Carol began to consider her client who had three sessions remaining out of the contracted twelve sessions provided. She was wondering how, in this remaining time, she could best support him to move into a more enlivened connection with his life. Suddenly, Carol stopped in her tracks, looking down at a dead mouse right on the edge of the path. I gave her time to take it in, allowing an expansion of the process to occur. As she stayed with her encounter, something appeared to soften in her body. 'It doesn't matter about the detail' she said, 'it's the essence of him that matters.' We stayed with the dead mouse as Carol contemplated how and what she was receiving from this experience.

Being in the natural environment supported her to slow her pace and her encounter with the dead mouse enabled her to acknowledge the role that 'deadening' had for her client. As her human supervisor, I could have encouraged her to reduce her pace and consider what else mattered here, but it would not have had the same vital relational and visceral impact that encountering the dead mouse had for Carol. We noticed together how she had not witnessed the alive animals that I had seen earlier and this felt to be significant. (Paying attention to how and what supervisees start their sessions with, often has relevance to their process later on.) She shared that she had wanted to see the aliveness around her, and similarly she sought to see this in her client. It's striking that it was in fact a dead animal that brought her into a more vital presence in connection with herself, the place and her client's process.

I enquired if there was anything else that needed to happen or be experienced here before departing from this spot. Carol felt to honour the dead mouse and placed it at the base of a tree, away from the path amongst vegetation. It felt like a moving ritual in which presence, honouring and acceptance was offered. On walking back, Carol clarified her reflections through her gathering-in process, stating she wanted to stay present with her client, recognize the work they had engaged in, and offer space for his therapy ending.

Encounters in natural environments can come unexpectedly, and be experienced in different ways by the supervisee: acknowledged, engaged with, ignored (consciously/

non-consciously) or perceived as an unwanted interruption. The former invites the more-than-human life to speak to the supervision process. Engaging with a nature encounter embraces the experience (allowing for expansion) and the supervisee may allow themselves to be impacted in their process or reflection. Ignoring or experiencing the encounter as an interruption most frequently happens when we are in a human-world-mindset and the flow of the place (and therefore the encompassing life) is not included in the relational awareness of the supervisee.

Notably, the root of the word *interrupt* shares '*rupt*' with the word rupture (*from the Latin Rumpere* meaning to break or burst) (Online Etymology Dictionary: 2024). In indoor settings, interruptions to clinical supervision are understandably viewed as unwelcome and efforts are made to avoid them. There are moments, however, when interruptions can offer a creative spark – *or break or burst* – providing new perspectives to otherwise stayed positions. When a Buzzard lands fleetingly on a nearby branch, unexpectedly close to an eco-supervision training group I am a participant of, is this an interruption breaking forth upon our fire-side conversation, or can we call it an intervention? What occurs within and between us all becomes part of our combined story. However we choose to define it, the experience of the intra- and inter-personal moment is a vital and enlivening one.

Paige

Talking with my supervisee, Paige, about monitoring self-care and walking at a slow pace, my gaze focused on the ground in front of me, it took me by surprise when suddenly (it seemed) a significantly sized branch 'appeared' before me taking up the space in front of me. 'Oh.. Hello!' I exclaimed, realizing my human-world-mind, I stopped in my tracks interrupting myself in mid-sentence. We paused to take in this branch with thick dark green foliage and bright red berries, marveling at its structure that looked strong with regular and ordered stems branching out from the main stem. I recall thinking it looked a bit out of place in amongst the entangled mass of brambles, honeysuckle and ferns (it was a self-seeded domesticated shrub).

We stayed a while with the branch, and the conversation changed tack as Paige began to focus on their clinical development and the training they had embarked on. They spoke of how well they were able to receive the theory due to the trainer's eloquence, and continuing to speak they slightly stumbled over their words and appeared less stable in their body. Moving into the evaluator role, I took the opportunity to reflect my observations that were becoming clearer to me about aspects of the way in which they saw themselves in the world. I put forward Siegel's 'River of Integration' model (2012) that describes healthy integration represented by the flow of the river, and when un-integrated we lean towards either chaos or rigidity (depicted in Seigel's model by the two banks either side of the river – see Figure 17.2). Using the path we were on to depict the river I invited my supervisee to speak from these three spaces. This provided helpful recognition and insights from an embodied place, as they recognized when they become

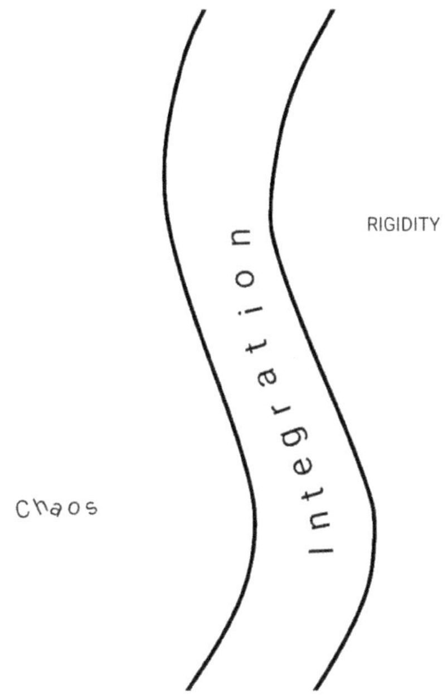

Figure 17.2 The river of integration – adapted from Daniel Siegel (2012).

anxious, they lean towards order and rigidity, and that from this (rigid) position, chaos looks appalling.

It's important to note that nature is, at least to most human eyes, not linear, ordered and neat and when this threat state occurs in my supervisee, they have doubts about nature-based supervision (being among what can often be messy, entangled plant life). We turned our focus back to the branch and acknowledged that the ordered beauty they saw in it were the qualities they were placing value in. Our encounter offered an opportunity for the supervision to turn towards valuable evaluative learning for their development.

Conclusion

In delivering nature-based supervision, we explicitly acknowledge our relationship with the more-than-human world. This nature-relatedness has key features, including embodiment, the development of an ecological mind (Barrow and Marshall 2023) and the recognition that, for the nature-based practitioner, our relationship within the living world requires an ongoing practice. My aim was to illustrate a creative and ecological supervision in an outdoor setting. I have shared examples from my nature-based supervision practice, my own supervision, and from an eco-supervision training group I am a participant in, to bring the concepts I discuss into a relatable frame. I discussed how supervision outdoors involves, what I call, an expansion and gathering in process. This sensory process, in which we expand in multidimensional relational planes and gather-in to our supervisory frame, combines the creative process with the ecological. I highlighted William's Four Roles model of supervision (1995) within an ecological context which, as Marshall's Living Third model (2021) describes, recognizes nature as co-facilitator – or co-supervisor. I have illustrated how working with practices within rites of passage can offer containment and a supportive frame within which supervisees can enter into an ecological mind, their creative supervision material and to acknowledge that, as my supervisor reminds us, *this place isn't just for the taking.*

References

Abram, D. (2017), *The Spell of the Sensuous*, New York: Vintage Books.

Barrow, G., and H. Marshall (2023), 'Revisiting Ecological Transactional Analysis: Emerging Perspectives', *Transactional Analysis Journal* 53: 1.

Capra, F. (1996), *The Web of Life: A New Scientific Understanding of Living Systems*, New York: Anchor Books.

Chesner, A., and L. Zografou (2014), 'Philosophical and Theoretical Underpinnings', in A. Chesner and L. Zografou (eds), *Creative Supervision across Modalities – Theory and Applications for Therapists, Counsellors and Other Helping Professionals*, London: Jessica Kingsley.

Lyons, C. O. (2016), 'Listening to Natural Law', in L. Vaughan-Lee (ed.), 2nd Edition, *Spiritual Ecology: The Cry of the Earth*, California: Golden Sufi Centre.

Hawkins, P., and R. Shohet (2010), *Supervision in the Helping Professions*, 3rd Edition, Berkshire, UK: Open University Press.

Jordan, M., and H. Marshall (2010), 'Taking Counselling and Psychotherapy Outside: Destruction or Enrichment of the Therapeutic Frame?', *Routledge European Journal of Psychotherapy and Counselling* 12 (4): 345–59.

Marshall, H. (2021), 'An Elemental Relationship: Nature-Based Trauma Therapy', in A. Chesner and S. lykou (eds), *Trauma in the Creative and Embodied Therapies: When Words Are Not Enough*, Oxford, UK: Routledge.

Marshall, H. (2023), 'A Place for the Ecological Third: Eco-TA in Therapeutic Practice', *Transactional Analysis Journal* 53 (1): 93–108. doi:10.1080/03621537.2023.2152567.

Online Etymology Dictionary (2024), https://www.etymonline.com/word/rupture (13/10/2024).

O'Driscoll, T. (2015), 'Eco Supervision: Toward an Ecological Consciousness in Supervision', *Inside Out Journal*, IAHIP https://iahip.org/page-1075600.

Plotkin, B. (2003), *Soulcraft – Crossing into the Mysteries of Nature and Psyche*, California: New World Library.
Siegel, D. (2012), *Pocket Guide to Interpersonal Neurobiology - An Integrative Handbook of the Mind*, New York: Norton.
Stoltenberg, C. D., and B. W. McNeill (2010), *IDM Supervision- An Integrative Developmental Model for Supervising Counselors and Therapists*, 3rd Edition, New York: Routledge.
Turner, V. (1969), *The Ritual Process – Structure and Anti-structure*, Chicago: Aldine.
Tselikas-Portmann E., ed. (1999), *Supervision and Dramatherapy*, London: Jessica Kingsley.
Van Gennep, A. (1960), *The Rites of Passage*, trans. G. Caffee and M. Vezedom, Chicago: The University of Chicago Press.
Wall Kimmerer, R. (2013), *Braiding Sweetgrass – Indigenous Wisdom, Scientific Knowledge and the Teachings of Plants*, London: Penguin Books.
Williams, A. (1995), *Visual and Active Supervision – Roles, Focus, Technique*, New York: W. W. Norton.

18

How to love this world: Becoming an ecological practitioner

Mary Dees

In this chapter, the author will provide the story of her journey to becoming an ecological practitioner. This will be a personal narrative from an experienced ecological psychotherapist who has developed her ecological practice by the weaving of many threads. The chapter will seek to show aspiring practitioners a route map, albeit a personal one, that may help them imagine what their own journey ahead might look like. It will include the role of the many threads, including trainers and supervisors, inspiring teachers, peers, clients and most importantly, the land itself.

Part 1

The journey into the world

In Herefordshire, the red soil tells the story of the Devonian red sandstone beneath. The Devonian period (400 million years ago) is known as the age of the fishes, so it seems fitting that the River Wye snakes its way through this landscape of my birth. I remember as a child watching swallows dart across the river, their red throats, the red riverbanks and my dark red hair getting mixed up into a deep and narcissistic belonging. I felt almost as if I had been moulded from the red clay soil that I squelched between my toes and fingertips. Here, in Herefordshire, my journey to becoming an ecological practitioner began.

I am seven.

The garage is dark, full of cobwebs, old rusty bikes, and junk.

I climb up through a broken window, scratch my leg, and emerge into the sunlight.

On the roof, I lean against the old sycamore tree and look around. I watch my family. No one can see me. I climb into its branches and settle into a comfortable sprawl. I play with the blood drying from the cut. I notice a fearless robin land near me, feasting on a worm.

I am eight.

I find a starling that has fallen down our chimney – shivering, pale pink and near death. Over the next few days, it grows stronger, fed from a pipette, and starts to develop feathers.

Fred is his name. The smell of his breath reaches out to me across the years.

Wild, sour and alive.

He grows into a beautiful, shiny starling that flies away and then, at the call of his name, comes crashing back through the garden to land on my head. One day, he doesn't return; I remember hoping he had found his flock and fearing something worse.

I loved him as deeply as any friend I've ever had (see Figure 18.1).

I am ten.

Birdwatching in Haugh Wood, Mordiford.

Just the two of us, my aunt and me.

This is a shared, intimate experience. Just as we are leaving, we see a flash of orange and a firecrest sitting on a pine tree. It takes my breath away. I carry that joy back into my crazy, chaotic home, where nine of us live.

It has always been about birds for me. They are an essential part of my life script (Berne 1972; Erskine 2018), of my belonging to this world and being a part of its aliveness. Birds play a large role in my life as an ecological practitioner, so I forewarn the reader, for they are often my co-therapist, working alongside me.

Client – Hawthorn: Forty-five years after my sighting of the firecrest, my client (Hawthorn) and I are sitting in a woodland area and they are talking about finding their voice in a world where they have often been silenced. Then a tiny bird lands in a hedge right next to my shoulder and starts to sing very loudly with a high-pitched joyful cry; I interrupt my client and shout out with surprise and joy – 'It's a goldcrest', I whisper – suddenly lowering my voice so I don't disturb it. It seems brazen in its determination to sing and captures our attention for many minutes. We spent the rest of the session talking about this encounter – my client, the goldcrest and I – all of us have a part to play – in this dance of ecological practice.

Figure 18.1 A photo of Fred and Mary. Photograph by Frances Dees.

From then onwards, the goldcrest became a talisman for my client – a small, shy bird able to find its voice and willing to demand to be heard. The goldcrest and its metaphorical significance supported my client in updating their beliefs about themselves, challenging their injunctions (Goulding and Goulding 1976) around taking up space and voicing opinions.

Mother nature

When I think back to my childhood, the memories of the outdoors are so visceral and feral; they are held in the tissues and sinews as much as synapses and neurons.

Many early experiences shaped me and my relationship with the ecological. Mixed up in them are being the fourth of five siblings, being a twin, and growing up in an intergenerational household where nine people lived, which was busy, loud and chaotic with a strong sense of love and belonging. Being a survivor of childhood sexual abuse by my older brother, abuse that happened in secret and silence for over three years. I never forgot the abuse, but I did compartmentalize it, what I now realize was a protective dissociation.

Nature was a place to escape to, to get lost in – an easy way to dissociate and bracket off my childhood trauma (Marshall 2016). Nature provided me with non-human others like the birds, trees and rivers that helped regulate confusing feelings – maybe providing a secure attachment (Bowlby 1979). The outside world was an important element in my early sub-symbolic protocol (pre-verbal, non-verbal), an implicit part of both my stimulation and soothing (Berne 1972; Marshall 2016). It became part of my parent ego-state (Berne 1961) during the symbolic or verbal stages of childhood – providing nurturing, holding and acceptance. It provided me with something vibrant, potent and full of vitality – sounds, colours, smells, textures, movement, a richness of experiences and relationships. Something that provided undemanding and unconditional healing of my unmet relational needs.

As a teenager, I took my love of nature and the outdoors and became an activist. I won the school election on behalf of the Green Party, and then I went on to study and work in environmental science.

I was determined to save the natural world, in a rather grandiose way, probably a projection of my desire to save myself or my natural 'mother'. I was an optimist, but the last forty years have seemed like an uphill battle against destructive forces. However, I do hold on to my belief that the human race is essentially decent. Bregman's (2020) book *Humankind* contains many tales of our true nature as a decent, sociable and friendly species. Belief in and hope for the human race are key motivators for my work as an ecological practitioner.

Healing tasks

When I was thirty-three, my Dad died; he was gentle and kind and loved me so deeply that I hadn't realized until he died that his love was holding me together. With him gone, all the unresolved trauma arose violently within my body, and the memories and secrets I'd kept hidden in a dark corner of my mind came rushing up to the surface. I wrote a poem at the time to express my experience of my visceral flashbacks of the abuse:

The Screaming Mute
Conscious thought frozen
in a moment of fear
retreats to safety
locked away
quietly

silent
on the surface
paralysed and mute
but shouting and screaming
painfully, incoherently, internally.

At thirty-five, I started psychotherapy to address my childhood trauma and, through that, found Transactional Analysis (TA: Berne 1961). The first six years of psychotherapy were incredibly tough as I set about the healing of my body–mind – set about the healing tasks of James Kepner (2013) – developing support and resources and undoing, redoing and mourning the trauma I had suffered. My psychotherapist provided an incredibly consistent and supportive space infused with love, care and an unwavering belief in me. He provided the conditions for my healing and growth and the blueprint for my later identity as a psychotherapist.

Going outdoors was an essential part of the healing process, a place to reconnect to myself, to soothe and heal my body. My last precious walk with my Dad through the orchards of Herefordshire was only six weeks before he died. Now, I trod those paths alone, opening myself up to both grief and the pain I'd locked away.

Becoming a psychotherapist

After six years of therapy, I trained as a TA psychotherapist. TA has given me a language and the basis for the philosophical thread that runs through my life and work. I discovered outdoor psychotherapy during a conference and met Hayley Marshall, a pioneer in the EcoTA movement (Barrow and Marshall 2019; Barrow and Marshall 2023). I knew this was the right direction for me – a chance to combine psychotherapy with my passion and love for the natural world.

My outdoor or ecological psychotherapist skills have developed in three main ways: in 2016, through TA and Outdoors: A two-day course introducing TA practitioners to working therapeutically outdoors. Since 2017, being a member of the Natural Reflections Group, a supervision and learning group for outdoor practitioners held four times a year in Shining Cliff Ancient Woods (see Thread 4). Also, since 2017, having individual outdoor supervision (See Thread 2). Through these learning and supervision experiences, I developed the confidence and skills to start taking clients outdoors. Over the last eight years, I have developed and honed these skills to develop my style of ecological practice. I am an eco-relational psychotherapist, and my work is inherently existential, embodied and emergent. Everything I do flows from a clear philosophy that has two key pillars:

> Pillar one: I'm OK. You're OK – my essential belief in the value, worth and decency of 99 per cent of humans (Bregman 2020). This includes a Martian (Berne 1972; Deaconu 2020), Bernian humility. 'The Martian', is a TA term for an observer who 'watches what happens without "preconceived ideas", … (and who) looks at things with the eye of innocence' (Hostie 1982: 1 quoting Berne 1972). Becoming Martian, therefore, involves being open to the somatic, the non-verbal, to a listening that relies on information provided by sensations and perception (Cornell 2016). For me, this includes an ecological take on

Standpoint theory (Keating and Merenda 2013) – from the ground up – where the greatest wisdom comes from the oppressed. This means clients are the experts on themselves, and I meet them in that way, including a strong focus on phenomenological inquiry and diagnosis and the transferential domain (Hargaden and Sills 2002).

Following this, I am drawn to the deep connection from Buber's 'I-Thou' (Cohn and Buber 1980). Buber says this happens when two people authentically engage in the here and now, truly 'showing up' to one another. This relational dimension is named 'the between' by Buber. In 'the between' dimension the whole (two people in a relationship) is greater than each individual. Buber described 'the between' as a courageous step into the experience of the other while simultaneously being open, present and authentic. I would go one step further and say the 'I-Thou' can also be experienced with non-human others and being part of ecosystems. In outdoor work, the ecological is an essential part of the I-Thou, and this can be further understood through Marshall's living third concept (Marshall 2016, 2023).

Pillar two: Ecosystemic mindset. An ecosystemic mindset is a deep appreciation and understanding at all structural levels (sub-symbolic, symbolic and verbal symbolic levels) (Cornell 2008, 2016) that humans are just one part of the natural world. Important to this are the ideas of autonomy and homonomy. Angyl's (1941) ideas have autonomy and homonomy as important poles within a biosphere: autonomy – the tendency to advance one's interests as a separate being. And homonomy – the tendency to fit oneself into something that is larger than the self. Therefore, the biosphere is a holistic entity or single reality, including both the individual and the environment. Marshall (2021), regarding homonomy, talks of the importance of interconnectedness and the wider embrace, humans realizing (or maybe remembering) that they are part of *and,* embedded in the wider web of life. In Berne (1964), he talks about autonomy as important to help people find their voice within families and systems of oppression. Salter (2006: 1) says 'If we can truly surrender ourselves to our fullest cosmic homonomy, we may find the courage to reach for new levels of autonomy.' The ability to balance these forces is an important challenge for individuals, communities and humans.

First steps outdoors

Taking my first clients outdoors was challenging; I'd been working indoors for many years, and there was a psychological barrier to taking my clients outdoors. As a kinaesthetic and experiential learner, my supervisor encouraged me to do it. My first experience was uncomfortable; I felt like I didn't know what to do. I enjoyed being outdoors, on the move and in one of my favourite places alongside the River

Goyt. But I felt exposed, very conscious of my body and how I moved, how I was perceived.

I no longer had the comfort of my room and of being able to 'disappear' into a therapeutic armchair. Even with my skills training, I felt like I was just taking a client for a walk. Was I doing it right? What was I supposed to do? Supervision helped me to tune into my curiosity about what was happening as I walked alongside my client. What did I notice? What thoughts, feelings and body sensations were coming up for me? What were we (my client and I) drawn towards in the environment? How did we move through the environment? I quickly realized that being fully embodied within an environment offered something special. It offered a more fully rounded understanding of the client. I started to notice how the landscape changed with different clients almost metaphysically.

Client – Raven: For example, my client, Raven (with a history of depression and low affect), came to a session feeling very passionate and frustrated, and he talked in a very animated and honest way. I was very struck by the level of vitality that he was starting to experience and the trust that now existed in our relationship that he could show this side of himself. I was also aware of his physicality, he seemed really solid. My countertransferential field extended to the landscape that stretched before us, it seemed to pop into an exaggerated 3D form, each tree in the woodland below showing its individual form, each a different shade of green. It seemed to me that the landscape was mirroring Raven's vibrancy, authenticity and move toward autonomy. Sharing this with him illustrated and specified his move towards a stronger sense of aliveness (Hargaden and Sills 2014).

I soon discovered the benefits of working outdoors for my clients. My experience supports the research showing that spending time outdoors in nature provides restorative benefits to our physical and mental health, including cognitive abilities (Kaplan 1995). I noticed in my clients a strengthened adult ego-state, a greater window of tolerance, space for feelings and the use of all senses. There seems to be easier access to early protocol or sub-symbolic material (pre-verbal, non-verbal and somatic)and the freeing of the natural child ego-state (Berne 1977). Marshall (2016: 154) talks about how the outdoors or nature provides a pathway into a client's protocol, the client being able to access their protocol experiences more readily and spontaneously 'as a result of the impact of dynamic natural environments on human body-mind'.

Co-therapist – River Goyt: I frequently sit with clients on rocks facing the large, fast-flowing river; both river banks are green with moss-covered rocks and mature trees covered in layers of moss, lichen and ferns. The sound of the river, which is very loud, seems to lubricate the human-to-human connection. The river often seems to run through us: its music, its movement, its vitality, its liminality, its potential and its metaphorical importance. It provides a green relational cushion and a dissociative space, as well as regulating and dosing (pers comm Marshall). Also a living third (Marshall 2016), an active part of the therapy, making the human-to-human encounter easier and helping clients connect to themselves, often helping them access their sub-symbolic material. Many tears, held in for decades, flow cathartically into the river and are carried away downstream.

With more experience taking clients outdoors, I started to enjoy the democratic nature of outdoor work, where I could bring more of myself and feel grounded and humble within the relationship. There is a natural mutuality to working outdoors, which means there are two people outdoors in the world with different roles in this relationship. No one is better than or an expert over the other, but each is of equal value – they both bring something important. They are both OK.

The impact of Covid

The Covid pandemic provided challenges. I caught Covid in March 2020 and was very ill, an illness that still lingers as Long Covid. This has hugely restricted my physical abilities, and, as an outdoor therapist, it is impossible to withhold from clients. I showed my vulnerability and limitations to my clients and worked with the impact of that within the therapeutic relationship, a source of important relational material but very challenging for me – as self-disclosure often is. Covid lockdowns also brought a wider range of clients outdoors, eager to stay in face-to-face contact. Clients who were disconnected from the outdoors opened themselves up to a new experience.

The journey continues

In 2023, thirteen years after starting my journey towards becoming a psychotherapist, I became a Certified Transactional Analyst (CTA: Level 7). This was through an oral exam on Giles Barrows' farm in Suffolk. My exam was based on my outdoor work, and it took place in a bell tent with the door wide open, with the fields and trees of Suffolk as part of my experience.

As an ecological practitioner, I have a thriving outdoor psychotherapy and supervision practice that includes individuals, groups and organizations.

Part 2

The five teachers – the threads of love

Thread 1: The land

I stand with my right cheek pressed up against the stone cliff. It is rough, pitted, damp and cool, and smells of the moss-filtered water that drips down. I take my hand

and hold it against this ancient, immovable rock. I feel both overwhelming gratitude and insignificance. I stay there like this for fifteen minutes or more, singly focused on the senses of smell and touch. Something is happening deep in my body, a deep remembering. Mary Oliver's poem 'Lingering in Happiness' captures a similar feeling '*and the dampness there, married now to gravity, falls branch to branch, leaf to leaf, down to the ground.*' … '*and soon so many small stones, buried for a thousand years, will feel themselves being touched*' (Oliver 2005).

One of the most important personal practices for me on my journey to becoming an ecological practitioner is regularly spending time outdoors without other humans and experiencing being part of or being embedded in this world. Abrams (2011), in his book *Becoming Animal*, provides an excellent manual for undertaking this practice. He talks of adopting an animistic world-view that assumes everything is alive and that others, whether spiders, wolves, oak trees or storm clouds, are experiencing the world in their own way, from their perspective and abilities.

He recommends contemplating the surrounding atmosphere as a living organ, or membrane, of the earth. We live enveloped by air, bodily immersed in this invisible atmosphere as thoroughly as fish are immersed in the sea. A realization that we do not live on the earth – we live in the earth! He talks of 'Becoming earth. Becoming animal. Becoming, in this manner, fully human' (Abram 2011: 3).

Spending extended periods of time outdoors (with no other humans), and being within my local environment is vital to my ecological identity, consciousness and psychological health. What I learn isn't something I can easily write about here; it's an organic unfurling and opening that includes healing, perspective, wonder and often a body-racking grief. It is about rhythm: of night and day from the dawn chorus to the deep dark of night, of the seasons from the return of the swifts to hoarfrost on the last of the hawthorn berries, of the celestial movements from new moon to full moon, of the sea from spring to the neap tides, of the trees from first willow leaf to last gasp of an old oak sinking into the bog. The closer I come to Abraham's *Becoming Animal* (2011), the more I learn about working outdoors with clients and the more resourced and supported I feel. But also the more exposed, raw and vulnerable as my dissociation melts away.

The local places I feel deeply embedded within include a fragment of temperate rainforest alongside the River Goyt and up high on the Peak District with vast 360-degree viewscapes mentored by skylarks, swallows, kestrels and buzzards. When I was first ill with Long Covid, I could not walk for more than ten minutes, and those places were lost to me. One day in late August, throwing off old thoughts of laziness, I lay for hours underneath a rowan tree in my garden and fell in love. This stunning tree provided me with shade just when I needed it, and the bright orange berries attracted a magical troupe of noisy and clumsy blackbirds, long-tailed tits and a hungry and battered baby robin very late from the nest.

Thread 2: Supervisors

It is April, and my supervisor and I are in a woodland near Buxton; for the first time in months, I feel well, and the fatigue has lifted from my muscles. The joy of being able to walk further into the woods pricks tears into my eyes, and I am determined to get to a particular spot. When we get there, we look around for somewhere to settle. This is a special place; I bring us here to think, to get clarity. There is a fast-flowing stream, tea-brown with peat. The canopy is starting to fill with spring green, the ground is covered with damp orange beech leaves, and there is an old beech tree that fell across the space decades ago but yet has kept on growing and thriving. The light is thick with beauty; there is energy here, the noise of the stream, and the vibrancy of colours, yet it also feels cosy and private.

I am bringing my doubts and fears to my supervisor. Since my CTA last summer, I have felt something is different in my client work. For the first time, I am questioning my future. She gently enquires, probes, expands, empathizes, and uses the energy and resonance of this particular place to draw out meaning. As we walk back through the woods, I feel light and optimistic. Over the next few days, I have a realization that shifts me back in touch with my work.

Supervision is essential and mandatory for psychotherapists. It is a core part of ethical practice and the continuing learning process that psychotherapy requires. Supervision outdoors and within an ecosystemic framework has enabled me to deepen my ecological practice. It is where I take my outdoor practice, particularly individual clients, and let them be bathed in the light of an autumnal wood, washed in a peaty stream or released to soar high in the sky with a kestrel. It is difficult to articulate what is happening outdoors, the subtlety of movement, and the experience of being within an ecosystem. Supervision is an interruption to the work where my supervisor helps shed light, helps me articulate and brings forth that which is a mystery. My supervisor, with their own ecological consciousness and gentle encouragement of my own, uses the living third (Marshall 2016) to help untangle the mysteries of the unknown.

O'Driscoll (2015, 2022) talks of the three elements of outdoor supervision, all of which I recognize in my own experience of being supervised:

- Emergent – the unfolding, evolving process and being receptive to what arises and open to its meaning.
- Embedded – being fully within the environment at this time in this place, the living third (ecological, more than human) providing new perspectives.
- Embodied – working with body and movement, where the whole sensing body is involved in the dynamic exploration; this has a strong reciprocal element.

Thread 3: Inspiring teachers

My first ecological teachers were my parents, aunts and grandmother. They deeply loved the countryside and can trace some of their ancestors back six generations as agricultural workers and stone masons. Then, there were the poets Emily Dickinson, Robert Frost and Goethe. For someone who trained as a scientist, it is interesting that my first thoughts are of the poets. I am disillusioned by the reductive nature of science and align with Goethe (writing 200 years ago) that Newtonian science, in looking at the individual parts, misses the big picture. I learned a quote from Goethe many years ago and have since failed to find the same translation, but it went something like this:

> *When observing nature, no thing is single if it lives but multiple its being. As nature has no heart and skin, all is outside, all is within. All at once, then you'll see the open sacred mystery.*

There are writers who have really shaped my understanding of the human race and helped me develop a clear philosophy about who we are. These include Berne's concept of I'm Ok, You're Ok (Berne 1961; Ernst 1971). I take Steiner's (2012) position that we all start life with a sense of OK-ness, a somatic sense in a newborn child that predates beliefs or decisions. Most of us keep some element of this fundamental core OK-ness into adulthood. I am confident in my positive stance on humanity; I believe, as Steiner said, 'in the absence of oppression, human beings will, due to their basic nature or soul, which is preservative of themselves and their species, live in harmony with nature and each other' (Steiner 2012: 10–11). Macdonald (2022) takes this further and suggests that humans are a cornerstone species, like the beaver or whale. Healthy ecosystems have a cornerstone species that plays a disproportionately large role in its diversity and equilibrium – keeping the whole ecosystem healthy. Humans have had this role in the past and I hope this is our future. Nick Totton (2021) supports this with his reminder that humans are also wild and that wilderness doesn't mean untouched by humans; it means humans are acting naturally as positive cornerstone species within a wide system that is interconnected and balanced.

Providing me with a theoretical and practical underpinning for my outdoor work has been the Ecological TA (Eco-TA) movement within the TA community, which has been growing and developing a definition and purpose over the last few years. Pioneered by Marshall and Barrow (2019) who offer a comprehensive definition at Eco-TA.dev. In summary: 'Eco-TA is the practice of transactional analysis in alliance with Earth.'

Thread 4: Outdoor supervision group

It's June 2024, and I am back in an ancient woodland on the edge of the Peak District; after such a wet spring, the woods are oozing, almost obscenely, with green foliage.

Words fail me as love fills my heart. How can I describe that green? Its sap-rising vigour, how it burns the eyes, twists the heart, lifts both the loins and the soul. I sit beneath an old oak tree, whose trunk is covered in lichen and look up. The sun comes out, and I notice the leaves are full of holes. Holes made by caterpillars that have fed the first brood of blue tits, great tits, warblers, tree creepers and more. Here in these ancient woods, this oak tree is an ecosystem within an ecosystem. A holobiont to its fullest extent. I feel at home, nestled within nature (holobiont (Gordon et al. 2013) is a new – albeit actually very old – biological concept where there are no individual species, just collective ecosystems.)

I joined the Natural Reflections Supervision Group in 2016 to increase my outdoor therapy knowledge and develop my ecological identity. For eight years, spending a whole weekend every season within an ancient woodland alongside a group of outdoor counsellors and psychotherapists has been a vital part of my journey to becoming an ecological practitioner. The group is a supportive community, facilitated by an experienced ecological practitioner and embedded within the ecological and incorporates learning, supervision, personal exploration and group processes. We are invited to work with movement, stories, art, dance, seasons, senses, elements, and always with the more than human at the heart of our group.

Over eight years, I have been in this group with many incredible outdoor counsellors and psychotherapists. At its heart, the group is a supportive learning community of people open to the ecological, willing to be vulnerable, and hungry to learn.

The interruption

We sit around the fire, surrounded on three sides by a steep cliff wall topped by trees and share stories of our work. It is exciting, fascinating and exposing. Suddenly, I notice a buzzard, all stripes, wings and flashes of white, land on a branch close by; it totters for a second and then quickly pushes off, flying low into the woodland beyond. I shout out to the group in delight and surprise. Only one other person sees it, but others see the branch bouncing around from the force of the take-off. I immediately apologize for the interruption, and the discussion continues where it left off.

The group facilitator jumps up, full of energy, and brings our attention back to the buzzard. An important part of ecological practice plays out in our group process. I talk about interrupting the discussion with the buzzard and relate it to my work with clients; a colleague points out wisely that I am not interrupting; I am merely acknowledging the interruption – an important distinction. Taking that further, another person says we are mistaking the other (more than human) for an interruption rather than an important active participant. If we are not allowing this buzzard into the work and paying attention to that living third (Marshall 2016), why are we working outdoors? But then another group member challenges the assumptions and doesn't understand the excitement of the buzzard, a shrug of 'meaergh' 'so what.' This is a really important reminder when working with clients: do not assume they have the same experience as you.

Client – Raven: This experience in the group helped me when working with my client, Raven, who was suffering from depression. We always sat on the same hillside and were often visited by a female kestrel. One week in winter, he was feeling very low, and the weather was grey and cold; suddenly, from the east, in flew our kestrel; she was looking splendid, her red-brown wings starkly contrasting with the grey skies and bleak landscape. It reminded me of the girl in the red coat at the end of the *Schindler's List* film, the only colour in a colourless world. I pointed her out to my client and asked about his experience. He talked about how he felt nothing in response to seeing the bird, and his body slumped at this realization; he talked about how he didn't deserve to see it. At that moment, it felt important for me to hold this flash of colour for him until he could see it, too. And I shared my thoughts with him. This became an important anchor point for our work; he started to calibrate how he felt using the natural world we were in. Knowing that I would hold the colour, the hope for him and belief in him on those days when he could not see and feel it, on those days when he believed he didn't deserve to see colour.

Thread 5: Clients

My work can be summed up by Mary Oliver's poem 'Wild Geese' (2004). My clients are not broken; they do not need fixing but they yearn for home, love, healing, growth, and finding their place in the family of things. Often, in honouring their reality and helping them understand, accept and love themselves and their needs, in all their unique glory, they find vitality and spontaneity.

As an experiential learner, my best teachers have been my clients. What a joyful experience of growth these lessons have been, especially the challenging experiences. I have learnt from them about myself, my ecological identity and ecological consciousness and I have been healed and changed by them all. I have learned about them and their wonderful, unique expression of life, learning about the infinite ways to see, feel, smell and hear the land, the air, the water, the trees, the birds (of course), and all the different natural processes.

What are my clients drawn towards? How are they experiencing the world? How do they move through the world? Where are they drawn to stop and stay awhile? Do they love the rain? Do they loathe the rain? Do they stand tall in the sun or retreat into shadows? Do they hear the birds as a cascade of colour and shape? Do they see through time? Do they make time stop or speed up? Does the kingfisher want to be seen when I am with them? What does the dipper say to them? Is the goldcrest here for me or them? Does the world feel washed clean and sparkly when I walk alongside them, or does all colour drain from the landscape? Who am I when I am with them? Do I feel protective of them as they walk through the landscape or fearful of their recklessness? Do I feel fragile or strong? How do they move – fast or slow? How do they use the outdoors: is it a safe place, a secure attachment, a source of narcissistic idealization, or a dissociative space?

Countertransference is a vital part of my psychotherapy. When outdoors, everything is an extension of my experience; everything is in the transferential field. I use nature like a radar, which provides me with sensory input, noticing and movement that provide a direct link to the stimulus from the client. 'This mechanism carries the therapist back to a protocol scene, reactivating script beliefs and the rackety feeling connected with that scene' (Novellino 1984 noting Erskine and Zalcman 1979: 22). I am so used to using the outdoors as a 'radar' that when I work online, I feel like a radio operator without an aerial, reaching for the imagination to fill the void (and using creative visualization of the outdoors to support the work).

The ecological context, particularly when outdoors, is always present at a psychological level. There is a lot of contracting between the two of us as we negotiate the landscape – a moment-to-moment dynamism that provides opportunities and challenges for the therapeutic encounter (Marshall 2013; 5).

Client – Douglas: In a previous session with my client, Douglas, I had clumsily made an assumption, which triggered a response in which he thought I was judging him. As he told me about his anger towards me, he walked slowly and slightly behind me. I knew that confrontation and conflict were very threatening to him. It seemed important that I was in front, out of eyeline, where he could control the distance between us and our relative positions. I matched my body to what I thought were his needs, and when I got an opportunity (not wanting to interrupt his flow), I asked if I was right about how he wanted us positioned as he expressed his anger. This dynamic contract on the move provided the conditions for an open, honest relational dialogue. My consideration of his needs was part of the relational repair needed during this rupture.

Mutuality is an important idea, where the client and I both make an active, considered decision to work together. And importantly the client knows that my stance is one of active curiosity about them – without the stance of 'expert' or thinking I know them or what is best for them. We are (as far as is possible) equals in this exploration towards greater awareness. Berne describes awareness:

> Awareness means the capacity to see a coffee pot and hear the birds sing in one's own way, and not the way one was taught. … Awareness requires living in the here and now, and not in the elsewhere, the past or the future. … [It] is the person who is aware, and who will not hurry because he is living in the present moment with the environment which is here: the sky and the trees as well as the feeling of motion. The aware person is alive because he knows how he feels, where he is and when it is. He knows that after he dies the trees will still be there, but he will not be there to look at them again, so he wants to see them now with as much poignancy as possible (Berne 1964: 178–80).

This quote is really important to me. It relates to us learning to live in the world in our own unique way. This quote also has ecological roots and emphasizes the importance of adult awareness – here and now.

Different ways of sensing the world

Some clients sense the world in a different way than most people, and it really provides a window into our narrow sensory perspectives. I have synaesthesia, both colour synaesthesia (where letters, words and numbers are perceived as inherently coloured) and spatial-sequence synaesthesia (where the months of the year are perceived as a counterclockwise three-dimensional map). It impacts how I perceive the world, particularly sensory experience. I think my synaesthesia may play a role in how the landscape changes for me with different clients and enriches the work and therapeutic relationship, but also, it is important to be mindful that it does not lead to assumptions and misunderstandings.

Client – Raven: My client Raven's form of synaesthesia is called chromesthesia. He experiences sounds in the form of colour and pattern. For example, the wind in the trees can be a grey wave-like pattern and the caw of a parliament of crows are circles of yellow. Associated with this is a gifted musical ability and a high sensory tolerance for noise. His experience of the natural world seems magical as I listen to him describing his colour and pattern perceptions in response to our soundscape. Like he has a glimpse into a different dimension. He has a gentle quality to him and feels so much part of the natural world we move through, being with him can feel like I am stepping more fully into this different realm. Our work together has many elements, but one key element has been exploring how alone and different he feels in the world – that loneliness sometimes feels like being burnt alive – such a viscerally painful experience. He often uses the natural world like a green cushion (Marshall pers com) – an idealized other that protects him from the pain of human disconnection. He describes the natural world as being like a painkiller. He connects first to the natural world (living third) and through that to me as he allows me to enter his realm.

Delving in the dark

Client – Hawthorn: We, my client Hawthorn and I, were working outside in my woodland area in the dark, with just light from a fire. They were talking about their cousin (who they loved very much) dying after a long illness when they were fourteen. Unprocessed grief was starting to emerge. They were challenging whether I was safe enough to express it in front of – did I care about them? As we explored their fears, a female tawny owl started to call for its mate 'ke-wick' 'ke-wick' 'ke-wick' over and over with no responding call ('hoo-hoo-oo'). The owl seemed increasingly desperate, and I said, 'She can't find her mate.' Hawthorn started to cry, turned their head away from me, and closed up their body in a signal of withdrawal. I said, 'I see your distress and know it is hard to show me.' Hawthorn nodded but remained quiet and we sat in silence, listening to the sounds of the woods. In the next session, they told me that the owl calling for its mate, with no response, had 'broken them apart'. They felt they had been calling out into the darkness since their cousin had died, and nobody was there to answer. The combination of the darkness, the owl and my attuned and caring relational presence had provided the conditions for them to unlock grief that had been locked away for a decade.

Within this encounter, outdoor space provides something unique: the darkness, the space to feel, the fire providing warmth and light. The place of therapy is very important; it stimulates or inhibits different parts of ourselves. Being in the dark allows for some feelings that being in the light doesn't; as I said to Ruth Allen and she writes about in her book *Weathering* (Allen 2024), 'I think (being in the dark) evokes that very early part of us. The imprint of us as humans. The outdoors can help with that, but outdoors in the dark specifically can make it quicker' (Allen 2024: 136). The dark can be daunting, provoking sub-symbolic fears, but with the presence of another, those primitive feelings can be tolerated and used therapeutically. As I tell Ruth 'The darkness provides an envelope of something that's very containing. It's just the two of you, and the fauna of course' (Allen 2024: 136). When I said this, I was thinking about Hawthorn and the owl who came to help us that dark night.

Conclusion – there is love

As Mary Oliver says in her poem, 'Spring', about a black bear rising from hibernation:

> '*There is only one question: how to love this world.*' And she ends the poem with
> '*all day I think of her –*
> *her white teeth,*
> *her wordlessness,*
> *her perfect love.*' (Oliver 2012)

Becoming an ecological practitioner has been a journey about love. At its essence, it is about fully loving this world – as an essential element within it. All is outside; all is within. I sit here in the woods in deep August, listening to the wind gently whispering through the tops of the tall trees, children shouting in the distance, watching the blackbirds seemingly delight in their discovery of bright orange rowan berries and noticing the light touch of the wind caressing my arms. I remember, I know and feel part of this world – and that knowing is love.

And to love is to be open fully to the darkness, to be willing to root around in murky sludge and be torn by thorny undergrowth – to grieve, wail and fight and to be alongside my clients as they wade through their own swamps and as they learn to love, be loved and flourish.

In the lyrics of Sam Evans in his song 'In Amongst':

In amongst all the damage
In amongst all the pain
In amongst all the fear
There's a change
In amongst all the laughter
In amongst all the trust
In amongst all the details
There is love

Acknowledgements

With special thanks to the teachers including my clients, Herefordshire, the River Wye and my ancestors of soil and stone.

References

Abram, D. (2011), *Becoming Animal: An Earthly Cosmology*, New York: Vintage Books.
Angyl, A. (1941), *Foundations for Science of Personality*, New York: Commonwealth.
Aldridge, B. (2021), 'Core Self, Sense of Self, and Whole Self: The Potential for Harm in Using Personality Disorder Diagnoses', *Transactional Analysis Journal* 51 (1): 49–62.
Allen, R. (2024), *Weathering*, London: Ebury Press.
Barrow, G., and H. Marshall (2019), https://Eco-TA.dev
Barrow, G., and H. Marshall (2023), 'Revisiting Ecological Transactional Analysis: Emerging Perspectives', *Transactional Analysis Journal* 53 (1): 7–20.
Berne, E. (1961), *Transactional Analysis in Psychotherapy*, New York: Grove Press.
Berne, E. (1964), *Games People Play*, New York: Grove Press.
Berne, E. (1972), *What Do You Say after You Say Hello? The Psychology of Human Destiny*, London: Corgi.
Berne E. (1977), 'Ego States in Psychotherapy', in P. McCormick (ed.), *Intuition and Ego States: The Origins of Transactional Analysis*, 121–44, San Francisco: TA Press. (Original work published in 1957.)

Bowlby, J. (1979), 'The Bowlby-Ainsworth Attachment Theory', *Behavioral and Brain Sciences* 2 (4): 637–8.
Bregman, R. (2020), *Humankind: A Hopeful History*, London: Bloomsbury Publishing.
Cohn, M., and R. Buber (1980), *Martin Buber: A Bibliography of His Writings;* 1897–1978, New York: Magnes Press.
Cornell, W. F. (2008), *Explorations in Transactional Analysis: The Meech Lake Papers*, Pleasanton, CA: TA Press.
Cornell, W. F., A. de Graaf, T. Newton and M. Thunnissen (2016), *Into TA: A Comprehensive Textbook on Transactional Analysis*, London: Karnac Books.
Deaconu, D. (2020), 'The Therapist's Agency as A Subsymbolic Working Tool in the Clinical Encounter: On the Phenomenology of Thinking Martian', *Transactional Analysis Journal* 50 (3): 193–206.
Ernst Jr, F. H. (1971), 'The OK Corral: The Grid for Get-on-with', *Transactional Analysis Journal* 1 (4): 33–42.
Erskine, R. G. (2018), 'Life Scripts: Unconscious Relational Patterns and Psychotherapeutic Involvement', in *Life Scripts*, 1–28, London: Routledge.
Erskine, R. G., and M. J. Zalcman (1979), 'The Racket System: A Model for Racket Analysis', *Transactional Analysis Journal* 9 (1): 51–9.
Goulding, R., and M. Goulding (1976), 'Injunctions, Decisions and Redecisions', *Transactional Analysis Journal* 6 (1): 41–8.
Gordon, J., N. Knowlton, D. A. Relman, F. Rohwer and M. Youle (2013), 'Superorganisms and Holobionts', *Microbe* 8 (4): 152–3.
Hargaden, H., and C. Sills (2002), *Transactional Analysis: A Relational Perspective*, London: Routledge.
Hostie, R. (1982), 'Eric Berne, the Martian', *Transactional Analysis Journal* 12 (2): 168–70.
Jordan, M. (2015), *Nature and Therapy: Understanding Counselling and Psychotherapy in Outdoor Spaces*, New York: Routledge.
Kaplan, S. (1995), 'The Restorative Benefits of Nature; Toward an Integrative Framework', *Journal of Environmental Psychology* 15: 169–82.
Keating, A., and K. Merenda (2013), 'Decentring the Human? Towards a Post-Anthropocentric Standpoint Theory', *Praktyka Teoretyczna* 10 (4): 65–88.
Kepner, J. I. (2013), *Healing Tasks: Psychotherapy with Adult Survivors of Childhood Abuse*, Cambridge, USA: Gestalt Press.
Marshall, H. (2016), 'A Vital Protocol–Embodied-relational Depth in Nature-Based Psychotherapy', *Ecotherapy: Theory, Research and Practice* 148.
Marshall, H. (2016), 'Taking Therapy Outside–Reaching for a Vital Connection', *Eco-Psychotherapy: Synthesising Ecology and Psychotherapy in Practice and Theory.*
Marshall, H. (2021), 'Ecological Transactional Analysis: Allowing the Leopards into the Temple', Keynote Address at UKATA National Conference 2021, *The Transactional Analyst*, Spring 2021.
Marshall, H. (2023), 'A Place for the Ecological Third: Eco-Ta in Therapeutic Practice', *Transactional Analysis Journal* 53 (1): 93–108.

Novellino, M. (1984), 'Self-analysis of Countertransference in Integrative Transactional Analysis', *Transactional Analysis Journal* 14 (1): 63–7.
O'Driscoll, T. (2015), 'Eco Supervision: Toward an Ecological Consciousness in Supervision', *Inside Out* 77: 41–51.
O'Driscoll, T. (2022), 'Eco Supervision: Embodied, Embedded, Emergence in Supervision', in *Embodied Approaches to Supervision*, 48–61, London: Routledge.
Oliver, M. (2004), *Wild Geese*, Northumberland: Bloodaxe Books.
Oliver, M. (2005), *Why I Wake Early: New Poems*, Boston: Beacon Press.
Oliver, M. (2012), *House of Light*, Boston: Beacon Press.
Salters, D. (2006), *The Script* 36 (5): 1–2.
Steiner, C. M. (2012), 'The OK Position: Freedom, Equality, and the Pursuit of Happiness', *Transactional Analysis Journal* 42 (4): 294–7.
Totton, N. (2021), *Wild Therapy: Rewilding Our Inner and Outer Worlds*, Monmouth: PCCS Books.

Afterword

Hayley Marshall and Joe Hinds

This volume of chapters represents an overview of the current developments, understandings and approaches within this broad discipline. Common to the chapters is the central importance of the natural world in its myriad forms and its relationship to human mental well-being. Although this relationship has traditionally been ignored or underplayed by Western psychology, there has been a growing recognition of the importance of it, evidenced by a growing body of theoretical, research, practice and educative initiatives. This book, while offering some perspectives on the theory, practice, research and education foci within the growing field of ecotherapy, is not a definitive statement on ecotherapy – there can never be a comprehensive coverage of the topic within one edition.

With a growing interest among the therapeutic community and beyond, the present volume, we hope, will provoke further theoretical, research, practice and education-based initiatives which will address explicit questions associated with specific groups, individuals and concerns within the field. We do recognize that the diversity of ideas and approaches makes the task of outlining one coherent epistemological base impossible. And as illustrated in many of the chapters, the work of ecotherapy is (perhaps even more so than traditional methods of psychological practice), an emergent practice, and so will probably never (nor should) be definitively categorized as following one method or 'way'.

In keeping with the holistic approach of ecotherapy, we feel the writings offered here provide an interesting and varied view on the practice which we would like to see encourage further insight and exploration to support the growing research and evidence base for ecotherapy. Although the methods used in the chapters cover some ground in terms of approaches and research philosophies, some will undoubtedly wish to make comparisons with other more 'robust' evaluations, such as randomized control trials and the like. Our position here is that there are no perfect 'gold standards' of assessment and that each has its own strengths and weakness; and that it's through longitudinal follow-up work that the true effect of any intervention may be determined, and we would issue a call for more of this work to be initiated. In particular the voice and experience of the 'client' in ecotherapy is currently still underrepresented in the research.

Ecotherapy represents a broadening of current theory and practice within the field of counselling and psychotherapy, and in doing so it also offers an important critique of current ways of thinking. By including the natural environment and the more-than-human world into therapeutic practice, it expands our understanding of relationships and mental health beyond the purely intrapsychic and interpersonal to include a matrix of relating and their potential for healing. In this sense it offers a much more holistic and reciprocal understanding of therapeutic practice beyond its traditional conceptions.

The chapters which explore the practice of ecotherapy again give an insight into the diverse nature of approaches and directions taken within ecotherapy. These chapters capture what might be, for some, central concerns in relation to ethical and professional practice such as the importance of boundaries and ethics for ecotherapy as a professional therapeutic practice. However, it is important to note that all the practitioners writing here will have engaged with these concerns in no less a rigorous manner than their indoor colleagues, specifically having to face a re-evaluation of the traditional therapeutic frame and therapeutic relationship, both greatly altered in ecotherapeutic work. We understand that as ever, practitioners should remain curious and open to further development on these matters.

A continually evolving issue of whether ecotherapy operates as an add-on to traditional forms of therapeutic work or presents a unique form of practice is an important topic. The diversity of approaches represented in the book raises further questions about the practice of ecotherapy in relation to 'being well' and what might be broadly termed 'therapy'. Undoubtedly some forms of 'depth' ecotherapy are close cousins to psychotherapy, whereas others may represent a new form of practice entirely. We view the chapters on education as forming a window into the kind of educative process required to support a newer kind of practice – the interplay between a practitioner's personal ecological development and the work they decide to offer being central to this. We hope and expect this educative aspect to develop further over the coming years.

Through continued developments and contributions in the areas we have outlined, we wish that ecotherapy may continue to carve its own unique place in the therapeutic world. We hope this book contributes to that development and that it acts as a clarion call for the value and necessity of ecotherapy, however it is interpreted or enacted, and for it to be further validated as an established and accepted practice.

Index

Note: Page numbers in *italics* and **bold** indicate figures and tables.

www.ingramcontent.com/pod-product-compliance
Ingram Content Group UK Ltd.
Pitfield, Milton Keynes, MK11 3LW, UK
UKHW052349170826
474521UK00005B/44

9 781350 459847